HERE WAS ROME

MODERN WALKS IN THE ANCIENT CITY

VICTOR SONKIN

SKYSCRAPER

First published 2017 by Skyscraper Publications
20 Crab Tree Close, Bloxham, Oxon OX15 4SE, U.K.
www.skyscraperpublications.com

A CIP catalogue record for this book is available from
the British Library.

ISBN-13: 978-1-911072-01-0

Cover concept and design by
gracefussellstudio.com

Maps created by Tatjana Russita

The publication of this book was effected under
the auspices of the Mikhail Prokhorov Foundation
TRANSCRIPT Programme to Support
Translations of Russian Literature

Designed and typeset by
Chandler Book Design

Printed in Malta
by Latitude Press

D · M
M · L · GASPAROVI
MAGISTRI · OPTIMI

CONTENTS

WHAT THIS BOOK
IS ABOUT

On the west bank of the Nile, near the ancient city of Thebes, there are two half-preserved statues. They portray the pharaoh Amenhotep III, but in Classical Antiquity they were known as "the Colossi of Memnon," after the Ethiopian warrior and half-god, who came with his army to help the doomed Trojans and fell at the hands of Achilles. They used to say that at dawn one of the statues produced a sound similar to that of a human voice.

For a few centuries, the statue was a popular spot for Greek and Roman tourists. The young general Germanicus went to Egypt officially "to learn about antiquity" (*cogonscendae antiquitatis*); so did the emperor Hadrian with his retinue. During the first two centuries after Christ, the huge legs of both Memnons were covered with more than a hundred inscriptions, including forty-five in Latin, sixty-three in Greek, and one bilingual.

In the 18th century, getting acquainted with the treasures of antiquity was a whole long ritual called "The Grand Tour"; without it, an upper-class British man was not properly educated. A short distance separates the Grand Tour and today's package tours "All the Treasures of Italy in a Week."

Nowadays, the books that tell stories about cities and countries for those with an interest in history fall into two categories. Some go into the details of buildings, ruins, methods of construction, size and architectural peculiarities of ancient monuments. Others consider time travelling possible and explain how to live in Ancient Rome on only five sestertii a day.

This book is written with a different goal in mind. It does not tell you only – not even a lot – about stones and pedestals; it prefers to tell you the stories behind them. To pass by the Palazzo delle Finanze, not very close to any ancient ruins, is one thing; a completely different thing is to know that this is where the "Cursed Field" was, this is where the failed Vestal Virgins were entombed, that their bones are somewhere underground, under your feet, quite near.

To call up the ghosts from the pages of ancient authors and chilly textbooks, to put them in the places where they loved, fought, made love, played the fool, sold and bought, dabbled in intrigue – this is this book's task. If you are on your way to the Eternal City or have recently returned from it, if you only dream about it or prefer to travel without leaving your comfortable armchair – then this book is for you.

ACKNOWLEDGEMENTS

The Roman emperor Mark Aurelius was also a stoicist philosopher. He began his philosophical treatise, which is usually called "Meditations" in English, with the list of people to whom he was grateful for his character and curiosity: "From my grandfather Verus I learned good morals and the government of my temper. From the reputation and remembrance of my father, modesty and a manly character. From my mother, piety and beneficence; from my great-grandfather, not to have frequented public schools. From my governor, to be neither of the green nor of the blue party [these were the main charioteering rivals] at the games in the Circus. From Diognetus… from Rusticus… from Apollonius… From Alexander the grammarian…"

The ancients understood well that a human was not unique, and that the results of his work were a part of the never-ending cycle of generations and communications. Let this book bear witness to the gratitude I have felt to anyone ever participating in the appearance of this book. I apologise to those not mentioned here due to my forgetfulness or distraction.

I am deeply grateful to the specialists who have read and corrected this book in various ways, especially to the late Grigory Dashevsky and the author of the only usable Russian guide to Rome, Olga Grinkrug. My students, old and new, offered help in some of the most baffling issues – especially the mathematician and translator Oleg Popov, linguist Alexander Piperski, and the literature scholar, medical scientist and now computer specialist, Andrei Azov.

The most important step in the life of this book was its publication in Russian, for which I am deeply grateful to Serguei Parkhomenko and the director of Corpus Publishing, an imprint of AST Publishing, Varvara Gornostaeva, who was the most understanding and generous editor-in-chief one could imagine. Her whole team played a great role in this book's Russian success. I am especially grateful to Yekaterina Vladimirskaya for her careful and thoughtful corrections, and to Yulia Revzina for her delicate and clever editing.

Present-day researchers, unlike the earlier ones, are blessed with the treasures of the Internet. It is impossible to acknowledge all my online sources, but some of the resources require a special acknowledgement: the wide-ranging Livius.org by the Dutch historian Jona Lenderling, the unimaginably rich and diverse Lacus Curtius of the American translator and lover of antiquity Bill Thayer, and the site about Rome's past and present, Romeartlover.it, created by Roberto Piperno.

I received help and guidance from my colleagues all over Europe – from Amanda Claridge, the author of a brilliant Oxford archaeological guide to Rome; from Susan Walker, the curator of the Ashmolean in Oxford; from Robert Coates-Stevens of the British Academy in Rome and Giovanni Ricci, who showed me new archaeological digs in the city; from Theresa de Bellis of the Villa Medici French Academy; and from Taylor Lansford, the author of a unique and wonderful to read guidebook to Rome's Latin inscriptions. I would also like to thank the staff of all the libraries, especially the ones in London, Oxford and Moscow, where I conducted my research. I am grateful to Robert Chandler for his kind words and editing of a couple of major passages, and to Boris Dralyuk for helping to translate Gogol's epigraph.

Slava Shvets showed me around the parts of Rome I never knew. Tatiana Russita, the author of the maps, invested much more time into the book than anyone (she included) expected in the beginning, heroically persevering through countless adjustments.

The appearance of this book in English is the result of the work of the Banke, Goumen & Smirnova literary agency (bgs-agency.com), especially my friend Natasha Banke. I am deeply grateful to Karl Sabbagh of Skyscraper Books for believing her words. I am also grateful to Elena Kostioukovich and her team for all the efforts.

With rare exceptions, the bulk of everyone's achievements comes from his family. I am happy not to be an exception, and I would like to share my joy about the book with my parents and their spouses, with my grandmother who taught me poetry, my brothers, my in-laws, my former wife and two sons, and now also to my grand-daughter. If they find this book interesting to read, in English or in Russian, I will consider my educator's task completed.

My most important partner throughout the preparation of this book, first in Russian and then in English, was my wife and companion Alexandra Borisenko. Without her support and patience, "Here Was Rome" could never see the light of day.

One person without whom this book would have been impossible is Mikhail Gasparov (1935–2005), an academician, scholar, sage, and the best master of Russian style of the last few decades. Unfortunately, he is much less known in the West than he should be – there is no one who resembles him. He had the gift of speaking simply about complex things, and this work about the Ancient Rome he loved so much is a humble gift to his memory.

THE HISTORY OF ANCIENT ROME IN ONE THOUSAND WORDS

Sometime around mid-8th century BC (tradition claimed that Rome was founded in 753 BC), a few tribes of Central Italy settled on a small patch of land at a strategically important intersection of trade roads and waterways. The hills on one side and the Tiber river on the other offered natural protection to the new settlement.

In the early years of Ancient Rome, the city (so the legends said) was ruled by kings. In 510 BC a sex scandal had brought monarchy to an end: the nobles, outraged by the indecent behaviour of a king's son, expelled the king and his relatives. A republic was founded, with supreme power entrusted to a pair of annually elected officials. The Roman system of checks and balances was so complex that legal historians have continued to produce volumes on the subject ever since.

Political power in Rome was concentrated in the hands of a few families with impressive pedigrees. As the state grew, members of other social groups started to question this group's supremacy. To overcome the resistance of aristocrats ('patricians' in Roman parlance), the humble people ('plebeians') threatened to abandon Rome, leaving it without a working population. After the conflict was resolved, the division into patricians and plebeians ceased to be politically meaningful.

The young state found itself overflowing beyond the confines of the Tiber valley. Neighbouring tribes soon fell under its power, and the rest of Italy followed suit, with only the Greek cities of the South holding out a little longer.

By mid-3rd century BC, Rome was ready to break out into the wider Mediterranean arena. She had a rival, though – Carthage, a North African empire founded by Phoenicians from the Middle East. The first clash between the two nations led to carving up their respective spheres of influence. The second clash came within a hair's breadth of pulling the plug on Roman history. If, after the catastrophic defeat at Cannae, the Romans had not rallied against their formidable foe, the course of European civilization would have been completely different. After the third war, which was nothing more than a mopping-up operation, former Carthaginian provinces – Sicily, Spain, parts of North Africa – came under Rome's control.

In spite of military victories, the economy was failing. The influx of cheap slaves from newly acquired lands unleashed a rampage of unemployment and defaulting on debts. The Gracchi brothers, scions of a noble family, attempted to institute land reforms against violent oligarchic opposition. While their programme was largely implemented, both brothers were killed by angry mobs.

The last hundred years of the Roman republic were turbulent and bloody. Wars raged on the borders of the expanding empire. In Rome itself, the political system collapsed: oligarchic and populist factions were at each other's throats, and the people clamoured for a strong hand. Their wish was soon granted: a new generation of Roman politicians realised that in an unbalanced society the most durable political solutions were brought about by the legionaries' swords. Charismatic strongmen came and went; every new one executed the followers of the former and confiscated their property. When a promising general called Julius Caesar made an unofficial three-way deal with two other contenders for supreme power and left for a protracted military campaign in Gaul, many people hoped that the murderous spree of civil wars was coming to an end. But nine years later Caesar brought his battle-hardened legions to the walls of Rome. Another round of strife followed, from which Caesar emerged victorious. Unfortunately, he lacked a clear plan, and his enemies suspected him of eying a royal crown. The Romans were extremely averse to kingly paraphernalia. Protectors of republican virtues joined up in a conspiracy and murdered Caesar on March 15, 44 BC.

The assassination did not save the republic. The conspirators and Caesar's supporters locked horns in yet another civil war. The conspirators lost. Ten years later, the victorious Caesarians, Caesar's lieutenant Mark Antony and Caesar's young grand-nephew Octavian, engaged in the final battle for superiority. The support of the Greek East, including the Egyptian queen Cleopatra, failed to ensure Antony's victory: Octavian won and became the sole and undisputed master of the empire.

At the threshold of the republican and imperial eras, Roman territorial expansion finally ran into insurmountable obstacles. The Romans suffered one crushing defeat in the Middle Eastern kingdom of Parthia and another in Germany, and the imperial spread was stemmed.

Octavian, bestowed with the honorific title "Augustus" in 27 BC, turned out to be a cunning and far-sighted politician. He did not abolish republican procedures or institutions, he never called himself king or dictator. His rule was allegedly based on his moral authority. When, in his old age, he started to feverishly grope for a successor, even the most optimistic republicans knew that there was no going back.

The system instituted by Augustus produced mixed results depending on the qualities of individual rulers. Under "bad emperors" things were bad: Nero set Rome on fire and executed everyone he disliked, Caligula made his horse a Senate member. Under "good emperors," living standards grew, taxes were collected, provinces flourished. In the early 2nd century AD, under the emperor Trajan, the Roman Empire had reached its greatest spatial extent, covering almost the whole known word from Scotland to Egypt, from Portugal to Armenia.

In the 3rd century AD, the empire was affected by a systemic crisis. Borders began to cave in under barbarian assaults, trade faltered, birth rates plummeted. Traditional Roman religion was challenged by Eastern cults, including Judaism and its spin-off, Christianity. The "soldier emperors" installed by their legions, often low-born provincials, murdered one another with clockwork regularity; virtually no one among them died of natural causes. Finally, the emperor Diocletian drastically overhauled the imperial government, from tax collection to administrative division. He no longer cared about preserving the republican façade. He also split the empire into western and eastern halves for better defensibility.

The Eastern half, called the Byzantine Empire by historians, had survived for about a thousand years, but the days of the Western Roman Empire were numbered. The army, staffed by barbarian mercenaries, could not and would not hold back the pressure on the borders. The traditional narrative assumes that ancient Roman history ended in 476 AD, when a Germanic chieftain called Odoacer deposed the last Roman emperor, a boy called Romulus Augustulus.

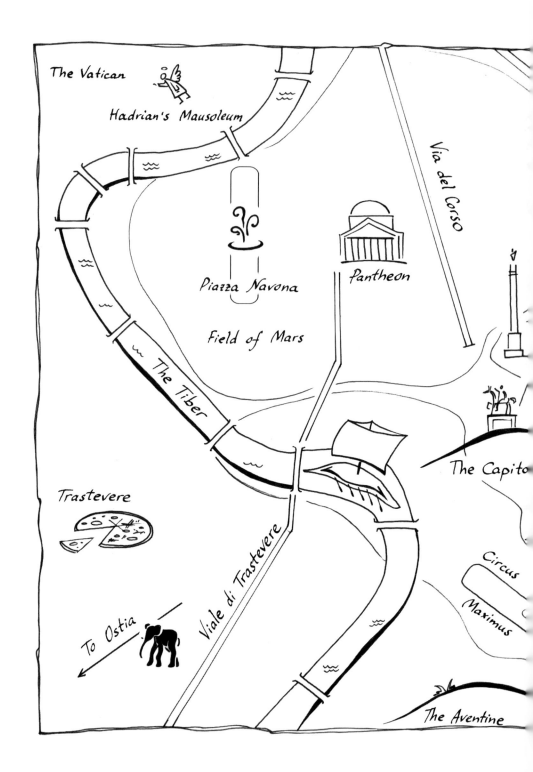

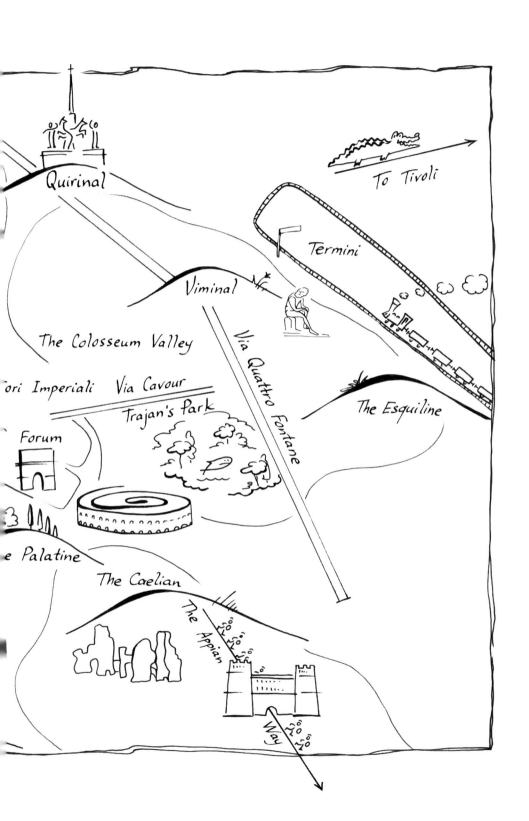

Quirinal

To Tivoli

Termini

Viminal

The Colosseum Valley

ori Imperiali   Via Cavour

Via Quattro Fontane

The Esquiline

Trajan's Park

Forum

e Palatine

The Caelian

The Appian

Way

hic sacra domus carique penates,
hic mihi Roma fuit.
Lucan

Here was Rome indeed at last; and such a Rome as no one can
imagine in its full and awful grandeur!
Charles Dickens

In short, he withdrew from everyone and set off exploring Rome on his
own, becoming, in this regard, not unlike one of the foreign tourists, who
are often, at first, taken aback by the dark, stained buildings and the
city's general air of dullness and pettiness, and keep asking themselves
bemusedly as they wander from alley to alley: "Where is Rome? Where
is grand, ancient Rome?" Only gradually, as it begins to emerge from
the cramped alleyways, do they recognise it — ancient Rome.
Nikolai Gogol

HERE WAS ROME

THE FORUM

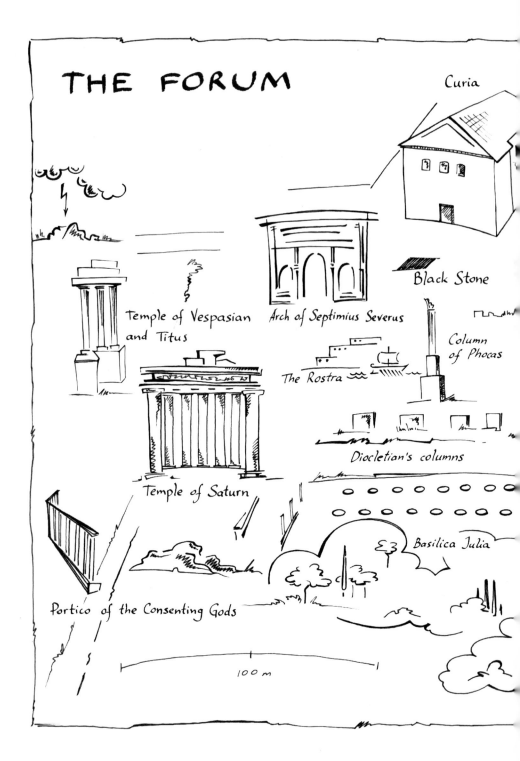

Curia

Black Stone

Temple of Vespasian and Titus

Arch of Septimius Severus

Column of Phocas

The Rostra

Diocletian's columns

Temple of Saturn

Basilica Julia

Portico of the Consenting Gods

100 m

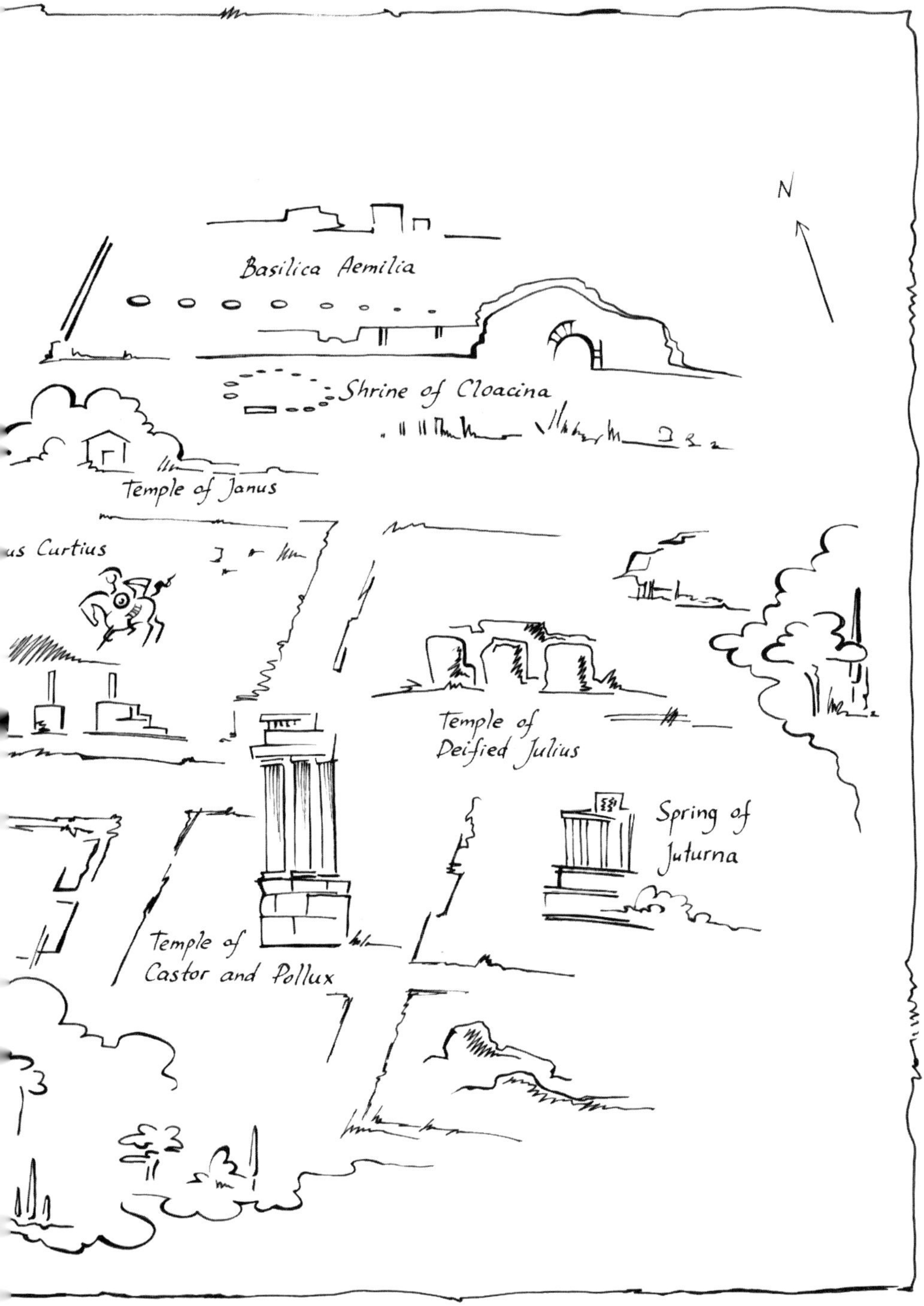

N

Basilica Aemilia

Shrine of Cloacina

Temple of Janus

us Curtius

Temple of
Deified Julius

Spring of
Juturna

Temple of
Castor and Pollux

CHAPTER I

THE FORUM
(THE HEART OF ROME)

N early every guidebook to Rome starts off with a description of the Forum, and nearly every author considers it necessary to apologise, in a manner of speaking, for the brick-and-marble jumble of ruins and stumps that is hard to navigate and harder to make sense of. Perhaps the bluntest of all is the observation of Amanda Claridge,

the author of the indispensable *Oxford Archaeological Guide to Rome*: "Today the area looks as though hit by a bomb."

This sentiment is nothing new. Two hundred years ago, Lord Byron wrote:

Chaos of ruins! who shall trace the void,
O'er the dim fragments cast a lunar light,
And say, "Here was, or is," where all is doubly night?

The double night of the poet is the night of old times and of ignorance. At least the ignorance can be partly rectified, which is what we will be trying to do. After all – and this is another point that no guidebook author fails to stress – no other public square in the world can rival this one in historic significance.

First of all, what exactly is the Roman Forum? It is a large rectangular space, stretching in a general east-to-west direction, and limited by the Capitol hill on the west, the Palatine hill on the south, the Imperial Fora (and the eponymous Via dei Fori Imperiali) on the north, and almost bumping into the Colosseum in the east. In many books, only the western half of that rectangle is considered Forum proper. Following that tradition, we will speak of the monuments on the Sacra Via in the next chapter.

Second of all, the guidebooks do not lie: there is hardly another plot of land in the known universe with such density of major historical events per square foot. The Renaissance writer Poggio Bracciolini describes how he would go to the Forum in the 1420s and find himself "dumbfounded with amazement, in imagination carrying myself back to the times when senatorial speeches were delivered here, and pretending that I am listening to Lucius Crassus, Hortensius or Cicero orating."[1]

In the 18th century the historian Edward Gibbon experienced similar emotions, recalling the impressions of his Grand Tour: "At the distance of twenty-five years I can neither forget nor express the strong emotions which agitated my mind as I first approached and entered the eternal City. After a sleepless night, I trod with a lofty step the ruins of the Forum; each memorable spot where Romulus stood, or Tully spoke, or Caesar fell, was at once present to my eye." Today, we know a lot more about the Forum monuments than was known to Renaissance humanists or even to Enlightenment historians: the building of the Senate was not where Poggio thought it was, and Caesar was not assassinated on the Forum. One thing remained unchanged: this is still the world's richest historical site.

It is necessary to keep in mind that no traces of whatever Caesar and Cicero, let alone Romulus, saw are preserved inn the Forum as we see it now (or, rather, they are concealed deep underground). In our best-case scenario, the oldest monuments here will be the ruins of late imperial buildings. (One famous classical scholar refused to visit the Forum on his trip to Rome: "Those are imperial age monuments, practically modernism in my book.") On the bright side, the Romans were very conservative; when they were restoring or even rebuilding their monuments, they were trying to keep as close to the original construction as they could. But again, that is the best-case scenario: at least half of the Forum's monuments owe their present-day appearance to radical restorations of the 19th and 20th centuries.

In prehistoric times, the future Forum was a marshy depression between the hills. Its oldest monuments are at the edges rather than in the middle, huddling at the foot of the Capitol and Palatine. The site of the future Temple of Antoninus and Faustina was occupied by a cemetery (while in historic times the Romans almost never buried their dead within the city). A stream was running through the marsh. Later, the marsh was drained, the square paved and cut through by the first road, later named Sacred, and the steam was diverted underground.

The Forum gradually transformed from the main market square into the hub of social and political life. It was there that the Senate convened, the laws were passed, alliances were struck, the destinies of the world decided. With the decline of the Roman republic and the establishment of emperors' rule, this function of the Forum had receded into the past. But outwardly, it became even grander, and in spite of proliferation of a whole string of new imperial fora within a short distance, it remained the principal among them, as "The Roman Forum" *(Forum Romanum)* or "The Great Forum" *(Forum Magnum)*.

When the Roman Empire fell at the hands of the barbarians, Rome's urban population shrank a hundredfold and concentrated at some distance from the Forum, on the Field of Mars. Ancient monuments began to slowly crumble. Natural and political disasters struck the Eternal City: devastating earthquakes in 847 and 1231, a massive sack in 1084 led by the Norman duke Robert Guiscard. And yet, life went on: mediaeval barons attached their fortresses to triumphal arches, monks converted pagan temples into Christian churches. During the Renaissance, the Forum's ancient structures became a quarry, pillaged by papal builders and architects for marble and other valuable material for their projects. In the 17th and 18th centuries, when the development fever abated, the Forum was one of the most rustic and idyllic parts of the city, known to travellers and artists as "The Cattle Field" *(Campo Vaccino)*.

*A view on "Campo Vaccino" in mid-17th century. Engraving
by Giovanni Battista Falda*

Systematic excavations began on the Forum in the early 19th century; a hundred years later, archaeologists were virtually the sole masters of the site. Houses were torn down, mediaeval ramparts dismantled, churches boarded up. In the course of the 20th century, the Forum was slowly turned into the bare archaeological area we are familiar with. The current fashion in conservation of old monuments puts an emphasis on preserving artistic achievements of all eras, but this insight is of no use to the Forum: in search of antiquity, the archaeologists destroyed almost all accretions of later times.

The main entrance to the archaeological area of the Roman Forum is from the side of the Via dei Fori Imperiali. Passing between the Senate House and the Basilica Aemilia, the tourists follow the course of an ancient Roman shopping street named Argiletum (possibly for the clay – *argilla* – that was mined nearby). The Argiletum led to the part of the Forum called Comitium, the place of popular assemblies. The Forum's oldest and most cryptic monuments are centered on it. But before we tackle each of them separately, we need to recall what was happening in Rome in the oldest times.

THE KINGS

"The City of Rome from its inception was held by kings" (*Urbem Romam a principio reges habuere*), begins one of the greatest Roman historical works, "The Annals" by Tacitus[2]. This simple fact was at one and the same time indisputable and legendary for the Romans. On the one hand, the history of Roman kings was well known: there were seven of them, and they had been ruling since the foundation of the city. Tradition ascribed the foundation to 753 BC (even the exact date was cited, April 21, which is still celebrated as the city's birthday). The royal rule ended in 510 or 509, when a group of aristocrats led by Lucius Junius Brutus expelled the last king and instituted republican rule. Since 509, the lists of consuls and other elected officials (magistrates) were kept in republican archives, and these lists (*fasti consulares*) have survived. Historians are inclined to consider them genuine: the lists of early republican magistrates feature a lot of names that never reappear in the historical record. If the fasti were later corrected by some Orwellian Ministry of Truth, the high and mighties would have certainly yielded to the temptation of padding them up with their own ancestors. As for the archives of kingly Rome, if they had ever existed, they perished in fire during the Gallic sack of the 390s BC.

The lists of consuls and triumphators – the victorious generals who led their troops through the city in a solemn procession called 'triumph' – were found in mid-16th century in the form of fifty marble fragments. At that time, any found marble was recycled for new churches and palaces in the best-case scenario; in the worst case, it was simply burned for lime. The papal librarian Onofrio Panvinio and his friend Michelangelo managed to salvage the fragments of the "Fasti" and preserve them for history. Today these marble tables, painstakingly assembled piece by piece (separate fragments continued to be found almost into the 20th century), are kept in the Capitoline Museums and are known, therefore, as *Fasti Capitolini*.

The first Roman king was Romulus, the founder of the city. The story of his (and his twin brother Remus's) life is pure fairy tale stuff. It has all the essential elements of magic: a treacherous coup (the twins' grandfather, Numitor, is overthrown by his evil brother Amulius); an ominous prophecy (Amulius receives an oracle that his grand-nephews would take his throne away from him); an attempt to introduce emergency security measures (Amulius forces Rhea Silvia, Numitor's daughter, to become a Vestal virgin and thus prevent her from procreating) which is, of course, thwarted (Rhea Silvia is raped, by the god Mars according to her testimony, and becomes pregnant); a murder attempt (new-born twins are thrown into the river); a miraculous salvation (Romulus and Remus are washed ashore, where a she-wolf suckles them); secret education (the children grow up in a shepherd's family, unaware of their royal lineage), overthrowing and murder of the granduncle, a quarrel between the brothers, Remus's death at the hand of Romulus. Interestingly, the Romans of enlightened times did not truly believe their own ancient legends. Thus, the historian Livy doubts the twins' divine paternity. He suspects that Rhea Silvia might have been touched by delusion of grandeur and actually think that it was the god Mars who had raped her, or, alternatively, might have dressed up the story as she did because, in her opinion, being raped by a god was less disgraceful. Livy even sacrilegiously muses that the twins' foster mother, the shepherd's wife called Larentia, was called *Lupa* ('she-wolf') by her husband's colleagues as a woman of easy virtue, hence the legend of miraculous lupine-assisted salvation.

Romulus had to contend for the supreme authority over the freshly founded city with Remus: they were equals in years and glory. They agreed to observe birds in flight (this might have been the first recorded case of birdwatching): whoever received the more convincing omen, would be the ruler. Romulus set up his observation post on the Palatine, the principal and oldest of Rome's hills; Remus chose a location a little to the south, on the Aventine. Vultures appeared in Remus's sector first; in Romulus's sector there were, however, twice as many. Not surprisingly, each of the brothers was ascribing victory to himself. In the ensuing scuffle Romulus killed Remus and became the sole ruler. There was another version of Remus's death: ridiculing his brother's engineering solutions, he easily hopped over the new city's defensive wall, and the enraged Romulus pierced him with the words "This will be the fate of anyone who jumps over my walls."

There were few people to live in the new city. To beef up the figures, Romulus used a trick typical of young ambitious states: he set up an asylum and invited the tired, the poor, the wretched refuse to join him. The resulting demographic imbalance soon grew out of proportion: for obvious reasons, there were many more men than women among the riff-raff who answered Romulus's call. Romulus sent embassies to the neighbours asking them to give their daughters in marriage to the Romans, but everyone eyed the Latin cutthroats with suspicion; someone mockingly suggested that Romulus open another asylum specifically for women. In a situation like that, there was no other choice but to hold a major sports event. Romulus announced the games; this time, the neighbours, driven by curiosity, arrived in droves – some of them, like the tribe of Sabines, in full force, with women and small children. Suddenly, at a prearranged cue, the Roman youths grabbed young Sabine women. The insulted Sabines went to war, but at the height of the fighting something unexpected happened. The Sabine women who got accustomed to their captors, in the first recorded case of Stockholm syndrome, "dared to go amongst the flying missiles, and … to part the hostile forces," [3] says Livy. The Romans and the Sabines made peace, Romulus and the Sabine king Titus Tatius became joint rulers, and it was already under them that Rome had first exhibited its imperial nature, subduing some of the nearby settlements.

Sabine women set apart the fighting warriors

The next king, Numa Pompilius, was pious and wise. According to one legend, he was a disciple of Pythagoras; unfortunately, when ancient historians started to compare timelines, they realised that a discrepancy of two hundred years would be too hard to patch up (also, what language they might have used between themselves, asks the sensible Livy). Numa was credited with establishing almost all of the state's religious institutions, including the priestly colleges and calendar.

The next king, Tullus Hostilius, was by contrast cruel and bellicose (even his name, Hostilius, means cruel, hostile). Under him, Rome went to war with its own mother city, Alba Longa. It was the custom of heroic times to solve such issues in single combat, and a variation thereof was held: three Horatii brothers against three Curiatii brothers (we will revisit that tragic story when we reach the Appian Way, the location of the fight). The Romans won; Alba Longa fell under the Roman rule and was razed soon after.

The next king, Ancus Martius, was a born Sabine. He expanded the Roman territory all the way to the Tyrrhenian Sea and founded the all-important seaport, Ostia, at the mouth of the Tiber. His successor, Tarquinius Priscus ("Tarquin the Elder") was an Etruscan immigrant; he instituted games and other forms of entertainment in Rome, increased the number of senators, strengthened the cavalry and successfully fought foreign enemies – including, by some accounts, his own countrymen.

The most mysterious king was Servius Tullius. His very provenance and appearance were shrouded in secret (we will revisit him shortly). Under him, Roman society was radically reorganised. He was the first to conduct a census, an all-important Roman procedure that recorded all the citizens and distributed them into classes according to their property. In essence, the reforms of Servius instituted the very notion of Roman citizenship. The army was also radically reorganised.

The last Roman king was Tarquinius Superbus ("Tarquin the Proud"). The son of the earlier Tarquin and son-in-law of Servius, he grabbed the throne by force, having murdered his father-in-law. Under him, Rome waged a series of successful wars, becoming the main stronghold of military and political power in Central Italy. The family's violent temper proved his undoing. His son Sextus raped the virtuous Lucretia, the wife of his relation; Lucretia convened a family council, recounted the sordid deed and stabbed herself. At that point, one of those present, a man called Lucius Junius Brutus, decided that enough was enough.

All of the above history is not true. Or, in any case, none of that could have happened the way Roman tradition describes it. Romulus is almost certainly a mythological figure, his name a back-formation from the name of the city. The story of a king afraid for his throne, the miraculous salvation of lawful heirs through a wolf and the subsequent fulfilment of prophecy is so archetypal that a rare nation does not have a myth to that effect.

One of the main problems with the Roman kings is the proportion between their number (seven: again, too conveniently magical) and the traditional combined length of their rule (244, an average of 35 years per king). There has never been a dynasty of such long-livers anywhere in the world, and there is no chance that these data could be genuine. In the 19th century, when scepticism was in vogue, many researchers doubted the very existence of regal rule in Rome, relegating all traditional accounts of the kings to the domain of untrustworthy tales. There is an additional problem of terminology. In the European mind of today, monarchy is a hereditary thing. Even these days, in the most developed democracies of the world, kings and queens are not elected, while utterly undistinguished young men and women become the fixtures of society columns for the mere fact of their birth to the purple. Roman monarchy, however, was not like that: there, kings were elected by direct popular vote, more or less like modern presidents. (This dynastic uncertainty would be much later inherited by Roman emperors, often with catastrophic consequences for themselves, their families and the state.) It was the Senate (the council of elders, from the word *senex*, 'old man') that managed the appointment, but the popular assembly could, at least theoretically, reject the proposed candidate. There was not one but two opportunities for doing so: one during the discussion of the candidate, and the other when the new king was invested with command authority (the word for this kind of authority, *imperium*, like many specifically Roman terms, cannot be adequately translated into modern languages). Before the king was elected in accordance with all the necessary rites, including divine omens, all power was wielded by a "transitional king" (*interrex*) who was one of the senators. He held the position for five days, when he had to yield it to the next senator, and so on until the proper king was elected.

Of the legendary seven kings, not one was a patrician, i. e. an aristocrat of the earliest Roman stock. Some were outsiders – like the two Tarquins from Etruria and Servius Tullius from virtually nowhere.

The legends that surround the names of the Roman kings mostly belong in the realm of mythology. But the institutions, conquests and buildings that are ascribed to them had actually existed.

THE COMITIUM AND THE CURIA

In regal and early republican times the most important location of the Forum (and thus of Rome) was the Comitium, the place of popular assemblies. It was an open site, sometimes covered by an awning in case of bad weather or excessive heat. Later a kind of amphitheatre was built there, and on its steps the members of various Roman tribes voted. The Romans remained standing during their meetings, and considered the Greek habit of sitting during popular gatherings a sign of effeminacy (but they did sit in the Senate).

An open-air site in Rome could be considered sacred – all that was needed was for the priests to properly consecrate it. A sacred place was called *templum*, which is usually translated as 'temple.' This usage confused modern-era archaeologists who thought that the Comitium was a building and spent much time searching for its traces.

There were a few monuments to various human heroes on the Comitium and one unusual monument to a botanical hero – a fig tree commemorating another fig tree, the one under which the she-wolf had found Romulus and Remus. When the tree withered, it was considered an important omen, and the priests solemnly replaced it with a new one.

Between the Comitium and the Forum proper (possibly on the place now occupied by the Arch of Septimius Severus) was an open platform intended for foreign ambassadors. It was a place of honour, but it was called with little reverence, Graecostasis (something along the lines of "the Greeks' parking spot"), because foreign ambassadors were usually from the Greek-speaking East.

The Comitium, in Livy's words, was "the lobby of the Curia." The Curia was the Senate House. The very first Curia was built on the Comitium in the legendary times of the king Tullus Hostilius. It must have been a simple house in austere republican taste. In 100 BC (the year when Julius Caesar was born) it saw the murder of Lucius Saturninus, tribune and darling of the people. The Roman republic at the time was already severely stressed. The dictator Gaius Marius who had amassed virtually all political power in his hands, owed a lot to his supporters, Glaucia and Saturninus, but their populist activity made his dealings with leading aristocrats increasingly difficult. When the thugs of Glaucia and Saturninus murdered a consular candidate, outraged notables told Marius to deal with the situation. Marius was torn between opposing forces; one night, he was paid a simultaneous visit by the senators telling him to rein in Saturninus, and Saturninus, who wanted to make short work of the senators. Marius was shuttling between the wings of his house, explaining his absences by an upset stomach to both parties and shamelessly lying to both. The next day, a real battle raged on the Forum. Saturninus and his clique were defeated and entrenched themselves on the Capitoline hill; their adversaries cut off all outside communications, and the Saturninians, left without food or water, were forced to surrender. The captured Saturninus was brought to the Curia with the intention to put him on senatorial trial, but many of the aristocrats were so enraged that they climbed to the roof, broke a hole in it and used that hole to stone Saturninus to death.

In 80 BC the Curia was restored by the next charismatic leader, Sulla, but his version was also unlucky: thirty years later the political struggle between the two demagogues, Clodius and Milo, erupted into the streets, and the factions engaged in hand-to-hand combat everywhere across Rome. Once, on the Appian Way, Milo's men ran into Clodius and murdered him. The outraged Clodians hauled the body of their leader to the Curia and set up a funeral pyre right there. That was the end of the Curia Hostilia: it burned down.

NAMES

In hoary antiquity a Roman might have just one name (such as 'Romulus' or 'Remus'), but in historic time any self-respecting citizen had three (*tria nomina*). They were the personal name (*praenomen*), family name or, strictly speaking, the name of one's *gens* (which is roughly equivalent to 'clan' or an extended family – that was *nomen*), and an additional name indicating the branch of the family (*cognomen*). Non-aristocratic Romans often made do with only the first two until the late republic. A Roman triple name looked like "Gaius Julius Caesar" or "Publius Ovidius Naso." There were very few personal names to choose from, maybe about three dozen; even of these, only a handful were used with any frequency: Gaius, Marcus, Lucius, Publius, Gnaeus, Quintus, Sextus.

A clan name harked back to very old time, to the founder of the gens. It ended with *-ius* or *-aeus*: Julius, Claudius, Horatius, Cornelius, Annaeus. The third name usually had its origins in a nickname attached to some quality of the founder of a family branch, for example Ahenobarbus ('red-bearded'), Cicero ('chickpea'), Celer ('swift'), Brutus ('dumb'), Scipio ('sceptre'). Sometimes the meaning of the cognomen was lost in the mist of ages: we do not know what 'Caesar' or 'Cato' means (though Romans themselves had lots of contradicting versions).

The third name, as a rule, was handed down from father to son, but a citizen could obtain yet another extra name (a second cognomen or *agnomen*) for some outstanding achievement – for example, Creticus ('Cretan') for bringing the island of Crete under the Roman power, or Africanus for distinguished military service in Africa. Sometimes such an agnomen was awarded posthumously – thus, one of the champions of the hopeless republican cause is known to posterity as Marcus Porcius Cato Uticensis, after the suicide he committed in the African city of Utica.

What about women? Women, strictly speaking, did not have names at all. This might sound strange, but indeed, all a regular woman had was a feminine version of the clan name. The daughter of Marcus Tullius Cicero was called Tullia ('Tulliola,' Little Tullia, to her immediate family), the daughter of Julius Caesar was Julia. If there was more than one daughter in the family, the first two were designated 'Elder' and 'Younger' (*Maior* and *Minor*), and then sequential numbers were employed: *Tertia*, *Quarta* and so on. Some women, though, did have family names, based on their father's or husband's cognomen (Caecilia Metella) or even some personal trait. In imperial times, a woman sometimes received her husband's personal name in marriage, but the idea was much older, reflected in the traditional language of the archaic wedding ceremony: "Where you are Gaius, I am Gaia" (*ubi tu Gaius, ego Gaia*).

Slaves of foreign extraction usually got by with one name only (if you think back to famous Ancient Greeks, you will see many examples of that: Plato, Aristotle, Themistocles and so on). If a master set them free (this was called 'manumission'), they took his personal and clan name and added their own original name as a cognomen; thus, Tyro, the freedman of Cicero and the inventor of shorthand, was called Marcus Tullius Tyro as a free man.

*Tomb inscription for Marcus Annaeus Paulus Petrus
from his father Marcus Annaeus Paulus*

You may sometimes see one of the most frequent Roman names spelled "Caius" instead of "Gaius." This is actually a misunderstanding. The languages from which Latin had borrowed its alphabet (Etruscan, for example) did not distinguish between the sounds [K] and [G] and therefore did not need separate letters for them. The Romans were happy with one letter, C, for a long time, but at some point a variation with an additional squiggle was introduced for the G-sound (always hard as in 'gift'). However, probably out of superstition (they were extremely conservative that way), the Romans never changed the spelling of the first letters in names like Gaius and Gnaeus, especially when those were shortened to C and CN·

Faustus, the nephew of Sulla, began building a new Senate House, but Julius Caesar did not let him finish the project, tore down what was built and started all over again. Caesar was killed before the Curia was complete, and the end of the works was overseen by Octavian (later known as Augustus). Augustus installed in the Senate a gold statue of Victory, brought from the Greek city of Tarentum in southern Italy. At the end of the 4th century AD, this statue was the centre of a violent controversy between a number of senators who were nostalgic about old pagan beliefs and Christians who by that time had gathered momentum. "Let us restore the religion that had been providing our state with proven benefits for ages," wrote the senator Simmachus. "How can we tolerate pagan sacrifices when there are Christians present?" complained Ambrose, the bishop of Milan, in a letter to the emperor Valentinian. The Christians won.

The Curia (church of Sant'Adriano). 19th-century drawing

After Augustus, the next large-scale reconstruction was carried out by Domitian in the late 1st century AD, and after him by Diocletian at the end of the 3rd century, when the building had been damaged by a major fire. The guidebooks usually call today's building Curia Julia, after Julius Caesar, but it is in fact Diocletian's. Of course, the Senate house did not stand on the main city square as we see it now, with simple brick walls and small windows; it is simply that all marble and stucco that lined it was lost.

Inside the Curia was a large hall with three rows of seats along its longer walls. That was where the senators sat, in armchairs or on benches. The upper tier was probably meant for junior senators who did not sit and were called *senatores pedarii*, pedestrian senators. A session was chaired, as a rule, by a consul or the doyen of the Senate; when it was time to vote, he either called out everyone present by name, or simply asked those who were pro and contra to move to the opposite sides of the hall – in this case it was often possible to gauge the outcome without the tally. Presiding officers were sitting opposite the doors (and that is where the statue of Victory was standing, too). Two doors behind their backs led onto the Forum of Caesar. Other statues stood in the niches of the hall, and stucco was designed so as to enhance the acoustic quality of the premises.

In the oldest times the Senate had consisted of only one hundred men – a relic of that era was the senatorial privilege of using special shoes marked with the letter C (possibly from *centum*, hundred). Then their numbers grew to three hundred, and by the end of republican times snowballed and almost reached a thousand under Caesar. Sorting out the affairs of the state, Augustus limited the number of senators to six hundred. But only about three hundred people could be easily accommodated on the three tiers of the Curia (perhaps a little more if we count pedestrians). Most likely, lots of senators were absent at any given time, and this was not considered a breach.

Some ancient Roman edifices were luckier than others for one simple reason: they were converted to Christian churches. This is how the Pantheon was saved, and this is why, compared to other buildings on the Forum, the Curia looks better. In 630, under Pope Honorius I, the building was consecrated to St. Adrian, a guard of one of the later emperors who was martyred together with his wife Natalia; today Adrian is considered the patron saint of soldiers, butchers and communication specialists. In the mid-17th century, the Curia was embellished in baroque style by the architect Martino Longhi the Younger; another architect, Francesco Borromini, removed the building's heavy bronze doors, ordered that they be restored (a few coins were found between its bronze plates) and then reinstalled them in the church of San Giovanni in Laterano. They are probably the oldest functioning doors in the world.

In the second half of the 19th century, archaeologists realised that the ancient Roman Senate was concealed beneath the baroque décor of Sant'Adriano. In 1935, the church was deconsecrated, and by 1938 all later accretions were removed, revealing bare brick walls. It is considered by some one of the best interiors that has come down to us from antiquity, but others object that doing away with Longhi's masterpiece has not brought us closer to appreciating ancient Roman art and architecture. A multicoloured mosaic floor made in lavish imperial style with several varieties of stone brought from all over the Roman world is an authentic trace of the Curia. Today the building is used for temporary exhibitions.

THE BLACK STONE

The Forum had finally and irrevocably become the fiefdom of archaeologists by the end of the 19th century, and it was around that time that some of the most sensational discoveries were made. In 1899, slabs of black marble were found in front of the Curia, and under them a number of monuments dating from different periods: a U-shaped altar, a small base of a lost statue, an oblong slab of volcanic rock (tufa), shards of pottery, archaic cult figurines. Artefacts were not layered in a clear chronological order; it seemed as if old and recent objects had been hastily dug up and buried under the black pavement in the 1st century BC, when the Forum and Comitium were massively overhauled (not for the first or last time). Archaeologists decided that what they had found was the so-called "Black Stone in the Comitium" (*Lapis Niger in Comitio*), known from written sources. New excavations are ongoing, and the whole space is currently covered by a rather horrible semi-translucent pavilion.

Ancient Romans considered the place a tomb, but they were not sure whose. Some said Romulus's; that seemed to contradict the legend about the deification of Romulus and his ascension to the immortals, but the ancients easily dismissed such paradoxes. In another version, the Black Stone marked the tomb of the shepherd Faustulus, foster father of Romulus and Remus, who was horrified when his former wards got into a fight and, gripped by a death wish, he joined in the melée himself. Or perhaps it was the tomb of old Hostilius, the grandfather of Rome's third king. Finally, it could be the Vulcanal, sanctuary of the underworld iron-forging god. This version is supported by a fragment of Greek black-figure vase found in the heap of other objects and debris in the Black Stone hole, with a picture of the god Hephaestus (Vulcan) on a donkey. This represents a well-known and widely reproduced story: Zeus, the father of Hephaestus, angry with his son, threw him from Mount

Olympus down to earth. Hephaestus fell for a whole day, landed on the island of Lemnos (that was the origin of his disability – he remained lame for life) and lived there for nine years, attended by local nymphs. At some point, his parents (Hephaestus was one of the few children of Zeus by his lawful wife, Hera) had second thoughts and invited him back, but he was understandably reluctant. Dionysus did the trick: he got the lame smith drunk, heaved him onto a donkey and triumphantly brought him back to Olympus. Which means that in the old times when the vase was made, the Romans had already made the connection between their Vulcan and the Greek Hephaestus. By the way, no traces of any burial were found under the Black Stone.

The most interesting find in the sanctuary was an inconspicuous piece of tufa. It had words inscribed on it, and the words were in Latin, but an extremely old version of the language. Indeed, the Greek historian Dionysius of Halicarnassus reported that Romulus had dedicated a bronze chariot to Hephaestus and set up a statue of himself nearby with an inscription "in Greek letters" (he does not say "in Greek," which might mean an archaic typeface used for Latin; indeed, the letter R in our inscription looks like a P, not like an R).

The inscription is partly preserved. The writing method used for it was also very archaic – not left-to right, not top-to-bottom, but first in one direction, then in the opposite (in this case, up and down). This type of writing is called *boustrophedon*, "ox-turning" (i.e. when ploughing a field). Only three words are more or less discernible: *kalatorem*, *iovxmenta* and *recei*. The first denotes an official, someone like a herald or messenger; the second describes beasts of burden; the third seems to be an archaic form of *rex*, 'king.' In 1899 this created a sensation, because it seemed to prove the reality of the regal era, at the time doubted by many.

In Cicero's time, a priest called *rex sacrorum* ('a king of sacred things') who was invested with religious functions of the long-ago kings, performed some rituals on that spot; as was often the case with Roman rites, their meaning had been long lost. For example, after completing the procedure, the *rex sacrorum* was supposed to go away in haste, as if pursued by enemies.

It is often assumed that the Black Stone is this inscribed bloc of tufa, but it is not; the name refers to the black marble pavement that used to cover the spot. Cautious scholars think that the Black Stone inscription describes some actions involving domestic animals performed by a king (or a priest) and his assistant. Those who are less cautious have a stab at translating the whole inscription, including its lost portions – for example, "the king forbids anyone from stepping on this sacred spot, and whoever does so acts at his own peril and runs the risk of being gored by beasts of burden." Whatever the inscription meant to say, it is definitely one of the earliest surviving examples of the Latin language.

LACUS CURTIUS

If we stand in the middle of the Comitium (or somewhere near it) and look at the opposite (south) side of the Forum, the first thing we see is a large solitary column, of which more later, and to the left of it a dip in the ground under a depressing squat cover. This is the Lake of Curtius, another very ancient and possibly the most mysterious monument of the Roman Forum.

First of all, it is obviously not a lake. Its name recalls the fabled times when the Forum was not yet drained or inhabitable. Says Ovid (in a rather charming 18th-century translation):

> *What now the **forum** is, was once a moor,*
> *The river us'd to float it heretofore;*
> *And where you see that holy altar stand,*
> *Was **Curtius'** lake, tho' now 'tis solid land[4].*

There is more than a grain of truth here: Rome stands on marshy soil, and it was only after a large-scale engineering effort of the Tarquins' time that the valleys between the hills became habitable along with the hilltops. But a lake amid the marshes, especially on such a tiny plot of land is, of course, a poetic exaggeration.

The Romans themselves had at least three explanations for the Lake of Curtius: the one pedestrian, the other legendary, and the third fantastic.

The pedestrian explanation said that in 445 BC lightning struck this spot, and that year's consul Gaius Curtius Philo ordered railings to be erected around the place. A bolt of lightning, in Roman tradition, meant that the gods wanted the site for themselves. If there was something supernatural about it, it was lightning striking level ground.

The second explanation was set in the times of the war between the Romans and Sabines. A battle was raging on the Forum; the Sabines were driving the enemy almost up the Palatine; Mettius Curtius, one of the Sabine leaders, was leading the charge on horseback. Romulus and a handful of audacious warriors managed to repel him, his horse bolted and got bogged down. While the Sabines were trying to help their comrade out of the mire, the Romans regrouped and used the lull to their advantage. Curtius was saved, the battle resumed – and it was at that point that the Sabine women rushed in and helped to settle the conflict peacefully.

Marcus Curtius jumping into the pit. Engraving
by Cherubino Alberti (?), 16th century

The third explanation was the most fantastic and the best known. In
362 BC a sinkhole opened up in the middle of the Forum – due to an
earthquake or for some other reason. It could not be filled in, however hard
everyone tried. Finally, the priests gave the traditionally vague oracle: the
most precious possession of the country should be thrown into the pit to
appease the gods of the underworld. While the senators were arguing what
that might be, the young warrior Marcus Curtius asked them reproachfully:
do we really possess anything more precious than our arms and valour?
With these words, in full armour, he spurred his horse into the pit, which
immediately closed.

Interestingly, the rather sceptical Livy prefers the last version (because
it is the latest one). There is a Sabine word *mediss* meaning 'leader' – perhaps
the name of the Sabine warrior was not an invention after all. But, of
course, the legend about the mysterious pit and salvation through Roman
virtue was the popular favourite. In Augustan time, a small relief was

set up on the Forum, depicting Marcus Curtius on horseback, ready to plunge into the hole. The slab with the relief is now kept at the Capitoline Museums, and a copy stands near the Lacus Curtius.

Augustus seemed to be partial to this spot: Suetonius says that "all sorts and conditions of men, in fulfilment of a vow for his welfare, each year threw a small coin into the Lacus Curtius."

In the "year of the four emperors" (69 AD), when several contenders fought for supreme power, the first of the four, Galba, was murdered near the Lake of Curtius. He came out to the Forum, confident of his victory, but that was actually a ploy to draw him out from the palace: even his own legionaries turned against him. Only recruits from Germany were willing to defend him, but they got lost in the unfamiliar city and reached the Forum when it was too late, and the emperor was lying in a pool of blood near the Lacus Curtius. The soldier who chopped off Galba's head could not lift it by the hair to carry it to contender number two, Otho: Galba was bald. So he had to thrust a thumb into the dead man's mouth and carry it by holding the head by the jaw.

JANUS AND CLOACINA

Literary sources unanimously claim that there was another very important Roman temple near the spot where the Argiletum joins the Forum, near the Curia – the temple of the two-faced Janus (*Ianus Geminus*). Perhaps it had occupied the place now taken by the small brick building used by the Forum's archaeological service.

As with many other Roman sanctuaries, this was not a temple in our sense of the word, but a narrow corridor with doors on both sides. There were various stories about its origin, but they all converged on the same conflict between the Romans and Sabines. According to one version, the sudden upwelling of a hot spring stopped the almost victorious Sabines in their tracks. According to another, after reconciliation, Romulus and Titus Tatius erected an altar to the double-faced god as a symbol of duality of the nation that embraced both Romans and Sabines. Finally, Livy and Pliny the Elder both claimed that the temple was founded by the wizard king Numa Pompilius as an "indicator of peace and war" (*index pacis bellique*). This explanation caught on better than the rest, and traditionally the gates of the Janus sanctuary were open when Rome was at war, and closed in peacetime. The latter was an exceedingly rare occasion: after the fabled times of Numa, that only happened after the end of the First Punic War in 235 BC, then after the Battle of Actium in 30 BC that made Augustus the master of the world, and twice more during his rule (Augustus very proudly mentions it in his autobiography). Stretches of peace were more frequent in imperial times, but the Roman republic had lived in a state of permanent mobilisation of its army.

In the sanctuary or near it stood a bronze statue of Janus that had, naturally, two faces (Ovid calls it 'two-faced,' Virgil 'two-fronted'). It was said to be erected by Numa Pompilius. The god had a staff in one hand, a key in the other, and still he somehow managed to display a finger combination that meant "355" – that was the number of days in a Roman year before Julius Caesar's calendar reform.

Janus occupied a special place in Roman mythology. God of thresholds, doors and borderline states, he was worshipped by the obsessive-compulsive Romans with a touch of fear. Plutarch writes that ancient coins had the two-faced Janus on one side, and a ship's prow on the other, because "Janus had erected a good frame of government among them … and the river being navigable afforded plenty of all necessary commodities."[5] Indeed, Roman children used to say *capita* and *navia* when tossing a coin, as we say 'heads' and 'tails,' irrespective of what is actually minted on the coin. The name of Janus began every Roman oath to the gods.

A little further to the west, before the portico of Basilica Aemilia (to which we will come in due course), there is a round marble rim approximately two and a half metres wide, with a small gully coming off it. The archaeologists working on the Forum at the end of the 19th century determined that it was the base of the Shrine of Cloacina. The shrine was dedicated to the stream that used to run across the Forum but was later diverted underground and became a part of a large-scale sewage system known as *Cloaca Maxima* ('the Great Drain'). The Romans believed (correctly, as it turned out) that good sewage was essential for public health; remarkably, they held this belief from a very early time. The Shrine of Cloacina is one of the oldest in the whole city; under the rim you see today are seven more layers of stone dating back to older times: the cultural layer was rising, and the foundation had to be raised correspondingly.

Tradition tied the appearance of the Shrine of Cloacina to the time of Romulus, or, more precisely, yet again to the end of the Roman-Sabine war. After the successful intervention of the women, the warriors of both tribes laid down their weapons and purified themselves with branches of myrtle in that very place. We know the general look of the shrine from coins of Julius Caesar's time.

But there is a caveat, when extrapolating from images on coins to complex ancient buildings. Even a small building would hold at least a few people; some buildings can accommodate hundreds or even thousands. But even the largest coin fits into a palm. Such a massive discrepancy of scale forces even the most meticulous coin designer to simplify the building, shave off details, change proportions, because a tiny image dictates a different set of composition rules. The result is a visual synopsis rather than a faithful depiction. Numismatics, however, is our primary source of information about many lost ancient constructions. This is very important and often unique data, but we have to treat it with caution.

The coins that show the Shrine of Cloacina display a small base (probably round), a latticed balustrade and two female statues in headgear. One of them holds a small object in her raised hand; traditionally, this object is thought to be a flower, but this is no more than a guess, the image is too small to make out any details. There are two figures, because at some point the cult of Cloacina got entwined with the cult of Venus; thus the two goddesses, one strictly local, the other national, graced the place where one of the openings of the Cloaca Maxima was.

The Shrine of Venus/Cloacina was the location of one of the tragedies of the early republican era, when the city, according to legend, was ruled by a council of decemviri ('ten men'). One of them, Appius Claudius (we will be meeting his namesakes and descendants more than once), became inflamed with passion for a chaste plebeian girl who was appropriately called Virginia. He made one of his cronies say publicly that the girl was not the daughter of the centurion Virginius (which she was) but only a slave girl. The trial deliberating the problem was presided

over by Claudius himself, and its outcome was obvious. On hearing the news, the girl's father Virginius surmounted lots of obstacles to get back to Rome from the military camp where he was and arrived in time for the trial; he asked the assembly for permission to speak to the girl in private and took her to food shops near the Cloacina shrine. As soon as they were out of reach of the crowd, the centurion grabbed a large bread knife from a bakery stall and stabbed the girl with the words "This is the only way I can protect your freedom." The people were shocked, and the autocratic rule of the decemviri came to an end.

In traditional accounts, the establishment of the Cloaca coincided with the rule of the last kings. The underground bed of this stream follows a very capricious course from the Forum to the river, and the Romans did not attempt to change it: for them, any mountain or brook was a deity, potentially a hostile one. Some of the canals dug for the Cloaca network were so large that a cart loaded with hay could easily pass through it. When Augustus's closest companion, Agrippa, was an aedile (official in charge of public construction), he ordered that Roman sewage be thoroughly cleaned. To monitor the works, he sailed around the Cloaca in a boat. In the later 19th century, enterprising Roman guides were happy to show the Cloaca tunnels to paying British and American customers. The future novelist Henry James wrote to his mother from Rome in 1869 that it was "the deepest and grimmest impression of antiquity" he had ever received.

In the 1st century AD the polymath Pliny the Elder wondered how it happened that the Cloaca, being 700 years old, was as good as new and "completely intact." He would have been even more surprised to know that after 2000 more years, the Cloaca Maxima is still in use (though, admittedly, to a very limited extent). An opening that was used in ancient times to discharge the sewage into the Tiber can be seen on the inner side of the embankment near the Palatine Bridge (*Ponte Palatino*).

THE ARCH OF SEPTIMIUS SEVERUS

In a discussion of the antiquities of Rome, one is inevitably forced to sacrifice either chronological or topographical continuity. When historians search for ancient or mediaeval records, they often stumble across so-called *palimpsests*, scrolls or codexes where the original text had been effaced (but remains somewhat legible to modern scientific methods) to make room for new writing. The whole of Rome is one huge palimpsest, a city which never hesitated to overbuild Classical walls with Renaissance towers.

In this spirit, a large triumphal arch sprang up in the early 3rd century next to the oldest monuments of the Forum (the Black Stone and Lacus Curtius). It remains, along with the Curia, one of the best-preserved ancient buildings on the Forum. Even the reason for its safe survival is the same: in the 7th century, Pope Agatho annexed it with a deaconry – a charitable community centre of sorts – dedicated to St. Sergius and Bacchus. It had survived until the early 17th century. In the Middle Ages, it was a common enough occurrence, and the pagan nature of the original buildings was not considered an obstacle. In the 12th century, local barons added fortifications to the arch, which remained there for the next five centuries.

The Arch of Septimius Severus. 16th-century engraving

The Arch of Septimius Severus is unpopular with art historians: its reliefs are considered schematic and lifeless compared to those that adorn, for example, Trajan's Column. Apart from the winged Victory, river deities and representations of the seasons, the arch tells the story of Septimius Severus's oriental expedition: an army marching out of the camp, people voluntarily submitting themselves to the Roman rule, a siege, an assault, a military council, the conquered cities of Edessa and Ctesiphon. One of the main visual motifs repeats in the form of Roman soldiers (or, sometimes, civilians), who rudely push in front of themselves the frightened, cap-wearing Parthian captives.

The expedition was one of the last successful military ventures of the Roman Empire. Parthia – the main adversary in the East – was vanquished, and over a hundred thousand people were taken prisoner and sold into slavery. The fortified capital of the Arabs, Hatra, had withstood the assault, but Severus added the victorious title 'Arabian,' along with 'Parthian,' to his name anyway: the words *Parthico* and *Arabico* can be seen in the upper line of the dedicatory inscription. The inscription itself glorifies the emperor and his sons Marcus (better known as the future emperor Caracalla) and Publius (better known for his future brief co-rulership with his brother under the name of Geta). When Caracalla had Geta assassinated, he launched a procedure known as *damnatio memoriae* ('damnation of memory'). As a result, the name of Geta on the arch was replaced with an abstract phrase about 'the best and strongest leaders' (*optimis fortissimisque principibus*). But a palimpsest is oblivion-resistant: the original inscription was easily deciphered using the position of the holes for the pegs that had held the original lettering.

Coins show that there used to be a huge sculptural composition on top of the arch: a triumphal chariot drawn by six (possibly eight) horses, led by the reins by two warriors (Caracalla and Geta?) and possibly two more knights riding at either flank, like police bikes in a presidential motorcade. No traces of this group have survived.

In ancient times, the arch was raised on a pediment, with stairs leading up to it. In contrast, many old paintings and engravings, from Piranesi to Canaletto, reveal that until the 19th century, the lower tier of the arch (containing the reliefs with captive Parthians manhandled by Roman soldiers) was completely concealed by a layer of soil.

THE TEMPLE OF SATURN

Behind the Arch of Septimius Severus (looking from the side of the Curia) stand eight columns. These are the remains of the Temple of Saturn, which used to compete with the Temple of Vesta and the Temple of Jupiter on the Capitol for the rank of the city's oldest sanctuary. The Romans were not quite sure who had founded it; they agree that it must have been someone very ancient, like the kings Tullus Hostilius and Tarquin the Proud, or Titus Lartius, the first Roman dictator.

Today's remains date back to the 1st century BC, when the temple was restored (probably built from scratch to old specifications) by the consul Lucius Munatius Plancus. Plancus was a man with an unbelievable career.

Caesar's officer in the Gallic wars, the organiser of the famous feast for Antony and Cleopatra (it was rumoured that he dressed up as a merman and danced in front of the quasi-royal couple, wagging a blue tail), the inventor of the title "Augustus" for Rome's first emperor, the very last Roman censor (the office was abolished and its responsibilities absorbed by the imperial administration), the founder of Basel and Lyon. A whimsical wooden statue of him graces the city hall of Basel.

Unfortunately, what we see today are not the remains of Augustan high art: eight columns of grey and pinkish Egyptian granite borrowed from other buildings and purpose-made Ionian capitals of mediocre quality were assembled in the 4th century AD. This is such a late date that some scholars consider this restoration one of the last desperate stands by Roman pagans in an era when the temples to Olympic gods had already been officially forbidden. The frieze says that the Senate and Roman people restored this temple, previously ravaged by fire; this is one of the handful of inscriptions, where the ubiquitous abbreviation SPQR is written out in full: *Senatus populusque romanus incendio consumptum restituit.*

Since the oldest times, the state treasury was kept under Saturn's sanctuary, which caused the temple to double as the headquarters of quaestors, magistrates responsible for state finances. At some point, the treasury was divided in two: one half served everyday budget purposes, the other was a "stabilisation fund" to be resorted to only in times of grave national peril. The Romans thought that the most likely threat was a war with the Gauls, but reality, as usual, thwarted their expectations. During the turbulent years of "the Roman revolution," the treasury was taken over by Julius Caesar. When a young tribune of the people tried to physically prevent him from robbing the vault, Caesar ominously told him: "Trust me, it's harder for me to threaten you than to kill you."

Like many other monuments on the Forum, the Temple of Saturn was worst hit by Renaissance builders. We have already mentioned Poggio Bracciolini's "On the Vicissitudes of Fortune" (*De Varietate Fortunae*); from this work we even know the exact time frame when the temple was pillaged:

> "Near the Capitol toward the Forum there survives the portico of the Temple of Concord [that was the common attribution of the Temple of Saturn in Poggio's time] which I saw almost intact and lined with excellent marble at the time when I first arrived at Rome [about 1405]; and then, Romans burned all the temple, part of the portico and broken columns for lime. The portico still [ca. 1447] displays the letters testifying that the Senate and Roman people restored the temple destroyed by fire."

Temple of Saturn. Engraving by Giovanni Battista Piranesi

On an engraving by Piranesi (second half of 18th century), the ruins of the Temple of Saturn are shown in idyllic settings long disappeared from the Forum: a now-gone street with residential houses recedes into the distance, a small building clings to outermost columns, and flowers in huge pots grow on its roof; goats graze on an earth bank, a clothes line is stretched between the columns.

Inside the temple was a statue of Saturn, made of gold and ivory and dressed in woollen clothes. Pliny the Elder says it was hollow inside, filled with olive oil, which was supposed to be beneficial for the ivory. In addition, the feet of the statue were bound with coarse ropes that were removed once a year, for the Saturnalia at the end of December. It was a boisterous, noisy holiday, "the best of days" as the poet Catullus said: slaves and masters traded places, everyone made visits and carried gifts, all business activity ceased. (Catilina and his co-conspirators planned their coup for the Saturnalia days, when the Romans relaxed their guard.) Pliny the Younger wrote to a friend that he had made a special study in his villa so as not to be in the way of his household celebrating the Saturnalia (also for the Saturnalia not to be in the way of his learned pursuits). There is a theory that the date of Christ's nativity was crammed into late December by early theologians in order to "reframe" the ineradicable custom of the Saturnalia.

THE TEMPLE OF CONCORD

Behind the Arch of Septimius Severus, near the western limit of the Forum, is a concrete core of a building that used to cover a much larger area and partially receded further toward today's stairs and Palazzo Senatorio. These remains of concrete (probably the oldest concrete in Rome) are left from the Temple of Concord *(Aedes Concordia)*.

The legend dates its foundation by 367 BC. Here is Ovid again in William Massey's translation:

> *When **Furius** victor from the **Tuscan** war*
> *Return'd, he vow'd to build **this temple** here;*
> *The reason was; a fatal diff'rence rose,*
> *The **people** would the **nobles** pow'r oppose;*
> *Of her own strength **Rome** justly was afraid,*
> *When that revolt was by **the people** made.*

Indeed, at that point Roman plebeians revolted against the existing order and threatened to leave the city and found a state of their own. After an arduous struggle, a number of laws were passed that ensured the plebeians' access to top magistracies, including consulship; moreover, according to those laws at least one consul of the year had to represent the plebeian order (no such provision was made for patricians, which made it possible, in theory, to have two concurrent plebeian consuls but not two patrician ones). The celebrated general and statesman Furius Camillus announced the settlement to the people and was met with general rejoicing and vowed to build a temple to honour the concord of the orders.

The next version of the temple arose in 121 BC. The cement for its foundation was probably sourced from crushed stones of the ancient temple of Camillus – such symbolic gestures had a profound meaning in Roman architectural practice. This temple was no longer dedicated to the concord of orders (the difference between patricians and plebeians was no longer politically relevant); rather, it glorified the concord of oligarchs. The construction was sanctioned by the consul Lucius Opimius. Shortly before, on the pretext of heeding the Senate's "final decree," he had drowned in blood the movement of the supporters of Gaius Gracchus. That was the turning point of Roman history: a century later the system of government that had functioned more or less properly for hundreds of years, broke down completely. The fact that Opimius marked one of the bloodiest and saddest episodes in the history of Roman republic with rebuilding the Temple of Concord did not escape anyone's attention, and very soon a street artist subscribed the dedicatory inscription on the temple with the slogan "The Temple of Concord, built by Discord." A few centuries later, St. Augustine was still sneering:

"Actually, the raising of a temple to that goddess merely made the gods a laughing-stock – for surely, if Concord had been in the city, it would not have been torn by so many disorders. Unless, of course, we prefer to say that the goddess Concord, guilty of deserting the lives of her fellow citizens, deserved to be shut up in that temple, as in a prison."[6]

The Temple of Concord is mentioned several times in literary sources in connection with various omens: once lightning struck the statue of the goddess of Victory on its roof, at another time blood-coloured rain was observed in the vicinity of the temple. In the turbulent years that the British historian Ronald Syme called "The Roman Revolution" (his approach defies our notion of a sudden and violent revolution – the transition from republic to empire was slow and used a variety of means, not all of them violent), the Senate often convened in this temple, especially in times of crisis. It was here that Cicero delivered his fourth and final Catilinian oration with an appeal for execution. The temple was rebuilt and decorated by the emperor Tiberius from the spoils of the military campaign in Germany.

Like some other temples in Rome, the Temple of Concord also served as a museum of sorts. In his old age, Augustus asked for a statue of Vesta from the island of Paros to be brought to the temple; there were also lots of other Greek statues and Roman paintings, four unique elephants made of obsidian (volcanic glass) – also the gift of Augustus – and a ring donated to the collection by Livia, the emperor's spouse. Tradition attached to this piece of jewellery claimed that it was the very ring that used to belong to Polycrates, the tyrant of Samos.

Since the terrain already had significant buildings on it, the architectural treatment of the structure was unusual: against convention, its width was greater than its length. During the reconstruction under Tiberius the builders wanted to enlarge it, but its length was limited by the Tabularium behind it and Comitium in front of it, so they had to widen it even more. Coins show that the temple was decorated with a variety of sculptures: Hercules and Mercury at the entrance and at least seven more figures on the roof (probably featuring the goddess of Concord, Tiberius, his brother Drusus and other dignitaries). A fragment of lavishly decorated entablature (the part of the building above the colonnade, consisting of a lintel that is directly above the columns, a frieze and a cornice) is on display at the Capitoline Museums.

The Ring of Polycrates

Polycrates was the ruler of the Ionian island of Samos in the 6th century BC, the fabled time of Greek wise men. He was the luckiest ruler alive, with a powerful army and navy, strong alliances with other potentates, and a court of great luxury and elegance. Once (recounts Herodotus, 'the father of history') he received a letter from his friend, the Egyptian king Amasis. Amasis wrote: "My friend, your happiness is too great; the gods will envy you. Take the thing you love most of all and part with it; perhaps it will help to avert a greater disaster."

Polycrates, though a tyrant, knew that the world was ruled by law, and law put moderation above all else. He had an emerald signet ring that he loved very much; he put it on, sailed into the open sea and in front of his whole retinue dropped the ring overboard.

A few days later, a fisherman came to the court. "I caught a fish so large that it is unheard of, and decided to bring it to you, Polycrates, as a gift." The tyrant thanked the fisherman and sent the fish to the kitchen. The slave who was cutting the fish suddenly cried out in surprise: something glittered at him from out of the fish's stomach. It was the ring of Polycrates that had returned to its owner.

Polycrates, amazed, wrote to Amasis, and Amasis wrote him back: "My friend, I see that the gods do not accept your sacrifices. You were spared a minor misfortune, now await a major one. I break the ties of our friendship because I do not want to see a friend suffer and be unable to help."

Soon after, Polycrates entered into negotiations with the Persian governor, Oroetus, who offered him a secret union. Polycrates went to discuss the deal against the premonitions of his own daughter, and Oroetus had him murdered and executed so cruelly that Greek historians did not have the heart to describe it.

When the famous ring of Polycrates was on display in the Temple of Concord in the more affluent times of Augustus, it was one of the collection's least ornate and expensive exhibits.

The Russian classical scholar Mikhail Gasparov, under the pen-name Klara Lemming, summarised the story in a poem:

> *The ring of Polycrates*
> *really loved Polycrates.*
> *When Polycrates threw it into the sea,*
> *it really wanted to take offence,*
> *but decided that love was above such things,*
> *crept into a fish*
> *and returned to Polycrates's finger.*
> *After the crucifixion of Polycrates,*
> *every trace of it is lost.*
> *Later it was on display in an Augustan museum*
> *and seemed of mediocre craftsmanship.*
> *This is how Pliny reports it.*

THE TEMPLE OF VESPASIAN

Next to the Temple of Concord (or, to be precise, the site of the Temple of Concord) stand three columns of white Italian marble. One of Piranesi's engravings shows them against a backdrop of another genre scene from the life of the "Cattle field." A tourist of today would barely recognise the monument: in the engraving, the soil reaches up almost to the capitals. When in 1810 it was decided to remove the cultural layer that had accrued since the times of the Roman Empire, it turned out that the surviving columns were not standing straight – they had veered off for almost a metre and were only held in place by the soil around it. The architects were forced to dismantle the columns and erect them on a new foundation, so the visitor needs to bear in mind that the stairs and base of this temple date back to 1811. At the end of the 19th century the famous archaeologist and educator Rodolfo Lanciani wrote, with a touch of exaggeration, that "the expectant public could see outlined against the sky those capitals and that frieze which, only a few months before, had been trodden by the feet of tourists."

Both Piranesi and early 19th-century architects thought that the three columns belonged to the Temple of Jupiter the Thunderer (which was not that far away, on the Capitol hill). The surviving portion of the frieze contains the letters ESTITVER. It was not difficult to surmise that this was a fragment of *restituerunt*, 'restored,' but for obvious reasons that did not really solve the attribution problem.

The key to the riddle was found in a unique document called "The Einsiedeln Itinerary." It is a portion of a 9th-century manuscript (the time of Charlemagne) with eleven routes for walking in Rome, from one set of gates in the ancient walls to the other, with a description of everything to be seen along the route. The learned monk also carefully copied out some of the inscriptions, of which many were in much better shape than today. The Temple of Vespasian, for instance, was adorned with the words "To the Divine Vespasian Augustus the Senate and Roman people," and on the second line "The Emperors and Caesars Severus and Antoninus Pius, the happy Augusti, [had this temple] restored." The document had been found in the Swiss monastery of Einsiedeln a long time ago, but it was only in 1827 that the archaeologist Antonio Nibby put two and two together.

It was now obvious that it was the temple begun by Titus after the death and deification of his father Vespasian. He did not end it, because he himself died two years later. Titus was also deified, and the construction was completed by his younger brother, the third and last of the Flavian emperors, Domitian. Ancient sources indicate that the temple was dedicated to both father and son (though only the father is mentioned in the inscription). Some books call it "The Temple of Vespasian and Titus."

The cynical and level-headed emperor was also a wit, though he probably would have been surprised to hear that. Two of his quips were especially well remembered by posterity; one was his retort to Titus who objected to a tax on public toilets; pushing a coin under his son's nose, Vespasian asked "Does it stink? No? And yet it comes from urine." The other was connected with the practice of deifying the emperors upon their death. It had started with Julius Caesar as a one-off honour, but by the time of Vespasian became almost routine. Therefore, when Vespasian felt that death was drawing near, he said: "Woe's me. Methinks I'm turning into a god" (*Vae, puto deus fio*).

The frieze of the temple was decorated with ox skulls (*bucrania*), a symbol of sacrifice which also protected from bad omens. Various sacrificial paraphernalia were placed between the skulls – helmets, axes, knives, plates, jugs. This elegant specimen of Roman decorative art is on display in the Capitoline Museums.

THE PORTICO OF THE CONSENTING GODS

Behind the Temple of Vespasian and opposite the Temple of Saturn lurks a strange monument which is often overlooked. It is a colonnade of twelve squat Corinthian columns that form an awkward blunt angle with its "back" toward the Capitol. The authors of architectural and archaeological guides, usually reserved, do not mince their words when they describe this – admittedly clumsy – structure.

This monument does not even have a firmly established name. It is known that it was dedicated to the twelve gods. The concept of some gods being more important than the others was taken by Romans from the Greeks (the Greeks called the supreme gods 'Olympians,' after their alleged residence on Mount Olympus in northern Greece), and it got entrenched, in all likelihood, during the war with Hannibal. When the state was in mortal danger, the senators and the people turned to the priests who delved into sacred books and announced that if Rome would stand, the whole generation of offspring of the first peaceful spring – all calves, lambs, piglets and chickens – would have to be sacrificed to the gods. It was an ancient Sabine rite called "Sacred spring" (*ver sacrum*). In addition, six couches were voted to be installed on the Forum, one for each couple of supreme gods. Titus Livius lists them in this order: Jupiter and Juno, Neptune and Minerva, Mars and Venus, Apollo and Diana, Vulcan and Vesta, Mercury and Ceres. The old Latin poet Ennius composed a virtuoso couplet (listing the necessary names to fit a metrical poetry line was close to impossible) in which he distributed all the Olympians by gender: first all the goddesses, then all the gods. He succeeded only by substituting the archaic *Iovis* for Iuppiter:

Iuno Vesta Minerva Ceres Diana Venus Mars
Mercurius Iovis Neptunus Volcanus Apollo.

In his treatise "On Agriculture," the polymath Varro also mentions the twelve consenting gods, but not "those urban gods, whose images stand around the Forum, bedecked with gold, six male and a like number female, but those twelve gods who are the special patrons of husbandmen."[7] They are, in Varro's reckoning, Jupiter and Tellus (the goddess of soil), Sol and Luna (sun and moon), Ceres and Bacchus, Robigus (the averter of grain disease) and Flora, Minerva and Venus, Lympha (the goddess of freshwater) and Bonus Eventus (the god of happy outcome).

Archaeologists assume that the images of the gods stood between the columns of the portico. It is not quite clear what purpose was served by seven small recesses – perhaps six of them were meant for the six pairs of gods, perhaps there were twelve but five somehow were never found. The surviving ruins date back to the Flavians, but the portico was restored and reconstructed many times since then.

The last reconstruction of Classical times is marked by an inscription on the lintel, and we know its organiser: it was the urban prefect Vettius Agorius Praetextatus in 367 AD. This is a very unexpected date for restoring such a blatantly pagan monument: all sacrifices were forbidden in 341, pagan temples were officially closed down in 356. However, many Romans, especially hereditary aristocrats, resisted the victorious onslaught of Christianity. Praetextatus was one of such die-hard conservatives (like his younger friend

Praetextatus

Symmachus, the one who tried to protect the statue of Victory in the Senate House). A bronze tablet that has come down to us outlines, on the right, Praetextatus's administrative career (governor of Lusitania, proconsul of Achaia, urban prefect) and on the left his religious titles (priest of Vesta, priest of Sol, hierophant, Father of mysteries).

Like Symmachus, Praetaxtatus was also an active opponent of the new religion. At the end of the 4th century AD, Christianity was no longer the faith of marginalised provincials; it was confidently striding to become a state-sponsored totalitarian doctrine, and the learned pagans of the time witnessed the predilection of Christian hierarchs for luxury, something that would later blossom on Roman soil. "Make me a pope, and I will take baptism post haste," sneered Praetextatus. The Christians had no sympathy for him, either: shortly after his death, St. Jerome wrote contentedly that the year's consul designate was now in Hell.

In the light of this deadly feud, the history of recent restoration of the monument seems paradoxical: it was excavated under the auspices of Pope Gregory XVI, and its current shape is the result of the efforts of Pope Pius IX: in 1858, he ordered that columns be assembled from fragments of greenish marble and the missing columns replaced with new ones (of travertine, not marble; these are the five non-fluted columns on the right-hand side of the portico). The contribution of both popes is recorded on commemorative tablets.

THE TWO BASILICAS

The central area of the Forum is taken up by an almost square-shaped and at first sight almost bare plot of land with a few columns and empty bases in the middle. The north and south sides of this square had been once fronted by two majestic basilicas.

The word 'basilica' is nowadays mostly used with one of the two meanings. It denotes a large Roman Catholic church with special rights given to it by the Pope. It also means (in art historians' parlance) any Christian church which looks like a Latin cross in plan view (according to this definition, St. Peter's is a shortened basilica, while San Marco in Venice is not a basilica at all). But before Christianity, the basilicas were purely secular buildings. The word itself means something like "royal house" or "kingly portico." The basilicas served as courthouses, business centres and shopping arcades: their luxurious halls were given to criminal and civil proceedings, while shadowy passages housed the shops selling all kinds of goods.

The rectangle at the north border of the Forum, with its side facing the Argiletum, was occupied by Basilica Aemilia. This is hard to believe today, but Pliny the Elder once wrote that it was one of the three principal architectural marvels of Rome (alongside the Forum of Augustus and the Temple of Peace). In the legendary times of the early republic there were shops there – meat shops at first, then money-changers. In the 2nd century BC the censor Marcus Fulvius Nobilior built there the first permanent structure. As often happens with Roman buildings, it is not clear whether the Basilica Fulvia was the same as Aemilia, and if yes, to what extent. One source even calls it "Basilica Aemilia and Fulvia." But either way, the building was quite important: the city's first water clock was installed in the basilica.

The new (or renovated) structure was named Aemilia in acknowledgement of a few members of the family who had spent a lot of money on restoring and embellishing it. One of those men was called Aemilius Paulus, and another version of the name, Basilica Pauli, was added to the building.

At some point, Paulus took money for the basilica from Julius Caesar. This struck a warning note with Pompey, Caesar's rival, who was unhappy about the concentration of money, power and propaganda clout in the hands of Caesar's supporters. That was one of the episodes that later spiralled into the final unravelling of the Roman republic. This is how Plutarch describes it:

"Caesar having now sent his Gallic wealth for all those in public life to draw from in copious streams ... and having given Paulus the consul fifteen hundred talents, out of which he adorned the forum with the Basilica, a famous monument, erected in place of the Fulvia, – under these circumstances Pompey took fright at the coalition, and openly now, by his own efforts and those of his friends, tried to have a successor appointed to Caesar in his government, and sent a demand to him for the return of the soldiers whom he had lent him for his Gallic contests."[8]

Augustus was proud that he had found Rome a city of brick and left it a city of marble, and he also directed his attention to the basilica. This attention was ideologically charged. One of the most burning problems facing Augustus in the later years of his rule was the problem of succession. The situation was further complicated by the fact that Augustus and his wife Livia had different ideas on who would best fill the most important position in the state. Augustus gravitated toward his biological progeny, Livia toward hers. Livia had a stronger hand: from her first marriage, she had a son, Tiberius Claudius, who was intelligent, morally irreproachable and a good soldier to boot. Augustus had only one child, a profligate daughter called Julia, and it was her sons, Gaius Caesar and Lucius Caesar, that Augustus was betting on. To inure the people to the thought, he adopted the grandsons and made the Senate proclaim them consuls designate when they were still in their teens – so as they could assume consulships the moment they turned twenty. Augustus also ordered a portico in their honour to be attached to the Basilica Aemilia. When this area of the Forum was excavated, a large slab with a dedicatory inscription was found; it now stands near the basilica. The portico was still standing in the early 16th century, when it was sketched by the architect Giuliano da Sangallo.

Portico of Gaius and Lucius. Drawing by Giuliano da Sangallo

An unenviable fate was in store for the two young men: one of them died at the age of eighteen, another at twenty-three, and Augustus was forced to adopt Tiberius, making him *de facto* successor in the people's eyes. In his restrained and formal autobiography a human emotion bursts out only once: "My sons whom fortune snatched away from me in their youth…"[9] The rumours, of course, accused Livia of engineering the death of Augustus's grandsons, but there was no proof, especially since the boys died far away from Rome: Gaius in Lycia, Lucius in Gaul.

In the early 5th century AD, the basilica suffered a fire. The fragments of the marble floor still preserve greenish traces of bronze coins that melted in the conflagration (perhaps there still were money-changing shops in the basilica). The fire could have been the result of the sack of Rome in 410, when Alaric's Goths took the city – the first time in over 800 years when Rome fell to an external enemy. Old people were shaking their heads and saying that it had been too hasty to reject the traditional gods in favour of the fashionable Christian heresy. (As a response to these doubts, a bishop from the North African city of Hippo called Augustine wrote his most important work, *De civitate Dei*, "The City of God.") In 847, under Pope Leo IV, the basilica was damaged by an earthquake. But the remains of the walls and the portico were pulled apart for building materials after Sangallo had managed to sketch them.

We can still see some of the buildings where these materials went. A straight street, Via della Conciliazione, leads from the Castle Sant'Angelo to St. Peter's Square, and it is lined by embassies to the Holy See. House number 30 is the so-called Giraud Torlonia Palace. Before Henry VIII, when England was another Roman Catholic country, this house was the English embassy; then it came into possession of French bankers, then to the Torlonia family, still prominent in Vatican administration. Many Roman antiquities were stored there, but since the 1960s they are unavailable to public and specialists alike. The lining of this palace consists of the remains of the famous basilica that was once one of the wonders of the world.

Another basilica stood just across the way from Aemilia. It also had a number of names: first, Sempronia; then Julius Caesar began a new building on the same footprint. It was Augustus who saw to completion of most of Julius Caesar's urban projects; this happened to the new basilica as well, which he called Basilica Julia in honour of his adoptive father. After the death of Gaius and Lucius the basilica was briefly renamed after them, but the new name did not stick.

Structurally, the basilicas were alike: both on two levels, with different columns downstairs and upstairs, with shopping arcades on the outside and business premises inside. The college of *centumviri* met at the Basilica Julia; this was a very old institution, founded allegedly in regal times. The word means "a hundred men," but there were actually 180 of them. They mostly dealt with property law, including inheritance cases. The lawyer and memoirist Pliny the Younger left a colourful description of a case he was pleading before the college:

"A woman of distinguished birth, married to a praetorian, was disinherited by her octogenarian father within eleven days of his bringing home to his daughter a stepmother with whom he had become infatuated. Attia was now seeking to recover her father's property in the assembly of four panels. The 180 judges (this is the sum of the four panels sitting together) took their seats. There were several advocates on the two sides, and the benches were jammed; and in addition a densely packed crowd of bystanders surrounded the very extensive court-room in a circle which was thronged. Then, too, the bench of judges was crowded, and in the gallery of the basilica both men and women loomed over us in their eagerness to hear (which was difficult) and to see (which was easy). Fathers, daughters, even stepmothers all awaited with great anticipation.

The outcome was divided, for we prevailed in two of the four panels, and were defeated in two. … The chance outcome was one that did not seem to happen by chance; the stepmother, heiress to a sixth of the estate, lost her case."[10]

Both basilicas were covered with wood; in poetic language, the Basilica Julia was even called "the Julian roof." The half-mad emperor Caligula used it in a rather unorthodox manner: he "scattered large sums of money among the commons from the roof of the basilica Julia for several days in succession."[11]

The floor of the Basilica Aemilia is famous for its melted coins, while the floor of the Basilica Julia is no less famous for its numerous game boards; according to some calculations, there are over eighty of them. Obviously, what we sometimes call 'table-top games' were 'floor games' for the Romans.

THE ROSTRA

The oldest military monument in the United States, the so-called Tripoli Monument in Annapolis, Maryland, honouring the heroes of the First Barbary War (a naval conflict of the early 19th century between the nascent United States and North African pirates), is adorned with two rows of prows of antique galleys. In St. Petersburg, Russia, two huge red columns that used to serve as beacons for river navigation also sprout ship prows. Such columns are called rostral (from Latin *rostrum*, plural *rostra* – prow of a ship).

The tradition of decorating architectural monuments with the prows of enemy ships dates back to Roman times. The very first rostral column was erected on the Forum in celebration of a naval victory off Antium (now Anzio, about fifty kilometres south of Rome on the shore of the Tyrrhenian Sea). Not knowing what to do with the bronze decorations of enemy ships, the Romans decided to install them in the middle of the Forum.

Another, better known column, was dedicated to the victory over Carthaginians in 260 BC in the battle of Mylae (now Milazzo, a small town on the north coast of Sicily). It was Rome's first major naval victory, and over an adversary whose supremacy on the seas was considered incontestable. The Romans were so clueless about naval warfare that they could only start building their own navy when a stray Carthaginian ship was wrecked in the Straits of Messina and fell into the hands of the Romans. Carthaginians, though, had been forewarned: shortly before the First Punic War, a Roman statesman was telling the Carthaginian ambassador that the Romans are quite used to defeating enemies on their home ground using their favourite methods. He concluded this warning with a direct threat: "Do not force the Romans to engage in affairs of the sea; for if we have need of naval forces we shall, in a short time, equip more and better ships than you, and we shall prove more effective in naval battles than people who have long practiced seafaring."

The Romans' military strength had so far been completely land-locked; even with a fleet, they did not have trained mariners. They decided to circumvent the difficulty by deploying troops skilled in ground operations to enemy ships. But how to get them onto enemy ships? Roman engineers came up with a special boarding device (probably called *harpago* by the Romans themselves, but later known as *corvus*, 'raven,' in history books); it consisted of a wooden bridge with a heavy spike at the end (that was the 'beak' meant to pierce the deck of the enemy ship). The rest was easy: board the Carthaginian galley and fight hand-to-hand as you're used to. The corvus could not be used on choppy seas, but by the end of the First Punic War the Romans had gained enough general naval experience to stop using it altogether.

The first man to actively use the corvus in battle was the commander of the rear fleet at Mylae (he was forced to advance to the thick of the battle after the commander had been captured by the Carthaginians), one Gaius Duilius, later a consul. In those times, this was a unique honour for a "new man" (*homo novus* was a technical term for a high-ranking magistrate whose direct ancestors had not been senators or consuls). The rostral column on the Forum was also named for his victory.

With the growing number of naval victories the Romans decorated a whole platform near the Comitium and the Curia with the prows, and called it simply *Rostra* ('the prows'). According to ancient historians, that was the most solemn spot on the Forum. There was no higher award for a statesman than a statue of him erected on the Rostra. Of course, with time, there were so many statues that old ones had to be removed to make way for the new. Something similar was happening to the Rostra themselves. The old platform was dismantled under Julius Caesar. Its back was convex to accommodate the stairs on the Comitium; the Julian Rostra were moved closer to the centre of the Forum, and the new structure faithfully replicated the shape of the previous one. Augustus added another platform a little to the east, and in late imperial years yet another was set up for the sake of balance on the other side of the Forum, in front of the Temple of Deified Julius. In the 19th century those last Rostra were erroneously identified as mediaeval (i.e. historically unimportant in the eyes of 19th-century archaeologists) and torn down.

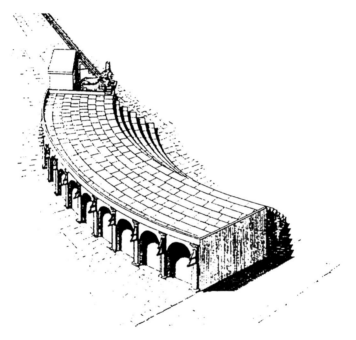

The Rostra. Reconstruction

Caesar's Rostra were reconstructed in 1904 almost from scratch, though some of the ancient blocks (like the ones with the holes for the ships' prows) were used. Near the Augustan Rostra there is a small brick annex with a poorly preserved dedicatory inscription. It seems that it commemorates some achievement of the urban prefect Junius Valentinus in the last years of the Western Roman Empire. The achievements of the time, especially if they were of a military nature, usually consisted of fighting the German tribe of Vandals, and this tenuous surmise has given the annex the name of the "Vandals' Rostra" (*Rostra Vandalica*).

THE FUNERAL

The Rostra served as the favourite spot for public speaking and funerals, which in Rome were also an occasion for public speaking on a grand scale. The most detailed description of Roman funeral customs was given by the historian Polybius. Polybius was a Greek nobleman taken to Rome as a hostage along with a thousand of other young man from Achaia in the 2nd century BC, when Rome was firmly establishing its political and military presence in Greece. "Hostage" in this case does not mean a bound and gagged man awaiting execution; hostage-taking was a form of cultural exchange. Polybius had spent seventeen years in Rome in that status, was received by the crème de la crème, became the tutor of the future general and politician Aemilius Paulus and formed a very flattering, if somewhat idealised, view of the Roman state, its mores, customs and culture. (Polybius was a shrewd thinker, and his ideas, especially on the separation of powers, were very influential with the Founding Fathers of the USA.) Polybius kept returning to the question that seemed an insoluble riddle to him and to most of his Greek contemporaries: how did it happen that a provincial barbarian town in West Mediterranean transformed itself into the lord and ruler of the known world within a span of two generations? As a Greek writing for Greek audiences, Polybius was more focused on ethnographic detail than later Roman historians, and his "Histories" are a priceless source of information on everyday life.

The death of a noble Roman, Polybius reports, becomes an important event for the whole city. The deceased is taken to the Forum and set up (in a standing position, not lying down) on the Rostra. In preparation, special craftsmen take his death mask, trying to be as life-like as possible, down to the complexion (later the mask takes pride of place in the house of the deceased). The funeral is supposed to extol the virtues of the newly departed, as well as the glorious past of his *gens* (family). His son (or other relative) delivers a speech, praising the man and telling the stories of his noble ancestors, down to the most ancient. This account is rather theatrical, because other relations of the deceased are sitting on the Rostra at that very moment, role-playing those ancient ancestors, in their death masks and corresponding attire (in a broad-stripe consular toga, for example, if the ancestor had been a consul).

It was from the Rostra that Mark Antony delivered his famous funeral oration over Caesar's dead body, best known to the posterity through its reconstruction (there is no record of the actual speech) in Shakespeare's tragedy. The historian Appian of Alexandria writes that Antony turned Caesar's funeral into a carefully staged show. At the end of his eulogy, when the crowd was sobbing fit to bust, a special rotating device hoisted the wax effigy of Caesar above the Rostra; it was dressed in a bloodied toga, complete with the marks of the twenty-three stab wounds inflicted by the conspirators. The agitated crowd rushed to avenge Caesar, and Mark Antony could now safely say that the people had found the amnesty he had promised the assassins unacceptable.

When Mark Antony joined the armed struggle for Caesar's legacy, the old Cicero decided to make the final stand in defence of the dying republic. In the Senate and on the Forum, he delivered fourteen venomous speeches against Antony which he called "Philippics" in memory of the speeches delivered by the Athenian orator Demosthenes against Philip II of Macedon. The young Octavian, the future Augustus, is treated kindly in these speeches, as the possible protector of the Senate and future guardian of the state. But when Octavian emerged victorious in the armed conflict, he joined forces with Antony and agreed the list of proscribed persons with him. Cicero's name on that list was undoubtedly Antony's idea, but Octavian acquiesced to that. Cicero made a half-hearted attempt at fleeing Italy, but was found and murdered. The orator's severed head and hands were brought to Antony; Fulvia, Antony's wife at the time, pierced Cicero's tongue with her own hairpin. The horrible spoils were nailed up on the Rostra, where Cicero's career had unfolded over several previous decades. "And more people came to see the dead man than used to listen to him when he was alive," says Appian.

At the beginning of the 4th century BC, five columns were erected on the Rostra to celebrate the twentieth anniversary of the rule of Diocletian and the tenth anniversary of the government system he had instituted, known as 'tetrarchy' (the rule of four). For this solemn occasion, Diocletian visited Rome for the first and last time in his life. The highest column was topped with the statue of Jupiter, the other four held the statues of the four rulers. In 1547, the pedestal of one of those columns was found (the so-called "Decennalia base"); it is currently placed near the Rostra. The pedestal shows processions and sacrifices honouring the tetrarchy's tenth anniversary, and the coat of arms held by winged goddesses says "Happy Caesars' decade!" (*Caesarum decennalia feliciter*)

Ten more huge brick bases (of course, they used to be lined with travertine or marble) stand at equal distances between one another along the south border of the Forum. They are the pedestals of commemorative columns set up for various victories of the late Roman era. Two of them were restored (though on wrong bases), and the one with visible holes apparently used to stand in a different corner of the Forum and was rostral (the holes are where the decorative prows were fastened).

On the sides of the Rostra were two monuments marking the centre of Rome (and, correspondingly, the world). One of them was "the navel of the city of Rome" (*Umbilicus urbis Romae*), with the only part of it preserved being a round concrete base between the Rostra and the Arch of Septimius Severus. The other was the Golden Milestone (*Milliarium aureum*), a column of gilded bronze erected in Augustan times. This signpost marked the most important cities of the empire and distances to them, and it was where, according to Plutarch, all the roads of Italy terminated.

THE COLUMN OF PHOCAS

Traditionally, the Column of Phocas is considered the last Classical monument on the Forum, even though the year of its appearance, 608 AD, may already qualify as belonging to early Middle Ages. This stand-alone Corinthian column had always been a convenient reference point on the Forum, even when it was a grazing field for cows and goats. The dedication on its base says that Smaragdus, the Exarch of Ravenna (a Byzantine governor of Italy) erected the monument to the "best, most clement and pious ruler, our lord Phocas the perpetual emperor, crowned by God, the forever august triumphator." Finding good stone masons and architects in Rome was difficult at the time, so the column was borrowed from an unknown 2nd century building.

Phocas was a soldier of the humblest possible birth who procured the Byzantine crown for himself by the most straightforward means: he murdered the emperor Maurice and his five sons, after which the army installed him on the throne. A few years later, the exarchs of Africa, father and son both named Heraclius, renounced their allegiance to Phocas and began a civil war. After a few bouts of fierce fighting, the younger Heraclius entered Constantinople without meeting any resistance – even the private imperial guard under the command of Phocas's son-in-law surrendered to the conqueror's mercy. The captured Phocas was brought before Heraclius. "That's how you ruled, rascal?" said the victor. Phocas snapped: "What, you will rule better?" The enraged Heraclius personally beheaded Phocas.

In spite of his cruel disposition, Phocas did a great service to Rome by giving the city at least two important monuments – apart from his column, also the Pantheon. It was on his orders that the Pantheon was given to Pope Boniface IV to use as a Christian church, which helped to preserve it into our days almost intact.

An inscription shedding light on the history of the column was found by Napoleon's archaeologists in 1813. Byron, writing a few years later, still called it "thou nameless column with the buried base" (it was more romantic that way). Further excavations were sponsored by an eccentric English noblewoman, Elizabeth Cavendish, the Duchess of Devonshire. Under her patronage, a mediaeval step pyramid was found beneath the brick base. It was dismantled in 1903.

THE TEMPLE OF CASTOR AND THE LAKE OF JUTURNA

To the west of the Basilica Julia is a path that was called "The Etruscan Lane" (*Vicus Tuscus*) in antiquity. The comedy writer Plautus warns in his lively description of Forum life that it was the favourite spot of those who were selling their bodies. On the other side of the lane, the Temple of Castor stood. Three remaining columns are not a latter-day reconstruction for a change: they are found in many vedutas (paintings with urban views) of the 18th century. In the 4th century AD the temple was in good condition, then there is no mention of it for a very long time, and in the 15th century the Etruscan Lane was called "The three-column street" (*Via Trium Columnarum*), which means that it looked more or less as it does now.

These three columns had been justly admired over a long period. In the 1760s the future architect John Dance wrote to his father, also an architect, that he had taken "a Model cast from the finest Example of the Corinthian order perhaps in the whole World."

A student of English architect John Soane measures the ruins of the
Temple of Castor and Pollux. Drawing by Henry Park, ca. 1810

To say that the columns were not a latter-day reconstruction is
accurate. The temple was, of course, restored in antiquity; it was very
ancient, but what we see now dates to Augustan times. Castor and Pollux
(the second brother was called Polydeuces in Greek), or *Dioskouroi* ('divine
young men,' or simply *Gemini*, 'the twins,' in Latin) were the children
of Leda, seduced by Zeus in the shape of a swan. That was a very old
myth. Divine or semi-divine brothers who are very good with horses is
a common Indo-European motif with parallels in Indian Vedic tradition.

Greek myths about the Dioskouroi are numerous and contradictory, another sign of their antiquity. Their cult flourished in Magna Graecia, the Greek cities of southern Italy. There were home-grown Roman myths about them as well; one of them connected Castor and Pollux with a battle that the Roman republic, freshly liberated from the rule of kings, fought with its neighbours.

Polydeuces/Pollux was an unlucky figure, similar to the vice-president in the American joke ("one brother was lost at sea, the other became the vice president of the United States, and both were never heard from again"). The temple is called "of Castor and Pollux" in some sources, but more often than not the second brother is forgotten. Already in antiquity, this injustice was a source of merriment: in the consulship of Julius Caesar and Marcus Bibulus, called by the wits of the time 'the consulship of Julius and Caesar,' Bibulus "openly said that … just as the temple erected in the Forum to the twin brethren bears only the name of Castor, so the joint liberality of Caesar and myself [was] credited to Caesar alone."[12]

The battle in question was semi-mythical, and Livy grumbles as he prepares to describe it that the order of magistrates and years is mixed up in different sources: "not only events but even authorities are so shrouded in antiquity." After the expulsion of the kings, the Tarquin family began to stir up neighbouring Latin tribes against Rome; when delaying the clash further became impossible, the Romans engaged the new rule of electing a dictator for dealing with a critical situation. In modern language, 'dictator' means an autocratic ruler who obtained power illegally, does not intend to relinquish it, and treats his subjects with cruelty. The Roman dictator was none of these things; it was, in effect, a crisis manager. The necessity of such a magistracy was caused by the dual nature of consular authority; great as it was, sometimes a strong single command was a dire necessity. So the Romans decided to appoint a man who would be in charge of a specific complex problem of national importance (it was usually a problem of military nature, but not necessarily, especially in later times). The appointment of a dictator was similar to present-day martial law: a dictator was bound to step down as soon as his work was completed (or, if he could not solve it fast, not later than in six months' time); he had the right to be protected by twenty-four bodyguards called lictors (twice as many as a consul); the authority of the consuls was not abolished for the time of dictatorship but the consuls reported to the dictator in the sphere of his competence. The Romans' fear of king-style absolutism was so strong that an appointed dictator had to immediately choose an assistant called "master of the horse" (*magister equitum*), who, though a subordinate, still limited the dictator's absolute rule.

To fight the Latins, Aulus Postumius was appointed dictator with Titus Aebutius as the master of the horse. The armies met near Lake Regillus in Etruria. It is difficult to say where the lake was – it was a shallow volcanic lake that had dried up by the 18th century. Most likely the battle occurred somewhere between today's towns of Frascati and Tuscolo. When the Romans wavered under enemy assault and turned their back, Aulus Postumius turned his best hand-picked cohort into a retreat-blocking unit with the threat to destroy deserters. Stripped of any choice, the Romans attacked the enemy, rolled up the enemy formation and captured their camp; the dictator and master of the horse triumphantly returned to the city.

At the most desperate moment of the battle, the Romans suddenly saw two handsome young men fighting alongside them on huge white steeds. When the victory was won, it was these same young men who brought news of it to Rome: miraculously, they appeared on the Forum and watered their weary horses by the spring of Juturna. Cicero tells another story: much later, in 168 BC, when the Roman general Aemilius Paulus trounced Perseus, the king of Macedon (and took a thousand hostages, including Polybius), the Dioscouroi appeared to the senator Vatinius and informed him about the victory. The frightened Senate put Vatinius under arrest for spreading false rumours. Many days later, a messenger from Paulus in Macedon confirmed the date of the victory, and Vatinius was released with apologies accompanied by awe and fear.

The temple of the twins was rededicated by Lucius Metellus Dalmaticus at the end of the 2nd century BC to celebrate a victory over Dalmatians (people, not dogs). The tribes of Dalmatians who lived on the shores of the Adriatic Sea had submitted to Rome shortly before and were not planning to fight at all; they were friendly toward Metellus and invited him to winter at Salona (now Solin, a suburb of Split in Croatia). On his return to Rome, Metellus celebrated his triumph. The podium of the temple probably dates back to his time. As for the three columns that are standing today, they were erected at the end of Augustus's rule by his adopted son and heir Tiberius.

In mid-July, a holiday honouring Castor was celebrated in Rome. Several thousand young men in full military dress participated in a procession headed by two riders on white horses acting as the Dioscouroi. Augustus 'privatised' that cult and made an attempt to tie the veneration of the twins to the imperial household: first with his his grandsons Gaius and Lucius, and after their untimely deaths, with Tiberius and his brother Drusus (who turned out to be remarkably unsuccessful as a Dioskouros and died after falling from a horse).

Behind the temple of Castor are the ruins of some structures of Domitian's and Caligula's time and a small house that had once been Rome's main Christian church. It is Santa Maria Antiqua with unique early mediaeval frescoes which are in such poor condition that tourists are not allowed inside. The church was abandoned (possibly after an earthquake) in the mid-9th century, and its main relic, a 5th-century fresco of Mary and the child, the so-called "Our Lady of Tenderness," was carefully cut out from the wall and transferred to the neighbouring church of Santa Maria Nova (now Santa Francesca Romana). The old building was completely forgotten and even had a chapel built over it, which was dismantled in 1901 during excavation work. Another nearby chapel commemorates the martyrdom of forty Roman soldiers who refused to renounce their Christian faith and were frozen alive on the ice of a mountain lake near the Armenian town of Sebastia (now on Turkish territory). The building itself dates from Roman times.

The chapel abuts a shrine and so-called "lake" of Juturna – it was the source used by Castor and Pollux for watering their horses after the battle of Lake Regillus. In the 2nd century BC, Aemilius Paulus erected there equestrian statues of the Dioskouroi to celebrate his victory over king Perseus. The water of the source was thought to have medicinal properties. In imperial times, Vestal virgins used it for their rites, and the building itself housed the office of water supply, the so-called *statio aquarum*.

The shrine we see today is a reconstruction from the 1950s that makes use of some ancient fragments; thus, a block that says IVTVRNAI S is set into the attic. In A. A. Milne's "Winnie-the-Pooh," Piglet has a piece of board near his house that says "TRESPASSERS WILL," which can be interpreted in a variety of ways; similarly, the Juturna inscription could have meant "The Shrine of Juturna" or "To Juturna from Senate and Roman People." Juturna is an obscure character of old Roman lore, a water nymph, a goddess of water supply, a wife of Janus. In "The Aeneid," Virgil gave that name to the sister of Turnus, the main adversary of Aeneas in the battles for Latium.

THE TEMPLE OF CAESAR

The assassination of Julius Caesar caused uproar in the hearts and minds of Roman citizens. There were those who celebrated the conspirators as tyrannicides, but most people sincerely grieved for the dictator. Then Caesar's will that had been safeguarded by Vestal virgins was publicly read;

according to its terms, he bequeathed his lavish gardens above the Tiber for public use and left 300 sesterces to every citizen of Rome. This magnanimity fanned the flames of people's grief and hatred. In the heat of the moment, the crowd mistook Caesar's friend Helvius Cinna, a poet, for Cornelius Cinna, one of the conspirators (not even his relative), and, in spite of his protestations ("I am Cinna the poet, I am Cinna the poet." – "Tear him for his bad verses, tear him for his bad verses") tore him to pieces (at least that is how Plutarch and Shakespeare tell the story).

Caesar's funeral was a two-stage affair. Initially the funeral pyre was set up on the Field of Mars; then it was transferred to the Forum and ignited near the Temple of Castor. People threw into the fire their clothes, surrounding benches, anything they could grab, including children's medallions which were supposed to be worn around the neck until legal adulthood and then devoted to the gods. In front of the mound of ashes was installed a column of Numidic marble, yellow as gold, with the inscription "The Father of the Fatherland," but it was soon removed by the anti-Caesar faction.

In July, an unusually bright star or comet appeared in the sky; it was widely rumoured to be the soul of Caesar ascending to the immortals. (Which comet that was remains unclear. In the 1990s two US researchers had burrowed through tons of materials, from ancient Chinese chronicles to chemical composition of Greenland ice and came up with a more or less coherent hypothesis, but many historians remain convinced that there was no comet at all, that it was all a later propaganda invention.) Under pressure from the young Gaius Octavius, to whom Caesar's will bequeathed the lion's share of his huge fortune and, implicitly, the dictator's political blessing, the Senate passed the law deifying Caesar. A temple was erected on the location of his funeral pyre – the first ever in Roman history that was not dedicated to a god of legends and old lore, but to a man who had a very short time ago walked among the living.

Gladiatorial games were given to celebrate the dedication of the temple, with even one of the senators taking up the sword; on that occasion, the Roman audiences saw a hippopotamus and a rhinoceros for the first time. The altar of the temple was endowed with the right of asylum, which meant that a fugitive slave or criminal who managed to reach the altar and demanded protection could legally count on clemency or at least postponement of the sentencing. In Rome, the right of asylum was traditionally given only to the altars of such gods that were known in times of Romulus; some guardians of tradition were outraged. The solution had all the hallmarks of Roman bureaucratic elegance: the right of asylum was not removed from Caesar's altar, but the temple was enclosed with a fence so high that it could not be accessed without a security check.

The temple stood very high, higher than the neighbouring Temple of Castor. Ovid mentions this in one of his epistles from exile: "the Twins of the neighbouring temple whom divine Julius views from his lofty shrine." Inside the temple was a huge statue of Caesar with a star or comet in his forehead. When the doors of the temple were open, the statue was visible from the Forum.

Like many other Roman sanctuaries, the Temple of Deified Julius exhibited works of art: paintings of the Dioskouroi twins, the goddess of Victory and Venus Anadyomene ('rising from the sea') by the greatest of Greek painters, Apelles. Unfortunately, not a single easel painting of antiquity has come down to us. The famous Venus was already damaged by dampness in antiquity, and Nero replaced it with a different picture.

Coins testify to a reconstruction of the temple in the times of Hadrian, but the unspectacular ruins that we can see today belong to the initial structure. The cult of Julius Caesar smoulders in Rome even today, and from time to time – especially on March 15, the anniversary of Caesar's assassination – fresh flowers appear on the temple's altar.

The Temple of Deified Julius. Reconstruction

Temple of Antoninus "Temple of Romulus"
and Faustina

Sacra Via

Regia

Temple of Vesta

House of the Vestals

silica of Maxentius

SACRA VIA

N

50 m

Santa Francesca Romana

Temple of Venus and Roma

Arch of Titus

CHAPTER II

SACRA VIA
(THE SACRED WAY)

Only two Roman streets had been called *via* since the oldest times – *Sacra Via*, 'the sacred way,' and *Nova Via*, 'the new way.' Both traversed the Forum valley. Sacra Via began from the small hill of Velia, an offshoot of the Palatine, at approximately the place where the Arch of Titus now stands. It ran its short course to the middle of the Forum, ending at the Temple of Vesta. Its special status was marked by a large number of important temples, but even more significantly, it was the final leg of the triumphal procession: victorious generals moved along the Sacra Via right before ascending to the Capitol for the thanksgiving sacrifice.

THE TEMPLE OF ANTONINUS AND FAUSTINA

The emperor Antoninus, called Pius for his pious behaviour, was truly fond of his wife Faustina. When she died in 141 AD, only a few years after his accession, the Senate offered to deify her, build a temple in her honour, appoint priests and cast statues of gold and silver. After the rule of the arrogant Hadrian, who died "hated by everyone," according to an ancient historian, the Senate enjoyed stable relations with the new sovereign and did its best to oblige.

Antoninus ordered that statues of Faustina be erected in circuses across the whole of Italy. He also continued to finance the charitable foundation for orphaned girls, a pet project of his spouse, and built the temple suggested by the Senate on the ultimate prestigious place, right on the Sacra Via at the north-eastern edge of the Forum. A dedicatory inscription was set on its architrave: DIVAE FAVSTINAE EX S.C. ("to the Deified Faustina by Senatorial Decree"). A giant statue of the empress was installed in the cella (the inner space).

Twenty years later, Antoninus Pius died peacefully in his seventieth year of life. The night before, he had over-indulged himself on Alpine cheese, and became sick. In the morning, he made final arrangements with the courtiers, gave the chief of his security detail the new password for the day – *aequanimitas*, 'equanimity' – and passed away.

The emperor's death plunged his subjects into deep and, apparently, sincere sorrow. His rule was the most tranquil in the whole history of the empire. He did not wage large-scale wars of conquest, did not engage in power play with the Senate or his own guard; his reign was not marked by major natural disasters (like the eruption of Vesuvius a hundred years before) or sweeping epidemics (like the Antonine Plague that started a few years later and raged for fifteen years). That remarkable stability was further buttressed by the emperor's long presence on the political scene: his rule was second in duration only to the record-setting longevity of Augustus.

The Senate deified Antoninus and rededicated the already standing temple on the Forum. Decorations on the frieze were torn down, and a new inscription appeared in their place: DIVO ANTONINO ET ("to the Deified Antoninus and") – thankfully, the rules of Latin (or English, for that matter) allowed for this innocent sleight of hand. Next to Faustina's statue, a huge statue of Antoninus appeared.

The façade of the building, eight stylish columns of green Carian marble, is still standing thanks to the building's later Christianisation. The church of San Lorenzo in Miranda had been installed in the building for a long time, possibly from the 7th century. In the 12th century, it is mentioned by the famous directory-cum-guidebook, "Marvels of the City of Rome" (*Mirabilia Urbis Romae*).

The church that grew in the cella of the ancient temple was dedicated to St. Lawrence because it was on that spot, according to the legend, that he was sentenced to death. It happened in 258 AD, during the persecutions under the emperor Valerian. St. Lawrence is one of the most venerated Catholic saints, especially beloved in Rome, the city of which he is the patron saint. He was burned alive on a gridiron and during the execution exchanged friendly banter with his torturers: "Turn me over, that side is already nicely done!" On the site of his martyrdom stands a small church of San Lorenzo in Panisperna. His remains are kept in the basilica of San Lorenzo fuori le mura founded by the emperor Constantine. Finally, those who want to see the actual instrument of execution, the gridiron, can do so in the church of San Lorenzo in Lucina, extant from no later than the 4th century. Today's building dates from much later, it is mostly in Baroque style, but the façade is relatively old, made in the early 12th century.

San Lorenzo in Miranda had largely assumed its present aspect in 1602, when the architect Orazio Torriani remodelled its façade and built new side chapels. Whether something had stood on that prestigious place before the construction of the Temple of Faustina, and if so, what exactly, remains unknown. Excavations in the early 20th century revealed traces of ancient marble pavement behind the remains of the colonnade; in late imperial times, it was built over with baths.

THE REGIA

Opposite San Lorenzo, on the other side of the Sacred Way, are the remains of the Regia. The very name tells us that we are dealing here with something regal (Regia, of course, is derived from *rex*, 'king'). Legend has it that the Regia was founded and built by Numa Pompilius, the second king of Rome. Ancient sources seem to indicate that the Regia combined the functions of a temple (*fanum*) and a residential house, though that kind of arrangement was untypical for Rome. Inside was the sanctuary of Mars; spears and shields belonging to the god of war were kept there. Another sanctuary was dedicated to the chthonic (which means 'underworld') goddess whom the Romans called Ops Consiva. *Ops* means 'power' and 'wealth,' it is the same Indo-European root that gives us words like 'office' and 'official.' *Consiva* derives from the verb *consero*, 'to sow.' In August, a holiday for this important deity was marked by solemn processions.

The Ops sanctuary in the Regia was off-limits to everyone, except the supreme pontiff (*Pontifex Maximus*, the most senior Roman priest) and Vestal virgins. As for the spears of Mars, they were used for divination: if they started to rumble all by themselves, it was considered a bad omen which required immediate expiatory sacrifices to be ordained by the priests. On the Ides of March in 44 BC, the day of Julius Caesar's assassination, the spears of Mars began to rumble, and Caesar, the supreme pontiff at the time, and living, at least part-time, in the Regia, carried out the necessary rites, but failed to avert the tragedy.

Excavations have shown that some kind of building had stood on this place since ancient times, 7th or 6th century BC. It seemed to be an affluent house in Etruscan style. The house was rebuilt and rearranged a few times, but since the early Republic, the general outlines of premises and walls had remained the same through all the reconstructions: a suite of three rooms, with the middle giving access to each of the side rooms (the sanctuaries of Mars and of Ops Consiva).

In the early years of Octavian's rule, the general Gnaeus Domitius Calvinus restored the Regia and lavishly decorated it with war trophies which he had collected in the cities of Spain. Gold alone, however, was not enough for a building of such importance, and Spain was still too barbarous to have worthy works of art. Calvinus asked Octavian for a loan of a few statues, and Octavian agreed. When the ruler demanded his property back, Calvinus told him: "Send your men and take the statues." This might have meant that his own labour force was tied up with construction, but it could be also construed as a refusal to part with the statues voluntarily. Octavian gave up on them and decreed that the statues were his offerings to the Regia. Calvinus got away with this impudence probably because he was one of the few Roman aristocrats who had always been staunchly loyal to Julius Caesar and later to his successor Octavian.

THE VESTAL VIRGINS: CULT AND RITUAL

When the poet Horace wanted to say that his poetry would never be forgotten, this is what came out (Od. 3, 30):

> *…dum Capitolium*
> *scandet cum tacita virgine pontifex –*

"while the Supreme pontiff shall ascend the Capitol with a silent virgin." It meant – while Rome stands; and Rome, as everyone knows, is eternal. And indeed, nothing better signified eternity in the eyes of Romans than the cult of Vestal virgins.

The cult was very old. It preceded the foundation of the city. According to legend, Romulus and Remus were sons of the god Mars and the Vestal virgin Rhea Sylvia. The half-legendary king Numa Pompilius instituted the college of Vestal virgins, apparently transferring it from Alba Longa, Rome's metropolis. The virgins' main duty was tending to the fire of Vesta and protecting sacred objects. The exact list of the objects is unknown, but it included *palladium*, a wooden image of Athena salvaged by Aeneas from the ashes of Troy. Thus, from the very beginning the Vestal cult combined several geographical components, each of them important to Romans: Alban, Trojan, Latin, and the one which was not limited to a specific area but covered the whole Mediterranean (Vesta had a Greek prototype – Hestia, the goddess of the hearth). The Romans loved to consider themselves first among equals in the family of peoples, but they understood that their priority was based on the "melting pot" where their nation was formed, not on any special purity of breed.

Originally there were four Vestal virgins; later their number increased to six. Girls were enlisted between six and ten years of age. The requirements were strict: candidates had to be free of any physical blemish, with both parents alive; their father had to live in Italy (which covered the broad definition of "being Roman"); neither parent could be a slave or a member of a dishonourable profession. Even a family quarrel could jeopardize a girl's chances. The selection was similar to an army draft. It was performed at the discretion of the supreme pontiff, and afterwards – by casting lots among the selected so as to confirm the human choice by divine will. In historical times – the times for which we have written records – the strict ritual was not necessary: influential parents were only too happy to offer their daughters for the service, and their requests were usually granted. And yet the cult was not always popular. The ageing Augustus reproached his senators who were reluctant to offer their daughters for the college; he said that if he had a granddaughter of suitable age, he wouldn't hesitate a moment.

Even in the most archaic period the Vestal virgins were selected impartially from patricians and plebeians; no one except them could confidently represent the Roman people as a whole before the gods.

A girl became a Vestal virgin in the course of a ritual called *captio* ('capture'). It resembled an archaic wedding custom but stopped halfway, not transferring the "bride" from the father's power into the husband's. A girl, sitting in her father's lap, was approached by the pontiff, grabbed by the arm and taken away "as if she had been taken in war," says the antiquarian Aulus Gellius (2C AD), who left the most detailed description of the ritual. While "capturing" the girl, the priest recited the following formula:

"I take thee, Amata, as one who has fulfilled all the legal requirements, to be priestess of Vesta, to perform the rites which it is lawful for a Vestal to perform for the Roman people, the Quirites."[13]

The formula was extremely archaic, and by Gellius's time many details had become hazy. For example, it is unclear what "all the legal requirements" (*optima lege*) means or why the future Vestal is called Amata. The simplest hypotheses are based on the meaning of the word in Latin ('the loved one') or on Gellius's own guess – that it was the name of the very first Vestal virgin. Later scholars added many different speculations – that *amata* was a Vedic term which meant "the younger" or a Latinized form of Greek *admeta* ('unconquered' or 'virginal'). None of these versions is very convincing.

Apart from keeping Vesta's fire and taking care of sacred objects, the Vestals performed many religious rites. On March 1, the traditional Roman New Year, they decorated the temple of Vesta with fresh laurel branches and lit a new fire on Vesta's altar. In June, Vestalia were celebrated, the main festival devoted to their goddess; on that day, the ashes from the sacred hearth were solemnly taken from the temple and thrown into the Tiber. In April they participated in sacrificing pregnant cows; also in April, during Parilia, ashes of a calf, blood of a horse and bean stalks were ritually burned; in May the Vestals threw human figurines made of reed from a bridge into the Tiber (the meaning of this ritual is unclear; Ovid vaguely says "images of people of yore"); in October, a horse was sacrificed to Mars, and the Vestal virgins burned its tail in a purification procedure; in December, Vesta's priestesses were among the main participants of the Good Goddess mysteries. Several times a year the Vestals prepared flour from special rare cereal, spelt (spelt is hexaploid wheat – it has six sets of chromosomes; today it enjoys popularity in Europe as "eco-food"). On September 13, two kinds of salt were added to the flour to make *mola salsa*, "salted flour," which was then used to prepare sacrificial bread. The meaning of all Vestal rituals boiled down to two things: purification and prosperity.

The Vestal virgins' safety (along with everything entrusted to their care) was of paramount importance to the Romans. A telling example was an event of 386 BC: the Gauls besieged the city, and the population fled in panic. The Vestals, together with their sacred objects, were among those trying to leave. A citizen named Lucius Albanius ordered his wife and children to dismount from his cart and took the Vestals instead; he then drove them to safety to the Etruscan city of Caere (today's Cerveteri).

The chief Vestal
(Virgo Vestalis maxima)

This story looks like many other patriotic Roman legends, if not for one crucial detail: this is the oldest extant record of the Vestal virgins which we have on good authority.

The Vestals' rules of conduct stressed their exclusivity. Roman priests were not a separate "order", as in ancient Egypt or in any Catholic country today; priestly offices were elective, and often, especially in turbulent times, politically important. The Vestal virgins, usually in their office for life (more on that later), did not fit into that scheme. First, the Vestals were the only women in Roman society who were not under the *patria potestas* – the authority of father, husband or other male guardian. Technically, the supreme pontiff exercised some fatherly functions towards them, but they were the only Roman women who freely managed their (sometimes quite substantial) property, drafted their wills or spoke in the court of law. Their testimony was so weighty that one Vestal virgin of early Imperial period refused to appear in court – the case was too trifling – and ordered that a praetor come and take her testimony instead. The praetor, one of the highest officials in state hierarchy, humbly obeyed. No one except for the Vestals could move in a vehicle within the city limits. They kept their own stables, and their horses could not be expropriated for military needs. In Imperial times, the priestesses were escorted by an armed bodyguard (lictor). A condemned criminal could appeal for pardon if he met a Vestal virgin in the street.

The virgins' religious, legal and financial status was unique for the Roman society. The Danish scholar Robin Wildfang says that the Vestal virgins were fully incorporated into Rome's social structure, remaining full citizens, but at the same time were excluded from family structure, which bound regular Romans of both sexes. This "marginal" status enabled the Vestals to represent the Roman people in their entirety, without direct allegiance to any caste or clan.

However, the alienation of Vestal virgins from their biological families was never complete. The rules disbarred a girl from the college if her sister was already serving: no one wanted one family to exert its influence through the priestesses. The first case of the Vestals meddling in state affairs (that we know of) happened in 143 BC. Consul Appius Claudius Pulcher attacked Salassians, an Alpine tribe dwelling not far from today's town of Aosta. The senate ruled that Roman losses were unacceptable, and denied the consul his triumph. The vainglorious Pulcher decided to stage a triumph at his own expense; when an official tried to stop the procession, a Vestal virgin called Claudia jumped onto the triumphal chariot, protecting the consul and his unauthorized triumph by her sanctity. It does not take a Sherlock Holmes to deduce that Claudius and Claudia were related (our ancient sources disagree whether she was his sister or daughter).

In the 1st century BC, the most turbulent hundred years in Roman history – at least as far as internal political struggle is concerned – the Vestals acted vigorously in that cruel world, not hesitating to enter the man's game. In 63 BC the Vestal virgin Licinia yielded her seat of honour at gladiatorial games to her cousin, Licinius Murena. Murena was contending for the next year's consulate, so the gesture was definitely a sign of support (from the immortal gods or from the candidate's family – depending on one's degree of cynicism). That same year, Roman matrons gathered for the Good Goddess festival in the home of the current consul, Cicero. In the course of the ritual the fire on the altar was extinguished according to the custom; suddenly it went ablaze again, and the Vestals present at the ceremony unanimously concluded that it was a good sign. They told their hostess to convey the goddess's goodwill to her husband and to urge him to proceed with whatever decisions he had in mind. One of the Vestal virgins was a half-sister to Cicero's wife. Taken together, the evidence suggests that the miracle was a prearranged pyrotechnical stunt. (A similar miracle occurs every year on the eve of Christian Orthodox Easter at the church of the Holy Sepulcre in Jerusalem; the "Holy Fire" has been attested since 1106 and remains a subject of bitter controversy between sceptics and believers.)

The next year, in 62 BC, the Vestal virgins supported Cicero and his party again. A college made of priests and Vestals had to ponder the punishment of Clodius, an up-and-coming politician who made it into Julius Caesar's home during the Good Goddess ritual, dressed in drag. The rituals were strictly forbidden to men – in fact, so strictly, that we don't even know the name of the goddess in question; "Good Goddess," *Bona Dea*, is nothing more than a men-safe nickname. The Vestals condemned Clodius and handed him over to a specially appointed tribunal. However, Clodius was very rich; in spite of Cicero's desperate invectives, the judges, thoroughly bribed, acquitted the young man.

In 73 BC the Vestal virgin Licinia was accused of an amorous liaison with her cousin Marcus Licinius Crassus (the general who around that time had his hands full with Spartacus's revolt). He managed to exonerate the woman, explaining that he only wanted to buy some real estate from her. Crassus had a bad reputation, but in this case it helped him: he used to arrive at the scene of a fire with his private fire brigade and offer the shocked owner to buy the house at a fraction of its pre-fire price. Should the owner refuse, Crassus left together with his henchmen; otherwise, the firemen hastily saved the new house of their inventive employer. What on earth could a man like that discuss with a Vestal virgin, apart from the cost of property?

So we have finally touched upon the best known and the most sinister element of the Vestal cult: the priestesses' virginity and the punishment for losing it. The girls were elected to the college when pre-pubescent, while the minimum term of service was thirty years. Throughout her tenure, the Vestal virgin had to be ritually pure – that included sexual purity, of course; only thus could she retain her status of a *virgo* which enabled her to deal with Vesta's fire and other sacred objects without defiling them. Any breach of the ritual could tip the delicate balance between this world and the divine (such balance was known as *pax deorum*, 'peace of the gods'). Consequently, any fault of the Vestal virgin was subject to purification sacrifices, while the worst fault of all, the loss of innocence, was punishable by death.

The Romans were usually reluctant to carry out executions, especially those for impiety. Thus, parricides were sown into a sack together with a dog, a monkey and a cock and thrown into the Tiber – technically, imposing the death penalty was left to the gods. When a Vestal virgin was accused of *incestum* (this technical term meant a breach of religious vows; the meaning 'fornication with a close relative' developed later), the execution procedure was even more convoluted. The condemned woman was taken in a carriage through the whole city to the Colline gate, to the place called *Campus sceleratus* ('the cursed field'; it was located near today's streets Venti Settembre and Goito, up the Quirinal, where the Ministry of Finance stands today). The Vestal was seen off by relatives and priests; in the 'cursed field' she descended into a specially prepared underground chamber that contained a bed, a lamp, some oil, bread, water and milk. The hole in the ground was filled in so as not to leave any trace. If her lover was known, he was whipped to death, in public, with willow branches.

Throughout the millennium of the Vestal service, the cases of interment were few, and most of them happened in turbulent times. For instance, two Vestal virgins, Opimia and Floronia, were accused of *incestum* and condemned in 216 BC, soon after the devastating defeat of the Roman army at Cannae. It was a moment when the stability and the very existence of the Roman order of things were threatened, and Rome was enveloped in horrible, incessant women's wail: every home lamented their dead. Condemning the Vestals served a double purpose: to expiate the (alleged) impiety before the gods, and to scare the women into silence: their howl could finish off the already shaken morale of their husbands, brothers and sons. In other cases, execution of a Vestal virgin could be directed against the social order she represented: thus, the cases in 483 and 337 BC could have been connected with the escalation of struggle between patricians and plebeians.

The accused priestess could do little to exonerate herself – the usual tenets of Roman law did not apply. Some, however, succeeded. The historians were especially fond of the stories where divine intervention seemed to be involved. The Vestal virgin Tuccia proved her innocence by fetching water from the Tiber to the Forum in a sieve. Aemilia put her garments onto the temple's hearth, and the extinguished embers suddenly went ablaze. There were less fantastic cases, too: the Vestal Postumia was accused of *incestum* for her lively wit and choice of clothes; she was lucky to escape with a reprimand from the supreme pontiff, who told her to steer her behaviour and dress code towards piety instead of frivolity.

Vestal virgin Tuccia with a sieve. 19th century engraving

The minimum priestly tenure of thirty years was divided into a decade of apprenticeship, a decade of service and a decade of mentoring. In principle, after that a Vestal virgin had the right to leave the college and to marry; at 36 to 40 years she was far from old even by Roman standards. However, those few who attempted this mid-life career change were unlucky in family life. Most Vestal virgins preferred to remain in service for life.

During the Imperial era, Rome's political life shifted from public places to palace lobbies. The status of Vestal virgins changed accordingly: they became closely associated with the Emperor's cult and were often responsible for the safekeeping of important state documents. A cursory remark by the historian Suetonius suggests that in 1C AD the vow of chastity was not strictly implemented, and the "good emperors" (Vespasian and Titus) turned a blind eye to it. Quite understandable: the well-educated, independent Vestals could well consider their chastity a relic of the archaic past and not take it seriously. The next emperor, Domitian, did not approve of such lenience, and as many as four Vestal virgins were condemned for *incestum* during his reign.

In the course of Rome's Christianization, the Vestal activity was becoming increasingly formal, until, at the end of 4C AD, the emperor Theodosius prohibited all pagan cults. In 394 the college was disbanded; its buildings and property went to the Emperor's administration.

THE TEMPLE OF VESTA AND THE HOUSE OF THE VESTAL VIRGINS

The Vestal virgins' regular activity was focused on a small part of the Roman Forum, or, rather, directly to its south. There stood a small, round temple of Vesta, its form reminiscent of the ancestral huts of Rome's founding fathers. Just like those huts, the temple was said to have initially a thatched roof. It later times it was adorned with Ionic columns with ornamental gratings between them. In the upper part of the conical roof an opening let out the smoke from Vesta's hearth. Most likely, the opening was protected from inclement weather by a metal construction of some kind. There are several coins which show what seems to be this temple. On some of them a sculpture stands on the roof, most likely of Vesta; on some others, a curule chair (a simple seat used by political or military notables) is seen inside the temple (which is not very realistic). Two of the most reliable images of this temple can be found in Uffizi gallery in Florence and on the pedestal of a statue in Sorrento archaeological museum.

Of the temple of Vesta, very little survives to this day. What we see now is a round concrete bump surrounded by several layers of tufa blocks. The rest was pillaged in mid-16th century, when papal builders swirled through the Forum, stripping off any marble they could find. Some of the fragments were later incorporated into various monuments, including St. Peter's Basilica; others were burnt for lye. What is left of the temple of Vesta are the ruins of relatively late date, from the time of the Empress Julia Domna who sponsored a reconstruction of the building after a fire in the early 3rd century. At some point between the late republican period (attested on coins) and the last reconstruction, Ionic columns were replaced with Corinthian. It is possible that the mosaic floor and pits for keeping the ashes are older. Some fragments of the temple, which by chance escaped the papal scavengers, were found during the excavations of the late 19th century, and in 1930 a small part of the temple's outer perimeter was reconstructed. The reconstruction proved to be a success: the monument is displayed on countless posters, calendars and postcards, and even made its way to the cover of the first edition of the prestigious Oxford archaeological guide to Rome.

For a long time it was thought that there was another temple of Vesta on the Palatine, but apparently this was a misunderstanding. When Augustus was elected supreme pontiff, custom required that he move to a residence in the Forum, the so-called *Domus Publica*; however, he did not want to. Instead, he donated a part of his Palatine home to the state and converted it to a shrine to Vesta, while *Domus Publica* went to the college of the Vestal virgins. In passing, the temple of Vesta in the Forum was not a real temple either. A proper temple had to house a statue of the god, while this one only had a symbolic fire. As for the so-called "temple of Vesta" on the Tiber bank, the round edifice near the mega-popular *bocca della verità* – it is pure misunderstanding caused by its round shape.

Next to the temple of Vesta is a large rectangular area which had once been the House of the Vestal virgins, *Atrium Vestae*. Its four sides ran parallel to the four streets – *Sacra via* ('sacred'), *Nova via* ('new'), *Vicus Vestae* ('Vesta lane'); the name of the fourth has not survived. Today's position and ground plan date to the time of Trajan (early 2C). The traces of earlier floors and walls can be seen on lower levels. The centre of the western wing is taken by a large room with three smaller chambers around it. It is unlikely to be a "flat" of any of the Vestal virgins – the house was so spacious that each of the priestesses must have had her own large apartments, including premises for servants and slaves; it might have been some place of ceremonial importance – a dining hall, for example. In republican times the outer sides of the house were a lively shopping arcade, whose revenues went to the college's budget.

The northern wall is lined with statues which were found there in a heap during the excavations of the 1880s. The statues are from the 2nd to 4th centuries AD; the pairing of statues and bases is arbitrary. Each of them represents a chief Vestal virgin (*Virgo Vestalis maxima*); the bases are covered with dedicatory inscriptions.

Two aspects of the Vestal cult have always piqued the curiosity of posterity: its mysterious antiquity and, of course, the virginity. The Vestals were venerated even when no one seriously believed in the importance of their duties: the Romans, very much like the British, were suckers for tradition. This attitude is reflected in the words of Konstantin Levin, the author's *alter ego* in Leo Tolstoy's "Anna Karenina": "we live without making anything, as though we were ancient Vestals set to keep in a fire."[14]

Virginity is an important cult element in many rituals. Some Eastern religions, including Christianity, have a motif of a virgin giving birth to a divine child. (The notion is less preposterous than it sounds. Asexual reproduction, known as parthenogenesis – from the Greek for 'virginal birth' – has been recorded in species as advanced as sharks, lizards and birds. The only hitch is that parthenogenesis can only produce female offspring.) In Nepal, a virgin girl known as *Kumari* is still worshipped as a goddess; the Kumari of Katmandu performs some important ceremonial state functions and attracts lots of tourists. The process of selecting a Kumari is even more rigorous than the one for the Vestals; among other things, candidates must spend a night in a deserted temple surrounded by heads of sacrificed goats and buffaloes. However, the girls only serve as Kumaris until their first menstruation; after that, the goddess is believed to have vacated their body, and they revert to normal life while new candidates are tested. Tradition has it that a husband of an ex-Kumari dies a painful death shortly after the wedding, but in reality most of the recent Kumaris led a perfectly healthy family life.

This never-ending obsession with virginity – still very much a part of human culture, even in industrial countries – made the Vestals the most memorable priestly figures of the Roman world. Indeed, who remembers the *flamines* or the *luperci*, or even the supreme pontiff (except as a title for the Pope)? But say "Vestal virgins", and people's imaginations will be stirred. It is not a coincidence that a ruined temple, with only three dubiously reconstructed columns standing, has become such an important symbol of ancient Rome today.

"THE TEMPLE OF ROMULUS"

Returning to the Sacra Via, we pass by the basilica of Santi Cosma e Damiano, also a recycled late Roman temple. This small building is usually identified with the shrine built by the emperor Maxentius in commemoration of his dead son, the teenage Valerius Romulus. This identification is tenuous: the coins confirm that Maxentius erected a similar-looking temple, with a domed roof and sculptures of naked youths, but it is difficult to connect it firmly to the Sacra Via building when the only evidence we have comes from coins. It is possible that this temple was the so-called "sanctuary of the city" (*urbis fanum*), known from literary sources. The temple was assembled in the early 4th century almost like a child's puzzle: the largest part of its architectural ornamentation was made up of spoils (*spolia*), fragments of earlier buildings. Among those were two columns of green marble, their capitals (pilfered from other columns), bronze doors and their marble framing (from Severan buildings of the early 3rd century), and the upper cornice, largely put together using blocks of the Augustan age.

When the Gothic king Theodoric conveyed a number of buildings on the Sacra Via to pope Felix IV as a gift, the pope dedicated "the Temple of Romulus" to the martyr brothers Cosmas and Damian, as a counterweight to the neighbouring temple of the pagan twins Castor and Pollux.

Cosmas and Damian were physicians working in the province of Cilicia, in the port city of Aegeae (now Yumurtalık in southern Turkey). They refused any payment for their work; in the Christian tradition the saints who scorn material comforts are called 'unmercenary', *anargyroi* in Greek. Legend ascribes to them a unique breakthrough in transplantology: when one of their patients was on the verge of losing his ulcerous leg, they grafted onto him a leg of a recently deceased Ethiopian. The contrast between the Ethiopian's black leg and the white body of the healed patient was used to a great effect by numerous painters who depicted this miracle, the brothers' best known achievement. Their magical skills did not save them from persecution under the emperor Diocletian: refusing to renounce their faith, the brothers were crucified, stoned, pierced with arrows and finally beheaded.

The brothers were venerated as patron saints of physicians, surgeons, farriers and apothecaries. The choice of place for their church was appropriate, because it was allegedly in that building – at the time, the library of the adjacent Temple of Peace – that Galen, the main medical authority of classical antiquity after Hippocrates, had once lectured. For many centuries, the doctors of Rome convened there to discuss professional business. San Lorenzo in Miranda next door had been assigned to a college of pharmacists and herbalists – Collegio degli speciali – since the 15th century, and the members of these professions to this day hold meetings in a small annex that belongs to their guild.

THE BASILICA OF MAXENTIUS

A ruined basilica stands next to the church of Santi Cosma e Damiano. Even in its present state, it is the largest edifice on the Forum and one of the most impressive ancient monuments of Rome. The concrete brick-faced walls are huge, up to six metres thick in places. The basilica was begun by the emperor Maxentius and completed by his luckier rival, emperor Constantine (we will revisit their momentous stand-off near the Milvian Bridge when our walk takes us to the Arch of Constantine). It is worth repeating that an ancient basilica was not a church, but a place of trading, dealing, bureaucracy and leisure. The kind of vaulted architecture used here was previously only employed for the baths. Even though the purpose of the basilica was not religious, there were statues of gods in recesses of the walls. In the western apse was set a huge – five times larger than life – seated acrolithic statue of Constantine. The head with its pious upward glance seems idealised (though it must have at least some similarity with the real emperor), but the hand with the index finger pointing up and the calloused feet are, by contrast, very realistic. Today the parts of the emperor's body are exhibited in the inner courtyard of Palazzo dei Conservatori of the Capitoline Museums, and there is no guidebook and almost no film about Rome that does not reference them in some way.

"Acrolithic" refers to an ancient technology; this Greek word means "with stone extremities." Only the head, arms and legs of the statue were carved from marble; the trunk was made of wood and covered with either metal plates or drapery. Of course, the metal was ransacked in the Middle Ages, but Constantine's marble head and extremities were rediscovered in the 15th century.

The basilica is variously called in different sources the Basilica of Maxentius (because he launched the construction), the Basilica of Constantine (because he finished it), or simply the New Basilica (*Basilica Nova*), to tell it apart from the Julia and Aemilia. It began to be dismantled in antiquity, and a couple of centuries after it was built no one remembered what it was. In the 6th century it was called "The Temple of Roma," the tutelary goddess of the city. In the 7th century, Pope Honorius used its bronze tiling for St. Peter's Basilica, founded in Constantine's time on the spot now occupied by the "new" St. Peter's Basilica, the famous work of Michelangelo and other titans of the Renaissance. In the 11th century, a section of the Basilica of Maxentius was destroyed by an earthquake.

There is a curious Christian tale that made its way into a hugely popular collection of mediaeval apocrypha called "The Golden Legend." According to this version, the Basilica of Constantine collapsed on the day of Christ's birth, together with the giant statue of Romulus which (so the legend says) stood there. Even if we disregard a three hundred years-wide anachronism, the legend chooses a very unfortunate target for divine vengeance: if there is any single person most responsible for the future world domination of Christianity, it was Constantine. In spite of that, the legend proved to be very tenacious. Many Nativity scenes are set in the ruins of a pagan temple, sometimes even bearing a vague resemblance to the Basilica of Maxentius/Constantine. This is also an echo of the Golden Legend.

In 1613 Pope Paul V transferred the only surviving column of the basilica to the square in front of the church of Santa Maria Maggiore. It stands there to this day, topped by a statue of The Virgin Mary by Guillaume Berthélot and Orazio Censore, and gives a good idea of the immensity of the original design.

Under Mussolini, the surviving northern wall of the basilica, facing the new pompous Via dell'Impero (which will be discussed in detail in a further chapter), was adorned with maps showing the spatial expansion of the Roman Empire. In 1960, during the Olympic games, the ancient building hosted wrestling competitions.

Near the Basilica of Maxentius, the Via Sacra bumps into a plot of land around the church of Santa Francesca Romana. The church is hardly small, but the surrounding area is huge. This is not very obvious from the pavement level, but if you look at it from the upper storeys of the Colosseum, you will be duly impressed. The emperor Nero straightened up the Via Sacra which, in his vision, had to pass through this plot leading to his palace, "The Golden House" *(Domus Aurea)*. It was on this straight section of the road that the colossal statue of Nero himself stood (we will come to it later). The emperor Hadrian took a liking to this space, too. He directed huge resources to clearing it and moved the Colossus of Nero further east, and then set about building a new temple on the vacated land.

THE TEMPLE OF VENUS AND ROMA

Hadrian was an intellectual and a hellenophile. Like every intellectual, he was acutely sensitive to criticism; like any hellenophile, he wanted to be celebrated as a creative spirit and not simply as a ruler. He had been deeply hurt by a casual remark of the great Greek architect Apollodorus, who had built a new forum with its famous column for the previous emperor, Trajan. Once, Hadrian had made an attempt to break into a conversation between Trajan and Apollodorus, and the architect snubbed him: "Don't meddle in this, go draw your pumpkins, you don't know the first thing about architecture." The cryptic pumpkin remark might refer to ribbed domes – Hadrian was partial to that style. Clenching his teeth, Hadrian in all probability thought: "Just wait till we take over." When he did take over, he launched a huge development project – a Greek-style temple of his own design. Affecting modesty, he sent blueprints to Apollodorus. Apollodorus returned them with a note: "The height of the building is incompatible with the size of the statues. If the goddess wanted to stand up and go out, her head would break through the roof."

To be fair, exactly the same criticism used to be directed at the statue of Zeus in Olympia by Phidias, long recognized as one of the wonders of the world.

Hadrian was furious. It was too late to introduce any substantial changes to the project; all he could do was send Apollodorus into exile, and later have him executed. This story has to be treated with caution: it was told by Cassius Dio, a Roman senator, though a Greek; Hadrian was perpetually at odds with the Senate, and the Senate hated him back.

The new temple was introducing a double cult of Venus and Roma (the embodiment of the city of Rome). Venus was presented in a new, previously unknown guise of Venus Felix, the happy Venus – as a sign of well-being and tranquillity of Roman subjects everywhere in the far-flung Roman domain (the empire was at the peak of expansion at the time). Each goddess was given her own cella, where they were sitting with backs to each other: Venus was facing east, toward the Colosseum, Roma was facing west, toward the Capitol. The next emperor, Antoninus Pius, issued a decree in memory of his deceased wife: newlyweds had to offer a sacrifice at the altar of Venus and Roma.

The temple, once the largest and grandest in the city, was slowly crumbling. Details are sketchy, but in the mid-9th century Pope Leo IV built a church, Santa Maria Nova, among its ruins. After a reconstruction of 1612 it was renamed Santa Francesca Romana. Details surviving from

Hadrian's project include partially preserved double apses and colonnades of the temple itself and its outside perimeter which covered an area of 1.5 hectares and served as a separate forum of sorts.

HADRIAN

In 2008, the British Museum in London staged an exhibition called "Hadrian: Empire and Conflict," which, rather unexpectedly, became one of the major cultural events of the year. Advertising for the event said that Hadrian's first act on coming to power "was to withdraw the Roman forces from Iraq." Of course, there was no Iraq in the 2nd century AD, but the drive to dress Hadrian in modern clothes was typical of the European culture of the last century. When in the middle of the 20th century the French author Marguerite Yourcenar wrote her novel "Memoirs of Hadrian," she was doing the same, only making the emperor into an existentialist *ante litteram*.

Gustave Flaubert wrote in a letter: "With the gods gone, and Christ not yet come, there was a unique moment, from Cicero to Marcus Aurelius, when man stood alone."[15] The feeling of god-forsakenness and loneliness was typical of Yourcenar's era ("to write poetry after Auschwitz is barbaric"),[16] as well as ours. It is not very surprising that Hadrian, one of the main characters of the era described by Flaubert, draws such attention.

We will see the traces of Hadrian's activity many times. He built the Temple of Venus and Roma on the forum and relocated the Colossus of Nero; he competed in architectural skill with Trajan's favourite architect, Apollodorus; he erected one of antiquity's principal monuments, the Pantheon, on the Field of Mars; his own mausoleum near the Vatican is now Castel Sant'Angelo. To complete the picture, we need to review his life.

We have very limited detailed information about Hadrian. His only full biography is in the so-called "Augustan History" (*Scriptores Historiae Augustae*), a source that is late in time and extremely unreliable. It was thought for a long time that there were four authors of the work, but current scholars increasingly think that all biographies from Hadrian to the succession of "soldier emperors" and pretenders at the end of the turbulent 3rd century were written by one person, who might have used four pseudonyms to make a stronger impression or who has multiplied in the imagination of the descendants. Cassius Dio also describes Hadrian's rule, but, unfortunately, this part of his work has only come down to us in a shortened Byzantine retelling. Apparently (and not just in Yourcenar's imagination), Hadrian actually wrote an autobiography – the author of "Augustan History" refers to it several times – but, unfortunately, it has fallen off the edge of the earth.

Hadrian came from Italica, a Roman colony in Spain, founded in the era of the Punic wars. Some sources claimed he was born in Rome, but this was most likely an invention. Roman colonists were often tightly connected with local provincial aristocracy by family connections, and Hadrian's ancestors included some Spaniards, or, to be more exact, Celts who were the main settlers of the Iberian peninsula then. Hadrian received a very good education, but his Latin pronunciation remained non-Roman for the rest of his life.

When he was an adolescent, his education and career were reviewed and supervised by his remote kinsman Trajan, the future emperor and also a native of Italica. From that time, Hadrian never came back to his native city. He quickly climbed the rungs of the traditional Roman career ladder, occupying both military and elective (sort of) civic duties: in the case of an emperor's protegé, honest elections were unthinkable. In 117, after a long illness, Trajan died in Cilicia (present-day Turkey) without leaving any clear indications about his successor. This episode and subsequent dealings with the main adversaries blighted the whole future of Hadrian's reign. Plotina, the widow of Trajan, presented a document signed by the emperor which said that he adopted Hadrian as a son; this almost automatically meant that after Trajan's death Hadrian would assume his powers. And yet, classical authors consistently consider Hadrian's victory a result of a court conspiracy: he was, they claim, a lover of Plotina, and the document was forged after Trajan's death and dictated by the faltering voice of a frontman (a plot later used by Dante, and, after him, by Giacomo Puccini in his brilliant one-act opera *Gianni Schicchi*). Modern historians consider Hadrian a plausible candidate, judging by his credentials, and the succession (very delicate and painful for the whole history of imperial Rome) was in this case accidental. The wish of Trajan to surrender the power to the Senate and Roman people, hinted at by the authors of the senatorial class, is a fantasy worthy of the Hollywood.

Having dealt with possible adversaries, Hadrian directed his attention to foreign policy. The first thing he did was, indeed, refusing to defend the freshly occupied provinces, Mesopotamia and Armenia (it was Mesopotamia that was later called "Iraq"). He allegedly referred to the example of Cato, who once proclaimed the Macedonians free because he could not subdue them.

Hadrian's external policy was based on a combination of diplomatic mastery and military threat. He did not conduct expansionist wars – for the first time in a few centuries, the territorial coverage of the empire shrank. He spoke with his neighbours, personally and through his companions, trying to achieve peace. One such treaty was made with the most dangerous adversary, the Parthian Empire. The legions were in constant combat readiness. Hadrian never attempted any downsizing of the army – on the contrary, the number and preparedness of his legions was constantly monitored.

What do soldiers do, when they have no one to fight? They build. Building projects included houses for the generals, schools, and frontier works. Under Hadrian, the campaign of drawing and fortifying Roman borders was in full swing. In many European regions (in the forests of Germany and Romania, on the Rhine and Danube) the remains of camps, checkpoints and watch towers are the only evidence of Roman civilisation in the area. But the best-known frontier wall was erected by Hadrian in Britain.

This construction is called Hadrian's Wall; its Latin name is unknown. In 2003, treasure-hunters found in Staffordshire a large enamel vase with a schematic depiction of several forts along the wall and inscriptions. Such vases were also found earlier, but this Moorlands patera, as it was called, shows, as the scholars think, the wall as a whole. In this case it was called Vallum Aelium (the source of the name is obvious from the emperor's full name: Publius Aelius Trajanus Hadrianus Augustus).

The construction of the wall fully corresponded to Hadrian's main military principles in the provinces: stop the conquests, strengthen the border. As a military site, Hadrian's Wall was not very efficient, but that wasn't its goal; the goal was to show both Barbarians and Romans where the Pax Romana begins and what kind of resources, if necessary, will be launched to protect it. Hadrian's successor, Antoninus Pius, neglected the wall, building a new border barrier – Antonine's Wall – further to the north, in today's Scotland. This territory soon became impossible to protect, so Roman garrisons moved back to Hadrian's border.

Hadrian's Wall stretches along the north of England from the North Sea in the east to the Irish Sea in the west. It does not coincide with the England/Scotland border, always remaining on the English territory, even though it is less that a kilometre away from Scotland in the west. Weather, time and people did not protect the wall, but in its central sector, especially in Northumberland, there are well-preserved remains of the stone works, gates, and sentry posts. A well-marked pedestrian route goes along the wall, and in the summer many tourists use it. Hadrian's Wall has been on the UNESCO list since 1987, but it is still unprotected and unfenced, which makes it a rare case where a walk along a Roman wall is still possible.

One of the most exciting finds connected with Hadrian's Wall are the Vindolanda tablets. They were found in 1973, and this was one of the most important discoveries of Roman epigraphic materials ever.

THE VINDOLANDA TABLETS

Almost all monuments of ancient literature came down to us through many hands of many generations of rewriters. Anyone who has played Chinese whispers understands how problematic it is. Specialists have ways to work through the layers of many centuries, but losses are unavoidable. We have first-hand accounts of architectural monuments or graffiti, mostly from Pompeii and Herculanum; both are very specific as genres go. Another source of knowledge about everyday life is documents written on papyrus, but this material is fragile, and European moisture is death to it. As a result, almost all Greek and Roman papyri we have are from Africa – Egypt, Libya and so on.

The Vindolanda tablets are very thin wooden boards with words written in ink on them. They were left in boggy soil and survived almost miraculously. An auxiliary cavalry cohort was quartered in Vindolanda, a few miles south of Hadrian's Wall. Most tablets are official military documents, such as business correspondence between procurement and delivery officers. But there are some more human documents on file, too, like the one in tablet 291:

"Claudia Severa to her Lepidina greetings. On 11 September, sister, for the day of the celebration of my birthday, I give you a warm invitation to make sure that you come to us, to make the day more enjoyable for me by your arrival, if you are present. Give my greetings to your Cerialis. My Aelius and my little son send him their greetings. [2nd hand] I shall expect you, sister. Farewell, sister, my dearest soul, as I hope to prosper, and hail."

This is one of the earliest surviving Latin texts written by a woman, one of the first written artefacts created in Britain, and probably the first woman's letter in history.

The Vindolanda tablets were a major landmark for antiquity studies. Scholars found out many things about Roman handwriting, received confirmations of their ideas regarding widespread Roman literacy and found out that the Romans had a bad word for the indigenous people – *Brittunculi*.

Almost the only place where active warfare was raging under Hadrian was Palestine (which, again, draws a sad parallel between Hadrian's time and ours). Initially, the relations between Hadrian and the Judeans were good, but when the emperor decided to rename Jerusalem as Colonia Aelia Capitolina, build a temple of Jupiter on the footprint of the destroyed Temple of Solomon, and forbid circumcision, a mutiny erupted. It was in preparation for a long time, because the Jews did not want to repeat the mistakes of the previous war 60 years ago. The head of the resistance was Simon bar Kokhba, who proclaimed himself a Messiah. The Romans underestimated the scope of the mutiny. When it became obvious that things were serious, Hadrian recalled one of his best generals from Britain and drew legions from the whole empire close to Palestine. The war went on for several years, with both sides suffering heavy losses. Addressing the Senate about the events, Hadrian even avoided the usual formula "I and my legions are fine."

In the end, bar Kohba's mutiny was quenched in blood. Ancient sources claimed that the Romans killed almost 600,000 Jews, destroyed fifty cities and a thousand settlements. Jews were banished from Jerusalem and forbidden to come near the city that was sacred to them. Hadrian tried to suppress the Jewish religion, which he now considered the source of mutinies and wars: a roll of Torah was solemnly burned on top of the Temple Mount, adorned with the statues of Jupiter and Hadrian himself. Learning the Torah and the Jewish calendar were also forbidden. The province was renamed and no longer called Judaea, but Syria Palaestina. This moment marks the beginning of Jewish dispersion around the world. In Judaic tradition, the name of Hadrian is never mentioned without adding *shkhik asamot*, "may his bones be crushed."

Hadrian wanted to be considered an intellectual. In Roman society, the attitude to what was later called science and engineering was ambivalent: on the one hand, it was impossible to rule an empire without engineers and administrators, on the other, a sentimental idea of the only noble occupations being war and agriculture was still strong, though had no longer any connection with reality. As for intellectual work – medicine or pedagogics – it was mostly the domain of the Eastern half of the empire and its citizens, who were thought to be Greek, irrespective of their skin or clothes colour. A Roman intellectual could thus only be a Hellenophile, which Hadrian, of course, was – so much so that history has preserved an insult directed at him, *Graeculus* (Greekling). He was the first of the emperors to wear a beard according to the Greek tradition – though caustic tongues claimed it was because of a skin defect.

Hadrian was eager to acquire any kind of knowledge and tried to surpass the acknowledged masters. He played musical instruments and sang, did mathematics, drew, composed poetry. The Apollodorus story shows that he was not successful in all of his attempts, but few were as brave as the famous architect. Once during a dinner the emperor criticised an expression used by the philosopher Favorinus, who immediately accepted the criticism. When, later, friends accused the philosopher of servility, he answered: "Is it possible not to consider the smartest man the one who commands thirty legions?"

The same thirst for knowledge made Hadrian travel. He wanted to see everything he read about. Of course, back then any trip was complex and, most importantly, very long. Even a government envoy changing horses at every station could not cover more than a hundred miles per day; an emperor with his retinue, of course, travelled much more slowly. That meant that for months, sometimes for whole years, Rome remained under the control of emperor's close aides – and the fact that Hadrian's power did not so much as stumble during his absences speaks more about his rule than any caustic comments of his biographers.

Hadrian travelled his endless empire, scrutinising the smallest cases, dealing with petty complaints, visiting the sights. In Sicily, he went up Aetna to see the sun rise as a multicoloured arc; in Attica, he participated in the famous Eleusinian mysteries, and forbade his bodyguards to enter Eleusis armed.

> The Eleusinian mysteries were celebrated in Eleusis, a day's travel from Athens, for almost two thousand years. They were dedicated to the goddess Demetra and the cult of eternal rebirth connected to her. The Greeks, and the Romans too, saw life after death as a very bleak affair, and the Eleusinian mysteries offered an alternative: as a grain of Demetra in the earth dies and is reborn in a new ear, thus the initiated could hope that they would be reborn into a new life. It was forbidden to describe the rituals, which is why we know very little of what happened there. The initiates drank a special drink called *kykeon* and took sacred objects from a special trunk – but we do not know what they were. Then the Eleusinian mysteries were more widely known, because even slaves could be initiated into them: everyone was equal before death.

During a visit to Bythinia (a province on the Black Sea coast of today's Turkey), Hadrian met a Greek boy called Antinous and included him in his retinue. The boy was very beautiful, Hadrian very passionate ("now draw your own conclusions," helpfully advises the author of "Augustan History"). Antinous spent a few years at the emperor's court and during one of the trips – this one in Egypt – he drowned in the Nile under mysterious circumstances. Some sources seem to claim that he was horribly sacrificed according to an ancient rite, or killed himself to avert a bad omen from the emperor. Hadrian was inconsolable; he founded a city in Egypt, which he called Antinopolis. The scientists who were brought to Egypt by Napoleon found the ruins of its temples and streets, but today no ruins are visible at its site, near the small village of El Sheikh Ibada. Hadrian also ordered the deification of Antinous, which was previously something only awarded to members of the imperial family.

*Antinous. Relief from the Roman villa or cardinal and
art patron Alessandro Albani*

Hadrian's last years were grim. His health deteriorated; to avoid the
ambiguity that had plagued his own accession, he appointed his successors
ahead of his death. Some old courtiers who had hoped to succeed Hadrian
were unhappy. Hadrian, who grew more suspicious with age, had them
executed for treason. One of those courtiers, an old man called Servianus,
made a wish going to his death that Hadrian would want to die but could
not. The wish came true: the emperor had to be stopped from committing
suicide several times. Finally, in 138 AD, he died, "hated by everyone"
(*invisus omnibus*), not in the Tibur villa he loved, but in Baiae near Naples,
and was buried on the estate that had once belonged to Cicero (before
being laid to a new mausoleum).

Before his death, Hadrian wrote a poem addressed to his soul, so
un-classical in shape and spirit that ancient authors claimed they did not
like it – but modern poets raved about it; Byron translated it into English
(see below), but there are over forty English translations from the 17th
century onwards.

Animula, vagula, blandula
Hospes comesque corporis
Quae nunc abibis in loca
Pallidula, rigida, nudula,
Nec, ut soles, dabis iocos…

Ah! gentle, fleeting, wav'ring sprite,
Friend and associate of this clay!
To what unknown region borne,
Wilt thou, now, wing thy distant flight?
No more, with wonted humour gay,
But pallid, cheerless, and forlorn.

THE ARCH OF TITUS

There is a story about a delegation of Israeli rabbis who visited the ailing Pope John Paul II in 2004 and asked his permission to take inventory of the Vatican dungeons with the aim of finding the treasure of the Second Temple. A year before that, the president of Israel officially requested a list of Judean treasures from Vatican, and the Minister of Religious Services demanded in 2001 that an official commission be formed with the task to search for the menorah.

The menorah is a ritual seven-candle lampstand of pure gold that used to stand in the Temple in Jerusalem. When Roman troops destroyed the Temple, Judean treasures fell into the hands of the victors. The fact is well attested by a unique architectural document, a triumphal arch, that stands on the Sacra Via. But what happened to the treasures later no one knows for sure. They might have fallen into the hands of the Vandals, the Germanic tribe, who could have taken them to their capital city at the time, Carthage in North Africa. Another version says that pirates hauled them from one end of the Mediterranean to the other, and returned them to Jerusalem just in time for them to fall to the Persians. Yet another story features the Byzantine general Belisarius who took the treasure to Constantinople and hid it under the Hagia Sophia church. There are madder versions as well; one of them says that the menorah fell down from the Milvian bridge into the Tiber on the day of the fateful battle between the two contenders for the imperial throne, Maxentius and Constantine, on October 28, 312 (how it got to be there in the first place is not explained). A persistent Jewish urban legend has claimed since at least the 18th century that the menorah and other relics are still in Rome, which explains official requests and rumours about the Vatican cellars.

THE TEMPLE IN JERUSALEM

In 66 AD a rebellion against foreign occupation broke out in the Roman province of Judaea. Things looked bleak for the Romans – so bleak, in fact, that the emperor Nero was forced to recall the elderly general Vespasian, who had once incautiously dozed off during the emperor's music session, and sent him to suppress the uprising. With difficulty and losses, Vespasian put pressure on the rebels, but in the year 69, after Nero's suicide, the empire began to fall apart: various legions were proclaiming their commanders 'emperor,' including Vespasian's. The old soldier suddenly became interested in the prospect of becoming the master of the known world; he made for Italy and left his son Titus to sort out Judaea. The year 69 AD went down in history as "the year of the four emperors"; it ended with the victory of Vespasian and the establishment of a dynasty called Flavian after his *nomen*.

Titus besieged Jerusalem for five months, and action was focused around the Jerusalem Temple. Four legions were camped by the city walls; small-time Oriental rulers and local chieftains sent their reinforcements; desperados from the disbanded armies of the losing imperial contenders, Otho and Galba, arrived from Italy. The defenders of Jerusalem did not stand a chance.

And yet, the struggle proved to be arduous. The city was enclosed in several perimeters of ramparts. The Romans had broken through two of them and captured the so-called "new city" in the course of fierce fighting. Titus realised that an assault would be risky and might not lead to the desired result. He changed tactics, cordoned Jerusalem off and cut down all the trees within a ten-mile radius. The city, already suffering from famine, was now afflicted by disease. Those who managed to break out and surrender sometimes gorged themselves to death when they saw food. Hoping that the defenders were weakened, Titus ordered an assault on the Antonia Fortress standing next to the Temple, but it turned out that yet another wall had been erected behind it. The Romans sent in a 24-strong commando squad. The defenders of the Temple overestimated the threat and retreated, leaving their underground communications unprotected; the Romans immediately seized that opportunity and poured into the opening. A few days later, the priests were forced to suspend ritual sacrifices in the Temple, and this information shattered the spirit of Judean fighters. The Temple was put to the torch. The historian Flavius Josephus says that it was a grassroots initiative coming from the Roman rank and file – but Josephus, a onetime freedom fighter, at the time of writing his histories had long become a loyal client of Titus and Vespasian, so he wouldn't have wanted to besmirch their reputation in the eyes of his Jewish audience. Other sources, citing a report by Tacitus that did not survive, claim that the order to destroy the Temple was issued by Titus himself.

The destruction of the Temple fell on the ninth day of the month of Av – the same date of the Jewish calendar when the Babylonians had destroyed the First Temple. This date, Tisha B'Av, is generally considered unlucky for the Jewish people, and various disasters were destined for that day in later times, such as the expulsion of Jews from England by Edward I in 1290 and the beginning of mass deportation to the Treblinka camp from the Warsaw ghetto in 1942.

The document that illustrates the pilfering of Jewish relics is the triumphal arch that stands on the upper point of the Sacra Via, at the exit from the Forum archaeological area. It is known as the Arch of Titus. The arch depicts the triumph in honour of the suppression of the Judean rebellion, celebrated by the old Vespasian and 40-years-old Titus in 71 AD. The inscription on the eastern face of the monument (the one facing the Colosseum) says: "Senate and the Roman people to the Divine Titus, son of the Divine Vespasian, Vespasian Augustus."

Standing under the span of the arch and looking at both sides, you can see the reliefs that document the looting. The legionaries are hauling the Menorah which is so heavy that cushions on the shoulders were necessary to soften the burden; they carry silver trumpets "for the calling of the assembly, and for the journeying of the camps" (Numbers 10:2) and, possibly, the gold-plated wooden table for the shewbread (Exodus 25:30). The soldiers are holding some signs in their hands, which probably used to contain some inscriptions. Since they were painted and not carved, they did not survive. They might have contained the names and numbers of the legions – a sore loss for military buffs, but manageable; if there were comments on the spoils, then, of course, the damage is much greater.

In the dedicatory inscription, Titus is called 'deified' (*divus*), which means that the arch was erected or at least completed after his death and subsequent deification. There is another vivid confirmation of that. If, standing between the pylons, you lift up your head, you will see a relief not noticed by most tourists: Jupiter's eagle carrying away a small man in his claws. This man is none other than the emperor Titus. This bizarre image shows us the very moment of apotheosis, becoming a god.

The symbolic connection of the Arch of Titus (and not in a good way) to Judaism and the Jewish people turned out remarkably strong. In 1555, Pope Paul IV issued a papal bulla *Cum nimis absurdum*, which renewed the lapsed anti-Jewish legislation in the Papal States. Jews were prohibited from living outside ghettoes, forced to wear special markings on their clothes and swear an oath of loyalty to the Christian authorities next to the Arch of Titus. To this day, the Jews of Rome avoid passing under or too close to it. An exception was the parade of 1948, when a large crowd of Roman Jews marched under the Arch of Titus, celebrating the creation of the state of Israel – but they did so in a direction opposite to the route of a Roman triumph.

The Arch of Titus is one of the best-preserved Classical monuments of the city, but this state of preservation is a result of painstaking restoration. In the Middle Ages it formed a part of the works of the Frangipane family, and saw a lot of fighting in the 12th and 13th centuries. The damage was so great that in the early 19th century serious rebuilding was called for. It was fortunate that the person given the task was the Classicist architect Giuseppe Valadier. He carefully dismantled the arch and then reassembled it with equal care; for the pieces that needed to be replaced, he used travertine instead of the showier marble, so that the modern replicas would be immediately spottable. The side facing the Forum received its own inscription, also in Latin, of course: "This monument, remarkable in terms of both religion and art, had weakened from age: Pius VII, Supreme Pontiff, by new works on the model of the ancient exemplar, ordered it reinforced and preserved in the year of his sacred rulership the 24th (i.e. 1821)."[17]

Septizodium

The Flavian palace

Aqueduct

Hippodrome garden

Via di San Gregorio

N

0   50   100 M

San Bonaventura

San Sebastiano

THE PALATINE

Via dei Cerchi

Temple of Apollo

Lupercal (?)

Palatine Museum

House of Augustus

The Cacus stairs

Temple of Cybele

House of Livia

Temple of Victoria

Farnese Gardens

Via di San Teodoro

C H A P T E R   I I I

THE PALATINE
(THE HILL OF THE EMPERORS)

T he Forum was the oldest of Roman squares, and the Palatine, according to tradition, was the most senior among the city's hills. The greatest of the Roman epics, 'The Aeneid,' is set in a time immediately following the fall of Troy — which had happened, in the traditional chronology, more than four hundred years before the founding of Rome. But Virgil's readers, including the most important among them, Augustus, certainly expected the poet to describe the city they lived in, which was becoming increasingly prettier under Augustus's urban planning programme. To circumvent this difficulty, Virgil populated the future site of

Rome with immigrants from the rugged Greek province of Arcadia who teamed up with Aeneas's Trojans in their fight against the Latins. Their small city was called Pallantium, and the Palatine was its core. The wise Evander, the ruler of Pallantium, shows Aeneas and his entourage around the places that were very familiar to the first readers (or, rather, listeners) of the poem.

Generations later, the descendant of Aeneas, Romulus, observed on this hill the flight of vultures – an omen that directed him to lay the foundation of the city. According to a version recounted by ancient chroniclers, it was there that he raised a wall of the so-called "square Rome" (*Roma Quadrata*), and up until the final triumph of Christianity, the "hut of Romulus" was venerated here – a simple wattle-and-daub cabin with thatched roof.

Archaeologists often discover that the oldest Roman legends are rooted in at least a modicum of actual fact. In this case, the tradition was correct again. When serious excavation work started on the Palatine in the early 20th century, it was discovered that people had lived there for a very long time; the hill had been settled at least a few centuries before the official date of the founding of Rome. The reputation of "the senior hill," the plexus of power and authority, has survived almost into the present. In the mid-1930s the Flavian Palace, the largest and grandest ancient building on the Palatine, was hurriedly (and rather arbitrarily) restored with the aim of impressing Hitler during his state visit to Italy in May 1938. The Führer was welcomed with Ancient Roman pomp: a sailpast of 200 navy ships was shown to him in the Bay of Naples, an exercise of army and air force troops in Rome. Hitler, however, was underwhelmed by all the show of muscle, and the relationship between the axis partners remained strained.

There is not much to remind us of imperial grandeur on today's Palatine. For a long time, the hill was closed to visitors completely and archaeologists had the place to themselves. The excavations continue with no end in sight: the majority of monuments remain buried underground. The Palatine, however, is one of the few archaeological areas in downtown Rome where one can simply walk, and while walking, it is easy to forget what this site meant for the people who used to live here two thousand years ago. The buildings on the Palatine are poorly preserved, even worse than on the Forum, and poorly labelled. The imposing, brick-faced ribs and vaults jutting out from the edges of the hill (especially on the northern slope, near the Forum, and on the south-western, near the Circus Maximus) are the remains of the foundations, not of the buildings as such. The Palatine was not only expanding, it also grew in height: in its central section, the cultural layer rises above the bedrock for fifteen metres.

THE GARDENS

The best place to begin a walk is in the Farnese gardens. This is where the emperor's palace had once stood – or, rather, the part that is known in archaeological tradition as Domus Tiberiana. It was, indeed, Tiberius who started the construction, but the emperors Gaius ('Caligula') and Nero were equally responsible for the end result. Then posterity denounced those two as bad rulers, and the name of the palace was scrubbed clean of their names.

The cardinal Alessandro Farnese, the future Pope Paul III, laid out a picturesque garden in this part of the hill. The garden was designed by the Mannerist architect Giacomo Barozzi da Vignola. In the 17th century, when the Palatine was provided with a water supply for the first time since antiquity, Girolamo Rainaldi set up fountains in the gardens. In the 19th century, a "Villa Mills" grew next to the sumptuous Farnese villa, a Neo-Gothic "gingerbread house" of Charles Mills, an eccentric Scotsman who imaginatively rebuilt the small 16th-century Villa Spada. Mr. Mills was the last homeowner to hold private receptions on the Palatine – a thin thread of tradition stretching all the way from the heyday of the Roman Empire to the decline of the British one. All those buildings met a sad fate: the King of Naples who inherited the Villa Farnese took most of its treasures to Naples; it was later bought by the French emperor Napoleon III, an ardent promoter of archaeology. It was on his orders that the archaeologist Pietro Rosa launched large-scale excavations in various places on the hill. When the gardens and the villa were taken over by the Italian government, almost all non-classical structures were torn down. Today, only a restored gate on the Via San Gregorio (which serves as an entrance to the archaeological area) and 16th-century stairs with a mossy fountain that rise to the Palatine from the Forum side testify to the luxury of times past.

The botanical rarities of the Farnese gardens were famous as early as the 17th century, but the modern landscape planning is mostly the work of another archaeologist of Napoleon III's time, Giacomo Boni. Boni was digging the Forum, but lived on the Palatine, and it was there, in the middle of a garden which he had himself reconstructed after the ancient Roman fashion, that he was buried.

The Farnese gardens are surrounded by temples. Of course, it was the Capitol that was Rome's primary religious hub, and the western sector of today's Farnese gardens would have afforded a majestic view on the Temple of Jupiter.

In the south, leading from the valley of Circus Maximus, a set of stairs wound its way up the Palatine. It was called 'The Stairs of Cacus' (*Scala Caci*) after a notorious episode of cattle stealing. Heracles, venerated by the Romans under the name of Hercules, lay down for a nap on the Tiber bank, and the local giant shepherd called Cacus used the opportunity to steal a few of the magical cows of Geryon, recently obtained by Heracles in the course of his tenth labour. There is logic in placing this story on the banks of the Tiber: according to legend, Geryon lived in the far West, in the Spanish Gades (now Cádiz), so, on his way back to his cousin and temporary master Eurystheus who lived in Tiryns on the Peloponnese, Heracles might well have passed through Italy. The crafty Cacus found a cave and pulled the stolen cows by their tails, so that the traces would seem to lead out of the cave. The confused Heracles saw that something was wrong when he woke up, but since he could not find the missing animals, he drove the remains of the herd on. However, the hidden cows started to moo, Heracles discovered the ploy, and Cacus paid dearly for his crime. The stairs marked the place where the events took place, though the Romans were unsure about the exact location and offered the Forum Boarium, the oldest market on the Tiber bank, as an alternative place of Cacus's demise.

Heracles and the cattle of Geryon. Ancient Greek vase

THE TEMPLES

The south-eastern corner of the Palatine, the one that the Stairs of Cacus lead to, is one of the few well-excavated parts of the hill. If we have anyone to thank for that, it is the robbers of the 15th–18th century who pillaged virtually all valuable materials (and probably a lot of ancient artefacts), laying bare the foundations of the buildings. Concrete was of no special interest to them, so the bases of the Temple of Magna Mater and the small temple of Victoria Virgo survived. A nearby Temple of Victoria (not the same as Victoria Virgo) fared worse: the robbers dismantled its travertine base down to the ground, all the way to the wells and water cisterns of old Republican times.

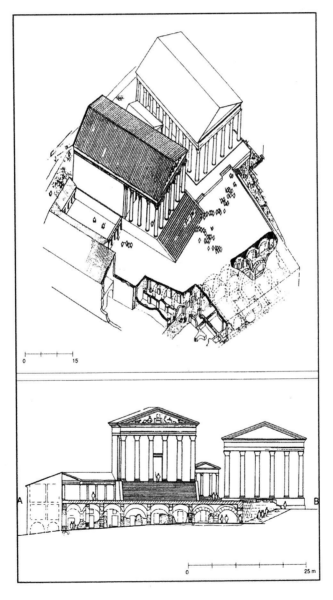

The temples of Victoria, Magna Mater and the small temple of Victoria Virgo (reconstruction)

Tradition ascribed the Temple of Victoria to the fairy-tale times of Evander. In reality, its foundations were laid in 307 BC by one Lucius Postumius Megellus from the fines he had collected as an aedile, an official responsible for public works. A few years later, this same Postumius Megellus was elected consul. His colleague Marcus Atilius Regulus went off to fight the Samnites, a rebellious Italic tribe with a long history of anti-Roman resistance (they managed to persist in their struggle into the times of the emperors). Megellus was sick and remained in the city. The enemies camped opposite each other, and during a foggy night the Samnites made a foray so audacious that the Romans were completely taken aback: they did not expect a head-on attack on their camp. The Romans, disoriented in the fog, were thrown back to the ramparts, and only the sonorous cursing of the consul Regulus ("Are you planning to besiege your own camp once you're thrown out of it?") made them rally and hurl back the foe. When news of the battle (much exaggerated) reached Rome, Megellus, sick though he was, rushed to the battlefield with an additional army, but not before he dedicated the Temple of Victoria. The Samnites, reluctant to fight on two fronts, withdrew.

Victoria was at the time becoming an increasingly important Roman deity. The conquest of Italy proceeded at full speed, and the first war with Carthage for domination in the Mediterranean (which effectively meant the whole known world) was on the horizon. The temple must have been majestic and luxurious. The few surviving fragments suggest a restoration of the 1st century BC, and a found fragment of an inscription records a reconstruction of Augustan date.

In 193 BC, soon after the exhausting Second Punic War that had stretched the resources of the state to their absolute limits, the Romans were still agitated, nervous with or without reason, and attentive to every minor portent. The historian Titus Livius records that in that year, some buildings collapsed and fell in ruins, there were showers of stones, and in Capua, swarm of wasps flew into the forum and settled in the temple of Mars and the insects were carefully collected and burned. The situation called for consulting the sacred books; "sacrifices were ordered for nine days... and the City underwent lustration (a purifying procedure). During this time [the important statesman] Marcus Portius Cato dedicated the chapel (aedicula) of Victoria Virgo near the temple of Victory, which he had vowed two years previously."[18]

As time passed, the cult of Victory became more and more fused to the cult of Rome's founders. It was a significant decision to allot the site for both Palatine temples to Victory next to the site of the simple cabin where the shepherd Faustulus and his wife were supposed to have brought up the foundlings Romulus and Remus. Cabins had indeed stood in that place for a very long time, and their remains are still visible if one looks from the temples toward the Circus Maximus. Whether *the* cabin was among them is of course impossible to say, but the Romans were absolutely positive on the matter. The historian Dionysius of Halicarnassus writes in his "Roman Antiquities" that the life of the oldest inhabitants of Latium was "that of herdsmen, and they lived by their own labour, generally upon the mountains in huts which they built, roofs and all, out of sticks and reeds. One of these, called the hut of Romulus, remained even to my day on the flank of the Palatine hill which faces towards the Circus, and it is preserved holy by those who have charge of these matters; they add nothing to it to render it more stately, but if any part of it is injured, either by storms or by the lapse of time, they repair the damage and restore the hut as nearly as possible to its former condition."[19] Like the perpetually restored ship of Theseus on the Acropolis in Athens, the hut of Romulus was a living example of a 'dialectical contradiction,' one of the favourite tenets of Marxist philosophy: a few centuries on, there was not a single original log in it, and yet, it remained "the same hut."

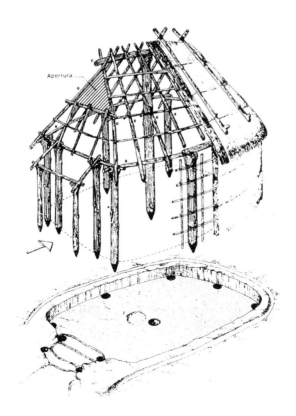

The hut of Romulus (reconstruction)

Next to the Temple of Victory, at a slight angle to it, oriented so that the two roofs almost touched, stood the temple of Magna Mater, the Great Mother of Gods. When Hannibal was standing by the very gates of Rome and the fall of the state seemed all but inevitable, the Romans consulted the Sybilline books and found an enigmatic demand to 'find and bring Mother.' Priestly commentators explained that Mother was the Phrygian Mother of Gods, the great Cybele who had been worshipped by the Trojans. The principal sanctuary of Cybele was on Mount Ida near the city of Pessinus in Anatolia, and the principal relic was a small triangular stone. Different accounts claimed that it either replaced the whole face of the goddess or was simply inserted into her mouth. Like many sacred stones, the stone of Cybele might have been a piece of a meteorite.

An embassy was sent to King Attalus, the ruler of that domain. The king wavered, probably unwilling to incur the wrath of Hannibal. At that time, a fortuitous earthquake supported the Romans' cause: they were quick to explain that it was a sign of Cybele's displeasure at the king. (Ovid also reports that the goddess personally addressed the king from the heavens, demanding that she be carried to Rome, the city worthy of housing all the gods.) The frightened Attalus agreed to part with the relic. With great care the precious cargo was delivered to Italy, but in the very mouth of the Tiber, near the port city of Ostia, the ship ran ashore. The welcomers, who included the most well-born men and women of Rome, were at a loss. Seeing this, a noble matron (a Vestal virgin, according to some sources) called Claudia Quinta, who always dressed a little bit flashier than modesty dictated and therefore was suspected of depravity, grabbed the ship's rope and jerked the ship afloat. The people were jubilant, Claudia was declared the people's heroine, and evil rumours were immediately forgotten.

The mysterious object was placed in the Temple of Victory. Several years later, a new temple was dedicated, and games honouring Mother Cybele were instituted. The offerings to her consisted of the simplest possible meal – cheese mixed with herbs.

The temple burned down twice, and both times the statue of Claudia Quinta remained miraculously intact. No part of it has survived, except a concrete plinth dating from a restoration of the late 2nd century BC. A statue in the Palatine Antiquarium Museum is thought to depict Cybele: the goddess is sitting on a throne flanked by two lions.

To the east of this temple cluster, beyond a small residential quarter (we will soon come back to it) stood another temple, the Temple of Apollo. It was the second Temple of Apollo in the city, and both were erected by Octavian (the future Augustus) in commemoration of his two most important naval victories, over Sextus Pompey at Naulochus off the shores of Sicily and over Antony and Cleopatra at Actium five years later, in the Ambracian Gulf off the western coast of Greece. Octavian venerated Apollo as his personal protector, and a separate temple to the god was built at Actium. It was rumoured that Octavian's mother Atia had spent a night in the sanctuary of Apollo nine months before her son was born, and there, the god penetrated her in the guise of a snake, leaving an indelible snake-coloured mark (Atia had since stopped frequenting public baths). Other elements of the Apollonian cult must have appealed to the ruler as well: the god patronised the arts and was merciless to his enemies. The doors of the Palatine temple were adorned with ivory reliefs which depicted the foes of Rome and Apollo suffering one defeat after another. One of them showed the expulsion of the Gauls from the Delphi sanctuary of Apollo in 278 BC, another the extermination of Niobe's children by the arrows of Apollo and his sister Artemis (known as Diana in Rome). The cult statues in the temple's cella – Apollo, Diana and their mother Leto (Latona) – were carved by the best Greek sculptors. The façade, facing east, featured the sun god Helios in his magical chariot.

Claudia Quinta pulling the ship. Mediaeval illustration

Around the temple was a portico called "The Portico of the Danaids." This was another veiled threat directed by Augustus at his potential enemies. It is not clear where exactly the portico was – in all probability, after the Great Fire of Nero's time it had burned down and was never rebuilt. While it stood, it was decorated with columns of Numidian yellow marble and the statues of the fifty Danaids and their father.

The Danaids were the daughters of King Danaus, who was considered the ancestor of the Greek nation. In Homer, the Greeks are collectively called Danaans (also Achaeans and Argives, and only twice Hellenes). Fifty daughters of Danaus all married their cousins, the sons of the king of Egypt, and during the wedding night forty-nine of them murdered their husbands on their father's orders (the fiftieth refused, and went on to engender the future Greek race). In the light of Augustus's victory over Antony and Cleopatra and annexation of Egypt the hint was less than subtle.

The Palatine Antiquarium has two Danaid statues of black Greek marble and one of red marble; red and black figures possibly alternated between the columns. Augustus added a library to the Temple of Apollo. It was large enough to accommodate Senate hearings, and the Senate convened in the library quite often, especially in the later years of Augustus's rule, when the old emperor found it hard to descend to the Forum. When Augustus accepted the office of Pontifex Maximus, a small shrine of Vesta was built nearby.

The importance of the new Temple of Apollo was sealed when Augustus chose it as the storage place for the Sybilline books. The prophecies were kept in chests of gold, and the chests were buried under the base of the statue of Apollo.

THE SIBYLS

Sibyl (*sibylla*) is a word of obscure origin that means 'prophetess.' The veneration of prophetic sibyls harks back to hoary antiquity, possibly pre-Indo-European. This partly explains the central position of women in this cult. The earliest written records of European antiquity belong to a time when life was already thoroughly patriarchal, and only the rudiments of the oldest rites suggested a civilisation unconquered by bloodthirsty horsemen from the steppes, a civilisation that worshipped its motherly deities. (Like all hypotheses about pre-Indo-European times, this one is controversial and tentative, and is likely to remain so until the invention of time travel.) The Vestal virgins in Rome and sibyls all across the Mediterranean were the priestesses of those ancient cults.

It is impossible to say how many sibyls there were – like all fairy-tale characters, they sprout doppelgängers and get confused with one another in the record. All sources agree on some of their typical traits: extreme longevity, aloofness from earthly concerns and the cryptic quality of their prophecies.

The sibyl most worshipped by the Romans used to live on the shores of the Bay of Naples. It was the place where the first seeds of civilisation had been sown on Italian soil, if we understand civilisation in the traditional sense as the beginnings of statehood and literacy. In the 8th century BC, the settlers from the Greek island of Euboea established there an outpost for trading with the local Italic tribes. As the colony grew, the outpost became a city – Cumae, the first permanent Greek settlement in mainland Italy.

The Romans told a variety of stories about the Cumaean Sibyl. The oldest of them was this. Once an old woman came to the king Tarquin the Elder and offered him nine prophetic books for sale. The king inquired about the price; the woman quoted an exorbitant sum, too much for the king, so she shrugged her shoulders and left. Some time passed, and she came again, claiming that she had burned three of the nine books and offering the remaining six for the same price. "This is crazy," thought Tarquin and chased her away again. When the persistent saleswoman arrived the third time, now with three books, something made the king pause. He called his advisers, and when they saw the books, they were in raptures: "These prophecies," they said, "lay out the future destinies of the Roman people, and they must be bought at any price. But where are the rest of the books? There should be more." The humbled king bought the remaining three books at the original asking price, and the Sibyl (for that's who she was) was never seen among the living again.

Cumaean Sibyl. A fragment of Michelangelo's fresco in the Sistine Chapel

Like all Roman legends about regal times, the story of the Sibylline books hovers between tradition and fairy tale. The books, however, did exist; they were kept in the sanctuary of the Capitoline Jupiter under the watchful eye of a special priestly college. When the state was threatened with imminent danger, the books were consulted for an answer vague enough to distract the people with the task of interpreting it for a while. The recommendations of the Sibylline books could be quite brutal. When the sacred writings were consulted after the catastrophic defeat at Cannae, the suggested remedy was to bury two Gauls and two Greeks in the Forum, alive, and the advice was followed. In 83 BC the Temple of Jupiter burned to the ground together with the prophecies. When the turbulent era of civil wars came to an end, Augustus ordered that the Sibylline books be reconstructed from quotations, copies, scraps, memories and other similar sources. It was these copies that were kept at the Temple of Apollo on the Palatine Hill.

Near the corner of the Flavian palace, next to the Barberini vineyards, was another temple. It is not known exactly what it was, though circumstantial evidence points at its dedication to Jupiter. It might have been the temple which the eccentric emperor Elagabalus turned into a sanctuary of his namesake god. As a child, Elagabalus was a priest of El-Gabal, a god worshipped in his native Emesa (now Homs in Syria). Finding himself on the Roman throne at the tender age of fourteen, he forced the Syrian cult on his new subjects, making the Senate and the people worship a new god under the name of *Sol Invictus*, 'the unconquerable Sun.' These Oriental fads displeased the Romans, and the young man was murdered by a cabal of conspirators egged on by his own grandmother.

Later emperors reinstated the worship of Jupiter, but not for long: another, more durable kind of monotheism was in the works. It is represented on the Palatine today by two small churches: San Bonaventura (late 17th century) and San Sebastiano (early 17th century, but with frescoes and many other details of an earlier building, approximately of the 10th century). The church of San Sebastiano used to be called Santa Maria in Pallara, because a legend claimed that it was the site of a pagan temple where the Palladium, the magical statue of Athena/Minerva taken by Aeneas out of Troy, was kept. The legend is hardly believable: everyone knows that the Palladium was in the care of the Vestal virgins in their Forum temple. But there are ruins of a late imperial temple between the two churches, and ancient Roman cisterns below the ruins. Both San Bonaventura and San Sebastiano are very popular wedding venues.

THE LIVING QUARTER

The Palatine, the central Roman hills, enveloped in an aura of old-time lore, formed the most prestigious residential quarter of the city. At the end of the republican era, it became a prestige symbol, and all politicians and lobbyists who cared about their status wanted to live on its slopes. Among those who made their home on the Palatine were the Gracchi family, Tiberius Claudius Nero, father of the emperor Tiberius, and Mark Antony of the Antony and Cleopatra fame.

Today, many of the highest-ranking politicians in the world come from legal backgrounds. In Rome, men with political ambitions began their careers with oratorial exercises. Of course, they also settled on the Palatine, close to the unofficial power seat. There was the home of Lucius Licinius Crassus, a famous orator and Cicero's teacher; also of Quintus Hortensius Hortalus, the most sought-after lawyer in Rome before Cicero's star lit up in earnest; and it was there, in dangerous proximity to his sworn enemy Clodius, that Cicero himself bought a house.

CICERO AND THE VERRES AFFAIR

Cicero's oratorial and political career kicked off with a corruption case. One of the politicians of the previous generation, Gaius Verres, was rewarded with a plum job for his service to the powers that be: he was sent to govern Sicily. It was a very lucrative posting, since Sicily had been long called "the breadbasket of the Republic." Its position in the centre of the Mediterranean, at the intersection of marine trade routes, ensured a constant flow of riches from all the ends of the habitable world.

Verres had used his sinecure to the hilt: he instituted unprecedented taxes for farmers, cancelled contracts as he saw fit, confiscated works of art from the islanders and amassed a huge private collection of great value. During the Spartacus uprising, he used to catch law-abiding slaves, accuse them of sympathy for the rebels and suggested to the owners that they could save their property from execution and even get it back if they make a donation to the governor.

The desperate Sicilians petitioned Rome with a request to bring Verres to trial. The young Cicero volunteered to represent them; Verres, confident of his plundered wealth, hired the infinitely more experienced Hortensius. Hortensius was famous for his florid style ("better to hear than to read," was Cicero's undoubtedly biased verdict), phenomenal memory, thespian skills (actors came to listen to his speeches with educational purposes), foppish approach to personal attire and a passion for luxury. Small wonder that a man like that had a house on the Palatine.

Cicero

Unfortunately for the accused, the judge in charge of the trial was Glabrio, a gentleman of the old school, unsusceptible to threats or bribery. Hortensius did his best to postpone the beginning of the trial so that it would fall to the new, more amenable judge. Cicero managed to work around this difficulty. The very first speech by the young orator made such an impression on everyone present, that Hortensius hastily laid down his arms, refused to object and told his client that it would be wise for him to leave the city. Verres had gone into self-imposed exile to Massilia (today's Marseilles), and lived there with part of his Sicilian spoils until Mark Antony got interested in some of his statues. It is not known how the deal went, but it was unlikely to end well for Verres.

Cicero was left with a bunch of undelivered speeches on his hands. Being an ambitious young man, he encouraged their circulation in privately-made copies, which is why students of law and elocution to this day use them in their training.

The Temple of Apollo is abutted by a residential compound traditionally connected to Rome's first imperial family – that of Augustus. The ruins usually called "The House of Livia" (who was Augustus's wife) might be the former house of Hortensius purchased by Augustus. Hortensius was known for his expensive taste, while the living standards of Augustus, as described by Suetonius, were remarkably humble: "The simplicity of his furniture and household goods may be seen from couches and tables still in existence, many of which are scarcely fine enough for a private citizen."[20] We should keep in mind, though, as Vladimir Nabokov once wrote, that "an ascetic may dream of a feast that would make an epicurean sick," and the luxury of Cicero's time might well have been treated as austerity fifty years later. For forty years, Augustus used the same bedroom in winter and summer (the Romans usually moved from the southern wing of their houses to the northern in summer) and kept an attic where he could work without interruption, which he called "Syracuse" and "little workshop." Only when he was sick, did he move to the villa of Maecenas on the Esquiline hill – the air was thought to be better there.

Surviving frescoes in "The House of Livia" depict garlands of flowers and fruit, Egyptian-style landscapes and, in the central room, mythological scenes. On one wall is the nymph Galatea and the sea giant Polyphemus pining after her; on the other Io, guarded by Argus. At each end of the long wall is a small painting in the Greek style of the type called *pinax*, "a plate"; those were very valuable and used to be protected with special doors. Both feature triple portraits of noble women. In the course of excavations, lead plumbing pipes were found, marked with a variety of names: the emperor Domitian, one Julia Augusta (that could be any of the noble ladies of the imperial house) and L. Pescennius Eros, a contractor of the Severan era.

The so-called "House of Augustus" nearby probably occupies the actual site which Augustus wanted to use to expand his residence, but changed his mind when lightning hit the construction site (a bolt of lightning meant that the gods claimed the place for themselves). Augustus yielded the site to the state, and used his own money to begin the construction of Apollo's temple with the portico. To compensate the emperor for his expenditures, the Senate offered to buy him a new house at public expense. We do not know whether Augustus accepted the offer, but in any event he continued to live in his old Palatine house, the one that had once belonged to Hortensius.

Finally, the house where Augustus was born had also stood in the Palatine quarter, near the Ox-Heads (it is not known what these were). Later, a young man called Gaius Laetorius, accused of adultery, begged the Senate for a milder punishment, citing in his defence, among other things, the fact that he was the owner and, as it were, warden of the spot which the deified Augustus first touched at his birth. (When Roman babies were delivered, they were placed at their fathers' feet, and if the father picked up the baby, he officially acknowledged his paternity.) The outcome of Laetorius's case was not recorded, but the Senate ordered the consecration of the exact location of the birth of Augustus.

ROMAN FOOD

What did the Romans eat? We usually picture exotic and richly decorated dishes, but the daily diet of most Romans, even those with some money (obviously, we know much less about the life of everyday people), was rather simple. Educated Romans treated culinary excesses as suspect. A household name was that of one Apicius, someone who lived in the 1st century AD and turned cooking into fine art, inventing many fantastic dishes like ragout of flamingoes' tongues or soup made from the tails of unborn piglets drawn from their mother's womb. It was reported that when after a long series of banquets he inspected his fortune and found that he only had ten million sesterces left (still a huge fortune), he killed himself. In around the 4th or 5th century, a large cookbook was published with Apicius's name as a tag (usually called *De re coquinaria*, "On the art of cooking"), the first collection of recipes in history. In spite of the real Apicius's reputation, many recipes from this book are simple, deal with only a handful of everyday ingredients, and generally look like current Italian cooking. We only have to keep in mind that the Romans did not know of potatoes, corn, or even tomatoes – all these things came from the New World. Sugar as such did not exist, and there were no sweet desserts typical of the East. Fresh fruit and vegetables, however, were quite popular, and honey played the role of culinary sweetener.

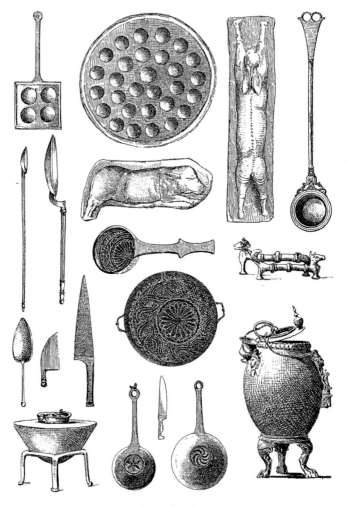

Cooking objects found in Pompeii

Sometimes we hear that the Romans loved gastronomic delights so much that saturation was of secondary importance; to eat as much as they could, they took emetics (or used a peacock's feather to induce vomiting) to empty the stomach. Indeed, the bilious Seneca wrote: "They vomit that they may eat, and eat that they may vomit, and do not even deign to digest the banquets which they ransack the globe to obtain."[21] It should be noted, though, that emetics were considered healthy even outside of gluttony. Julius Caesar, for example, was a modest and low-maintenance man, which even his enemies grudgingly acknowledged – and yet, when he dined with Cicero, he took an emetic.

The classical philologist and historian Mary Beard invented a jocular method of testing popular books on Roman culture and history (as well as documentaries and movies on the same topic). She suggests a simple "dormouse test." "How long is it before the characters adopt an uncomfortably horizontal position in front of tables, usually festooned with grapes, and one says to another: 'Can I pass you a dormouse?'" – she writes. Still, facts are brutal: a large rodent called a dormouse (*Glis glis*) was a part of the Romans' ration and, probably, was even considered a delicacy. In 115 BC a special law forbade the consumption of dormice, molluscs and imported birds – but such laws were often ignored or quickly fell out of use.

By the way, dormice are still caught and eaten in Slovenia and some parts of Croatia – since these were Roman provinces, it is tempting to think that the tradition has survived since the Roman times.

One of the residential houses on the southern slope of the Palatine, the one offering a view on the Circus Maximus, belonged to a certain Gelotius and became known in the literature as *Domus Gelotiana*. It was often visited by the emperor Caligula, an avid fan of chariot races who rooted for the Greens (we will revisit the circus games and rival factions when we come closer to the Circus Maximus). In 1857, an ancient grafitto was discovered in the house of Gelotius; it is probably the first surviving depiction of Christ. The depiction is utterly irreverent, to put it mildly. On the section of the wall is crudely drawn a human figure on a T-shaped cross. The figure has a donkey's head, a man is standing in front of it in a posture of devotion, and the inscription explains, in half-literate Greek, that *Alexamenos sebete theon*, 'Alexamenos worships [his] god.'

It is common for people, nations and ideologies to ridicule something they perceive as alien and do not understand. Classical Antiquity was baffled by Judaism and Christianity and tried to laugh them off. The Alexamenos graffito is a striking example of that strategy. For some reason, a donkey often becomes an instrument of such mockery. Greeks and Romans thought (or pretended to think) that Jews and Christians worshipped donkeys. This superstition had even acquired a specialist term, onolatry, from the Greek words *onos*, 'donkey,' and *latris*, 'worshipper.'

THE PALACE

True palaces only appeared on the Palatine in the times of Tiberius and Nero. In the Augustan era, such extravagance was unheard of, and the ruler of Rome used to invite himself to the houses of his friends and freedmen that were strategically located on the southern slope and whose upper storeys afforded the best views of the chariot races. Later emperors claimed for the palace the present-day site of the Farnese gardens. In the basement of the palace was a dungeon where, in 33 AD, Tiberius had starved to death his grand-nephew Drusus who was accused of being a part of a conspiracy. Historians note the interesting detail that the despairing young man chewed on the straw from the mat before he died.

The Flavian Palace (also called the Palace of Domitian) takes up the major part of the archaeological area of the Palatine. It is not fully excavated, and what lies in its north-eastern sector, near the San Bonaventura church, is quite unclear. However, the currently accessible portion takes up over three hectares. Before the Flavian Palace, there were simply no buildings on that scale in Rome.

The reputation of the emperor Domitian has suffered at the hands of later historians. The bulk of what we know comes from the works of the next generation – both Suetonius and Tacitus wrote under the emperors of the next (Nerva-Antonine) dynasty. The transition from the Flavians to Nerva was violent, and the succession was broken. To avoid painting the new rulers as a dynasty of usurpers, court historians were encouraged to show Domitian in an unfavourable light. This is how after the two almost picture-perfect Flavians, the third unexpectedly turned out to be a monster.

A few telling examples. In the first days of his reign he allegedly used to spend hours in seclusion, entertaining himself with catching flies and stabbing them with a sharp stylus (a court wit, when asked whether anyone was in there with Caesar, replied "Not even a fly"). He executed people arbitrarily and eagerly; for the first time in centuries, he invoked the brutal ancient rite of burying a Vestal for breaking her vow of chastity. Perhaps even more impressive is a brief personal note by Suetonius, something that he rarely indulges in, when he describes Domitian's rigour in levying the so-called "Jewish tax." In the best anti-Semitic tradition, the emperor extended the practice to those Jews who had long abandoned their religion and sometimes even concealed their origin. "I recall being present in my youth," Suetonius writes, "when the person of a man ninety years old was examined before the procurator and a very crowded court, to see whether he was circumcised."[22]

The extravagance of the palace was mind-boggling. Its dining hall was huge. Domitian's court poet Statius wrote about "Caesar reclining with the best of the best, among a thousand tables." (Unlucky as Domitian was in later historiography, he displayed remarkable skills in his day-to-day PR management.) The walls were decorated with three tiers of multicoloured columns. Marble and polished granite sparkled. No expense was spared in achieving the grandeur of the assignment and the builders made no attempt to respect the work of their predecessors. For example, the beautiful marble floor of the previous palace that had occupied that site, Nero's, with a floral design, one of the best known examples of Roman decorative art, was simply broken up where they needed to lay foundations, and covered with earth elsewhere. Now, some parts of that floor are visible again.

The dining hall was surrounded by gardens and fountains. Open courtyards were laid out, each as large as a palace. One of the courtyards ('the third,' near the Antiquarium) contained a garden, and today's reconstruction tries to follow the few rules of Classical horticulture that have come down to us. To the east of all that luxury was another gigantic garden in the shape of a 'stadium' or 'hippodrome,' one of the most impressive sights on the Palatine. Domitian seemed to be partial to such shapes: in Rome, he had built an actual stadium, whose contours are still visible in the shape of the prettiest of the city's squares, Piazza Navona. In his suburban villa, there was another garden of similar shape. We do not know what the Palatine 'stadium' was decorated with (apart from fountains on both sides). Perhaps those statues of gold and silver representing the emperor, the only ones Domitian allowed, with a fixed weight.

By the end of his life, Domitian had become distrustful. The day of his death had been predicted to him, and he awaited it anxiously. Bad omens started as scheduled. Lightning began to strike various buildings including the Palatine palace and even the emperor's bedroom; the oracles were increasingly gloomy. The final blow was dealt by the fate of the astrologer Ascletarion. Eager to check the veracity of the predictions, Domitian asked the astrologer what his own end would be. Ascletarion answered that he would be shortly torn apart by dogs. Domitian immediately ordered the execution of the magician and his careful burial. However, during the funeral a storm swept away the funeral pyre, and the charred corpse was, indeed, torn apart by dogs. Well-wishers immediately reported it to the already jumpy emperor.

The porticoes of the palace where Domitian usually walked were lined on the emperor's orders with moonstone – mirror-like translucent white marble, discovered in Cappadocia shortly before his reign. He hoped it would prevent an assault from behind. This did not help: bypassing the emperor's vigilance, the conspirators stabbed him to death in his own bedroom. Even Suetonius, biased against Domitian, says that he fought back valiantly and that the legionaries, on learning about his death, were prepared to tear the conspirators to shreds: Domitian was very popular with the troops.

In the later imperial era the palatial complex founded by Augustus and expanded with each new dynasty occupied virtually the whole hill. The very words 'palatial,' 'palace,' 'palazzo' are all derived from 'Palatine.'

SEPTIZODIUM AND LUPERCAL

The eastern part of the palace was rebuilt and expanded under the Severan emperors. Today, this section looks rather modest, but in its day it was grander in scale and decoration even than Domitian's development. At the approach to the palatial quarter, the Severans had erected in the early 3rd century AD a bizarre structure called Septizodium. The name is unclear: perhaps it was a reference to the seven planetary gods, perhaps it simply reflected the fact that it was divided to seven tiers. The Septizodium was a huge freestanding façade without any building attached to it, lavishly decorated with the statues of gods and the members of the imperial family. It might have been a purely propaganda project, meant to inspire awe in everyone who approached the Palatine from the south, along the Appian Way. Even today, when the Septizodium is long gone, the view of verdant slopes in the rays of the setting sun, if you look from the Circus Maximus side, is not to be missed.

One section of that strange façade, three tiers of Corinthian columns, survived for a very long time, until the end of the 16th century. In the end, under Pope Sixtus V, it was demolished: such a quantity of white and coloured stone lying around was a sore in the eye for papal architects. One hundred and four blocks of off-white Proconnesian marble from the Septizodium were used to restore the Column of Marcus Aurelius.

The emperors of later times continued to live on the Palatine, but did very little in terms of infrastructure. Maxentius left behind a modest bath complex, tucked in between San Bonaventura and the 'hippodrome' garden of Domitian. Perhaps he had more ambitious plans, but they never came to fruition. After the centre of imperial gravity moved to Constantinople, the Palatine was slowly turning into a monument to its past glory. However, those emperors of the West who still preferred to live in Rome (and not, let us say, Treveri or Mediolan) continued to favour the Palatine. When the Gothic rulers Odoacer and Theodoric visited the Eternal City, that was also their preferred residential choice. A Byzantine garrison stationed in Rome continued to appoint a "warden of the Palatine palaces" until the 7th century.

In November 2007, a team of Italian archaeologists led by Iren Jacopi and Andrea Carandini announced a discovery. A middle-sized grotto was found under "the House of Livia." Its cupola-like ceiling was decorated by a colourful mosaic made of smalt, pumice and seashells, with a white eagle in the middle. The researchers solemnly proclaimed that they had found the legendary Lupercal, the sanctuary of Romulus, Remus and the she-wolf who suckled them. Italian newspapers published long, gushing articles. The grotto is still off-limits to people, because it is chock-full of two millennia of construction rubble and could easily collapse. But modern technology came to the rescue, and the lovers of antiquity could enjoy colour photos taken with a special camera probe.

THE LUPERCALIA

The Lupercal was supposed to be on the very spot where the she-wolf had suckled the babies Romulus and Remus. This sanctuary was connected to one of the most ancient and whimsical of Roman festivals, the Lupercalia. The Lupercalia were celebrated in mid-February. Having sacrificed two goats and a dog, the members of the priestly college of Luperci, dressed in freshly flayed goat skins and with thongs made of the same goat skins ran around the whole city, whipping everyone left, right, and centre. No one ran away from them; on the contrary, noble matrons willingly held out their hands to be struck ("like children in school," notes Plutarch in a businesslike manner): the strikes of Lupercalia thongs were supposed to enhance fertility and alleviate labour pain. In the fateful year, 44 BC, Mark Antony was the consul – the highest-ranking state official; and yet, he did not think it beneath himself to run with the Luperci. Naked under the goat skin, he ran up to the Forum and offered a kingly diadem to Julius Caesar. Caesar gauged the reaction of the crowd (which was wildly negative: the idea of kingship was anathema to the Romans) and declined the royal honours – but that, it turned out, was not enough to save him.

The festival remained wildly popular, and when Pope Gelasius I decided to abolish it at the very end of the 5th century, he encountered intense opposition. The pope persuaded his opponents by offering them, since they were so free-thinking, to run around the city in blood-soaked goat skins. By that time, centuries after the Luperci consuls, the Lupercalia was a festival of the rabble, and aristocratic defenders of the holiday bit their tongues. Today's mass media often derive Valentine's Day, celebrated at around the same time, from Lupercalia, but there is no evidence for that. Indeed, there is no connection between the feast of St. Valentine and any notion of romantic or courtly love before a couple of Chaucer's poems created the link at the end of the 14th century.

Many researchers remained unconvinced about the identification of the newly discovered grotto. Ancient sources placed Lupercal closer to the Temple of Victory and Magna Mater than to the Temple of Apollo, the site of the new discovery, (though the distance is negligible, and the writers, especially Greek writers, could have easily mixed things up). There is no altar in the new room (it might be buried under the debris or dismantled by robbers). Finally – and this is a serious objection – mosaic ceilings were a novelty even in the times of Pliny the Younger, in the 2nd century AD, while the Lupercal, our sources agree, had been restored in Augustan times. On the other hand, records of a later restoration might have been simply lost.

The Lupercal deniers did not belittle the discovery itself: finding any ancient building with its décor intact in central Rome is a massive stroke of luck. They only put forward other theories, like the grotto being a private dining room of one of the emperors (Nero's, for example). But in 2009 a unique cylindrical brick construction was found in the Barberini Vineyards, which was immediately proclaimed the famous rotating dining room of the Golden House, Nero's post-fire palace. Of course, that claim was also immediately challenged: why on earth, the critics said, would this all-important room be so far from the main compound? (We will visit the Golden House in Chapter Six.) Recently, after a long break, the Barberini Vineyards were reopened to the public, and now the tourists can enjoy a great view of the Colosseum and see the mysterious cylinder with their own eyes.

Perhaps new research will shed light on the attribution of newly discovered buildings, but it is much more likely that we will never know the answers. Be as it may, sensational discoveries facilitate the financing of archaeological work, and it is not unthinkable that the oldest hill of Rome will have even more treasures and mysteries to dazzle us.

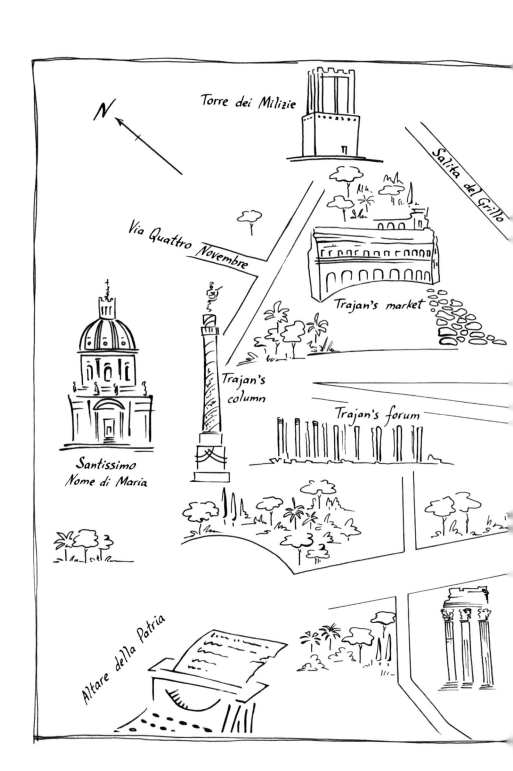

Torre dei Milizie

Salita del Grillo

N

Via Quattro Novembre

Trajan's market

Trajan's column

Trajan's forum

Santissimo Nome di Maria

Altare della Patria

FORI IMPERIALI

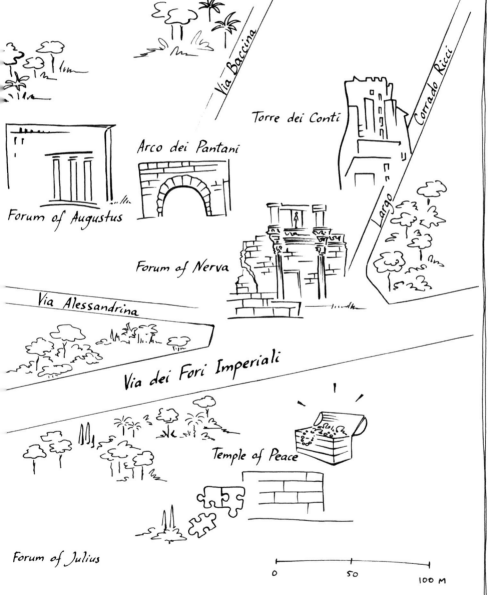

Via Baccina

Corrado Ricci

Torre dei Conti

Arco dei Pantani

Forum of Augustus

Largo

Forum of Nerva

Via Alessandrina

Via dei Fori Imperiali

Temple of Peace

Forum of Julius

0   50   100 M

CHAPTER IV

THE IMPERIAL FORA
(MUSSOLINI'S AVENUE)

A straight street running through the middle of an ancient city
is always suspicious. Cities that are hundreds of years (let alone
millennia) old are never built to a unified master layout. They
sprout residential neighbourhoods, public buildings and churches using
every available plot of land. Old streets in almost any ancient European
town are winding and narrow. If an arrow-straight thoroughfare is found
in the centre, beware: most likely a chunk of old "impractical" urban tissue
was sacrificed for the sake of this novelty.

Some areas of Rome are two thousand years old, and straight streets there are even more suspect than anywhere else. There are those which, like the Via del Corso, can boast of a venerable age: it is the continuation of Via Flaminia, in ancient times the main road linking Rome with the Adriatic coast. But most of the others are a hundred years old or less: Via Nazionale (from Piazza della Repubblica to Piazza Venezia) was cut through in the late 19th century, Via della Conciliazione (from St. Peter's Square to the bridge across the Tiber) in the early 20th. The most audacious among them is probably the Via dei Fori Imperiali running from the Colosseum to Piazza Venezia. It cuts through the very heart of imperial Rome, the arena that had served as a showcase of the ambitions, luxury, artistic taste and architectural grandeur of Rome's rulers for two hundred years.

The inauguration of the Imperial Fora Street (under the name of Via dell'Impero, "The Empire Street") took place on October 28, 1932. The event commemorated the tenth anniversary of "The March on Rome," the coup that forced King Victor Emmanuel III to hand over power to the leader of Italian fascists, Benito Mussolini. Though a native of the northern province of Emilia-Romagna, Mussolini thought of himself as an ancient Roman and treated everything ancient, especially imperial, with veneration bordering on mania. The inauguration of the new street thus became a central event of the festivities, just as important as the opening of "The Exhibition of the Fascist Revolution," meant to advertise fascist achievement of the previous ten years.

Benito Mussolini (1883–1945) was the head of Italy's fascist government from 1922 until 1943. In 1943, after Allied forces invaded Italy, he was ousted and arrested, but later rescued by German special ops. In 1945, when the defeat of Hitler's Germany was no longer in doubt, Mussolini made an attempt to escape to Switzerland, but was apprehended by Communist partisans, executed and hung upside down, together with his mistress Clara Petacci, at a petrol station in Milan.

Mussolini's urban planning programme involved the 'liberation' of ancient monuments. This meant that layers of residential and other buildings accreted through the centuries around ancient ruins were treated as 'slums' by fascist architects and were subject to demolition. The Theatre of Marcellus had already been 'liberated' in that manner; now was the turn of the Imperial Fora.

What exactly are the Imperial Fora? The name is traditionally applied to five architectural compounds to the north of the 'old' Forum. (The original Forum is sometimes called *Forum Romanum*, 'the Roman Forum,' to distinguish it from the later squares. This is, of course, deeply misleading: the imperial fora are just as Roman.)

The first of the imperial fora was conceived, if not quite constructed, by Julius Caesar at the sunset of the republican era. The last, Trajan's Forum, marked the historical moment which a later tradition would consider the apogee of the Roman Empire, the climax of its greatness.

THE FORUM OF CAESAR

The first of the imperial fora, the Forum of Caesar (also called *Forum Iulium*) was planned by Julius Caesar at a time when he was far removed from metropolitan creature comforts. He was busy chasing long-haired, trouser-clad Gauls all across present-day France (with occasional forays further afield, like the two abortive invasions of Britain). He was also getting a great deal wealthier along the way (a successful war was, and remains, a highly lucrative business). Caesar needed that money: first, he was in debt to some very no-nonsense people in Rome; second, he was planning a lot of expenses for propaganda purposes so as to bolster his standing in Rome. The construction of the new forum was a part of that propaganda campaign.

The existing Forum had indeed grown inadequate for the capital of the world. Popular assemblies and solemn religious ceremonies were crowding it beyond capacity. While Caesar was still fighting in Gaul, Cicero, whose attitude toward Caesar was complicated to say the least, wrote to his close friend Atticus that Caesar's friends were buying land plots for the future forum at his request – 'and you may explode with laughter, Atticus, but for the purposes of the deal I am one of Caesar's friends.'

Caesar was able to embark on his building programme only after defeating external and (so he thought) internal enemies. Before the Battle of Pharsalus which broke the resistance of his political opponents he made a promise in full accordance with the old Roman custom, vowing to build a temple to his protector goddess, Venus, should he emerge victorious.

The association of the man still considered one of the greatest generals of all time and the carefree goddess of love and sex might seem frivolous and bizarre. But it had an important dynastic meaning. The line of Caesar – a noble but impoverished family without any staggering achievements before Caesar – claimed descent from Iulus (also known as Ascanius), the son of the Trojan hero Aeneas who was widely considered the founder of the Roman nation and glory (even before Virgil's epic poem turned him into a mega-celebrity a generation later). Aeneas, in his turn, was a son of the goddess Venus. By referencing Venus, Julius Caesar was saying that his family line was directly descended from the Olympian gods. To press the point home, the temple goddess was called *Venus Genetrix*, the mother Venus.

The type of statue called 'Venus Genetrix' was created by the great Greek sculptor Callimachus. A statue in Caesar's temple was made after that model. This type depicts Venus when she is raising her right arm to cover her head in a gesture of devotion; her left breast is bare, she is holding an apple – the judgement of Paris prize – in her left hand. Callimachus's original statue has not survived, but Venus Genetrix was multiplied in Roman copies and on coins. One such copy was found in Fréjus, France. Now in the Louvre's Greco-Roman collection, it is considered by many to be the best Roman copy of a lost Greek original. Another, larger, variation on the theme was acquired by The Hermitage in St. Petersburg from the the famous Italian collector Giampietro Campana. The Hermitage statue is more modest, with both breasts covered.

How should we define a birthday of a temple, a street, or a square? Since Roman times until today there exists a special ceremony whose purpose is to shift an object from the state of non-existence into existence. The Romans called such a ceremony *dedicatio* (the Christian tradition replaced 'dedication' with 'consecration'). The Temple of Venus and the whole of Caesar's Forum were dedicated on the last day of Caesar's great triumph, on September 26, 46 BC. The temple standing at the back of the square overwhelmed the whole space, turning the forum into a sort of a solemn walkway leading up to the temple. This scheme had set a pattern for all the subsequent imperial fora.

THE TRIUMPH

A triumph was the most important event in any Roman statesman's life, an assurance of posthumous immortality of sorts. The Senate and the Roman people bestowed this supreme honour on victorious generals. To be deemed worthy of a triumph, a military campaign had to meet a number of the most stringent requirements: enemy losses had to be overwhelmingly larger than Rome's, the war had to be "just" (which is why victories in civil wars, with rare exceptions, were not awarded triumphs), the territory of the empire had to have increased. In expectation of the decision, the general and his army camped outside the city walls, and the decision itself was taken by senators outside the city limits. Armed soldiers could officially cross the sacred boundary of Rome – the so-called pomerium – only in a triumphal procession.

Once greenlit by the Senate, the general entered the city through the triumphal gate and proceeded along the "triumphal route" toward the Forum and the Capitol. Historians are divided about the actual route of the procession. It is possible that it varied, and whichever gate was used by a specific commander was considered "triumphal" for the occasion. The procession was followed by trumpeters, heralds, flautists, senators and other public officials. The triumphator himself rode in a special four-horse chariot, his face painted red, and the most prominent prisoners of war with their families went before him. War booty, gold and jewellery, works of art, models of conquered cities were carried on special litters. Temporary scaffolding was erected along the whole length of the procession, and people of Rome greeted the victor from it.

A triumph was accompanied by bizarre rituals whose general purpose was to avert bad luck and to prevent the triumphator from getting above himself. Soldiers sang bawdy and mocking songs about their commander. A government-appointed slave stood behind him on the chariot holding a gold wreath above his head and repeating now and then: "Remember you're mortal" (*memento mori*). A sculpted phallus dangled beneath the chariot as protection against evil eye. It should be noted, though, that most of the descriptions of these curious customs have come down to us through late and often unreliable sources.

Celebrations did not always go smoothly. Pompey decided to replace the traditional horse-drawn quadriga by four elephants, who got stuck in the triumphal gate. An axle of Julius Caesar's chariot broke, and he had to walk part of the route.

Whichever course the triumphal procession took, it ended up on the Via Sacra and from there ascended the Capitol, where the general and his entourage offered a thanksgiving sacrifice to the Capitoline Jupiter.

Triumphal procession

What became of triumphal ceremonies was one of the most telling signs of transition from the republic to the empire. Already under Augustus, a triumph became an honour awarded exclusively to the members of the emperor's household. Generals had since then to make do with the so-called 'triumphal regalia,' but even those, over time, began to reflect the emperor's good graces rather than military prowess.

Caesar did not live to see his urban planning campaign through; the task of completing the Forum Iulium fell to his successor Octavian (later known as Augustus).

Almost no traces of the Temple of Venus survived. Its foundations, together with some pieces of the columns and frieze, were discovered during 16th-century excavations. Vitruvius, the author of the only classical treatise on architecture to have come down to us, wrote that the columns of that temple were standing very close together. Such placement is known as *pycnostyle*, from the Greek word *pyknos* meaning 'dense.' The temple was made of marble, still a rarity at the time. Inside, or perhaps outside, a statue of Venus by the Greek sculptor Archesilaos stood. The temple, as often happened, served as a cabinet of curiosities and art museum with a collection of objects related to the life and legacy of Julius Caesar. Among them were a gilded statue of Cleopatra, a set of cameos, a breastplate beset with British pearls (Pliny the Elder says the pearls were small and dark). The space around the temple was adorned with statues. One of them depicted either Caesar on a horse or Caesar's horse *sans* the rider. The horse was unique: its front legs were humanlike (*humanis similes pedes priores*). Later, a statue of the emperor Tiberius was installed next to the temple, a gift from fourteen cities of Asia Minor which had received financial help from Tiberius after a devastating earthquake. Caesar had also "allowed" a statue of himself in chain mail to be set on the forum in his lifetime.

The Forum of Caesar adjoins the Altare della Patria, a monument honouring the king Victor Emmanuel II, which is also known as the "wedding cake" or the "typewriter" (the building was "dedicated" in 1911 and completed in 1935). Three columns of the Temple of Venus, restored in the 1930s, are clearly visible from the Via dei Fori Imperiali. A Fascist-era statue of Caesar stands before the forum. Every year on March 15, the anniversary of the Ides of March when the dictator was assassinated, flowers appear on its pedestal.

THE FORUM OF AUGUSTUS

Like the Forum Iulium, Augustus's forum was the fruit of a military victory. In 42 BC the future Augustus (at the time still known as Octavian – or, rather, as Gaius Julius Caesar, the name he had acquired on his posthumous adoption by the "proper" Julius Caesar) prevailed over the republican army led by the conspirators who had assassinated Caesar. The battle took place near a Macedonian town called Philippi (in northern Greece, about a hundred kilometres to the east of Thessaloniki). Before the battle, Octavian, as was the custom, vowed to build a temple to Mars, the god of war, if Mars would help him avenge the adoptive father. To build a temple, a site had to be cleared. The new forum became such a site.

The site of the forum was bought with the proceeds of another military victory (it is not known which). Historians say that there was not enough money to buy as much land as Octavian wanted, and he was reluctant to use administrative leverage to wrestle the business from local shopkeepers. (Most modern autocrats would not care to display that kind of restraint; ancient historians, though, remarked that it was unusually virtuous of Octavian.) In his brief autobiography, under the modest title "The Deeds of Divine Augustus," the emperor also pressed this point: "I built the temple of Mars Ultor on private ground."

Construction materials for the forum were subjected to careful scrutiny. Pliny the Elder says that the timber was sourced in the Rhaetian (that is, Swiss) Alps during the hottest days of the year to ensure top quality. The technology proved successful: in the 16th century, the beams were found in a condition suitable for reuse.

In antiquity, the hottest days of the year were called "dog days" because when the high season approached (by mid-July), Sirius, the brightest star of Canis Major (Great Dog), was rising above the horizon together with the sun. Today this happens about two weeks later due to a complex process called "precession of the equinoxes," a continuous re-alignment of the earth's rotational axis. The Romans called Sirius *canicula* – a little bitch. Today, in the dog days of August, the whole of Italy shuts down: shops, restaurants, even churches close, large cities empty out, leaving only the tourists and those who service them. In Rome, August is considered a minor low season, and some of the tourist-related prices go down.

When the forum was eventually built, pride of place was given to the temple of the Avenging Mars (*Mars Ultor*), with the implication that Octavian, under the auspices of the war god, had avenged the murder of Julius Caesar. The temple, in compliance with the already familiar example of Caesar's Forum, stood deep inside the forum, and the square itself was enclosed from three sides by a huge firewall. It offered protection from fire-prone slums of the adjacent bad neighbourhood of Subura. A two-storey portico went along the walls. Octavian ordered statues of all Roman triumphators to be erected on the square. Their line began with Aeneas, the legendary founder of the Roman nation (also a hint at family ties between the founder hero and the Julian clan), and continued into Augustus's own day. The base of each statue was inscribed with the respective person's service record – something that Roman tradition termed *cursus honorum*.

Augustus was one of the least belligerent Roman rulers. Wars were waged under his government, some of them successfully, but, unlike his adoptive father, he was not personally inclined or partial to military life. The event that probably provided an impetus for the construction of the forum was heralded as a great military victory, but was in fact a success of Roman diplomacy: the emissaries of Augustus managed to negotiate the return of Roman eagles (legionary standards) lost by Marcus Crassus and his army in a devastating defeat at Carrhae in 53 BC. In spite of Augustus's generally peaceful demeanour, his forum became one of the most militarised locations of the city. Young men first donned their grown-up garments (*toga virilis*) there, which traditionally meant readiness to go to war. The itinerary of Roman governors departing to their posts had its official starting point there – and the governors' service to a large degree consisted of suppressing mutinies and military control of local tribes. Victorious Roman generals brought their spoils to the Forum of Augustus; and when the censors' term of office was coming to an end, they marked it with hammering in a symbolic nail at that forum.

Forum of Augustus

Like any other public space in Rome, the Forum of Augustus served as a place of judicial and religious ceremonies. These two functions are intertwined in the curious testimony of Suetonius who relates the story about the emperor Claudius: "Once when he was holding court in the forum of Augustus and had smelled a meal which was preparing for the Salii in the temple of Mars hard by, he left the tribunal, went up where the priests were, and took his place at their table."[23] The biographer, of course, simply recounts an anecdote about the slightly autistic emperor to stress his point – that Claudius "was eager for food and drink at all times and in all places"; but the resulting picture of Roman social life is very vivid.

What remains of the forum today is not too impressive: three columns of white marble – all that is left of the Temple of Mars – and the firewall. Also visible are the foundations of stairs and lots of debris in the form of expressive pieces of columns, like elsewhere on the imperial fora. There is a relief kept at Villa Medici, the seat of the French Academy in Rome (about a mile to the north, near the Spanish Steps), which might depict the façade of the Temple of Mars. There is also a huge statue in one of the galleries of the Capitoline Museums, known as "Pyrrhus" – but it could actually be the cult statue of Mars from the temple built by Augustus.

The Forum of Augustus can be also approached from the opposite side, where the firewall is pierced by the only surviving arch, Arco dei Pantani (at the intersection of Via Bacchina that bumps into the wall at a right angle, and Via di Tor di Conti that follows the line of the wall). These streets are mediaeval; if you compare their level with the level of the imperial fora, excavated more or less to their original floor, you will see that the cultural layer (as the archaeologists say) has risen quite a few metres in the last thousand years or so. Even if the arch were not protected by a grating on Tor de Conti street, it would take an athletic (or a reckless) person to jump down to the forum.

If you stand facing the arch, the Conti Tower, which gave the street its name, will be on your left. It was commissioned by the family of Pope Innocent III (the pope's birth name was Lotario dei Conti di Segni) in the 13th century. In its day it was one of the tallest buildings in Rome. Material for the facing was pilfered, as was customary, from the nearest ruins – and the nearest ruins were those of the imperial fora. The Conti Tower, in its turn, fell prey to the plunderers of a later age: its veneer was recycled once again for the Porta Pia, a gate in the city walls.

Walking a little further, toward the small Piazza del Grillo, we find another mediaeval construction built into the wall – the Roman headquarters of the Knights Hospitaller (variously known in different times, as well as today, as the Knights of Saint John of Jerusalem, Knights of Malta, Knights of Cyprus and Rhodes and so on). The house, built in the 12th century, holds a number of works of art, including artefacts found during the excavation of the imperial fora.

TEMPLE OF PEACE

The large sector between the church of Santi Cosma e Damiano and the Forum of Nerva was only acknowledged as a "forum" in late antiquity. Before that, it had been known as the Temple of Peace, because a huge temple used to occupy the space. Unfortunately, Mussolini's Via dell'Impero cut right through it. Cars probably swoosh by directly above the crypt that once kept the treasures of Solomon's Temple.

Why Solomon's Temple? you might ask. The Temple of Peace (*Templum Pacis*) was conceived by the emperor Vespasian in 71 AD and dedicated in 75, after suppressing the revolt in the turbulent province of Judaea. Roman temples were not, as a rule, places of religious service – cult ceremonies usually took place in the open. As a result, the temples took on many other functions. The Temple of Peace was, among other things, a library, an art museum, and a bank. The museum exhibited the gold treasure removed from Jerusalem. The historian Flavius Josephus says that the most precious objects – the Torah scroll and the purple curtain that used to protect the inner sanctum of the Jerusalem temple – were kept under stricter security in the emperor's palace.

Rome's wealthiest people used to deposit their gold and silver jewellery in the Temple of Peace. As is often the case, the bank was not the perfect place for keeping one's fortune – at the end of the rule of the emperor Commodus (about 191 AD), the whole quarter around the temple burned down, leaving the richest Romans without their money.

In the times of the Severan dynasty (late 2nd – early 3rd century AD), a wall was added to the temple, and the so-called Severan Marble Plan was affixed to it. It was a huge topographic map on a scale of 1:240, drawn upside down (from today's perspective), with the north at the bottom and south at the top. Its fragments were first found and identified in mid-16th century; over a thousand have been found by today. Unfortunately, the surviving pieces of this gigantic puzzle cover no more than 10% of the map, much to the chagrin of architects and historians. Strangely, the surviving pieces indicate that the plan, surely a very prestigious commission, was a sloppy piece of work, with engineering precision and technical execution well below the best Roman examples.

The Severan Marble Plan is known in scholarly literature under a variety of names; one of the generally accepted is the Neo-Latin *Forma Urbis Romae* ('an image of the city of Rome'). It collapses into a rather unfortunate acronym, FUR, which means 'thief' in Latin. This short word was sometimes used for branding criminals.

The pieces of the Severan Marble Plan are kept at Palazzo dei Conservatori, a part of the Capitoline Museums. Placing them on the hypothetical map of Ancient Rome has been occupying historians for a few centuries. In recent years, new digital technologies have been deployed for the task, including a team working at Stanford University in California; even so, the progress is slow.

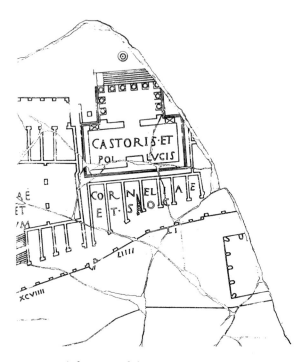

A fragment of the Severan Marble Plan

By a coincidence, the area around the Temple of Peace has been preserved remarkably well on the Severan Marble Plan, down to the letters CIS, the tail end of '*Pacis.*' There is a mystery about it, though. The map shows some interconnected rectangles around the temple. No one can explain what they are with any degree of confidence. They might be flower beds or trees (trees are very useful in protecting the people of Rome from the scorching summer sun). They might be shops – it is known that a farmers' market (*Macellum*) had occupied that space before the temple.

It is also unclear where was the main approach to the temple. Perhaps its lobby was in the place now occupied by the church of Santi Cosma e Damiano; perhaps between the Basilica Aemilia and the Temple of Antoninus and Faustina (the church of San Lorenzo in Miranda).

The Byzantine scholar Procopius of Caesarea, the last great historian of the ancient world, says that many statues stood around the Temple of Peace, including the cow by Myron and a powerful bull by some other famous Greek. That bronze bull, Procopius continues, was once mounted by a gelded steer when a herd of cattle passed through the forum. A passer-by who happened to be Etruscan ("even down to my day the Etruscans are skilled in the art of prophecy,"[24] notes Procopius) prophesied that one day a eunuch would bring down the ruler of Rome. Of course, this is what eventually happened: in 522 AD, the Ostrogothic king Totila was defeated by the eunuch Narses, an Armenian general in the service of the Byzantine emperor Justinian I.

Perhaps Procopius's story should not be taken at face value. There are many stories about birds flocking to peck at painted grapes or bulls trying to mount bronze heifers. Edward Gibbon ranted that Myron's cow alone was "celebrated by the false wit of thirty-six Greek epigrams."

> Feed, gentle swain, thy cattle far away,
> Lest they too near the cow of Myron stray.
> And thou, if chance fallacious judgment err'd,
> Drive home the breathing statue with the herd.[25]

THE FORUM OF NERVA

The Temple of Peace was ill-starred, but the Forum of Nerva got it even worse. First of all, it is also largely concealed under the asphalt of the Via dei Fori Imperiali. Second, it had not been a fully-fledged forum even in ancient times. Its construction widened the lacklustre but very old street of Argiletum, which made it a thoroughfare rather than a square. This function was reflected in its other name, also in frequent use – 'the transit forum" *(Forum Transitorium)*. Finally, it got labelled with the name of the emperor Nerva by chance – Nerva did dedicate it (in early 97 AD), but it was built under Domitian, the last emperor of the Flavian dynasty.

A section of a wall of this half-forum still stands today. The wall was intentionally made in the style of the Forum of Augustus, with somewhat larger stones. A long colonnade of about twenty columns used to follow the wall along the south-eastern edge of the forum, framing the entrance to the Temple of Peace. Two columns with a section of frieze are all that remain. They are quite conspicuous at the T-junction of Via Cavour and Via dei Fori Imperiali. The Italians had long given that chunk of antiquity an untranslatable nickname, *Le Colonnacce* ('huge ugly columns,' more or less). They do not seem all that disproportional now; however, if you imagine them not excavated to the base but jutting out from the level of Via dei Fori Imperiali – which was exactly what they did not so long ago – you will better understand the emotion hidden in the name.

A very interesting frieze runs above those columns, with women engaged in various womanly activities (spinning, knitting, giving birth). Above them, as if in a separate attic, is a relief depiction of the goddess Minerva. There are few fragments of such figurative antiquity in Rome that are still *in situ*.

The Forum of Nerva, like every other forum, had a temple on it. The Emperor Domitian was a fervent worshipper of Minerva and, of course, built a temple to honour her. Shortly before an assassination ended Domitian's rule and life, Minerva had appeared to him in a dream and told him with sadness that she would no longer be able to protect him, because Jupiter had taken away her weapons. A piece of that temple is visible on the Severan Marble Plan. It survived for a very long time, until 1606, and Renaissance artists had a chance to record it. Then Pope Paul V dismantled it for construction materials.

MINERVA MEDICA

A traveller who arrives in Rome by train is met by an unattractive neighbourhood of cheap hotels, Chinese souvenir shops and Middle Eastern eateries. It is not easy to see Classical antiquity behind this squalid façade. But it is there, in quantity – one should only pay attention. The street running right in front of the Termini station is called Via Giovanni Giolitti. If you follow its course in a south-eastern direction, in about a kilometre you will see on your left a large brick-faced concrete building. There is nothing solemn or museum-like in the area; a chance passer-by probably would not realise that the construction is 1700 years old. There is charm in such desolation; it reminds us of the time when ancient ruins were unguarded and unattended.

This shell of a building is traditionally called the temple of Minerva Medica, though the real temple was elsewhere, on the Esquiline hill. The confusion was due to the fact that these ruins were rumoured to be the finding-place of a famous statue of Minerva ("Athena Giustiniani"). The statue, first discovered in the 16th century, was probably found somewhere else. After passing through many hands, it ended up in the Vatican museums. But statues *were* found here, although much later, in the 1870s: two toga-clad officials, one young, one old (father and son?), holding a piece of cloth which they are going to drop, signalling the beginning of a horse race. They are on display at Centrale Montemartini, a branch of the Capitoline Museums.

The building had long been thought a decorative nymphaeum (fountain), but it is more likely to have been a luxurious dining pavilion with fountains and pools. Its decagonal hall was covered by a dome with light cells between brick stiffeners. "Minerva's" dome, one of the few surviving domes of antiquity, was admired, studied, and drawn by artists, including Piranesi. Unfortunately, it suddenly collapsed in 1828.

The original pavilion was so unusual architecturally that a few decades after its construction it was given a few buttresses, a semicircular niche and a portico; in this guise, which was more traditional, it has continued to crumble amid the growing urban sprawl.

The Minerva Medica used to stand in more picturesque surroundings, in the so-called Licinii gardens. The emperor Gallienus, himself a member of the Licinii family, loved to entertain his courtiers there, in the last third of the 3rd century AD, approximately when the pavilion was built. Perhaps a historian's moralistic reproaches refer to the orgies that unfolded in it. "Whenever he went to the gardens named after him, all the staff of the Palace followed him. And there went with him, too, the prefects and the chiefs of all the staffs, and they were invited to his banquets and bathed in the pools along with the prince. Women, too, were often sent in, beautiful girls with the emperor, but with the others ugly old hags. And he used to say that he was making merry, whereas he had brought the world on all sides to ruin."[26]

Stones and columns from the Forum of Nerva were used for a monumental fountain whose inauguration marked the relaunching of an aqueduct dating back to the emperor Trajan. The aqueduct partially solved the problem of water supply on the right bank of the Tiber (including the Vatican), which had been quite inadequate. The fountain is sometimes called *Acqua Traiana* after the emperor, but more often *Acqua Paola* after Pope Paul V. Its impressive façade was finalised by the aptly named architect Carlo Fontana, and the locals dubbed the whole construction *Il Fontanone*, 'the huge fountain.' For some reason there is an aura of gigantism attached to everything related to Nerva's forum.

A four-faced statue of Janus stood on the Forum of Nerva (the traditional two faces were apparently not enough, in keeping with the mentioned gigantomania). Alexander Severus used the place to erect the statues of posthumously deified emperors. They were either in heroic style (meaning that the rulers were depicted idealised and naked) or equestrian (those were tastefully clothed). A significant part of the forum has not been excavated, and new surprising discoveries are a real possibility.

THE FORUM OF TRAJAN

In 357 AD, Constantius II, by that time the sole ruler of the Western and Eastern Roman Empire, set foot in Rome. For the 40-year-old native of Sirmium (now Sremska Mitrovica in Serbia), it was the first visit to the Eternal City. Rome no longer was central to the politics of the Mediterranean area: the centre of gravity was increasingly moving east, toward Constantinople, and in the west such cities as Mediolanum (Milan) and Augusta Treverorum (Trier) were rising in prominence, often due to the presence of the imperial court. However, for a passing tourist, even if of the highest imaginable rank, the city was still a powerful source of awe. Constantius gave a speech at the Senate, chatted to the people on the (old) Forum, marvelled at public baths, the huge bulk of the amphitheatre (later known as the Colosseum), the Pantheon and other temples. "But when he came to the Forum of Trajan," writes the historian Ammianus Marcellinus, "a creation which in my view has no like under the cope of heaven and which even the gods themselves must agree to admire, he stood transfixed with astonishment, surveying the gigantic fabric around him; its grandeur defies description and can never again be approached by mortal men."[27]

Trajan's buildings have survived somewhat better than the other imperial fora. Mustering all our creative resources, let us try to follow Constantius II and be enthralled together with him. After all, "historical reenactment" of such kind is the purpose of our book.

Approximately halfway between the Colosseum and Piazza Venezia, the Via dei Fori Imperiali splits in two. Its left fork continues in a straight line under the same name; the right branches off at a sharp angle as Via Alessandrina (in memory of a demolished quarter) and later simply Foro Traiano. These both streets dissect the original living tissue of the imperial fora. If the triangle formed by them was walkable, then reaching the 20th-century statue of August we would have found ourselves by a triumphal arch. It was through that arch that Constantius II emerged onto the square. A narrow passage leading to a huge open space is a very showy architectural device; anyone who has first navigated the maze of Venetian streets to come out onto San Marco or walked under the General Staff arch into the Palace Square in St. Petersburg will remember the impression forever. Certainly Constantius experienced it, too. On the arch, which only survives as an image on coins, the emperor Trajan was controlling a chariot drawn by six gold-plated horses.

No one expected that the ailing emperor Nerva would name Marcus Ulpius Trajanus as his successor. A provincial from Spain, a career military man without any serious connections in political circles, he seemed an unlikely choice for the supreme ruler. And yet, he was popular with the army, his reputation was spotless, and low birth in Rome had never been an obstacle to upward social mobility. After Nerva's death, Trajan ruled the empire for almost twenty years – firmly, but sensibly.

The Christian tradition has created an aura of a "virtuous pagan" around Trajan. Some authors even tried to dress him up as a Christian, or at least a crypto-Christian. But the only reliable source indicates that Trajan's attitude toward Christians was neutral at best. When the lawyer and literary man Pliny the Younger was the propraetor of Bithynia, a province on the southern shore of the Black Sea, he used to ask the emperor for advice in all matters large and small, thus providing us with a unique window onto the workings of Roman provincial administration. One of his letters concerned the fate of a group of people denounced to him as Christians. Religious observances of the subjects were of no interest to

Roman officials. However, tightly knit religious communities were suspect as potential hotbeds of criminal activity (Christians were rumoured to practice cannibalism and torturing babies – allegations almost invariably thrown at "the others"). Another grave offence was their avoidance of civic duties: Christians refused to perform sacrifices to the emperor and state deities. Trajan's response to Pliny was brief and dry: Christians are not to be sought out, those who recant should be pardoned, those who persist should be punished; anonymous accusations must be disregarded in all cases ("this is both a dangerous kind of precedent and out of keeping with the spirit of our age"[28]).

The square that opened up before Constantius was different from the other imperial fora. Most importantly, it did not contain a temple – on the contrary, the space was huge and empty. It was flanked by colonnades, one of them called "a purple portico" (*porticus purpuretica*), probably because the columns were made of red Egyptian porphyry. In the centre was Trajan's equestrian statue; its pedestal was recently discovered, and it seems to indicate that the statue, too, was huge, three times as big as Marcus Aurelius's on the Capitol. The sculpture so impressed Constantius that he decided to make a replica of it somewhere in his domain. A member of the emperor's retinue, the Persian defector Hormisdas, remarked ("with Oriental subtlety," says Ammianus Marcellinus) that a horse like that should need a similar stable.

What Constantius and us would see after surveying the square was a basilica of many columns. It was called Basilica Ulpia, after Trajan's family name. We remember that an ancient Roman basilica is a completely secular affair, meant for judiciary hearing and other bureaucratic pastimes. The floor of this basilica was raised about one metre above the pavement, yellowish stairs led inside, columns were gaudily multicoloured. The upper level was adorned with quadrigas and statues of emperors, 96 columns of white and yellow marble bedecked the grand hall. Some of the columns from the Ulpian basilica still stand, and they seem like quite a few, but it is of course but a tiny speck of past grandeur. The roof of the building was laid with tiles of gold-plated bronze.

Constantius certainly walked all the way through the basilica, admiring the translucent marble, listening to the murmur of business negotiations and forensic speeches. In a corner, a slave manumission ceremony was unfolding: when the basilica was built, the "courtyard of freedom" (*atrium libertatis*), a place for this specific purpose, was transferred to the new premises. Where the old premises were is unknown.

Upon exiting the basilica on the other side, he would have found himself in a more restricted space. Immediately in front of us loomed a huge column, 100 Roman feet (30 metres) high with a gold-plated statue on the top. On either side of it, two small library buildings stood. Libraries in Rome were usually designed as twin premises, one for Latin books, the other for Greek ones. The author of the biography of Tacitus, a briefly reigning emperor (not to be confused with the great historian), writes with a touch of hurt feelings: "And now, lest anyone consider that I have rashly put faith in some Greek or Latin writer, there is in the Ulpian Library, in the sixth case, an ivory book, in which is written out this decree of the senate, signed by Tacitus himself with his own hand."[29]

What was beyond the column is an unresolved issue. Recently, traces of a luxurious building were found there while laying underground tracks. Some archaeologists think that it is the Atheneum, an academy founded by the emperor Hadrian.

Opposite the column is the church Santissimo Nome di Maria al Foro Traiano (of the Most Sacred Name of Maria). It was perhaps in this part of the forum that Hadrian built a temple commemorating his deified predecessor. It has long been believed that the foundations of the temple lie beyond Palazzo Valentini, a small elegant palace of the late 16th century, but so far excavations have revealed nothing except the remains of some villas and a small cluster of baths.

TRAJAN'S COLUMN

Trajan's column, on the contrary, has come down to us in excellent condition and became one of Rome's principal sights. It's the bearer of a huge two-part comic strip about the conquest of Dacia – a Black Sea region in the lower course of the Danube, roughly equivalent to present-day Romania. It is in two parts because the fight against the Dacians took two separate campaigns. The sculptors placed an image of the goddess of Victory between the two halves of this marble narrative. Both campaigns are described in painstaking detail, from the first skirmishes, logistic support, loading provisions to building bridges across the Danube, hand-to-hand combat and the triumphal return. The emperor Trajan is depicted as a man (not as a superman, which was perfectly acceptable in Roman visual arts) and on the column he can be found among his troops 59 times. The overall number of figures on the column totals about 2,500 humans – and that tally does not include horses, mules, sheep, ships, buildings, trees, siege towers… The narrative winds up in a continuous spiral, wrapping the column 23 times. Spread out in a line, the frieze would be almost 200 metres long.

Trajan's column is a bizarre object. What is so bizarre about it is that its monumental tale cannot be read quite to the end. This is obvious today: if you go round the column, you will be able to make out the lower parts in detail (unless they are obscured by scaffolding), but the closer to the top, the less you see of the reliefs. Perhaps the emperor Constantius II on his walk had an opportunity to go up to the roof of the basilica or either of the neighbouring libraries, but all of those buildings were much lower than the column, and its uppermost fragments remained virtually invisible even in antiquity.

The architectural compound of Trajan's Forum was dedicated to the Dacian victories and paid for from the war booty. All that splendour (possibly including the monumental sculptural ribbon of the column) was designed by Apollodorus of Damascus, one of the few ancient architects known to us by name. Appolodorus was not only an inspired urban planner, but also a military engineer. It was he who spanned the Danube with a huge bridge for Trajan's troops near the Iron Gates gorge, where the river marks today's boundary between Romania and Serbia. For a thousand years, it remained unequalled among arch bridges in total length. The emperor Aurelian ordered the destruction of the bridge when he withdrew the legions from Dacia, but its end pillars on both sides are still visible, and twelve more lie beneath the waves of the Danube.

It could be argued that the unorthodox application of sculptural and architectural features was a manifestation of that untranslatable Roman virtue, *pietas*. *Pietas* was not simply piety – it also included veneration of older relatives and the state, and was closely connected with a sense of duty. Erecting a column was an act of *pietas*, not of improving tourist attractiveness. In more recent times, a similar emotion was allegedly expressed by the great Catalan architect Antoni Gaudí. When criticized for spending a lot of time and effort on the details of Sagrada Familia spires, invisible from the ground, he answered: "The angels will see them."

Impracticality aside, Trajan's Column is a unique monument. It is made of twenty huge cylindrical blocks of Carrara marble stacked upon one another, each weighing about forty tons. It looks as if the column had been first carved into blocks and only then adorned with the sculptural frieze, with a substantial degree of improvisation. The sculptors did not know for sure how much space they had, and their work was not marked by clockwork precision. The edges of the ribbon feature a few sharp bends, its width changes arbitrarily – at first it becomes narrower as it climbs from the lower curls of the spiral to the upper, which is not very logical from the viewer's perspective on the ground; then, in the last two revolutions, it widens again, as if it suddenly became obvious that there would be enough space after all. The combination of the blocks with the narrative spiral also posed problems here and there. The blocks were fastened with heavy metal clamps which were removed in the Middle Ages.

Trajan's Column is not only a monument of the visual arts; in a sense, it is also a literary work (in our days, "graphic novel" has long become a literary genre in its own right). It serves as an irreplaceable and unique source of information on everyday life, composition and modus operandi of the Roman army in the 2nd century AD. Of course, treating solemn propaganda as a historical source is not without its problems; "Gone with the Wind" is not the most reliable source on the American Civil War. On the other hand, a picture is worth a thousand words – and when no words have come down to us, the pictures assume even greater importance.

By conquering Dacia, the Roman Empire gained access to the country's gold mines, so the financial outcome of the campaign was solid. As for geopolitical consequences, they were less auspicious: after a mere hundred years, the Romans were forced to withdraw from the province. The most durable result of the Dacian wars lies in the domain of language: thanks to Trajan's conquest, the inhabitants of today's Romania and Moldova speak a Romance language (from *romanus*, Roman). Trajan is a popular name in Romania.

> After the collapse of the Roman Empire, its principal language, Latin, continued to exist. In its written form it remained a live medium of science and religion until the 18th and 19th centuries. The oral expression started to change, adjusting to variations in pronunciation and influences of other languages. A few hundred years later, an Italian and a Portuguese, each speaking a Latin-derived language, could no longer understand each other. Today there are about twenty-five Romance languages in the world, including Italian, French, Spanish, Portuguese, Catalan, and Romanian.

Inside Trajan's column is another engineering wonder, a marble spiral staircase going all the way to the top. The few small windows are designed to open on nothing but the sky. We live in a world of skyscrapers, glass-walled lifts and Eiffel towers, but imagine the vertigo experienced by Constantius II when he had climbed 185 stairs, went out on the observation platform and saw the city of Rome from a vantage point like no other. In those days the column was, of course, topped by a gold-plated statue of Trajan. It disappeared in the Middle Ages together with its iron clamps. In the late 16th century, Pope Sixtus V installed a bronze statue of Saint Peter on top of Trajan's Column, and it stands there to this day. It is a pity that unless we are accompanied by the emperor the archaeological authorities are unlikely to let us climb to the top.

If you want to have a closer look at the reliefs on Trajan's Column – and they are worth it – it can be done. Full plaster casts are kept in at least three museums of the world – the Museum of Roman Civilization in EUR, a suburb of Rome (currently closed for renovation), London's

Victoria and Albert Museum, and the National Museum of Romanian History in Bucharest. There are also a number of web sites with detailed drawings and explanations of the images on the column.

Having climbed down, let us have a look at the base of the column. Gold urns with the ashes of Trajan and his wife Plotina were encased in it once; needless to say, they are long gone. A Latin inscription reminds of the scope and complexity of work that was needed to construct the column and the forum: "as an illustration of the height which this hill and place attained, now removed for such great works as these." It was long assumed that Trajan had completely removed the "saddle" between the Capitol and Quirinal hills which was just about the column's height, 30 metres or so. But under the base, remains of older houses and streets were found, which means that there was no hill. Scholars surmise that the inscription (especially the word *mons*, 'hill' or 'mountain') refers to some other location. Perhaps Trajan had razed the eastern slope of the Quirinal (if you stand between the basilica and the column, it is behind you on the right).

In 1989 the American typeface designer Carol Twombly used the letterforms of this inscription for a typeface called Trajan which she designed for Adobe. If you google American movie posters of the last twenty years, you will find that many of them use this font for movie titles. The mysterious dominance of the Ancient Roman typeface in film industry has produced a few jokes and parodies.

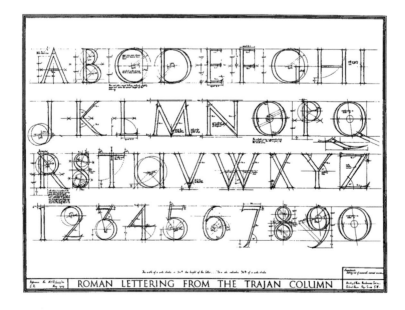

ROMAN LETTERING FROM THE TRAJAN COLUMN

A tourist experience would be incomplete without shopping, especially in Rome. Having climbed down from the column and caught his breath, Constantius could have directed his steps toward the so-called Trajan's Market (*Mercatus Traiani*). Shopping stalls were a fixture of Roman forums from time immemorial, but Appolodorus was the first to have built a real multilevel shopping mall. It was made of decorative brick and faced with travertine. In the Middle Ages parts of the compound were built over – the high square tower, Torre dei Milizie, is mediaeval. If you pass between Trajan's Column and the church of Santissimo Nome di Maria, you will see stairs going up the slope of the Quirinal hill. It is Magnanapoli street, and as you go up, you will cross an ancient street called Via Biberatica. This is one of the few places in the world with multi-storeyed houses surviving from classical antiquity.

Saying his goodbyes to Rome, Constantius II probably thought how fleeting the glory of the world was. Two hundred years before his time, in the age of Trajan, the might of the Eternal City had seemed, indeed, eternal. Under Trajan, the Roman Empire reached its greatest extent. This state of things was not to last: very soon, Armenia and Mesopotamia had to be given up; a hundred years after the Dacian wars, the emperor Aurelian recalled Roman troops from there as well. The memory of Trajan's blessed rule proved to be a long one. According to Edward Gibbon, it was under him (and other "good emperors" of the 2nd century AD) that "the condition of the human race was most happy and prosperous." A series of fascist era maps depicting the territorial expansion of the Roman Empire (they still hang on the wall of the Basilica of Maxentius facing the Via dei Fori Imperiali) ends with Trajan's reign. Mussolini's own "Italian Empire" used to complete the sequence, but after World War II it was removed.

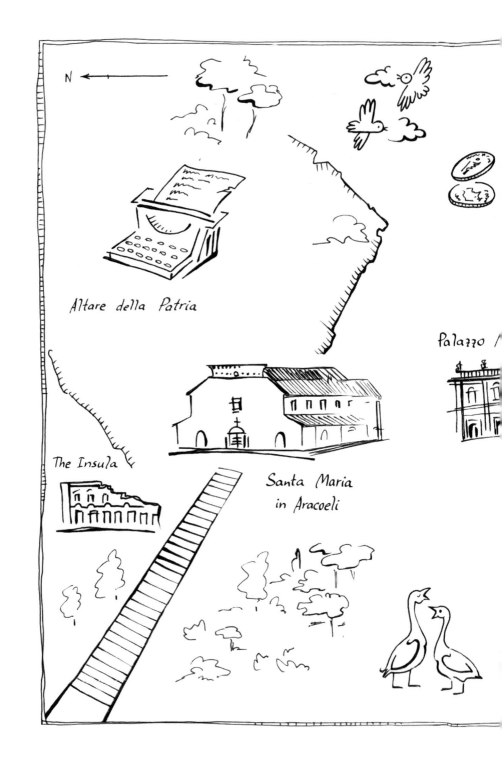

N

Altare della Patria

The Insula

Santa Maria
in Aracoeli

Palazzo /

San Pietro
in Carcere

THE CAPITOL

Palazzo   Senatorio

Palazzo   dei Conservatori

Cordonata

CHAPTER V

THE CAPITOL
(TEMPLES AND STAIRS)

The Capitoline Hill today is as close to being the city's secular centre as it gets. Its beautiful Renaissance square is flanked by three elegant palaces. The one in the centre, Palazzo Senatorio, houses Rome's city council (they say the best view on the Forum is from the mayor's window); the other two, Palazzo dei Conservatori and Palazzo Nuovo (not that new, really, at 400+ years) contain the collections of the Capitoline Museums, a must-see for any lover of antiquity. What's more secular than museums and red tape? And that's where the typically Roman irony kicks in. In ancient times the Capitol was the symbolic heart of the city, its sacred core, and, first and foremost, the abode of the gods.

TEMPLE OF TEMPLES

Do you remember how the poet Horace expressed his notion of eternity? "While pontiff and the vestal shall / the Capitol ascend" (this translation was written by the British prime minister William Gladstone, and its accuracy, at least in these lines, is commendable). So where did they go? They were ascending the hill to offer prayers for the well-being of the Roman people, and their destination was the Temple of Jupiter Optimus Maximus (Jove the Best and Greatest). There was no such thing as 'Cathedral' in an ancient city, but that temple came pretty close.

The temple was very old. It was vowed by the half-legendary Roman king Tarquin the Elder during the war with the Sabines, whose tribe had been merging with the Romans, on and off, since the times of Romulus. Tarquin promised to build a temple to three gods – Jupiter, Juno and Minerva. The legend fits nicely with the king's alleged Etruscan roots, because the trinity of Roman supreme gods was indeed an Etruscan import (only the Etruscans called them Tinia, Uni and Menrva, respectively). Every Etruscan town had its own capitol – a centre of statehood located on a high point.

Before the construction started, it was decided to clear the site of all other shrines and to devote the hill exclusively to Jupiter. The augurs observed the birds' flight and consented to the demolition of all temples except the temple of Terminus, the god of borders and thresholds. Thus the temple of Terminus was simply incorporated into the new building as a symbol of the longevity and strength of the young Roman state. Laying the foundations, the diggers found a human head with its face untouched by decay, which was also interpreted as a prophecy: one day, Rome will be the head of the whole world.

The Roman legend about the temple's construction and dedication conveniently places the work in the regal era, but pushes the solemn dedication a couple of years forward, in the early days of the Republic. Tarquin the Proud, the last king of Rome, even ordered a four-horse terracotta chariot for the temple's roof in the town of Veii in his native Etruria, but the Romans had ousted him before he could pick up his order. While the sculpture was baking it grew in size so much that the workers had to dismantle both the furnace and the workshop. With the new appreciation of this sacred object, the Etruscans resorted to a legal technicality to keep the sculpture in their possession: our contract was with Tarquin, they said, not with the city that sent him into exile. The temple would have been left quadriga-less, but during a horse race in Veii, the victorious chariot rushed away from the hippodrome, and the driver could not rein it in before it stopped at the foot of the Capitoline hill in Rome. Etruscans never questioned divine intervention, and the terracotta chariot was handed over to the Romans.

Veii is an Etruscan town 15 kilometres north-west of Rome, near today's village of Isola Farnese. During the early era of Roman history, Veii was Rome's archrival, and it took a long string of wars to finally subdue it. In the 19C the most ancient known Etruscan frescoes were found in the Veian necropolis.

On the Western side of Piazza Colonna (opposite the Corso) stands Palazzo Wedekind. Its columns are spoils taken from Veii.

The temple was dedicated in the first year of the Republic (509 BC). Both consuls – Poplicola and Horatius – vied for the honour, but Poplicola had to leave the city for a military campaign. As Horatius was leading the dedication rites, Poplicola's brother whispered to him: "Consul, your son became sick and died in the camp." It wasn't true; it was a ruse meant to throw the official off the track, but Horatius just said: "I don't care, just get rid of his body – grief cannot touch me now," and the ceremony was successfully completed.

This temple stood for about four hundred years and burned down during the civil wars of the first century BC, together with the prophetic Sibylline books, which the Romans consulted in times of national crises (they were later restored from scraps and quotes and transferred to the Temple of Apollo on the Palatine hill). Consul Lutatius Catulus rebuilt the temple in a richer and more up-to-date manner; bronze roof tiles were now covered with gold. Old-timers did not approve. Seneca Major, the philosopher who never missed a chance to be grumpy, wrote: "We did not descend into civil wars before the Temple of Jupiter was gold-plated" (not true, but who cares when you have a moral point to make). The second temple had a short life, and burned down in the ominous 'year of the four emperors,' 69 AD, when several factions fought for the control of the city. The third version, restored even more lavishly on the same footprint (as was the Roman custom), was built by the Flavian dynasty – Vespasian and his sons.

The third temple fared much better than the second. In early Middle Ages it was enthusiastically despoiled (first of all gold, then of gold-plated tiles, then of all statues), but as late as 13C a papal document mentions it as still standing ('a big temple facing the Elephas').

> Elephas Herbarium — the herbal Elephant — was the cryptic name of an object, possibly a statue, standing near the vegetable market, by the church of San Nicola in Carcere.

For many centuries, the Temple of Jupiter remained one of the main centres of Roman ceremonial life. There, consuls made sacrifices to gods when they assumed office; important international treaties were kept in the temple's vaults; the Senate convened there for its most solemn sessions. The Temple was the final point of triumphal processions when successful generals celebrated military victories.

Today, only pieces of foundation remain. One of them, a massive tufa podium inside Palazzo dei Conservatori, gives an idea of the building's size and alignment. Another piece can be seen in a ditch running along the Via del Tempio di Giove ('the street of Jupiter's temple'). And, of course, in strict accordance with Roman custom, bits and pieces of former grandeur are scattered around the Eternal City. For instance, there is a lovely Baroque church not far from Piazza Navona called Santa Maria della Pace, with a cloister by Bramante. It is rumoured that the statues inside were chiseled out of Pentelic marble that had been used for the facing of the Temple of Jupiter.

> Pentelic marble is white with a tinge of yellow. It was quarried on Mount Pentelikon (now Penteli) near Athens. It is the same stone that was used for the Parthenon.

…AND MORE TEMPLES

The Temple of Jupiter the Best and Greatest was not the only temple on the Capitol – moreover, it was not even the only temple of Jupiter. As many as three shrines to the Roman supreme deity stood on the hill. The oldest among them was the temple of Jupiter Feretrius (legend had it that it was the oldest temple in the whole of Rome). It was founded by Romulus himself. In the battle with the tribe of Caeninenses, he killed their leader Acron and took off his armour. From that moment on, the main function of this small temple was to store the so-called 'rich spoils' (*spolia opima*). The spoils were considered 'rich' only if stripped off the enemy commander by the Roman commander's own hand. In all of post-Romulan history, this only occurred twice: in 437 BC Cornelius Cossus got the armour of the Etruscan general Tolumnius (who hailed from the now familiar town of Veii), and in 222 BC Marcus Claudius Marcellus defeated the Belgian

chieftain Britomartus in single combat. Apparently, the temple did not
have as much as a statue of Jupiter – only the spoils, a sceptre and a sacred
flint. A coin from the times of Julius Caesar shows Marcellus with the spoils
in front of a temple – probably that one. But it is impossible to say where
exactly on the Capitoline hill it stood.

At the dawn of the imperial era, if we are to believe a cursory remark
of the Greek historian Cassius Dio, Augustus was granted the right to
pronounce the spoils of his choice 'rich' and to introduce them into the
temple of Jupiter Feretrius. However, Augustus must have been especially
partial to yet another Jupiter's temple on the hill – that of Jupiter Tonans
('the Thunderer'). The thing is, Rome's first emperor had a morbid fear of
thunderstorms, and with good reason: during the Spanish campaign a bolt of
lightning narrowly missed him, killing one of the slaves who was carrying
his litter. To commemorate his miraculous escape, Augustus dedicated a
lavish temple to Jove the Thunderer with walls made of solid marble and

lots of statuary inside and outside. His brontophobic panic attacks did not subside, though, and whenever the sky turned a darker shade, he hastened to don a seal's skin, supposed to protect from lightning strikes.

Suetonius says that one night Jupiter appeared to Augustus in a dream and complained that the new luxurious temple was stealing the thunder (rather literally) of the Capitol's main sanctuary. Augustus (still in his sleep) hastily explained that the Thunderer was but a doorman to Jupiter the Best and Greatest. On waking up, he gave orders for the roof of the new temple to be adorned with doorbells. The concrete core, possibly related to that building, was found near Via di Monte Tarpeo.

When a new gallery was being constructed between the wings of the Capitoline museums in 1939, another fascinating temple was found, partly preserved under the layers of later buildings. Even its cult statue was found. The god turned out to be young, beardless, with a she-goat and some arrows by his side. From these details, the scholars deduced that it was the temple of Veiovis. Veiovis was a god of unclear origin, function or etymology; two thousand years ago, Roman antiquarians had little to say about him. He might have been a version of Apollo, or a younger Jupiter, or an anti-Jupiter. One thing the sources were sure about was his dark nature: sacrifices made in his honour were meant to ward off evil, not to court anything propitious. An unclear but sinister fact is mentioned by the antiquarian Aulus Gellius: a she-goat was sacrificed to Veiovis according to a human rite (*ritu humano*).

Ancient authors wrote that the temple of Veiovis stood 'between two groves,' *inter duos lucos*. There was, indeed, a grove on each of the summits of the Capitoline hill. The southern summit was Capitol proper; the northern was Arx – the Citadel.

THE CITADEL

Nothing remains of the buildings that once covered the Capitoline citadel. At least, nothing substantial was found during the construction of Vittoriano, the monument dedicated to King Victor Emmanuel II, Italy's unifier. It is possible that something is hiding beneath the church of Santa Maria in Aracoeli. These two buildings – the church and the Vittoriano – cover the entire area of the Capitoline arx.

A citadel's primary function is defence. The Arx remained in military use until at least the first century BC, but the most famous skirmish happened in 387 BC. In that year (or so the legend says), the Cisalpine Gauls ('Cisalpine' means 'living on our side of the Alps') from what is today Northern Italy ran into a conflict with Roman emissaries. Not willing (or unable) to resolve the matter diplomatically, the Gauls launched an offensive on Rome. It was completely unexpected, and the Romans panicked. Leaving behind their houses, slaves, jewellery and elderly relatives, they poured out of the City into the surrounding countryside and neighbouring Etruscan towns. So few able-bodied men remained within the walls that a decision was made to relinquish the city and entrench on the Capitol. The oldest patricians volunteered to stay in the unprotected city and accept martyrdom so as not to dilute the defenders' fighting force. The Gauls entered the City. They were wary, fearful of traps and provocations. They did not dare storm the citadel, but one night some Gallic scouts managed to creep up the Arx so quietly that neither the sentries nor the dogs heard them. Luckily for the Romans, the geese heard something and woke up the defenders with their cackling. (The geese were kept in the Temple of Juno as the goddess's sacred birds, the only reason why they hadn't been eaten by the starving troops.) Roused by the geese, the Romans counter-attacked and quickly threw the Gallic vanguard off the hill.

"Woe to the vanquished!" An etching by Paul Lehugeur (1886)

The Gauls were led by a chieftain called Brennus. He carved himself a niche in every compendium of famous quotes thanks to his famous remark 'Woe to the vanquished' (*Vae victis*). He allegedly said it when the Romans were measuring their war indemnity in gold into one pan of the scales, and Brennus placed his heavy sword in the other pan, thus increasing the ransom. The Celtic *bren* or *bran* means 'raven,' and the common Irish surname 'Brennan' is cognate.

During that skirmish, the Romans were led by an ex-consul called Marcus Manlius Capitolinus. He was called 'Capitolinus' because his family had for a long time been in possession of a house on the Capitol. A few years passed, and his birth-place, the place of his glory, became the spot of his execution. Here's how it happened.

After driving back the Gauls, Manlius began to suspect that something was rotten in the state of Rome. The external enemy was gone, at least for the time being; war booty was filling the treasury, but the common folk (or the plebeians; in those archaic times – but not later – it was almost one and the same) still lived from hand to mouth. Some were so heavily in debt that the only solution was to sell themselves into slavery. Manlius capitalised on his reputation as the saviour of the nation, and styled himself the defender of plebeian rights. He hinted that the top bureaucracy, the senators, had quietly divided the war trophies between themselves. The patricians did not like it a bit. Quite soon, Manlius was confronted with the commonest accusation used against subversive activists: high treason (and, of course, corruption). The trial was conducted on the Field of Mars. The Capitol was in full view of the crowd, and Manlius responded to the prosecution's every move with a silent but meaningful gesture: he was pointing at the Arx, as if saying: look, citizens, what I have saved for you with my blood. The trial had to be rescheduled and removed outside city limits, where the public could not see the Capitol. There, the prosecution finally had its way, and Manlius was condemned to death. To avoid outbursts of plebeian revenge, the Senate passed a special edict prohibiting patricians from living on the Capitoline hill. Manlius's house was demolished. Later a new temple of Juno – the so-called Juno Moneta – was built on that spot.

As was the custom, enemies of the state (including the ill-fated Manlius) were thrown off the Tarpeian Rock. That place-name had a legend of its own attached to it. When the Romans kidnapped ('raped' was the old term) the Sabine women, Sabine men marched on Rome. The Vestal virgin Tarpeia treacherously opened the city gate to them. Sabine warriors had gold bracelets on their left wrists; Tarpeia rashly asked them, in return for the services rendered, 'what you carry on your left arm.' She forgot that every Sabine warrior had a heavy-duty shield. Nobody loves a traitor (and the Sabines must have been somewhat humiliated by the method they used to enter the city); the warriors buried Tarpeia under an avalanche of their shields. The traitor was buried on the rock which then acquired her name, and since then the Romans used the place for punishing traitors and other dangerous offenders. The Tarpeian-style execution was worse than death, because it entailed eternal disgrace. That's what the patrician enemies of Manlius hastened to do to him.

> The Capitoline temple of Juno for a while doubled as state mint, and the word *moneta* came to mean 'coinage' or 'means of payment' in many languages; that's where the English word 'money' comes from. The etymology of *moneta*, though, is far from certain. The Romans believed it was derived from the verb *moneo*, 'to warn': apparently, after an earthquake, a voice was heard on the Arx; it demanded an expiatory sacrifice, specifically a pig. The sacrifice was made, and a temple to The Warning Juno erected. During the construction of 'the Typewriter,' no traces of any such building were found.

The rock did not survive into our days, but we can make a guess about its location. All sources agree that the whole city gathered to watch the execution of traitors. Where? On the Forum, of course. Which means that the Tarpeian rock was somewhere in the south-eastern sector of the Capitoline hill. Today, a short street called Via di Monte Tarpeo meanders its way down the slope in that place. Had the executions continued until this day, the nearby Piazza della Consolazione might have provided a better vantage point than the Forum.

The Capitoline Arx was the scene for yet another important state affair: the auspices, or bird-watching. In later enlightened times, the sceptical Cicero (who'd served a stint as a bird-watcher himself) wrote: fancy how two augurs can meet and refrain from laughing. However, divination in Rome was always a matter of state importance, and a special site – the Auguraculum – was reserved for it on the Capitol. Most likely, the Auguraculum was a small open space; in Roman terms, a consecrated area was a temple (*templum*) even if no building stood there.

The augurs' spot was most likely in the north-eastern sector of the citadel, overlooking the Forum – not far from today's apse of Santa Maria in Aracoeli.

> Actually, Cicero did not mention the augurs, who read omens in the flight of birds; he referred to an even more esoteric sect of haruspices, who read the entrails of sacrificial animals, especially the liver. But for some reason posterity chose to remember 'the laughing augurs.' As for liver-based divination, this method was Etruscan in origin. One of the lengthiest surviving texts of the half-deciphered Etruscan language is the so-called Piacenza liver, a bronze model of a sheep liver with names of gods written upon it.

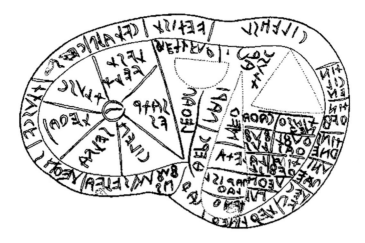

The Piacenza liver

THE CHURCH, THE APARTMENT BLOCK AND THE ARCHIVE

Today, the easiest access to the Capitoline hill is from the west. Two sets of stairs lead there from Via del Teatro Marcello: Michelangelo's Cordonata (on which more later) and the steep, 122-step flight of stairs to Santa Maria in Aracoeli. If the church is open, you can walk through it and emerge on the central Capitoline square.

Twenty-two ancient columns stand in the church on both sides of the central nave. The third from the left bears a curious inscription – *a cubiculo Augustorum*, 'from the Emperor's bedroom.' It refers to a mediaeval legend. On the day of Christ's birth, the Virgin Mary with baby Jesus appeared to the Emperor Augustus. The impressed emperor dedicated to them an altar right inside his bedroom. It was 'found' that his bedroom had stood on the spot of the Chapel of Saint Helen in the Aracoeli church (the real Augustus had his house on the Palatine, but that's nitpicking). Thus, according to this legend, Santa Maria in Aracoeli is the oldest Christian church in existence, and the Latin inscription above the chapel's altar drives this point home:

> You who climb to this kindly church of the Mother of Light,
> which was founded first of all in the world,
> know that at that time Caesar Octavian built this altar
> when the holy progeny of heaven appeared to him.[30]

Before making your way up to the church, look left. Behind the tree a unique monument is hiding; there is nothing like it in the whole of Rome. It is a multi-storey and multi-flat house which is approximately 1900 years old. The Romans called such houses *insula* ('island'), because they were isolated from the surrounding urban environment (the word 'isolated' is related to 'insula,' but the word 'island,' contrary to popular belief, is not). There are many examples of such real estate development in Ostia and Pompeii, but the Capitoline insula in the only well-preserved specimen in Rome.

The design of the insula is typical for Roman houses, and it's popular to this day: ground floor is taken up by shops and storage, while the upper floors are for tenants. Unlike today, the further up you go, the worse your housing conditions would be, with more and more people per square foot. Lower floors could have some sanitation facilities, like running water or sewer drains (but probably not in this specific insula). Food was prepared right there in the rooms, on portable stoves. Small wonder that insula-filled city blocks presented a major fire hazard. Epidemics spread through them with the speed of wind, too. Landlords collected the tenants' measly payments, which often totalled enough for a comfortable life somewhere on the Bay of Naples.

Santa Maria in Aracoeli

Insulas (or *insulae*, if you want to be a stickler for the original Latin) were often built around a courtyard, like an American motel. The ground floor of the Capitoline insula is nine metres below today's pavement. As is often the case, the building survived by accident: it was buried under several layers of successive churches. The oldest one, dating back to the 11C, was built right into the ancient structure. The small bell-tower and the Deposition fresco are still *in situ*. The latest, 17C, church was dedicated to Saint Rita of Cascia (a small town in Umbria), but during the mass-scale reconstructions under Mussolini it was dismantled, piece by piece, and moved to another nearby location, in Via Montanara. That's when the ancient apartment block was found beneath it.

That is the western slope of the hill. The eastern slope breaks off towards the Forum, and the stone wall that covers it used to be the Tabularium, the storing place for tables (*tabula*) – a state archive of sorts. There's not a single mention of such a building in ancient literary sources, and the only information available to historians and archaeologists are two inscriptions chiselled in stone. They indicate that in 78 BC the consul Quintus Lutatius Catulus 'built the underground structure and the Tabularium as decreed by the Senate.' One of these two inscriptions is only known from a mediaeval copy, while the other may still be viewed on the northern wall of Palazzo Senatorio, near the street of Via di San Pietro in Carcere.

The only possible reference to the Tabularium in Roman literature is two lines from *Georgics*, Virgil's agricultural poem. In one passage, the author sings praise to the bliss of country life, far away from strife and rhythm of the big city – a thought dear to any downsizer, from the emperor Diocletian until today. The farmer, says Virgil, 'does not care for the iron laws; he is unfamiliar with the crazy Forum, nor does he see the national archives' (2.501-2). The word used by Virgil here is *tabularia*, plural of *tabularium* – and its proximity to the Forum argues for its identification as our building.

The Tabularium made for a great backdrop to the Forum, all until the efficient simplicity was diluted by the Temple of Vespasian and Titus and the extended Portico of the Consenting Gods. In late 11C, Pope Boniface VIII (who was Dante's bitter enemy) built a tower over the Tabularium. Later, Michelangelo demolished the upper and western parts of this superstructure, and added another level – what we know today as Palazzo Senatorio.

The preserved lower part of the Tabularium is made of sturdy Republican-style masonry, the so-called *opus quadratum* with huge square stone slabs piling up. The inner part of the Tabularium is accessible from Palazzo Senatorio, but there's not much to see: concrete vaults, badly eroded by time (for a while, these basements were used for storing salt). The Tabularium is bordered by the temple of Veiovis.

PRISON AND STAIRS

A block of flats, a state archive – all peaceful things. But if you start walking down the Capitol towards the Forum along Via San Pietro in Carcere, you'll soon reach less congenial places: the state prison and the stairs that were worse than prison.

The prison was called Tullianum, and the Romans usually ascribed the name to the half-legendary king Servius Tullius. The more meticulous antiquarians derived the word from the archaic Latin *tullus*, a spring. Indeed, there was a small spring in the prison – actually, still is.

The practically-minded Romans did not recognize imprisonment as a valid form of punishment. Exile, confiscation of property, suppression of civil rights, and, finally, slavery and death – that's what was in store for a condemned criminal. But keeping costly and inefficient establishments to contain wrongdoers? Thanks but no thanks. So the Tullianum always was a place of short-term confinement for the most dangerous enemies of the state – in other words, the death row. In today's United States, inmates may be waiting for the lethal injection for years or even decades on end, but few people spent more than a few days in the Tullianum.

There are some exceptions, though. The archaic poet Gnaeus Nevius was a troublesome man; when the Metelli brothers, whom he disfavoured, were elected consuls, he reacted with an ambiguous verse: "Fate sends the Metelli to be Rome's consuls." The Metelli answered with a much less ambiguous verse: "Nevius the poet will get hell from the Metelli." For that, or something like that, Nevius was thrown into prison, and stayed there long enough to write two plays.

The Captive Jugurtha before Sulla. Joaquin Ibarra, 1772

Most commonly, the prison held foreign generals who had lost a military campaign against the Romans. That's what happened to the African king Jugurtha. He was thrown into the death row cell after being stripped of his clothes and even his earrings. Jugurtha kept a remarkably level head and even managed to crack a joke: "By Heracles, this bath of yours is really cold!" Six days later he died of hunger.

A controversial event in the history of the prison followed the exposure of Catiline's conspiracy. Having caught the culprits, Cicero, the consul of that year, threw them in prison and gave orders for them to be executed. Then, emerging onto the Forum full of people, he announced his famous '*vixerunt.*'

> *Vixerunt* is plural past perfect of *vivere*, 'to live.' In Latin, one can stuff into one word something like 'they have lived their due,' meaning – 'they're dead.'

Later, Cicero's enemies used this episode as a pretext to hunt him down: to summarily execute Roman citizens was a grave breach of protocol and custom. Recounting the story of the Catiline's plot, the historian Sallust gives us the most detailed surviving description of the prison. "In the prison, when you have gone up a little way towards the left, there is a place called the Tullianum, about twelve feet below the surface of the ground. It is enclosed on all sides by walls, and above it is a chamber with a vaulted roof of stone. Neglect, darkness, and stench make it hideous and fearsome to behold."[31]

Apart from Jugurtha and the Catilinarians (not Catiline himself, who died in a desperate battle after the execution of his comrades), the prison witnessed the last breath of the Gallic chieftain Vercingetorix (beheaded), Sejanus, the ambitious upstart from the time of emperor Tiberius (beheaded), a number of supporters of the Gracchi brothers (strangled), the augur Herennius Siculus (slipped, fell and smashed his head on the floor before the execution). But the Tullianum's most famous prisoner was reputed to be St. Peter.

There's not a shred of evidence to confirm that St. Peter was actually a prisoner in the Tullianum. But a legend, by definition, has a life of its own. The incarcerated apostle reportedly performed a miracle: he made a spring appear at the foot of the column he was chained to. In the waters of this spring he baptized his repentant jailers, Processus and Martinianus (later also executed for their newly found faith).

The uppermost level of the Roman prison had long been converted into a chapel called San Pietro in Carcere ('Saint Peter in Prison'). It holds a relief depicting the baptism of Processus and Martinianus, a spring, an altar and a small upside-down cross on the altar – a reminder that St. Peter was crucified head down. From this chapel you can go further down, but keep in mind that the stairs, the door, and the brick floor were all constructed in the seventeenth century, when the church of San Giuseppe di Falegnami was erected above Peter's chapel. In classical times, there were no stairs between levels: the prisoners were literally *thrown* into jail – through a hole in the floor.

The Tullianum is often called 'the Mamertine prison'. This word is just as obscure as 'Tullianum' (something to do with the god Mars, perhaps), but it certainly does not predate the Middle Ages.

The Rev. Edward Burton, professor of divinity from Oxford, wrote in his *Description of the Antiquities and Other Curiosities of Rome from Personal Observations and a Visit to Italy in the Years 1818-1819:* "A more horrible place for the confinement of a human being can hardly be imagined." One can't disagree.

As if this was not enough, a flight of stairs in the near vicinity (probably running up today's Via di San Pietro in Carcere) had a reputation worse than the prison. It was called 'the Gemonian stairs' (*scalae Gemoniae*), which the Romans explained through the verb *gemo*, 'to groan.' This etymology, though almost certainly false, was more than appropriate: the Gemonian stairs were used for exposing the bodies of the executed. For a Roman or a

Greek the very idea that a body might be left unburied was a nightmare and disgrace. That was the whole point: the macabre spectacle of the stairs was meant to threaten and disturb. In 'good old' Republican days such impiety was unheard of; the first evidence of the Gemonian stairs dates to the civil wars. The most heart-rending story was told by the historian Tacitus. It was about the inglorious end of the imperial minion Sejanus. First, as an omen of the future misfortunes, Sejanus's bodyguards, walking down from the Capitol after a sacrifice, were forced back from their master, slipped and fell on the Gemonian stairs. Later, following a unanimous Senate decree, Sejanus himself was executed and thrown onto the stairs. This did not stop the retribution machine. "It was decided," writes Tacitus, "to move against his two surviving children next. And so they were carried off to the Prison, the boy old enough to understand what lay in store for them, the girl however so innocent that she kept on asking what she had done wrong and where she was being taken; she promised she would never do it again – a spanking had always seen to that in the past. Writers of that time say that because it was unheard of to apply capital punishment to a maiden, the girl was first raped, with the rope at her side. Afterwards, she and her brother were strangled and thrown out, young as they were, onto the Gemonian steps."[32]

MICHELANGELO AND THE NEW CAPITOL

From the western side – from Via del Teatro Marcello – the Capitol square (Piazza del Campidoglio) may be reached by an unusual flight of stairs: its steps are very wide and very low. The goal was to make the slope accessible not just to people, but to horse- and mule-driven carts as well. Not too necessary these days, but the *Cordonata* – that's the name of the flight of stairs – makes a good location for a blockbuster car chase.

On the upper step of the Cordonata, when the Capitol square is lying before you in full splendour, stand the statues of the twins Castor and Pollux (whom we remember from our walk in the Forum). There is some heavy armour at the feet of each, but it's not really theirs. These shields and swords are called 'the trophies of Marius,' though they have nothing to do with the general Gaius Marius, either. They actually date to the time of the emperor Domitian (late first century AD). Pope Sixtus V, who ordered city magistrates to install the newly found trophies on the square, must have heard something about Julius Caesar restoring the trophies of Marius after his political opponents had put them in storage. Through a quirk of Latin syntax (no doubt intentional), the names of the magistrates are relegated to the back side of the shields, while the Pope's name proudly opens the inscription.

The square is paved with dark grey and off-white stones, whose combination creates an unusual pattern to be enjoyed from the upper floors of the museums – or on satellite photos. In the centre of the pattern sits a twelve-point star, and in the centre of the star a bronze bearded man on horseback with a rather rueful face is extending his right arm, while the horse is raising its right leg.

All this grandeur, including three magnificent palaces, was created by Michelangelo in the mid-16th century. Construction work dragged on for a long time, and the architect did not live to see the square in its final form. Many architectural ideas tried out on the Capitoline hill were revolutionary – such as the so-called 'giant order' of palaces, when the columns span two or more stories. The base for the equestrian statue of Marcus Aurelius was also designed by Michelangelo. Roman guides say: if you're not sure who built a palace or a church, say 'Michelangelo,' and half of the times you'd get it right.

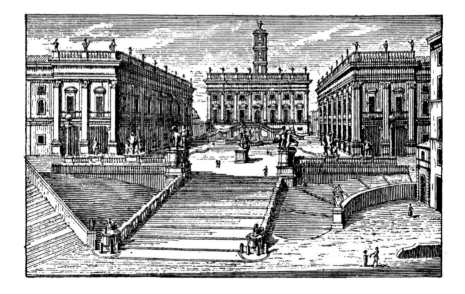

Very few Classical bronze statues survive — in many centuries, metal was more valuable than works of art. A pre-Christian *equestrian* bronze statue is rarer still; actually, the one you can see on the Capitol hill is the only one. (Technically, that's not quite true, either. The real statue now stands in one of the halls of the Capitoline museums. On the square, a masterful replica — some call it 'disappointing' for no obvious reason — has been doubling for the real thing since 1997. In 1979, right-wing radicals planted a bomb next to the city council, which at the time was headed by a Communist politician. The statue was not damaged, but Palazzo Senatorio had to undergo some repainting.)

The statue was saved from the melting pot because in the Middle Ages it was thought to be the image of Constantine, the first Christian ruler of Rome and the empire. Michelangelo transferred it to the Capitol from the square in front of the church of St. John Lateran; before, it stood somewhere else, probably on the Forum. The statue might have been coated with a thin layer of gold, and an urban legend says that on the Judgement Day the gold cover will be miraculously restored.

Note that the emperor sits in the saddle without any stirrups. This is because stirrups were not invented until much later: the Greeks and Romans did not know them.

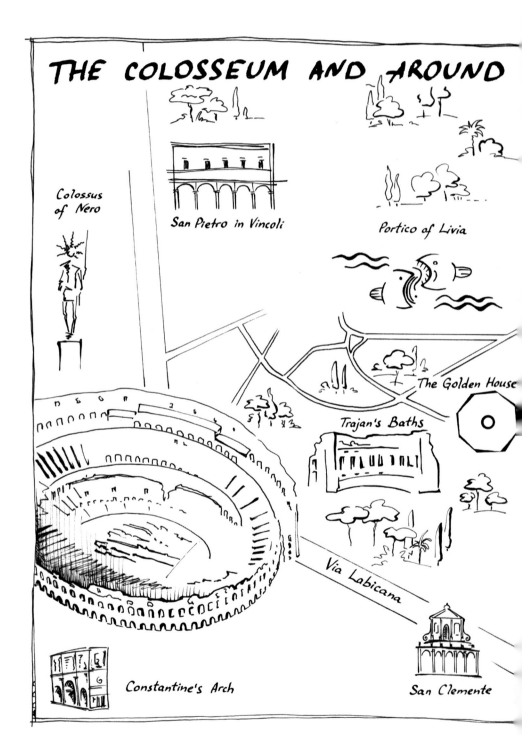

THE COLOSSEUM AND AROUND

Colossus of Nero

San Pietro in Vincoli

Portico of Livia

The Golden House

Trajan's Baths

Via Labicana

Constantine's Arch

San Clemente

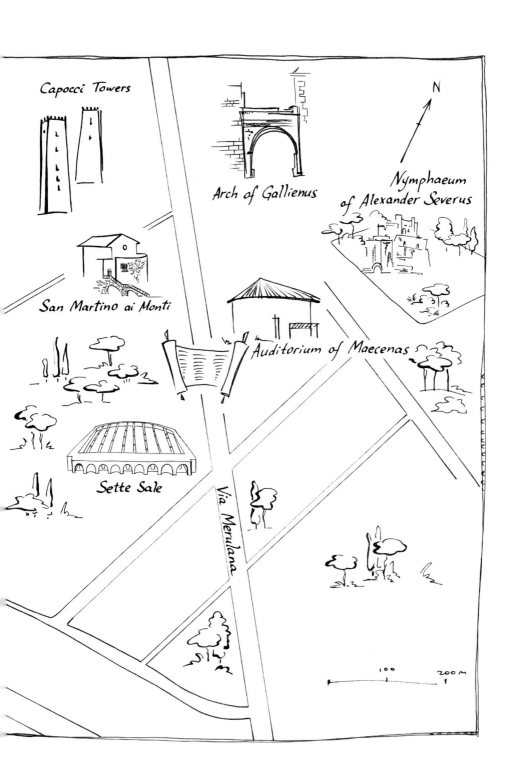

Capocci Towers

Arch of Gallienus

N

Nymphaeum
of Alexander Severus

San Martino ai Monti

Auditorium of Maecenas

Sette Sale

Via Merulana

100   200 M

CHAPTER VI

THE COLOSSEUM
(BLOOD AND SAND)

I f you type 'Rome' or 'Roma' in an online image search engine, at least a quarter of the results will display the Colosseum in some shape or form. Lots of historical books and guidebooks about Rome have the Colosseum on their covers. The Colosseum is the only architectural monument of the whole of Europe that made it to the list "New 7 Wonders of the World."

New 7 Wonders of the World was an initiative aiming to select, through a global voting campaign (using phones, texting and the Internet), seven existing architectural monuments. The model for the list was, of course, the Seven Wonders of the Ancient World – of those, only the Great Pyramid of Giza has survived and was granted honorary status on the new list. Voting results were announced in July 2007 in Lisbon. The new wonders are: Great Wall of China, the Machu Picchu complex in Peru, the stone city of Petra in Jordan, the Taj Mahal mausoleum in India, Christ the Redeemer in Rio de Janeiro, Chichen Itza pyramids in Mexico and the Colosseum.

In short, mass culture has long equated Rome with the Colosseum. This is not surprising at all; but before we tackle the history and legends of the famous amphitheatre, let us walk around it – the whole neighbourhood is full of stories.

"Colosseum valley and the Esquiline hill" is what archaeological guidebooks term the area of Ancient Rome we are about to walk through. On a map, it is an irregular quadrangle. The Colosseum square is certainly the focus of the area, but topographically it is in its lower left corner. The longer sides of the quadrangle are formed by Via Cavour (and its extension, Via Giovanni Lanza) on the top and Via Labicana on the bottom; the top right corner is occupied by Piazza Vittorio Emanuele II. In the centre of the rectangle a large chunk of space is taken by the Colle Oppio park.

THE PORTICO

The first monument we encounter if we walk the course of the Ancient Roman street called "The Subura Slope" (*Clivus Suburanus*, today's Via in Selci) is, unfortunately, absolutely virtual: no part of it survives. It is the Portico of Livia, the wife of Augustus, built in the last years of the 1st century BC.

Livia Drusilla came from a noble patrician family; both her father and first husband had fought against Augustus (here and elsewhere the anachronistic use of the title "Augustus" is for simplicity's sake) – first with Brutus and the 'liberators,' then with Mark Antony. When the victorious Augustus proclaimed amnesty, Livia and her husband returned to Rome from exile. As soon as Augustus laid eyes on her, he immediately decided to be her lawful wedded husband, divorced his second wife Scribonia on the day she gave birth to his only biological child, a girl called Julia, and persuaded or forced Livia's husband to grant her a divorce. Livia at the time was heavily pregnant with her second son, and the wedding took place on the third day after his successful delivery, with Livia's former husband giving her away to Augustus "as a father would." Both contemporaries and historians were inclined to see the union of Augustus and Livia as one of convenience, but the two of them lived more than half a century together and seemed a perfect couple. They did not have any children together. While Augustus was still alive, Livia was busy scheming to bestow the supreme power of Rome upon her descendants from the first marriage. She succeeded: the next four emperors, Tiberius, Caligula, Claudius and Nero, were her son, great-grandson, grandson and great-great-grandson respectively.

In Rome, a portico was not simply a covered colonnade for pleasant walks. People made appointments there, talked about lofty subjects, concluded deals – in short, just like a basilica, a portico was intended for various socially useful things. Covered colonnades provided protection from bad weather and scorching sun. We should keep in mind that the Romans conducted almost all of their working activities outside, in the sun – someone who avoided this and failed to receive his share of healthy suntan was branded an *umbrarius*, 'a shady person' – but protection from sun and heat was nevertheless necessary, especially in summer.

The portico was erected on a place already rich with history. It used to be the estate of one Vedius Pollio (at a time when it was on the outskirts, almost in the country). Pollio was *nouveau riche*, a man of obscure origin, perhaps even a freedman, but a close associate of Augustus nevertheless. Augustus assigned him to a number of important positions – he was, among other things, a governor of the province of Asia, an unheard-of honour for someone of so humble an origin. As a diligent courtier should, Pollio bequeathed most of his property to Augustus. The emperor kept the villa in Campania, but tore down the urban estate to clear ground for the new portico.

Ancient authors tell the same scary story about Pollio. This rich upstart, they say, was very cruel to his slaves. There was a pond on his estate, and the pond swarmed with lampreys. Pollio used to throw disobedient slaves into the pond, feeding the blood-sucking fish. Once, when Augustus himself was on a visit, a slave waiting at the table broke a glass goblet (glass was an expensive rarity). Pollio immediately ordered that the clumsy slave be thrown to the lampreys. Augustus tried to intercede on the slave's behalf, but the master was adamant. Seeing this, Augustus asked that all valuable crockery of the household be brought to him, and made a show of smashing it all. Pollio now felt it would be impolite to execute someone for an offence replicated many times over by the emperor, and he reluctantly pardoned the slave.

The story, of course, is fantastic enough to ascribe its perseverance in multiple sources to its status of an urban legend rather than to authenticity. Pliny the Elder, who was not a big fan of Augustus, drops the part about his clemency, while Tertullian, in a show of Christian rhetoric, adds chilling details: Pollio, he says, fed human flesh to the lampreys on purpose so as to eat the fish later and thus engage in a sort of secondary cannibalism.

Glass was widely used and highly valued in Roman times, but it suffered from the same problem that plagues glassware today: it broke easily. There is another legend preserved in a number of ancient accounts about an inventor who came to show an unbreakable glass cup to the emperor (sources disagree about which emperor it was). He threw the goblet on the floor, but it only received a tiny dent, which the master immediately removed using a little hammer. The emperor then asked whether anyone else knew the secret of the new technology, and the inventor said no, hoping for an ample reward. The emperor chose to execute the genius instead, claiming that the proliferation of this technology would have rendered gold and silver worthless.

Though later authors tried to find a rational solution to the story, claiming, for example, that the mysterious cup could have been made of aluminium, it is likely to be a myth. What is true, however, is an amazing glass cup of Roman times kept at the British Museum. Known as "the Lycurgus cup," it has a unique feature: it is green when lighted from the outside but red when the light source is behind or inside it. Only relatively recently, in the 1990s, did technologists sort out the mystery of the 'dichroic glass,' as it is known: the secret turned out to be in the nanoparticles of gold and silver suspended in the glass. Perhaps the Romans did not have unbreakable plastic cups, but they did use nanotechnology.

There is a problem with biological nomenclature in ancient authors. A lot of Latin words that have survived from classical antiquity occur only once in Pliny the Elder's monumental "Natural History" and denote animals, plants and minerals that are notoriously difficult to identify. There is a possibility that the fish who ate the less lucky among Pollio's slaves were moray eels, not lampreys.

Lampreys are still considered a delicacy in Baltic countries and parts of the Mediterranean. Also, there is another curious coincidence that makes lampreys especially appropriate in a chapter on the Colosseum: there is nothing more resembling a bird's eye view of a Roman amphitheatre than a gaping mouth of a lamprey.

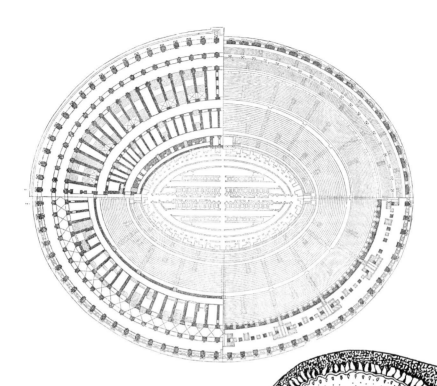

Though nothing survives of Livia's portico, not even ruins, it is marked on the Forma Urbis Romae, the engraved plan mentioned in the chapter on the Imperial fora. The plan shows that the portico was enclosed with a wall, that its main entrance was on the northern side, where the once noisy and crowded Clivus Suburanus went up in a stepped slope. Now the main thoroughfare of the neighbourhood is the Via Giovanni Lanza, while the Via in Selci that follows the course of Clivus Suburanus, became, on the contrary, an oasis of peaceful slumber in the midst of a city. The plan also shows that there was an architectural structure of sorts in the middle of the portico – perhaps a fountain or an altar.

Construction of a useful urban amenity in the place where a cruel man of property used to live was a subtle ideological move of the kind Augustus excelled in. In his *Fasti*, Ovid describes this noble deed thus:

But where we Livia's portico behold,
A grand and spacious palace stood of old;
Such piles of buildings join'd together, rose,
A lesser space does many a town inclose;
But level with the ground these piles were laid,
Too great a show of sumptuous pomp they made;
Great Caesar, Pollio's heir, that loss sustain'd,
(But by the deed immortal glory gain'd;)
The censor thus set up himself to view,
In actions he was to his precepts true,
His own example show'd what others ought to do.[33]

This is not the only mention of this architectural compound in Ovid's poetry, but the second one, in *Ars Amatoria*, is rather tactless. In the poem, Ovid describes in more detail the beautiful interior decoration of the portico.

…let not the Portico of Livia be shunned by you,
which, here and there adorned with ancient paintings,
bears the name of its founder.
Where, too, are the grand-daughters of Belus,
who dared to plot death for their wretched cousins,
and their enraged father stands with his drawn sword.[34]

Who is, though, being encouraged to visit the Portico? Is it us, the curious tourists? Unfortunately, not at all – it is the young playboy looking for a good pick-up venue: "First learn in what spot the fair are to be met with." Augustus had certainly meant to celebrate family values with the new portico, and this unintended function would have angered him. It was probably such straightforward approach – singing Augustus's regime for what it was, not for what it wanted to appear as – that in the end doomed Ovid to exile on the joyless frosty shores of the Black Sea.

THE HOUSE OF EQUITIUS

Not far from the place where the narrow Via in Selci flows into Piazza di San Martino ai Monti, you will see a house of brown brick on your right. Look carefully, and you will see that apart from small windows and a walled-in door, its façade once featured much larger windows and wide arches, now completely bricked in. The lowest part of the building, without any traces of arches, was faced in the 17th century, but the façade as a whole is that of a late Roman building, possibly of a large house of Late Empire (4th or 5th century AD), when the Esquiline was favoured by the affluent crowd. It is hard to believe that anyone today could live in a house whose age is counted in millennia, and yet this building is still used for residential purposes. It belongs to the monastery attached to the church of Santa Lucia in Selci, and the nuns treat their home as their castle: the Roman underbelly of their property has never been seriously studied. There is, though, a frivolous ancient detail (pious in the classical sense of the word, but certainly not from a Christian perspective) on the wall of the house. The lower tier of the house (as mentioned, faced with new brick at a relatively late date) sports the remains of four travertine pillars, and the second one on the right features a half-erased anthropomorphic figure. This is Priapus, a fertility deity who is easily recognizable by his large phallus. Images of Priapus were often placed near parks, gardens and intersections, and Priapus of Via in Selci meets all of these requirements.

On the square, there is a heavily restored mediaeval tower known as the "Capocci tower." On the other side of the street, squeezed in by modern buildings, is its twin. The southern side of the square is dominated by a squat structure made of ancient brick, not easily recognizable as a church. This is because it stands with its back end turned to the square; to see the baroque façade, one needs to walk down the tiny Via Equizia to the left of the church.

San Martino ai Monti is one of the oldest Roman churches. The first Christian shrine on that spot was built by pope Simmachus in the 5th century; before, Pope Sylvester had served in the home church there. The present-day structure is also rather old, dating to the 9th century. This is not very obvious from the interior or façade, due to a 17th-century reconstruction, but the general plan and some of the outer walls remained almost intact, and this is quite obvious from the square. Twenty-four columns in the nave are also ancient, probably even salvaged from the 5th-century church. The sacristy holds a silver lamp that belonged to St. Sylvester.

> The church of San Martino ai Monti is named after St. Martin of Tours, one of the most beloved popular saints of France (when the Armistice was signed on St. Martin's day, 11 November 1918, it was seen by many in France as a sign of the saint's intercession). His best-known good deed is from the time when, still a pagan legionary, he gave half of his coat to a beggar and was then visited by Christ in his dream and praised for his charity.

The basement of San Martino is an ancient Roman house of the late 2nd and early 3rd century AD. It is not located directly under the church, but to its west, though theoretically one can get there through the church's crypt. Legend claims that it was the house of a rich Roman called Equitius who, being a Christian, offered his dwelling for the meetings of the local Christian community (the side lane is called Via Equizia in his honour). Such 'house church' is called a *titulus* in Roman Catholic tradition.

Originally, 'titulus' was simply a tablet with an inscription. In Ancient Rome, as in an English village, such tablets were often used to mark private houses, and later the meaning was transferred to a meeting-place for fellow believers. Gospel stories and archaeological data show that in early Christian times such premises were not used for exclusively religious purposes (the only house church that was used only or mainly as a church was found in the Roman military camp Dura Europos in present-day Syria). "The house of Equitius," judging by its structure and size of rooms, looks more like a barn or granary than living quarters – which, of course, does not preclude its use for Christian meetings and sacraments.

It is possible that in the house of Equitius, in the presence of Emperor Constantine, were announced the results of the Nicaean Council – the first ever ecumenical council that attempted to bring together the Christians of the whole known world and made them agree on common dogmas and rites. The success was partial and short-lived: the heretical Arians, at the time the principal opposition force within the church, were temporarily subdued but far from exterminated. However, their heretical scriptures were solemnly burned, which makes San Martino the first place to witness this – later exceedingly popular – method of fighting dissent.

COMPITAL ALTAR

On the other side of the square, where it changes into a street of the same name, there is an inconspicuous door of a residential house, No. 8 (the house number shows up nicely on the keystone of decorative brickwork). In the late 19th century, when the whole neighbourhood was under construction, the remains of an altar were found on this place while building a foundation of the new house. Many monuments of the kind were immediately transferred to museums, but this one was left *in situ*. The altar is made of typical Roman travertine; there are a few tufa blocks in front of it and pieces of sundry stones and columns behind. The inscription indicates that it is a so-called *compital altar* – a small shrine on the crossroads dedicated to the Lares, the gods of liminal places and states.

> The Lares are deities of obscure origin. Their cult could have evolved from the cult of dead ancestors, deified heroes, house spirits. The Lares were supposed to guard their plots: a house, a settlement, an urban block. (There is a similar notion in Jewish tradition, *eruv* – a symbolic limit of a house or a community equated to a house, within which the moving of objects is allowed on a Sabbath.) In classical times, the Lares were depicted as young men in simple village clothes (Plutarch claims the clothes are of dogskin), with a goblet in one hand and a libation cup in the other. They stand in an almost dancing posture and most often come in pairs.

By the end of his rule, Augustus had reorganised the administrative layout of the city of Rome, dividing it into 14 regions. Inhabitants of each region elected officials (usually of low birth, like freedmen) responsible for fire brigades and 'well-organised militias' to fight street crime.

Those officials were also supposed to take care of compital altars. The inscription on the San Martino altar says there used to be a statue of Mercury, the god of travel and commerce – which Augustus had personally given to the neighbourhood. The funds for the statue came from donations offered to Augustus by his grateful subjects on the occasion of a New Year.

ESQUILINE GATE (THE ARCH OF GALLIENUS)

Moving further east, you will cross the broad Via Merulana and, leaving a neo-Gothic St. Alphonsus church designed by the Scottish architect George Wigley on your right, you will come directly to an ancient arch, squeezed between the church of Santi Vito e Modesto and a 19th-century building. It is the Arch of Gallienus, marking the old Esquiline gate that had been here since the times of the kings. If you pass through it, you will find yourself outside the oldest city limit. It was here that the Roman military once put an end to Etruscan raids. A tactical ruse was used: cattle, usually grazing within the safety of city walls, was deliberately let out, and when the greedy Etruscans rushed to capture them, the Romans ambushed them and cut them down, putting an end to Etruscan incursions.

It is not entirely fair that the arch bears the name of Gallienus. It was built, or at least rebuilt, in Augustan times, flanked on both sides by small pedestrian arches, which were, of course, pillaged for building materials during the Renaissance. In the 3rd century AD, a rich courtier named Aurelius Victor had the original Augustan inscription chiselled off and installed thin marble panels with a dedication of his own devising: "His Eminence Aurelius Victor to Gallienus, most merciful prince, whose invincible valour is surpassed by his goodness alone, and to Salonina, most blameless Augusta, in greatest dedication to their authority and majesty."[35] The abundance of -issimus and -issime superlatives did not save the emperor Gallienus from the usual lot of soldier emperors of the 3rd century: he was killed during the siege of Milan.

The inscription has not survived intact. The missing portion probably mentioned Gallienus's father Valerian, whose lot was even more tragic than his son's: in 260 AD, to the horror of the whole Roman world, he was taken prisoner by the troops of Persian king Shapur I and two years later died (or was murdered) in captivity. Roman POWs built the city of Bishapur in the Persian desert, in the south of modern-day Iran, not far from the shores of the Persian Gulf, with walls sporting majestic reliefs with the scenes of the Roman army's demise. It is one of those rare occasions when we can see Roman wars through the eyes of 'barbarians.'

Arch of Gallienus. The Nymphaeum of Alexander Severus is seen through its opening. Engraving by Giuseppe Vasi, 18th century

NYMPHAEUM OF ALEXANDER SEVERUS

The route through the Esquiline Gate by the Ss.Vito e Modesto church along the Via Carlo Alberto leads into the square of Vittorio Emanuele II and virtually runs into a very monumental but for some reason poorly known ancient Roman monument. It is the so-called Nymphaeum of Alexander Severus.

The nymphaeum is a structure as tall as a five-story house lined with typical Roman brick (the core is concrete). It is difficult to guess at its purpose at first sight, but walking around its enclosure, you will sooner or later see a large entrance opening for the aqueduct. It was a giant fountain.

Fountains of that kind were called 'nymphaea' in Rome because of an ancient legend. Numa Pompilius, the wisest and most devout of Roman kings, decided that inuring his rather wild people to piety was best done through fairy tales. So he pretended that he had a secret wife and advisor, the nymph Egeria, who was instructing him in the intricacies of various cults, while he was simply transmitting it to his people. This is the rational and pragmatic angle of the legend as presented by the historian Titus Livius. Ovid in Metamorphoses, however, seems to have taken the story at face value; he describes that after Numa's death the gods, moved by compassion, turned the mourning Egeria into a fountain that was forever shedding tears.

The shrine of Egeria exists to this day, and it is even decently preserved. It used to be a sacred grove with a brook, but in the 2nd century AD a fountain was built inside, and upper-class travellers of the 17th and 18th centuries considered it their duty to make a pilgrimage to the sacred place. A sketch of Egeria's nymphaeum by Goethe survives, as well as an expressively scary engraving by Piranesi. The nymphaeum is in the area of the Appian Way Regional Park, covered in Chapter 9.

A nymphaeum was supposed to be more natural than a regular fountain, whether this 'naturalness' is real or pretend, but with time, nymphaea transformed into large water-distribution nodes, from which aqueducts carried water to different neighbourhoods of the city.

The nymphaeum stands between two belts of defensive walls (the old, Servian, and the new, Aurelian) and on the intersection of two major roads – Via Tiburtina and Via Labicana. The name of emperor Alexander Severus was ascribed to it conditionally, based on the date of some of its building materials. However, those materials were likely to have been used for repairs, while the original fountain had been erected in the times of Domitian. It looked very much like a three-span triumphal arch with huge exedras instead of arch spans. These were niches inhabited by statues, which were not specifically made for the monument but borrowed from some other monument of an earlier date. We have seen examples of such practices before, and will see more of it. The central exedra was likely adorned with a statue of a god or goddess (Jupiter or Victoria), or perhaps the emperor as a god. As for side niches, their content is known positively: they were occupied by reliefs of weapons and armour. Such architectural ornaments were known as 'trophies,' and these specific trophies were for some reason connected in the Middle Ages with the victory scored by the general Marius over the Germanic tribes of the Cimbri and Teutones in the late 2nd century BC, while the nymphaeum itself was renamed as a temple (or 'trophy') of Marius (no one remembered that it had once been a fountain). In 1590, Pope Sixtus V transferred the reliefs to the upper landing of the stairs leading to the summit of the Capitoline Hill, and this is where they have been standing to this day.

GARDENS AND AUDITORIUM OF MAECENAS

After the square you can turn right and take the Via Leopardi. On our right is a park – *Parco Oppio* – with a name derived from ancient Roman topography (Oppian is the southern spur of the Esquiline hill). The northern part of the park, the one that will be on our way, is connected to a man whose name became synonymous with art patronage and sponsorship in many languages of the world. The name is Maecenas.

Gaius Cilnius Maecenas was one of the closest friends and associates of the emperor Augustus, his lifelong companion. After a century of exhausting civil wars, the rule of Augustus was genuinely welcomed by contemporaries as a golden age. Augustus used the fruits of peace as deftly as he used his generals' military victories: the doors of the Temple of Janus were closed with much pomp to signify the absence of any wars on the whole Roman territory – something that had last happened in half-legendary ancient times.

A richer state needed a larger and more efficient bureaucracy, but there were few good managers among old senatorial aristocracy: the upper classes had long spurned any practical activity, especially if commerce was involved. That led to unprecedented social mobility. The equestrian (knightly) order, wealthy but politically disadvantaged, had gained wide access to the Senate, to provincial government, and to the highest political offices.

It was from that order that Maecenas sprang. Of course, he was rumoured to be a descendant of mysterious Etruscan kings (this compliment opens every collection of odes by Horace: "Maecenas! scion of a kingly line, / Safeguard and hope and pride art thou of mine"[36]) – but a claim to obscure aristocratic ancestry is a favourite practice of all rootless upstarts of all eras.

Maecenas had travelled a long way alongside Augustus: he fought with him, he stayed in charge in Rome while the ruler was away in the provinces, he interceded in Augustus's legal and punitive decisions, always with a view on mitigating them, and Augustus was grateful for such intercession. But his main role, which guaranteed him a place in history and language, was in the domain of culture.

We said 'culture,' but it could just as easily be 'cultural policy' or 'propaganda.' Obviously, it was the propaganda side that was important for Augustus. But that was where the genius of Maecenas was at its best: he did not employ enthusiastic versifiers, always a dime a dozen, but recruited poets of such calibre for the tasks of state-building that their work continues to be read, studied, parodied and translated today, after two thousand years. He did not neglect the propaganda side, either: the literature of the era is called "the golden" or "Augustan" age of Roman literature. Augustus would have liked it.

Maecenas was a close friend and protector of two of the greatest poets of Rome (and civilisation in general), Virgil and Horace. Both enjoyed his financial support, including juicy real estate (Horace received as a gift an estate in the Sabine hills); both read their poetry, at his invitation, before the top officials of the state. Virgil died before he had a chance to prepare his magnum opus, the epic *Aeneid* for publication, and the task fell to his friends, who were also members of Maecenas's circle. Augustus was probably not too thrilled with the epic – it turned out to be saying too little about himself and too much about mythical times before Rome was even founded. There is little doubt that the emperor was keenly, and not always benevolently, interested in literary matters. Ovid, exiled in circumstances that have remained obscure ever since, bore the brunt of Augustan wrath; but Horace was also affected by princely interference. When, at the age of 40, the poet decided to retire, stop writing poetry and study philosophy, Augustus, through Maecenas, conveyed to him his polite but unequivocal displeasure: the poet, after all, did not only report to the Muses, but also to his benefactors, whom he was supposed to praise. With a heavy heart, Horace was forced to keep calm and carry on writing poetry.

Virgil inspired by the muse of history Clio and the muse of tragedy Melpomene. 3rd century AD, mosaic from the province of Africa, now in the Bardo National Museum, Tunisia

Maecenas received a large land plot on the Oppian summit of the Esquiline hill. This unhealthy locality had served as a poor man's cemetery since times immemorial (archaeologists have discovered multiple graves along Via Giovanni Lanza). Horace even writes that, before the innovations of Maecenas, sun-whitened human bones were scattered in the open near a local wall. Maecenas gentrified the neighbourhood, laid out a park and settled there himself. In the summer, when the Roman climate became especially unbearable, Augustus used to come and stay with his friend. Somewhere on the estate, the famous public readings were held – but where?

In 1874, during the redevelopment of the quarter, architects Virginio Vespignani and Carlo Ludovico Visconti discovered near Via Merulana an ancient Roman building with a floor with bricks arranged in a fishtail design (such brickwork is called *opus spicatum*), mosaics and seven stairs forming a semicircle. False windows were painted in the niches, which appeared to open on lush vegetation, fountains and birds. In the late 19th century the frescoes were quite vivid, but now they are unfortunately almost invisible.

Knowing the connection of the neighbourhood with the name of Maecenas, the discoverers decided that the semicircle was a miniature auditorium, and that they had chanced upon the very place where the courtier's guests listened to poets and musicians. No written evidence of such a structure survives, but it does not mean it could not have existed. If you visit the auditorium, keep in mind that the structure has undergone a string of reconstructions since antiquity; for example, the roof is a recent addition, because the original one was lost.

A structure that *was* mentioned in literary sources was the tower of Maecenas, the tallest point of the Esquiline at the time. Horace calls it 'a heap under the clouds,' while Suetonius claims that Nero had used that very tower as an observation point during the great fire, singing a poem about the fall of Troy of his own composition. Unfortunately, no traces of the tower survive, and its exact location is unknown. Most researchers think it could have stood opposite the Auditorium, on the place now occupied by the Brancaccio theatre.

At the end of his life, Maecenas removed himself from affairs of the state. He lived out his days in the Esquiline estate, worn out by nervous disease and insomnia, only able to doze off to the unhurried gurgling of the fountains. Maecenas was buried on the Esquiline; two months later, Horace died, too – he had almost kept the promise, once expressed in a poem, not to survive his friend.

THE MAD NERO

On October 13, 54 BC, the emperor Claudius died. Rumours attributed his sudden death to a poisoned dish of porcini mushrooms, offered to him by his wife Agrippina. (When Claudius felt dizzy, a bribed doctor inserted a feather into his mouth, ostensibly to induce vomiting, while the feather was actually covered in an even stronger poison; at least this is how Tacitus reports the events.)

The emperor's son Britannicus was not yet fourteen and thus was considered a legal minor, so a stepson of Claudius, son of Agrippina, took up the reins of government. His birth name was Lucius Domitius Ahenobarbus, but history remembers him as Nero.

Ahenobarbus means 'bronze-beard.' According to a legend, a distant ancestor of Nero's had met two young men of divine appearance on the road and was told to inform the people of the Roman victory at Lake Regillus. To prove their superhuman powers, one of the men touched the chosen herald's beard, making it fiery red. (They were Castor and Pollux, the horse-taming twins.) Fair complexion and hair remained a family feature of the Ahenobarbi down to Nero. It is not very clear today whether this was unusual in the ancient Romans. Literary sources usually find it necessary to mention that someone was blond, but do not display any extraordinary amazement about it. Surviving frescoes and mosaics usually depict Romans as typical Mediterraneans — swarthy and dark-haired. (Interestingly, this only applies to men — erotic Pompeian frescoes often seem to show interracial couples, but this is no more than an artistic convention: a proper man should be spending his time outdoors, lest he be branded an unsavoury *umbrarius*, whereas a women's virtue was, on the contrary, in being homebound. This resulted in double standards of beauty for the sexes: men were supposed to be well-tanned, women decidedly were not.)

A significant number of Nero's sculptural portraits have come down to us. They show obvious affinity with other representatives of the Julio-Claudian line: thin lips, small mouth, weak chin. With Nero, these features are supplemented by a tentative beard which mostly grows on the neck, adolescent-style. It should be kept in mind that Nero ascended to power at the age of 16 and died at 30.

Few happy thoughts are with the name of Nero in the modern reader's mind. It is mostly associated with various horrors and crimes: Nero builds a special self-destructing ship to drown his power-hungry mother, and when she swims for her life, sends assassins with daggers to finish her off; Nero conducts a long series of experiments with poisons in order to make no mistake when poisoning his stepbrother Britannicus; Nero accuses Christians of setting Rome on fire and makes human torches out of them. Many of those accusations might be true, but things are never straightforward with historical evidence. With the death of Nero, the Julio-Claudian dynasty, sprung from Julius Caesar, came to an end (a fact predicted by a menacing prophecy: "Last of the sons of Aeneas, a matricide shall govern"). New emperors had to work hard to prove their legitimacy; one of the ways to do that was smearing their predecessors. Also, emperors were not always on the friendliest terms with the Senate, and Nero was especially at odds with it, while Tacitus and Cassius Dio, our principal sources for Nero's time, had belonged to the senatorial order and protected its ideological interests. In the Greek East, quite a few false Neros had popped up after the death of Nero, which shows that the late emperor enjoyed a modicum of popularity, at least among Greek speakers.

This is hardly surprising: Nero seemed to scorn political and military activity, the only two things considered worthy of a Roman, but was a huge fan of arts and sports, the traditional domains of the Greeks. In his early years, he indulged in them quietly, privately, with tutors, then he started performing for his close circle, and, finally, having acquired a taste for the spotlight, began forcing his one-man shows on the people. Not an avid traveller, he did go to the worshipped Greece, ordering all the panhellenic games to be held together, because he wanted to participate in all of them and win. At the Olympic games, he rode a chariot drawn by ten horses. This was an impossibly difficult feat even for a skilled professional, so Nero promptly fell off the chariot. The attendants picked him up, brushed him down and reinstalled him, but he was too shaken to stay in the race. In spite of that, the judges awarded him a victory (how could they not?), and he, in turn, awarded liberty to the whole province of Achaia (Greece) – a gesture completely devoid of any political meaning, but pleasant for the Greeks nonetheless.

Delusions of grandeur, something that certainly afflicted Nero, was reflected in his architectural and development projects. Some remained unrealised, like the huge canal from Ostia to the Bay of Naples (which would have made it possible to sail from Rome to Italy's best seaside resorts without taking to the open sea) – even though construction started, and Nero ordered that all exiles and even criminal convicts be conscripted for it.

Nero realised, though, his dream of a palace without equal in the world. Initially he had been simply expanding the imperial residence on the Palatine, but with such abandon that the lobby of the palace ended up somewhere in the eastern section of the Forum. For its spread, the palace was called 'house of passage' (*Domus Transitoria*). But then the fire struck.

THE FIRE

There are many things that are unclear about the so-called "Great Fire of Rome." It broke out on the night of 18/19 July, 64 AD, in the shops near the Circus Maximus and quickly spread across a few neighbourhoods. Contemporaries are either silent or very laconic about the event. We learn about the horrors and destruction mostly from the historians of the following generation. Tacitus claimed that out of Rome's 14 Augustan regions, four were utterly gutted, seven severely damaged and only three came out unscathed. Archaeologists have for a long time considered this report a serious exaggeration.

The main question of the fire of 64 AD is whether it was an accidental fire, like the Great Fire of London of 1666, or an act of arson, like the Great Fire of Moscow of 1812, so vividly described in Tolstoy's *War and Peace*. Those who supported the latter version were saying that the city was flooded with people setting houses on fire, preventing citizens from putting out whatever was already burning and invoking orders from above whenever someone tried to stop them. Of course, the rumour quickly ascribed the arson to Nero himself. The gossip sprouted increasingly picturesque details: Nero allegedly sent his agents, armed with torches, and ordered them to pretend to be drunk; Nero donned a stage costume and sang a poem of the fall of Troy (evidently composed by himself) from the top of Maecenas's tower on the Esquiline. Tacitus, however, says that Nero was not even in Rome during the fire, and the sources do not try to deny the huge relief effort (both rebuilding and helping the victims) immediately undertaken by Nero. Among other things, he opened up the surviving parts of his palace to the people left homeless by the fire, and paid for extra deliveries of food from his own money.

Still, Nero saw it fit to deflect the unfavourable public reaction and pointed a finger at the newfangled sect of Christians as the likely arsonists. The importance of this accusation cannot be overestimated: it is the very first appearance of Christians in historical tradition. Roman historians, who had no sympathy for Christians whatsoever, never for a moment entertained the thought that there might have been a grain of truth in Nero's accusations, and unanimously agreed that the emperor's smear campaign had backfired, promoting and glorifying the Christians.

Whether Nero set Rome on fire or not, he certainly used the aftermath to the hilt. When it became clear that the Domus Transitoria could not be saved, Nero ordered two architects, Severus and Celer, to build a new residence for him. This turned out to be a major political mistake.

Positivist historians of the 19th century denied the historicity of Christ and doubted that the few mentions of Christians in ancient authors (Tacitus and Suetonius, in connection with the Neronian fire; Pliny the Younger and Flavius Josephus, on a different subject) were interpolations, that is to say later inserts by Christian transcribers. Today, scholars only have doubts about the gushing passage from Josephus (*testimonium Flavianum*), while the other three easily pass the test for the so-called 'criterion of embarrassment.' This means roughly the following: if an insert had come from a later Christian apologist, he would have certainly written something good about the Christians, even as he tried to imitate the impartiality of an ancient historian. And yet, Pliny writes about the Christians with bureaucratic indifference, Tacitus does not conceal his disgust, while Suetonius possibly does not speak of Christians at all but simply mentions a member of an unknown Jewish sect called Chrestus. Imagining such testimonies as produced by the pen of an early (and certainly very zealous) Christian demands an impossible leap of faith.

THE GOLDEN HOUSE

Travellers coming to any large imperial city often find, somewhere in the suburbs, a large imperial series of palaces and gardens with the alleys, fountains and all the other paraphernalia. Think El Escorial near Madrid, Schönbrunn Palace near Vienna, Versailles near Paris, and quite a few around St. Petersburg. There are such estates in the environs of Rome, too, like the sprawling Tivoli villa of the emperor Hadrian. But even the craziest among the French kings did not attempt to clear half of Paris to build a residence – alleys, fountains and all – smack in the centre of the city. Nero did.

By that time Romans had grown more or less used to luxury, palatial and otherwise. But it was sheer scale and location that enraged them. The Golden House covered an area from the Palatine to the suburban Esquiline and the city walls. The parks were more like wild forests, where exotic beasts roamed, brought on special orders from exotic lands. The place later occupied by the Colosseum was used for a huge artificial reservoir, with miniature cities around it, designed with careful attention to architectural and landscape features of their originals. A triple portico leading to the entrance was a mile long. At some points of the estate, a visitor could experience the illusion of being far away from a city with a million-strong population: all one could see was open skies and faraway rustic hills, without any residential quarters in sight. Moving to the new residence, Nero humbly remarked that he would finally start living like a human being (*quasi homo*).

We have mentioned already that the Romans' life mostly unfolded in the squares, streets and fora of the city, not at home. The fact that one citizen (even though he was an emperor) gobbled up such a huge chunk of public space was not to anyone's liking. Versified insults began to proliferate, like this one:

> *Rome has become a palace; citizens, run to Veii,*
> *Unless Veii has not become part of that palace, too.*

Nero's new 'human' life apparently involved perpetual gluttony. The palatial structure that has survived better than others and forms today the central element of the archaeological monument, the so-called 'octagonal room,' was surrounded by dozens of rooms that are all considered to be for dining. Suetonius describes the main dining hall, which rotated miraculously in accordance with the celestial movements. Until recently this hall was considered to be the octagonal room, but the recent discovery of a structure on the Palatine, mentioned in Chapter 3, made archaeologists change their minds.

Suetonius writes that the ceiling in Nero's banquet hall revolved like the heavens, and was equipped with special pipes that showered down flowers and perfumes on his guests. Nero obviously was fond of such contraptions: he made two attempts on his mother's life (both times unsuccessfully) using collapsible mechanisms – a ceiling and a boat.

The Golden House was not Nero's only city-planning project. After the fire he had the whole centre of Rome rebuilt with no attention to costs. It was rumoured that a certain equestrian assured him of Dido's countless treasure buried in Africa which would be very easy to dig up for the imperial budget. The treasure was never found, but Rome did become a great deal more luxurious. Not everyone was happy, though: in the pre-fire city, the scorching sun was easily avoidable by hiding in the city dungeons, in narrow streets, or in the shades of multistoreyed insulae. Now, wide prospects and majestic squares found themselves defenceless before the scorching Italian heat. It was similar to the mistakes made by the French architect, Le Corbusier, in India, when he redesigned the city of Chandigarh with open spaces and long walks between the domestic housing and the town's amenities.

The Golden House was discovered by chance at the end of the 15th century, but when exactly and under what circumstances remains rather unclear. The usual story is that of a local man suddenly falling underground in 1488 and finding himself in a richly decorated room. Italian painters who heard about the wonder rushed to inspect it. In the middle (or probably in the beginning) of the 1480s, some frescoes and paintings began to feature ornamental motifs which could not be taken from anywhere else except Nero's palace – hence the doubts about the date. In the Santa Maria in Aracoeli on the Capitol, the Bufalini Chapel has frescoes by Pinturicchio depicting the life of St. Bernardino of Siena, which show obvious knowledge of the newly discovered style. Indeed, Pinturicchio (just as Ghirlandaio and Raphael) was one of the first to use ropes to lower himself into the cellar of the Golden House, study the frescoes under the weak light of lamps and leave his signature on the ceiling (art historians later collected a whole catalogue of such graffiti).

Before the discovery of Pompeii (similarly by chance), the Golden House was almost the only source to provide any information about ancient painting. The artists of the Renaissance were not that impressed by pictures whose themes were mythological – compared to their own work, those were primitive, perspectiveless, schematic and, on top of that, mostly poorly preserved. The ornaments, though, immediately became highly prized.

The classical design in the Golden House style was marked by vivid fantasy: geometric and floral motifs freely intertwined with animalistic designs, with mythical chimerae hiding in the thicket of mythological bushes. This method of decoration was called 'grotesque,' from the Italian 'grotta' (grotto). Benvenuto Cellini, a jeweller with rampant imagination, thought differently about the creatures: "their real name is monsters, not grotesques." In any case, grotesque-style decorations became fashionable. When in the early 16th century Pope Julius II ordered the architect Donato Bramante to plan – and Raphael to paint – a few of the Vatican halls, the young artist took Neronian grotesques as his model.

The Russian empress Catherine II ordered her architects to imitate the Vatican galleries of Bramante and Raphael. But this is not the only thing that connects the empress with the Golden House. In 1768, a British architect called Charles Cameron worked in Rome for his book on Roman baths. He studied – very extensively – the premises which he considered the baths of the emperor Titus. While he researched them, he went underground and studied several rooms (of the baths, he thought; actually of the palace). One of the rooms was especially interesting, with grooves on the ceiling and paintings that showed musical instruments. "It was with great difficulty I got into this room: I was obliged to cut a hole through the wall and to let myself down by a rope, and afterwards to creep through a hole in [another] wall, upon my hands and knees. It was nearly full of earth to the ceiling."

Interestingly, after Cameron's visit this room was forgotten again and never heard of for 150 years. It was only rediscovered in the early 20th century. Today it is one of the best-known parts of the Golden House, "The room of Achilles on Skyros."

But why Catherine the Great? Well, upon his return to London, Charles Cameron acquired a tarnished reputation (enhanced by putting his own father into a debtor's prison) and was forced to look for work abroad. Luckily for him, Catherine's agents were at this very time hiring architects in Europe. This turned out to be the beginning of a beautiful friendship: Cameron built the palace in Pavlovsk and the famous Cameron's Gallery in Tsarskoe Selo, while the "Cold Baths" were a direct nod to his Roman sources of inspiration. Catherine valued Cameron's archaeological activity; in 1779 she wrote: "I am enjoying Mr. Cameron... We are fashioning here with him a terraced garden with pools beneath, an arcade beneath; this will be beautiful, beautiful." Under the following Russian Tsar, Paul I, Cameron fell out of favour (he had a knack of alienating people and making enemies) and lived quietly for the rest of his days, dying in 1812, shortly before Napoleon's invasion.

The artist who painted the Golden House, according to Pliny the Elder, was called Fabullus (or Famulus). He worked dressed in a toga (which is more or less equivalent to painting in a dinner jacket in modern times). Unfortunately, the frescoes of the palace are deteriorating every day due to air pollution and humidity; the day when they will be completely undetectable is drawing close. What can be seen today does not seem very impressive even to the imaginative. And yet, we must keep in mind that we can see today only a tiny portion of the Golden House adornment (to say nothing of precious gems, gold and pearl that used to decorate it). A lay person finds it difficult to appreciate a beautiful human being when all he can see is a poorly preserved skeleton.

During the last decades, the Golden House has been undergoing permanent renovation; it is almost always closed. If you are lucky in spite of that, keep in mind that there are more than 140 rooms thought to be part of Nero's palace. On the east side one of the best known rooms is the Nymphaeum of Polyphemus, so named after a fresco in the upper part of the vaulted ceiling (all ceilings in the Golden House are very high, 10–11 metres). In this room, which was also probably a dining room, fountains sprinkled the walls, filling pools in other rooms. Another famous room is the 'Room of the Golden Vault.'

It was ravaged by time more than most – some stucco with traces of paint is visible here and there, but mythological paintings are gone and only known from Renaissance copies preserved in the library of the Spanish royal palace. Room No. 119 (the one explored by Cameron), known as 'Chamber of Achilles on Skyros,' still amazes with its multicoloured frescoes and 'grotesques' where Fabullus's favourite colours dominate – blue, ochre, yellow. Satellite photos show the Octagonal Room with a huge hole in the ceiling and one of the most impressive Roman-era concrete domes.

> The mother of Achilles, the goddess Thetis, knew that her son was doomed to die in the Trojan war and tried to help him avoid the draft. (Interestingly, in 'The Iliad' Achilles seems to be the only hero who has a choice: he can either live a long uneventful life and die in obscurity or be cut down in his prime but perpetuate his glory for millennia; the destiny of everyone else is more or less written in stone.) Thetis sent her son to Lycomedes, a king of the island of Scyros; when Odysseus and Diomedes made it to Scyros in their search for the draft dodger, Achilles put on female clothes and blended in with a crowd of girls. The crafty Odysseus found it easy to expose the pretender, and off to war Achilles went. Suetonius says that the emperor Tiberius had a taste for idle literary exercises; one of the questions that interested him was – which female name did Achilles take up on Scyros?

The end of Nero's rule was marred by conspiracies, revolts in the provinces and general instability. Describing the last hours of the emperor's life, the usually dry Suetonius rises to a high degree of dramatic art:

Changing his purpose again [after having contemplated suicide], he sought for some retired place, where he could hide and collect his thoughts; and when his freedman Phaon offered his villa in the suburbs between the Via Nomentana and the Via Salaria near the fourth milestone, just as he was, barefooted and in his tunic, he put on a faded cloak, covered his head, and holding a handkerchief before his eyes, mounted a horse with only four attendants... At once he was startled by a shock of earthquake and a flash of lightning full in his face, and he heard the shouts of the soldiers from the camp hard by, as they prophesied destruction for him and success for [the rebel general] Galba. He also heard one of the wayfarers whom he met say: "These men are after Nero," and another ask: "Is there anything new in the city about Nero?" Then his horse took fright at the smell of a corpse which had been thrown out into the road, his face was exposed, and a retired soldier of the Guard recognised him and saluted him. When they came to a by-path leading to the villa, they turned the horses loose and he made his way amid bushes and brambles and along a path through a thicket of reeds to the back wall of the house, with great difficulty and only when a robe was thrown down for him to walk on. Here the aforesaid Phaon urged him to hide for a time in a pit, from which sand had been dug, but he declared that he would not go underground while still alive, and after waiting for a while until a secret entrance into the villa could be made, he scooped up in his hand some water to drink from a pool close by, saying: "This is Nero's distilled water." Then, as his cloak had been torn by the thorns, he pulled out the twigs which had pierced it, and crawling on all fours through a narrow passage that had been dug, he entered the villa and lay down in the first room he came to, on a couch with a common mattress, over which an old cloak had been thrown. Though suffering from hunger and renewed thirst, he refused some coarse bread which was offered him, but drank a little lukewarm water.[37]

"Nero's distilled water" (decocta Neronis) is boiled water cooled with snow, an extravagant luxury for the time.

It is impossible to render faithfully in most modern languages the famous phrase Nero used, exhorting himself to commit suicide: *Qualis artifex pereo* (in Rolfe's translation "What an artist the world is losing!"). In Latin the verb stands in the first person, literally "What an artist I perish."

In the end, lacking the courage to commit suicide himself, Nero asked his private secretary Epaphroditos to kill him.

"Although Nero's death had at first been welcomed with outbursts of joy," writes Tacitus, "it roused varying emotions, not only in the city among the senators and people and the city soldiery, but also among all the legions and generals, for the secret of empire was now revealed, that an emperor could be made elsewhere than at Rome."[38] As a result of the newly divulged secret, different legions continued to put forward their generals for the first position of the state, until one of those generals – Vespasian – had mastered the situation enough to stop the commotion.

The new dynasty founded by Vespasian hurried to dispel the harm to traditional Roman values that Nero had caused to the city and the world with his Golden House. Gold and pearls were confiscated and deposited in the state treasury, countless statues were distributed among temples and suburban villas, wild animals were probably auctioned off to circus managers. Praising these efforts, the poet Martial sucked up to the new rulers in words like these:

> Rome restored to herself! What were the delights of a tyrant,
> Now, under your rule, Caesar, belong to the people.

THE BATHS

A sprawling bath complex gradually grew over the footprint of the Golden House. The first bath buildings were hastily erected by the son of Vespasian, Titus (whose rule was brief, from 79 to 81 AD). He timed their inauguration with that of the Colosseum (indeed, one had to have a wash after a hot afternoon in the amphitheatre). The baths were possibly not built from scratch, but were actually refurbished and reconstructed baths of Nero's palace (the luxuries of the Golden House included hot and sulphurous springs). A huge granite bowl found in the ruins of the baths still stands in Vatican's Portico Belvedere.

The next stage in dismantling the memory of Nero and his palace was a good deal more radical. Archaeologists are uncertain about the exact time when it was launched – perhaps still under the Flavians (who were Vespasian, Titus and Domitian), perhaps later, under Trajan. A huge platform was set above the former Golden House, and a huge bath complex grew on that platform. These were the first Roman baths built on such a scale. They were located northeast of Titus's unprepossessing baths and oriented differently from all other buildings on the Oppian hill, at approximately 45-degree angle. The purpose was to maximise the exposure to the sun of the bath premises, especially the hottest rooms. This environmental principle was later used by other architects as well.

We will talk in more detail about baths and their importance in the life of ancient Romans when we reach the much better preserved Baths of Caracalla. As for the compound of imperial-era baths on the Oppian, they were called 'Baths of Trajan' until the 16th century, but then this attribution was forgotten, and people started to call them Baths of Titus. In the 16th century, the great architect Andrea Palladio made sketches of the surviving ruins. When Palladio worked on his sketches, and even when Charles Cameron was scouting the basements, the ruins were much more impressive than in the late 19th century, when the name of Trajan was restored to the baths. All that is visible today are a few exedras (semicircular constructions). Two of them, the north-eastern one (near Via Luigi Cremona) and the south-western one (near Viale Serapide) probably belonged to library buildings: in the 1990s, during excavations, niches and shelves were found on the walls – they could hold scrolls and manuscripts. A large distance between one wing of the library to the other was regular Roman practice, since libraries used to come in pairs, for Greek and Latin books.

Another amazing discovery was made during the same excavations. An underground passage (cryptoportico) was found under the south-western exedra. That was not surprising in itself, and not quite a new discovery – the passage was used for the production of saltpetre in the early 19th century, when Napoleon's troops were stationed in Rome. In 1997 the earth that had accumulated in the passage was removed, and a much earlier brick wall was found – dating back to Flavian or even Nero's times. The wall was painted with a fresco showing a port city. This painting, known as 'The painted city' (*città dipinta*), is unique for Classical antiquity. First of all, Greek and Roman artists preferred to paint mythological, rustic and wild landscapes; urban subjects did not move them. Second, the city on the fresco is empty. We see porticoes with sculptures, a theatre, fortified seaside docks, a huge gold statue ('a colossus'?) – and that's it. Quite possibly, this is not simply a work of art, but a depiction of a specific city, a map of sorts. (The nearest analogy might be the early Byzantine mosaic from Madaba in Jordan, showing a simplified view of Jerusalem.)

Which city is shown on the fresco? There was no lack of guesses: Ostia, the port of Rome? Antioch in Syria (now Antakya in Turkey)? Arelata in Gaul (now Arles in France)? Londinium in Britain (no need to translate)? We'll probably never know.

To the east of the baths (on the opposite side of Via delle Terme di Traiano) are the remains of a water supply system – not underwater plumbing, but giant reservoirs. To create pressure sufficient for this complex (Trajan's baths occupy an area of 25,000 square metres), cisterns had to be much higher than ground level. This is how Sette Sale ('Seven Halls') came about. The name is misleading: there are nine cisterns. Their orientation is different from that of the baths, and they were considered to be part of the Golden House, until the analysis of brick stamps had shown that they were, indeed, built under Trajan.

The engineering brilliance of the cisterns' design is impressive even for today. Openings for water flow in the walls are never in the same plane, to avoid unnecessary currents; the concrete-and-brick interior is covered with waterproof terracotta paste; the only function of the robust lower level is to support the upper one, which could hold up to eight million litres of water; all nine cisterns are of exactly the same width (5 metres 30 centimetres).

Trajan's Baths remained in function until the 5th or 6th century AD. In late antiquity, an opulent villa stood near Sette Sale; in the Middle Ages, one of the cisterns served as a cemetery, and more than a thousand skeletons were found there in the course of excavations.

LAOCOÖN

On January 14, 1506, farmer Felice de Freddis was ploughing his vineyard on the slope of the Esquiline when he stumbled upon a piece of marble protruding from the soil.

The news of the discovery quickly made it to the pope, who dispatched his court architect, Giuliano da Sangallo, to the site. Sangallo took along his 11-year-old son Francesco (who wrote an account of the events sixty years later) and the young Michelangelo Buonarotti, who during that period used to hang out at the Sangallos' all the time.

When the statue was unearthed, it turned out to depict a large bearded man and two youths, all writhing in the embrace of two giant snakes. Sangallo at once said: "This is Laocoön described by Pliny." Indeed, the polymath Pliny the Elder had mentioned a sculpture of Laocoön carved by three masters from the Greek island of Rhodes, which he considered the most perfect example of visual art.

Laocoön is a character in the Trojan myths, but he is not featured in Homer's *Iliad*. His star turn occurs in Book II of Virgil's *Aeneid*, when he tries to explain to his compatriots, who are completely taken in by the sight of the wooden horse, the dangers of trusting the Greeks, even when they bear gifts *(timeo Danaos et dona ferentes)*. To neutralise this unexpected resistance, the goddess Minerva (Athena) who roots for the Greeks sends two formidable serpents to take care of Laocoön and his two sons.

The newly discovered statue achieved star status in no time. Ten or fifteen years later, plaster, bronze and terracotta copies of Laocoön spread across the whole of Italy. When the interest in classical antiquity moved out of the antiquarian curiosity phase into serious scholarship (largely through the efforts of the Germans), Laocoön was cast in a star part again; he became a subject of works by G. E. Lessing, J. W. Goethe, and the father of art criticism J. J. Winckelmann. In the early 19th century, the sculpture made a brief journey to Paris as Napoleonic war booty, but was soon returned.

The archaeological circumstances of the find are poorly known: we do not know exactly where De Freddis's vineyard was; Sangallo Junior says "near Santa Maria Maggiore." Pliny is of little help, too: he says that Laocoön had stood "in the house of the emperor Titus," which could mean the Golden House (occupied by Titus for a while) or something else entirely.

The sculptural group found in 1506 was missing a few extremities, including the right arm of Laocoön himself. Michelangelo made a guess that Laocoön was holding that arm behind his neck, caught in the losing fight with the serpent. Pope Julius II launched a restoration competition with a jury presided over by Raphael. The winning version had an arm that was heroically raised above the head. It was in that posture that Laocoön remained known to the public for a few centuries.

In the early 20th century, archaeologist and curator Ludwig Pollak found (literally in a scrap yard) a piece of an ancient marble arm and thought that it might fit Laocoön. His guess was only checked in the 1950s, after Pollak had perished in Auschwitz, and the arm was a match. It turned out that it was, indeed, thrown behind the head, just as Michelangelo thought. The arm was returned to its proper place, restored extremities were removed, and now Laocoön and his sons stand in the Octagonal Court of the Vatican Museums in their original shape (excluding the missing hands and arms). However, there are lots of 'heroic' versions all over the world, based on the Renaissance reconstruction.

SAINT CLEMENT

St. Clement was one of the first successors to St. Peter as the bishop of Rome, that is to say, one of the first popes. Strangely enough, there is no official list of the popes with their ordinal numbers, which means that it is not exactly known whether Clement was the second, third, or fourth pope. Among early Christian writings, only an epistle to the Corinthians is reliably attributable to him, but it has the distinction of being one of the earliest Christian works which are not in the New Testament. St. Clement is worshipped by many Christian churches and is considered one of the 'apostolic fathers' – the few early Christians who were directly instructed by Christ's disciples.

> Clement was a popular name among the popes, they have used it fourteen times so far. The last of them, the Franciscan Giovanni Ganganelli, occupied the Holy See from 1769 to 1774.

The life of St. Clement is known mostly from the legends recorded a few centuries after his death, not before the 4th century. It was at that time that he was identified with the 'fellow labourer' of apostle Paul, mentioned in the Epistle to the Philippians: "help those women which laboured with me in the gospel, with Clement also, and with other my fellow labourers, whose names are in the book of life." It was claimed that Clement led an active and successful conversion campaign, provoking the ire of emperor Trajan (who was not otherwise known for atrocities or religious intolerance). The emperor banished Clement to the shores of the desolate Euxinus Pontus, to Chersonesus in Taurica (near today's Sebastopol in the Crimea). He was condemned to forced labour in the quarry. The convicts were suffering from thirst (a realistic touch: there is very little fresh water in the Crimea). When Clement saw a lamb on a mountain slope, he knelt, prayed, then climbed the mountain, struck it with his hammer, and a spring miraculously gushed out from the stones. Seeing the miracle, the exiles began converting to Christianity in droves; the enraged authorities further condemned Clement to be tied to an anchor and thrown into the sea. After that, the sea used to recede every year for a short time, uncovering the incorruptible relics of the saint.

St. Clement had a special relationship with the Slavic world, because it was St. Cyril (his secular name was Constantine), the inventor of Slavic writing, who had rediscovered his remains. He found the bones in Crimea in an abandoned cemetery and identified them by the anchor buried with them. Now the relics are kept in the church which is the subject of our story. One year after his return from the Crimea, St. Cyril died in Rome. His brother and colleague Methodius wanted to take his remains home to Thessaloniki, but ended up burying them in the same church. The relics of St. Cyril were lost at the turn of the 19th century, and a fragment was recovered and returned only in the 1960s. John Paul II, himself a Slav, came to the resting place of St. Cyril to pray for Slavic countries.

St. Clement, pope of Rome. An eastern Orthodox icon

The Cyrillic alphabet is used for a number of Slavic languages. Most people recognise Cyrillic as the Russian script, but it is also used by Ukrainian, Belarusan, Bulgarian, Macedonian, and Serbian – though Serbian is one of those rare languages that officially use two scripts, in this case Cyrillic and Latin. Through the influence of the Soviet Union during the Communist era, use of the alphabet spread to a number of other languages of Eurasia, none of them Slavic (Mari, Buryat, Tatar, Kazakh and many others). The alphabet is named after St. Cyril, but, counter-intuitively, Cyrillic is not what Cyril and Methodius invented. They were Greeks with sound knowledge of a Slavic dialect spoken locally near their birthplace in Thessaloniki (historically the Macedon of Alexander the Great), and were dispatched to Great Moravia (now in the Czech Republic) to evangelise local Slavs. Upon arrival, the brothers found that their prospective flock spoke no Greek or Latin. They decided to translate the most important Christian books into Slavic, and invented an entirely new script for this purpose. It is called Glagolitic (or *Glagolitsa*), from the Slavic word for, well, 'word.' Later, however, most Slavs adopted either a modified Latin or a modified Greek script, and the latter gradually transformed into what is known today as Cyrillic. Glagolitic continued to be used in religious contexts, in some regions (notably in Croatia) up to the 19th century.

Contrary to popular perception, Cyrillic is quite easy – along with Greek and Latin scripts, it ultimately stems from the same Western Semitic (Phoenician) alphabet which was the origin of most European alphabets of the last three millennia.

St. Clement's church (or, to be exact, basilica) is a palimpsest, that is to say, a number of layers belonging to different eras that overlie without completely destroying one another. The lowest level is occupied by a Roman house of Republican times, burned down, apparently, in the fire of 64 AD. A rich 1st-century house was built upon it, with a large square courtyard inside. Tradition connects this house to the politician Titus Flavius Clemens.

The Clemens in question was a consul (an honorary but decorative function in imperial times) and a relative of emperor Domitian. He is often mentioned as the first Christian senator and martyr (Domitian had him executed for 'atheism and drifting into Jewish ways,' which almost certainly indicates Christian sympathies). There were even some attempts to identify him with St. Clemens, not very successfully. An ingenious version makes St. Clemens, of Jewish origin, a slave and later freedman of Clemens the consul. Indeed, Roman freedmen, on gaining their freedom, adopted the name of their former master, though it was not the cognomen (Clemens in this case), but the first two names, praenomen and nomen; that means that a freedman would have been called Titus Flavius and preserved his own name, Greek, Jewish, or whatever, as his cognomen.

(glagolitic inscription in the cathedral of Zagreb)

(the prayer "Ave Maria")

A simpler house stood next to the opulent one – a residential insula; its basement is also under St. Clement's basilica now. In the late 2nd and early 3rd century, the basement was used for meetings by adherents of another Eastern cult, Mithraism (we will cover this mysterious religion in more detail in another chapter, but it should be noted that the mithraeum under St. Clement's is the most accessible and best preserved among the Roman mithraea).

The basilica has stood on this spot since the 4th century, if not earlier. In 1084 it was sacked and burned by the invading Normans, but it was restored already in the early 12th century and preserved more or less intact since then. Unfortunately, its austere mediaeval aspect was spoiled by frivolous gilded stucco added by Pope Clement XI, elected to the pontificate on St. Clement's name day in 1700.

However, the lower church with its amazing old frescoes gives a very good idea of Christian art of the late antiquity and early Middle Ages. One of the niches of the right wing holds a unique Byzantine Holy Virgin (it might have initially been a portrait of the empress Theodora) and an unusual cleanly shaven Christ. In the forechurch are 11th-century frescoes: one of them depicts St. Clement's miracle in the Crimea, another, the arrival (the official term is 'translation') of St. Cyril's relics to Rome.

When Roman Catholicism was virtually outlawed in England under Charles II, Catholic priests fled to the Continent in droves from all the parts of the country (including Ireland). Irish Dominicans found refuge with Pope Urban VIII, who handed St. Clement's basilica over to them. In the 19th century, Father Joseph Mullooly, superior of San Clemente, conducted the first thorough archaeological research into the lower levels of the basilica, and found the sanctuary of Mithra among other things. Father Mullooly was devoted to his church: when Garibaldi's revolutionary forces took Rome in 1848, he defended San Clemente and its artefacts even after the pope had fled the Vatican. His 1873 book "Saint Clement, Pope and Martyr, and His Basilica in Rome" remains an important source to this day. As recently as the 1950s, the Dominicans preferred to conduct excavations in the church themselves, with some help from young Italian archaeologists.

LUDUS MAGNUS

Ludus Magnus, the gladiatorial school, may be observed from either Via San Giovanni in Laterano or Via Labicana. Next to the Colosseum its ruins are not that impressive, and yet the training arena whose half-oval is easily discernible (the other half is concealed beneath the pavement and neighbouring buildings) is just as big as the average arena of a provincial amphitheatre. There are two kinds of ruins around it: first, spectators' seats with a capacity of about three thousand people, and, second, small cells of gladiators' barracks.

Historians and Roman buffs had many qualms about Ridley Scott's 2000 movie *Gladiator* (though, frankly, I find exposing historical errors in film and literature a fool's errand). And yet, one of the most improbable plot lines, the one about the emperor who personally fights in the arena, is based on real events. The real Commodus (who ruled from 180 to 192 AD) was strangled in his own bath, not stabbed by Russell Crowe in the Colosseum, but historians say that by the end of his reign he had completely neglected the affairs of the state and was only interested in gladiatorial profession. He even expressed a wish (and possibly acted upon it) to move from the imperial palace to the barracks. One of the tiny cells around the Ludus Magnus arena might have housed the half-mad emperor.

Historians write that Commodus fought in the Colosseum's arena many times, steadily winning every fight (of course, it was mortally dangerous not to play into the emperor's hands). He was especially fond of animal hunts. He hired the best coaches to instruct him in archery and javelin-throwing, and mastered those skills to such a degree that he easily struck lions, ostriches, elephants and other exotic beasts with one blow. The historian Herodian claims that during one of his shows he hurled one hundred javelins at a pack of one hundred lions and killed each of them dead without a single miss. It should be noted that Commodus performed his exploits from a specially constructed terrace, where he was safe from the beasts and displayed, according to the same historian, "skill rather than courage."

It was the emperor Domitian who surrounded the Colosseum with gladiatorial schools. There were four of them. Ludus Magnus was, obviously, the biggest; a special underground passage connected it to the Colosseum, which meant that gladiators could dash onto the arena right from their barracks. Ludus Gallicus and Ludus Dacicus were named after communities of gladiators from their respective provinces. Finally, Ludus Matutinus ('the morning school'), as almost all books say, was meant for handling wild animals. This conclusion is based on the fact that animal hunts were mostly scheduled before noon, before gladiators' fights – but, of course, there might have been many other reasons to call the school a morning one.

The primary definition of the Latin word *ludus* is 'play, game, diversion,' while the Greek *schole*, the source of our word 'school', means 'leisure.' Serious educational institutions have rather light-hearted roots.

META SUDANS

There is a circle overgrown with grass directly behind the Arch of Constantine. It is the trace of a monument called *Meta Sudans*, 'the sweating meta.' What is a meta and why is it sweating?

In Latin, *meta* means any kind of boundary or signpost, and this meaning is further extended to the conical turning-post in the circus (hippodrome), which the chariots must skirt without crushing into it. The meta near the Colosseum was shaped like the circus meta and it marked the boundary of a few city neighbourhoods – four (perhaps even five) of the 14 urban regions of Augustus met near the Colosseum. It might have even served as an actual turning post, because on that spot triumphal processions changed their course and embarked upon the homestretch toward the Capitol.

Now why is it sweating? In English and most modern European languages, the word 'sweat' is associated with something clammy, smelly and unpleasant. The Latin word is neutral, able to function in poetic contexts; Catullus writes about "a pine with sweating bark" (*sudanti cortice pinum*). If a fountain 'sweats,' it means that its waters do not gush out of it, but slowly trickle down its conical slope. The phrase *meta sudans* did not mean this fountain specifically, but all fountains of that type; it is known that a similar 'meta' had stood in the resort town of Baiae, and a later one, dated to the 3rd century AD, still stands at Djemila in Algeria.

Meta Sudans. Reconstruction.

The meta in Rome had stood for a long time. Sprays of water and glistening marble were long gone, but as recently as 1930s its brick-and-concrete core was still towering in the original place. Mussolini's master plan called for a road junction near the Colosseum, and the meta was in the way; it was removed, and a memorial plaque was installed in its place. In the 1980s, excavations uncovered some underground structures, which probably had to do with water supply to the fountain. In the mid-1990s Mussolini's roundabout was abolished and the whole area around the amphitheatre was pedestrianised. It turns out that the skeleton of the ancient fountain was needlessly removed.

THE COLOSSUS OF NERO

On the other side of the Colosseum, with more than half of it buried by the Via dei Fori Imperiali, is the foundation of another monument that does not survive. It was excavated in 1828, but more than a hundred years later Mussolini erased what little of it remained in the course of the same transport reconstruction of the square. It was the place where Rome's largest statue, the Colossus of Nero, had once stood.

Actually, its initial position was elsewhere, in front of the Golden House entrance. We know for a fact that during the rule of the emperor Hadrian the colossus was obstructing the projected space for the Temple of Venus and Roma, so it had to be moved. The moving distance was short, but the size and weight of the statue were such that Hadrian's engineers had to employ no fewer than 24 elephants for the task. The original foundation of the colossus may still be concealed under the church of Santa Francesca Romana.

The statue was created, on a commission from Nero, by the sculptor called Zenodorus. The name is Greek, but he was mostly famed for a monumental statue of Mercury in Gaul, and it was thanks to that new wonder that Nero invited the promising artisan to Rome.

There are many contradictory pieces of evidence in classical sources that mention the Colossus of Nero. The most detailed account is from Pliny the Elder. He seems to indicate that the sculptor made the statue's face resemble Nero's, but later it was changed into a more abstract visage of 'the indomitable Sun' (*Sol Invictus*). Later authors say that the head of the colossus was changed more than once – from Nero to Sun-god or perhaps the emperor Titus, then to Commodus as Hercules, then back again. It is possible that Zenodorus didn't assemble the huge bronze statue in his workshop, but right on the spot, forging it piece by piece from bottom up. In any case, that was the technology described by one Greek author when he wrote about the Colossus of Rhodes. This explains the move involving 24 elephants: a statue assembled that way cannot be disassembled and moved piecemeal.

In this case, however, a period of four years from the arrival of Zenodorus in Rome to Nero's suicide would not have been enough to complete the task. That would mean that the colossus was completed under the Flavians, and its face was changed before it was ever put in place. A more ingenious guess is that the statue had depicted a sun god all along, and any similarity to persons living or dead was only imagined by contemporaries.

How tall Nero's colossus was is another riddle. Pliny's text is corrupted at this point. Other sources cite figures that are consistent enough; it seems the colossus was about 30 metres high (to put this in perspective, Nelson's

Column in Trafalgar Square is just above 50 metres). The rays of the sun crown on the colossus's head were 6 to 7 metres long. The satirist Martial possibly writes about this statue (in the original he calls it 'the Palatine colossus') when mocking a girl of Amazon stature:

> *At the Coloss imperial thou might'st laugh,*
> *Claudia, if shorter by a foot and half.*[39]

Until recently, the tallest statue in the world was "The Motherland Calls" by Yevgeny Vuchetich (87 metres), a statue commemorating the Battle of Stalingrad. But starting with the late 1980s, a number of much taller statues were built in various Asian countries. At the time of writing, the crown is held by Spring Temple Buddha, 128 metres tall, in the Chinese province of Lushan.

Ancient colossi

What did the colossus look like? Unfortunately, the souvenir trade in small-scale copies of famous monuments had not been invented or, at least, no examples of it have survived. We know the most majestic sculptures of antiquity, such as the Colossus of Rhodes or the famous Zeus in Olympia, only by descriptions. The Colossus of Nero falls almost in the same category; almost, but not quite, because we have the likeness of that monument on coins. Their testimony indicates that the Colossus was a naked man who stood propping himself on a column with his one hand, and held a ship's rudder, a symbol of the goddess Fortuna, in the other.

The latest evidence of Nero's colossus still standing dates to 354 AD. Whether it fell during the sack of Rome by the Gothic hordes of Alaric, or during one of the numerous earthquakes of the 5th century is not known, but by the Middle Ages it was certainly dismembered for scrap metal.

This poses an interesting question about a well-known quotation. It is often attributed to the Venerable Bede, an English monk of the 8th century, but, most likely, its real author is some other Anglo-Saxon who made a pilgrimage to Rome (Bede seemed not to have ever ventured to the Continent). It goes like this: *Quamdiu stabit Colyseus, stabit et Roma; quando cadet Colyseus, cadet Roma; quando cadet Roma, cadet et mundus.* In *Childe Harold's Pilgrimage*, Lord Byron offers an exact translation:

"While stands the Coliseum, Rome shall stand;
When falls the Coliseum, Rome shall fall;
And when Rome falls—the World." From our own land
Thus spake the pilgrims o'er this mighty wall
In Saxon times…

Most scholars agree that the 'Colyseus' of this quotation is not the amphitheatre (it was not called that in classical times, not even once), but Nero's Colossus; when the statue did fall, the pragmatic Romans simply transferred the name to the nearest large structure. And yet, in the 8th century, when the English pilgrims made their observation, there was certainly no colossus left standing. Perhaps they did mean the amphitheatre after all, and, if we are to take their prophecy at face value, the world should take great care of the Colosseum.

Before we end the chapter with a close look at the most famous of all Roman monuments, let us inspect its current nearest neighbour, the Arch of Constantine. It is one of the oddest and most controversial structures of Imperial times.

ARCH OF CONSTANTINE

First of all, architecture historians and archaeologists have not reached a unanimous conclusion about the date of its construction. This might seem strange: over each of the small archways in the upper part of the arch there are inscriptions that say *VOTIS X* and *SIC X*, meaning, approximately, "In honour of the tenth anniversary." Constantine celebrated the tenth anniversary of his rule in 315 AD – it was in 306, after the death of his father Constantius, that the British legions in Eboracum (York) proclaimed him emperor. (Yes, it is nine years from 306 to 315, but the Romans counted anniversaries from the beginning of the year in question, not its end, so this tallies up.)

And yet, whenever scaffolding embraces the arch, and scholars embark on new research, arguments flare up again. After all, why couldn't Constantine use an existing arch for his purposes, the way he turned a few of his predecessors into himself (more on that later)? The problem is exacerbated by a complete absence of the Arch of Constantine from any written sources of Classical antiquity. Experts had made various guesses: that the arch was erected under Marcus Aurelius, even under Domitian. Most historians agree to date it to the time of Constantine himself, but this attribution is not set in stone, so to speak.

Recently, art historians of the world were shocked to hear that the famous Capitoline Wolf, long considered to be an Etruscan statue of the 5th–4th centuries BC (except for the twins, which were added during the Renaissance) was in fact a much later mediaeval work, possibly dating to the 13th century. Though the Italian researchers were pretty sure about their conclusions (based on complex material analysis, moulding technique and spectrography), it was not widely advertised, and most guidebooks and museum booklets still list the Lupa as a genuine Etruscan statue.

Such controversies are rarely settled with 100% certainty, and many ancient artifacts will keep their shroud of mystery for a long time to come.

Even an untrained eye will easily spot the difference between reliefs and sculptures on the arch – from the intensely realistic barbarians of the upper tier to the schematically flat reliefs above the side spans. The Arch of Constantine is a hodgepodge of fragments from different styles and eras that struggle to form a coherent whole. The word *spolia* that means spoils or trophies began to be used in the 16th century for fragments of structures or architectural decoration that were reused in a new context. Rome is chock-full of such examples, but even in Roman terms, the Arch of Constantine is in a class of its own, deserving the nickname *cornacchia d'Esopo* (Aesop's magpie).

This peculiarity of the arch made it an easy target for the fans of high art. Raphael was among the first to be disparaging about it; in his report on ancient monuments compiled for Pope Leo X circa 1519, he wrote:

Although literature, sculpture, painting, and almost all the other arts had long been declining and had grown worse and worse until the time of the last emperors, architecture was still studied and practised according to the good rules and buildings were erected in the same style as before... Of this there are many evidences: among others, the Arch of Constantine, which is well designed and well-built as far as architecture is concerned. But the sculptures of the same arch are very feeble and destitute of all art and good design. Those, however, that come from the spoils of Trajan and Antoninus Pius are extremely fine and done in perfect style.[40]

So what does this DIY arch consist of? Let us try and be thorough. On the upper tier, on both wide sides – northern and southern – stand barbarian captives, four men on each side. The fact that they are barbarians is evident from their sullen postures, bizarre headwear and especially trousers. The barbarians, carved from light-coloured Italian marble and partially restored, are taken from some monument of Trajan's time, perhaps from Trajan's forum, which means that they are most likely Dacians.

Two upper reliefs on the shorter sides of the arch and two more on the inner sides of the central span also date back to Trajan's campaigns. These four fragments are of identical size; they used to be parts of a monumental relief band, known as the Great Trajanic Frieze. This frieze had probably adorned the Basilica Ulpia. The principal motif of these reliefs is the death and humiliation of enemies under the hooves of Roman horses. On each of the four fragments we see at least one barbarian, either smashed by the cavalry charge or humbly bowed before the victors. A little later we will see how these images fit into Constantine's ideological agenda.

One tier lower there are eight roundels, four on each side. When art historians made out the faces of Antinous (the young favourite of emperor Hadrian) and Antoninus Pius, Hadrian's successor, they decided that the roundels were taken from an unknown monument of Hadrianic time (Raphael ascribed them to the time of Antoninus Pius). We do not see Hadrian himself on these reliefs, because his face was recarved into a likeness of Constantine.

The roundels alternate in a strict sequence: hunt, sacrifice, hunt, sacrifice. On the southern side (if you are looking at it, the Colosseum is a little to the right in front of you) the emperor first goes hunting; another character (headless) holds a horse by the bridles, another, suspiciously underdressed, leads a dog on a leash. The next scene is a sacrifice to the forest god Silvanus (Pan); if you look carefully, you will see its permanent attribute, the syrinx (also known as Pan flute, pipes of increasing length), in the branches of the tree. Then follows a poorly preserved roundel with bear hunt (apparently bears were smallish in Classical times). After that there is a sacrifice to Diana, the hunter goddess.

On the northern side (the Colosseum is behind your left shoulder) the first scene is a very dynamic boar hunt (the boar is, on the contrary, gigantic). After that is a roundel with the calmest and most harmonic composition, a sacrifice to Apollo. A lion hunt scene follows. Or, rather, the hunt is over, and a very exhausted lion is lying under the hunters' feet. This is the only roundel where something else other than the emperor's head was modified; one can easily notice that on all other roundels the characters are standing on an unadorned straight line, and here they stand on a lion, which was added in Constantine's time. The faces are, however, those of Hadrian's entourage: in the background is Antoninus Pius, to the right, with a horse, is Antinous. Finally, on the rightmost image the whole crowd sacrifices to Hercules. Note the porphyry background of the two last roundels – this precious stone had been long stripped down from the other six.

Porphyry is igneous rock whose composition is close to that of granite. It is unimpressive in its raw form, but when polished, it acquires a noble burgundy hue. In ancient Roman times the only known porphyry mine was in Egypt, and the fad for this material was also of Egyptian origin. The sarcophagi of Helena, the mother of Constantine, and his daughter Constantia, kept at the Vatican Museums, are made of porphyry. Another famous example is the tomb of Napoleon at Les Invalides in Paris – but this porphyry was not sourced in Egypt; instead, the stone came from Karelia in Northwestern Russia.

One hypothesis claims that the Hadrianic roundels are not spoils from some other monument, but parts of the arch's original décor, and that the arch – at least up to the roundel tier – was actually built under Hadrian.

On the upper tier there are eight reliefs (two double panels on the northern and southern sides) depicting Germanic campaigns of Marcus Aurelius. They might have been taken from two lost triumphal arches which Commodus, the lover of gladiatorial entertainment, erected in his father's honour. On the southern side, the enemy leader is brought to the emperor; then, unceremoniously, other captives; in the next frame, the emperor addresses the troops with a morale-boosting speech (a ceremony known as *adlocutio*), and then, also in military settings, a solemn procession leads smallish animals – a pig, a sheep and a bull – to be sacrificed. This procedure is called *suovetaurilia*, from *sus* 'swine,' *ovis* (sheep, as in 'ovine') and *taurus* 'bull.'

On the northern side the emperor arrives at a city in a ceremonial procession and then, no less ceremoniously, sets off for war. The last two reliefs show a procedure of handing out money to the people and – again – the surrender of an enemy leader (only this time the emperor is standing on a pediment, which makes his superiority even more tangible). Just as with the Hadrianic reliefs, the emperor here is recarved into Constantine.

Finally – the long relief of a Constantinian date, encircling the whole arch. It begins on the western side (the Colosseum is in front of you, on your left): the troops depart for the campaign. It continues on the southern side (the Colosseum is in front of you, on your right): the siege of a city, most likely Verona. A little further to the right is the tipping point of Constantine's life and career, the Battle of the Milvian Bridge: the enemies crumble under the assault of the victorious army and drown in the river; the trumpeters of the vanquished sound the call for retreat. On the eastern side of the arch (the Colosseum is behind your back, on the right), Constantine's army triumphantly marches into Rome. On the northern side (the Colosseum is behind your back, on the left) we see the emperor busy with peacetime things: addressing the nation from the rostra, handing out money (on these two reliefs, the emperor's head is missing). The lateral sides of the arch have two more roundels of the same time with sun and moon, and some more allegorical figures in the spandrels.

It is hard to disagree with Raphael while contemplating the Constantinian frieze. After the life-like realism and exquisite composition of early reliefs, the comic strip about Constantine's deeds and victories seems primitive: the carving is shallow, proportions are off, no individual features anywhere, the horses are dog-sized, all scenes are stretched across a flat surface without a hint of depth or perspective. And yet, one can see them differently: yes, the classical plasticity is gone, but there is focus, ideology, a foreboding of a new era in these reliefs. The Arch of Constantine is a monument where antiquity metamorphoses into the Middle Ages.

To better understand why Constantine's time was such a watershed, let us read the inscription about the main span of the arch (it is identical on both sides):

THE SENATE AND PEOPLE OF ROME DEDICATED THIS ARCH, DISTINGUISHED BY HIS TRIUMPHS, TO IMPERATOR CAESAR FLAVIUS CONSTANTINUS MAXIMUS PIUS FELIX AUGUSTUS, FOR HAVING HIS ARMY, WITH DIVINE PROMPTING AND GREATNESS OF MIND, AVENGED THE STATE WITH RIGHTEOUS ARMS AT ONCE AGAINST BOTH THE TYRANT AND HIS ENTIRE FACTION.[41]

What is carved in stone is rarely incidental. Using the methods of 'monumental propaganda,' Constantine here broadcasts at least three very important things. First, he calls his former co-ruler and rival in factional strife, Maxentius, 'a tyrant,' while old reliefs on the arch indicate that the insubordinate shall be dealt with summarily: they are basically no better than barbarians. Second, Constantine styles himself an avenger of the state (*res publica*), in an almost Augustan manner. Finally, and most interestingly, he touches upon the subject of supernatural reasons for his victory with outstanding diplomatic skill and caution.

Whether Constantine was a Christian, whether he was ever baptised, whether his baptism, if it happened, was orthodox and valid – these issues have been hotly debated by both church and secular historians for centuries. Be that as it may, in the early 4th century any perspicacious politician knew that the new religion was there to stay, and it was impossible to act as if it did not exist. Unlike traditional Roman paganism, Christianity was not tolerant of other religions. At the same time, the millennium-long pagan tradition could not be simply tossed aside, not by the Romans with their passion for all things ancient. That is why the inscription does not say *diis faventibus* ('through the benevolence of the gods') or something like that, but vaguely refers to *instinctu divinitatis* ('divine prompting'). At the same time, Constantine, even though he is remodelled from previous emperors, offers pagan sacrifices and does other things typical of a Roman ruler. We do not see any bishops or Christian symbols on the arch – which is, of course, only a matter of time. The Arch of Constantine, in a sense, concludes the architectural history of Ancient Rome.

On the eve of the Battle of the Milvian Bridge, which took place on October 28, 312, Constantine had a vision, and then an explanatory dream instructing him to use a certain symbol. We know the story from an account of the Greek-speaking historian Eusebius of Caesarea, so the instruction also came down to us in Greek: *en toutoi nika*. It was usually translated into Latin as *in hoc signo vinces* ('in this sign thou shalt conquer').

In the so-called Room of Constantine of the Vatican Palace there is a large fresco completed by Raphael's pupils and collaborators after the artist's sketches when he died. It is called The Vision of the Cross, and it shows a very dramatic demonstration of a fiery cross to the numerous troops. To avoid confusion, a large ray with a Greek instruction emanates from the vision as well. However, the use of a cross as a Christian emblem only became established later; if Constantine had actually used a symbol of the new religion, it would have been the Greek monogram of the two first letters of the word 'Christ,' Chi-Rho (XP).

THE ARENA

"It is no fiction, but plain, sober, honest Truth, to say: so suggestive and distinct is it at this hour: that, for a moment – actually in passing in – they who will, may have the whole great pile before them, as it used to be, with thousands of eager faces staring down into the arena, and such a whirl of strife, and blood, and dust going on there, as no language can describe. Its solitude, its awful beauty, and its utter desolation, strike upon the stranger the next moment, like a softened sorrow; and never in his life, perhaps, will he be so moved and overcome by any sight, not immediately connected with his own affections and afflictions."

Thus wrote Charles Dickens in 1846 in his travelogue titled "Pictures from Italy." In the century and a half that elapsed since the heyday of Queen Victoria, we have got used to gigantic structures, and yet the Colosseum still has the power to amaze – perhaps not so much with sheer size (though that, too, remains a factor) as with the pressing question – how did they do it?

THE WALLS

To appreciate the scale and structure of the Colosseum, walk around it. Start from the western side, where the Arch of Constantine stands (and where the Meta Sudans and the Colossus of Nero no longer stand). Walk counterclockwise. It is important to remember that only on the side you are passing now – on the north – the external wall of the amphitheatre survives. Look at it closely, and you will see that the upper, fourth tier is distinct from the lower three: it looks less elaborate, it is made from stone of a different colour, and there are no arches in it, only windows in every other section (there used to be decorative shields between the windows). This tier was constructed somewhat later than the first three.

Now look at the columns, which are different in each tier. They belong to the down-to-earth Tuscan order in the lowest tier; in Roman times, it was associated with hoary and noble antiquity. One level higher, we see the elegant Ionic order (which is not often found in Rome), then the Corinthian. Such a sequence says a lot about the structure of the whole building. The Tuscan order of the lower tier (which is very similar to the Doric order of the Greeks) exudes robustness and readiness to bear weight. The Ionic is elegant rather than powerful, which is why it decorates the middle tier, whose proportions are the most delicate. Finally, the ornate Corinthian order offers a touch of lightness to the third tier. This Colosseum sequence was adopted by architects from the Renaissance times on whenever they needed to decorate a multi-tier façade.

Moving further along the outer wall, you will reach the spot where it ends. You will not miss it: at that point, the wall of the monument is supported by a huge brick buttress which protects it from crumbling. The erection of this support in 1807 at the expense of the Vatican was one of the first examples of architecture conservation in history.

Disregarding the buttress, this is where the signs of antiquity have best persevered. The entrances are numbered above the arches (the numbers from LI to LIV, that is from 51 to 54, are especially clear), under your feet is a piece of ancient pavement, and if you look right, you will see large stone bollards. They used to encircle the whole amphitheatre, but only these five survive. Their purpose is not completely clear. They could be used to fix the ropes that hoisted a sun protection awning above the seats; perhaps chains were attached to them to mark a protective boundary around the site as a means of crowd control.

Greek and Roman columns. Upper row: Tuscan and Doric order; middle row: Ionic order; lower row: Corinthian and composite order

The external wall collapsed in the 14th century after an earthquake, and the stones were quickly ransacked for various construction purposes. When you walk further, you will be seeing things not originally intended to be seen – the interior of the amphitheatre, its 'cross-section.' This is why that wall is bereft of columns or decorations; the numerous holes are the places where separate stone blocks were fastened with metal clamps. Metal was a precious and rare commodity in the Middle Ages, and the clamps were removed, but, apparently, their protective function was redundant: the structure remained standing without them.

On the western side of the Colosseum there is another buttress, also dating from the 19th century (1852), but less monumental.

The Colosseum (for the sake of convenience we will use the common name, even though the amphitheatre was not called that in antiquity, not even once) was built in the late 70s and early 80s of the 1st century AD, during the rule of the Flavian dynasty. Since time immemorial, a large stone block commemorating a restoration of the 5th century had been lying in the arena. Recently, archaeologists scrutinised the stone and found that the commemorative inscription was made above a previous one, and that older inscription could be reconstructed using the positions of holes holding bronze letters. The reconstruction yielded this: EMPEROR CAESAR VESPASIAN ORDERED A NEW AMPHITHEATRE TO BE BUILT USING MONEY FROM MILITARY SPOILS. The reconstruction is suspiciously neat, which threw off some of the experts. If it is true, though, it only confirms what historians had been suspecting all along: Vespasian and his sons used the untold looted riches of Jerusalem to finance the Colosseum.

The amphitheatre was dedicated (apparently under Titus) with unprecedented pomp and circumstance, admiringly remembered long after. There were gladiatorial fights and animal hunts, with five thousand animals killed. This brings us to one of the Colosseum's riddles.

Some ancient authors, notably Cassius Dio and Suetonius, claim that mock naval battles were staged at the Colosseum, including its inauguration days. Titus, Dio says, suddenly flooded the arena with water where specially trained horses and bulls performed, followed by a re-enactment of the famous battle that had precipitated the Peloponnesian War, that of the Corcyreans and Corinthians. Many popular guidebooks will tell you, without going into too much detail, that the Colosseum could have been almost instantly transformed into a pool.

But the amphitheatre whose ruins survive could not be flooded. Under the arena lies a *hypogeum*, a complex substructure of passageways, cells and lifts about six metres deep, which made spectacular appearances of huge packs of lions and similar marvels possible. The hypogeum was constructed not later than under Domitian, and it would have made any flooding impossible (also, even without the hypogeum, flooding the arena with all the available capacity of the nearby Aqua Claudia would have taken about an hour, which is not quite 'instant'). It is well documented that other locations, such as an Augustan pond a bit outside the city constructed specifically for the purpose were used for *'naumachia'* (mock sea battles), but the Colosseum might have not, and Cassius Dio, writing a century after the inauguration, could have mixed up the venues.

The amphitheatre offered the Romans spectacles of two principal types: gladiatorial fights and animal hunts. Each of those had lots of subtypes and versions, and the boundaries between them were fuzzy, and yet they were two distinct kinds of shows.

Let us have a look at the gladiators first.

THE GLADIATORS

Gladiatorial fights were not a native Roman custom; like many other things, it was adopted from neighbouring tribes, probably from Etruscans. The Etruscans with their focused and serious attitude to death used to organize fights between armed warriors during the funerals of their noblemen; the main weapon was a sword (*gladius* in Latin). It was a version of a funerary sacrifice: without excessive bloodshed, the spirit of the deceased could not hope for a decent life beyond the grave. The connection of gladiatorial fights with commemoration of the dead had held for a long time. When in 65 BC Julius Caesar presented to the awe-struck Romans 320 pairs of gladiators in armour of silver-plated bronze, it was at funeral games in honour of his father – dead for twenty years by that time.

Etruscan funeral games. Tomb painting

Even language preserved the memory of the fights' sepulchral origin: theatre and racecourse performances were simply called *ludi*, 'games,' while gladiatorial performances (and their spinoff, the animal hunts) were *munus* (commonly *munera*, in the plural). This word could take many meanings, including 'obligation,' 'offering,' 'duty,' 'gift.'

During the late Republic and early Empire, gladiatorial fights became a veritable showbiz industry. Gladiators lived and trained in purpose-built barracks (one of them, Ludus Magnus, we have just seen) under the guidance of a manager called *lanista*. The job of a lanista was not respectable – a lanista fared no better on the social scale than a pimp – but it was quite profitable. Technically, only slaves could fight in the arena; volunteers from the equestrian or even senatorial order had to renounce their freedom formally before taking up the sword; evidence of such cases is contradictory and muddled. Of course, in the case of emperors everyone was prepared to look the other way. Commodus was by far the most enthusiastic among them, but certainly not the only one; even the eccentric and intellectual Claudius fought a whale who was confined in a narrow pool.

The evidence of gladiators' life suffers from the lopsided nature of our sources: literary works that came down to us were almost exclusively written by upper-class men, which is why we know of emperor gladiators (which is thrilling, but a mere curiosity), we know something of the spectators' impressions (our authors, especially if they are Christian, often condemn the carnage, but describe it with sadistic thoroughness). The impressions of the simple folk are known primarily from Pompeian graffiti, while gladiators themselves speak to us only from their tombstones.

This makes our knowledge of such exciting subjects as the social and ethnic composition of the gladiator world, as well as its economic side, very scanty. The gladiatorial pool was fed by the influx of captives (initially armed fighters of different kinds were called by the names of hostile peoples – Samnite, Gaul, Fracian) and sentenced criminals (who could be sent to fight in the arena or simply to be mauled by wild beasts).

It is hard to estimate the number of people who fought for the money, glory and adrenaline rush – the number of professionals in a deadly job. It is even harder to evaluate a gladiator's chances of surviving a fight. That, of course, hung on specific circumstances: rivals, luck, the mood of the crowd, which could demand that a defeated gladiator be either dealt a final blow or spared. (Apparently, the spectators indicated their decision by turning their thumbs, but it is not known *how* they turned it; the idea of a downturned thumb meaning 'finish off' is pure speculation.) Games 'without mercy' (*sine missione*) meant that the organisers were prepared to splurge: recruiting and training new gladiators was a very costly affair. Some got lucky: tombstones claim that there were gladiators with a hundred or more fights under their belt (if those are not cases of exaggerated bragging). Such figures, however, are very rare, and it is clear that surviving twenty games was a massive stroke of luck.

In spite of their low social status, gladiators were insanely popular and easily became pop stars and sex idols of their day. The satirist Juvenal mocks a noble lady who ran away from her senator husband with a gladiator, who was not young, or handsome, who was disfigured in fights, but he was a gladiator, which explained everything. "They love the blade," remarks the poet with completely deliberate Freudian suggestiveness.

In a video commercial from 2004, Pink, Beyoncé and Britney Spears strut out onto the Colosseum arena, but instead of fighting they launch into a rendition of *We Will Rock You*, secure for themselves the emperor's stash of Pepsi and accidentally hurl the emperor himself to the lions. This is an example of gladiatorial and arena symbolism preserving their commercial value after almost two millennia.

Did women fight in the arena, though? Cassius Dio says that they did even at the inauguration ceremonies ('women of no importance,' he adds hastily). There is a relief from the Eastern Roman Empire in the British Museum, which depicts two unmistakeable women in a staged fight.

ANIMAL HUNTS

Animal hunts grew in popularity simultaneously with gladiatorial contests. In austere Republican times, wild beasts were used only during springtime fertility holidays. For the Cerealia, foxes with torches attached to their tails were released into the city; for the Floralia, hares and does were allowed to run wild in the circus (not the amphitheatre – there was no permanent amphitheatre in Rome at the time).

The hunts (*venatio*, plural *venationes*) gave game sponsors a chance to show various animals to the Roman public and boost their own popularity. The offering was huge; spectators were shown virtually the whole fauna of the inhabited world, with an emphasis on exotic beasts. The main supplier of those was North Africa. In the years of the Colosseum shows, the audiences saw elephants, rhinoceros, camels, giraffes, hippos, ostriches, aurochs, elks, leopards, antelopes of every kind, and, of course, countless lions, tigers, bears and boars.

In 1850, a young hippo was delivered to the London Zoo in Regent's Park – the first hippopotamus in Europe since Roman times. His journey from the shores of the Nile to those of the Thames was long and arduous, expensive and fraught with security and logistic problems (a whole herd of cows was necessary to provide milk to the beast in transit). It is still unclear how the Romans managed to perform such feats on a regular basis, with their inferior technology, navigation and zoology skills. Most likely, the majority of animals died on the way. Environmental damage inflicted by Roman shows on the provinces, especially in Africa, was huge, and its consequences have never been overcome.

When Cicero was the governor of Cilicia, a province in Asia Minor, his friend and relation Caelius Rufus pestered him with requests for panthers. Rufus had just won the elections and was eager to set up an appropriately lavish performance. Cicero was consistently evasive: panthers, he wrote back, are now few and far between; those there are have fled from my province to the neighbouring Caria; didn't I recently send you some panthers already? There are no panthers in today's Turkey – neither in historic Caria, nor in Cilicia.

You may find accounts in scholarly literature of a fight between seals and polar bears organised in the times of Nero. Seals were procurable, but the presence of polar bears in Rome is highly doubtful, unless the range of these animals had contracted dramatically since Roman times. The polar bear (*Ursus maritimus*) is found in a narrow swathe of Arctic Eurasia, from Novaya Zemlya to the Chukchi Peninsula. Even given the ingeniousness of Roman entrepreneurs, envisaging their trade with the Chukchis is a stretch. This seems to be a misunderstanding: a poem by Calpurnius Siculus, the source of confusion, mentions regular brown bears, who were reimagined as polar thanks to their proximity to the seals.

SPECTATORS

Anyone who has ever visited a large theatre or stadium knows that getting to your seat is not that simple. You have to constantly adjust your position against the number of sector, row, seat on the ticket, look around, work out the tangle of floors and passages, and in the end you might need a seat attendant's assistance anyway. Architects and engineers have to take countless other things into account: spectators must not block the stage or arena from one another; a row must have the designated number of seats without making it too crowded for anyone; it should be possible to pass between the rows; finally, in case of fire or other emergency, evacuation must be completed within minutes.

The structure of the Colosseum takes all those considerations into account – plus some more, unknown to modern builders. Like today, the seats closest to the arena were the most prestigious, while the upper gallery was not. Today, class distribution of spectators is regulated by the cost of tickets. But public games in Rome were usually free for all: the costs were borne by officials, private sponsors, the imperial treasury. Also (the British should understand this detail better than most), the relationship between one's fortune and social status was far from direct. As a result, the distribution of spectators across the amphitheatre's tiers was pre-ordained: the best spots were occupied by senators, higher up were members of the equestrian order, higher still those called simply 'the people' (*plebs*; this is not the same as plebeians, who could well be senators) – the people were Roman citizens with a right to wear a toga; further up were those who could not afford the official attire of a Roman citizen. At the highest gallery, standing places were occupied by urban proletariat, migrants and immigrants, slaves. Women were not admitted to the Colosseum in all eras of its existence, but when they were, it was to those upper rows. Members of certain taboo professions were banned from ever coming to the games – for instance, anyone who had ever fought in the arena as a gladiator (excluding Commodus and other emperors, of course). Does that mean that a retired fighter could not come and see the young generation in action? In theory, yes, but the ban was probably not strictly enforced.

There were separate boxes for the emperor and his retinue on one side, and for the Vestal virgins on the other. (We have already seen that the Vestals were not considered fully female or, for that matter, fully human, and as such were exempt from any mundane prohibitions.) The honorary boxes were in the middle of the longer sides of the oval, affording the best views of the arena. A separate entrance on the northern side was reserved for the emperor.

The ravages of time give us a chance to see the Colosseum from inside, the way ancient Romans never saw it. We have already mentioned the internal southern wall, but the arena itself is an even more telling example. Of course it did not look the way it does today. What we see (apart from the smaller covered section) are internal underground mechanisms and passages that brought gladiators and beasts to the arena. Mythologically-themed performances were a popular fixture of the Colosseum: the siege of Troy, the rape of Europa, Dirce dragged to death by a bull, Thisbe ravaged by a lion. The organisers could afford a high degree of realism (that is, actually killing the actors), and to raise it even higher, suitable theatrical scenery was necessary. The mountains, forests and cities erected for such shows were raised from under the arena.

In Monty Python's *Life of Brian*, the title character walks around the rows of a Roman amphitheatre in Judaea, offering the spectators larks' tongues, otters' noses and ocelot spleens. These snacks are invented (an ocelot is, after all, an American cat), but certainly it was not unusual for vendors to offer snacks and drinks during the breaks.

The shows at the Colosseum often went on for hours (a hunt in the morning, a gladiatorial fight in the afternoon), which is why taking care of the spectators' comfort was of paramount importance. Apart from food and toilets, they needed to be protected from the scorching sun. To that end, the amphitheatre could be covered with a special canvas awning. To service the contraption, a separate detachment of sailors from Misenum, Rome's primary naval base, was stationed with the Colosseum. An awning certainly boosted the attractiveness of any spectacle: when Julius Caesar protected the Forum from the sun during the games he had sponsored, it was talked about more than the games themselves. A famous graffito from Pompeii that advertises a forthcoming fight makes a point of saying "There will be cover" (*vela erunt*).

CHRISTIANS AND LIONS

In popular consciousness, the Colosseum is inextricably linked with Christian martyrs. The amphitheatre forms the silent background to countless stories, guidebooks, cartoons and jokes in poor taste along the lines of "Lions v. Christians, 5:0." The connection is so strong that the Colosseum is often perceived as a Neronian construction (because Nero is perceived as the Christians' enemy No. 1) – even though Nero never saw the Colosseum founded, let alone completed.

This link, however, was what finally protected the amphitheatre from complete demolition. In the 16th century, Pope Pius V recommended a sacred procession around the Colosseum, because its arena was soaked in the martyrs' blood (the tradition survives to this day). In the mid-

18th century, Pope Benedict XIV erected several crosses in the arena which remained there until the 1870s and were only removed to demonstrate that the Vatican's hold on the city had come to an end. Under Mussolini, a cross was re-erected on the northern side of the arena, to mark the end of hostilities between the church and the Fascist government. This cross is still standing.

There is, however, no evidence at all of Christians ever suffering a martyr's death on the Colosseum arena. Persecutions of Christians flared up a few times in Ancient Rome, but quickly subsided. Contrary to widespread opinion, the persecutions were not religious in nature: the Roman administration was deeply indifferent to the bizarre gods their subjects chose to worship or not. But the unity and functioning of the empire was based, among other things, on the unity of religious rites. It was okay not to believe in Jupiter or Venus (educated people did not, not really), but it was impossible to imagine that in certain prescribed situations citizens would not perform certain strictly prescribed and customary actions. Roman religion was very neurotic that way.

The Jews with their strict monotheism and a ban on worshipping foreign gods had asserted their right to abstain from some Roman rituals, but with the growth of Christianity, Jewish quirks began to spread across the empire. Worse than that: unlike the Jews, Christians lured into their sect new members, not necessarily of Middle Eastern origin, and suddenly respectable matrons refused to perform rites and acknowledge the divine nature of the emperor, citing a religious taboo. It was only at that point that the Roman administration's patience came to an end.

Christians often chose martyrdom consciously, even with bravado. The bishop Ignatius of Antioch, one of the Christian protomartyrs (depicted as devoured by lions on icons) wrote in an epistle: "I am writing to all the churches to let it be known that I will gladly die for God if only you do not stand in my way. I plead with you: show me no untimely kindness. Let me be food for the wild beasts, for they are my way to God. I am God's wheat and shall be ground by their teeth so that I may become Christ's pure bread. Pray to Christ for me that the animals will be the means of making me a sacrificial victim for God. No earthly pleasures, no kingdoms of this world can benefit me in any way."

THE COLOSSEUM WITHOUT GLADIATORS

Christians might have succumbed to the lions in the arena, but they won the ideological war. In 325 AD, the emperor Constantine banned gladiatorial combat. By the late 4th century, all gladiator schools were shut down, in the early 5th century animal hunts were banned as well. Romans, true to themselves, continued to organise and watch both fights and hunts for a long time after the official ban, but finally the emperors' power had waned, too, the city was depopulated, and public-crammed shows simply petered out. In 1332, the tradition was briefly revived with a bullfight in the Colosseum. It was a one-off thing: until modern times, the Colosseum was used as a monastic dormitory, a workshop, a part of defensive fortifications and, of course, as a quarry, but blood sports never made a return.

Even in its state of complete abandonment and desolation, the Colosseum still staggered the imagination. With time, Romans forgot what the structure was meant for. In the Middle Ages, one of the more popular opinions was that it was the temple of Sun God and a dwelling-place of demons, built by none other than the poet Virgil, a famous necromancer. Another version said that it was the palace of emperors Vespasian and Titus (which at least got the dynasty right).

Only during the Renaissance, when humanists started to read and understand ancient sources, was the Colosseum acknowledged as a show business amphitheatre. Its connection to necromancy and demons remained strong. The famous jeweller and sculptor Benvenuto Cellini describes in his boastful and gory memoirs two visits to the Colosseum with a certain Sicilian priest with the goal of invoking demons. Their second attempt turned out to be more successful than they hoped for, so much so that an apprentice boy whom Cellini had taken along shouted out: "The whole Colosseum is in flames, and the fire is advancing on us," but, thankfully, one of the participants in the ritual "let fly such a volley from his breech" that the demons were chased away, otherwise things might have taken a nasty turn. While the dunderhead necromancers walked home, a couple of stray demons followed them in huge leaps, moving across the streets and roofs.[42]

In the 18th and 19th centuries, Europe saw the beginnings of mass tourism. It was not, of course, mass by modern standards, but the Italian pilgrimage of affluent men, especially from Northern Europe and Great Britain, was no longer undertaken exclusively by eccentric loners. Rome was, as a rule, the climax of "The Grand Tour," and the Colosseum remained Rome's most celebrated sight. Small wonder that all famous tourists of the time, from Goethe to Byron, wrote heartfelt passages about the Colosseum, further enhancing its popularity.

ROMAN HOLIDAY

Lord Byron, one of the great Romantic poets of the 19th century, only briefly passed through Rome, but a Romantic poet does not need too much fodder to feed his imagination: he left a description of the Colosseum in his dramatic poem *Manfred* and translated from Latin the memorable saying of Anglo-Saxon pilgrims quoted earlier.

One line from Canto IV of his *Childe Harold's Pilgrimage* had a curious afterlife, connected with a film where Audrey Hepburn plays a young princess who has a brief and doomed fling with an American journalist. The title of the film, *Roman Holiday*, is a quote from Byron when he describes a gladiator dying in the Colosseum:

> *He reck'd not of the life he lost nor prize,*
> *But where his rude hut by the Danube lay,*
> *There were his young barbarians all at play,*
> *There was their Dacian mother – he, their sire,*
> *Butcher'd to make a Roman holiday –*
> *All this rush'd with his blood – Shall he expire*
> *And unavenged? – Arise! ye Goths, and glut your ire!*

Now here is what Mark Twain writes in his 1869 book *The Innocents Abroad* that catapulted him into a successful writing career:

> "So far, good. If any man has a right to feel proud of himself, and satisfied, surely it is I. For I have written about the Coliseum, and the gladiators, the martyrs, and the lions, and yet have never once used the phrase "butchered to make a Roman holiday." I am the only free white man of mature age, who has accomplished this since Byron originated the expression. *Butchered to make a Roman holiday* sounds well for the first seventeen or eighteen hundred thousand times one sees it in print, but after that it begins to grow tiresome. I find it in all the books concerning Rome…"

In 19th-century novels, authors on both sides of the Atlantic loved to portray the Colosseum as a romantic but dangerous place of trysts and secret moonlit walks. In the Colosseum, characters were likely to lose their mind, catch the 'Roman fever' (which usually meant malaria) or a deadly cold after sitting on a block of marble.

At the same time, the Colosseum was undergoing increasingly close scrutiny by scientists. A few volumes were dedicated to the unexpectedly rich subject of the Colosseum flora. A peculiar microclimate inside the amphitheatre encouraged the proliferation of plants not found anywhere else in Italy. Richard Deakin in his *Flora of the Colosseum of Rome* (London, 1855) thought that exotic seeds could have been brought by exotic beasts (on their fur or in their intestines) who had once fought and died in the arena. These precious plants, he wrote, "form a link in the memory, and teach us hopeful and soothing lessons, amid the sadness of bygone ages: and cold indeed must be the heart that does not respond to their silent appeal; for though without speech, they tell us of the regenerating power which animates the dust of mouldering greatness." Such was the style of botanical books in mid-19th century.

By the end of the same century, in spite of vocal opposition on the side of the romantically inclined, the amphitheatre was cleared of vegetation: the archaeologists decided that they posed a serious threat to ancient stones.

Today, surrounded by idle street actors in pseudo-gladiator suits, with queues at the entrance, often encrusted by scaffolding, the Colosseum has lost some of its romantic appeal, but it still remains a powerful symbol, used (sometimes destroyed) in many movies that want to tell you as succinctly as possible – "Here is Rome." Whenever a death sentence is carried out anywhere in the world, the Colosseum, the arena of death, is lit up in protest in the spirit of true Italian paradox.

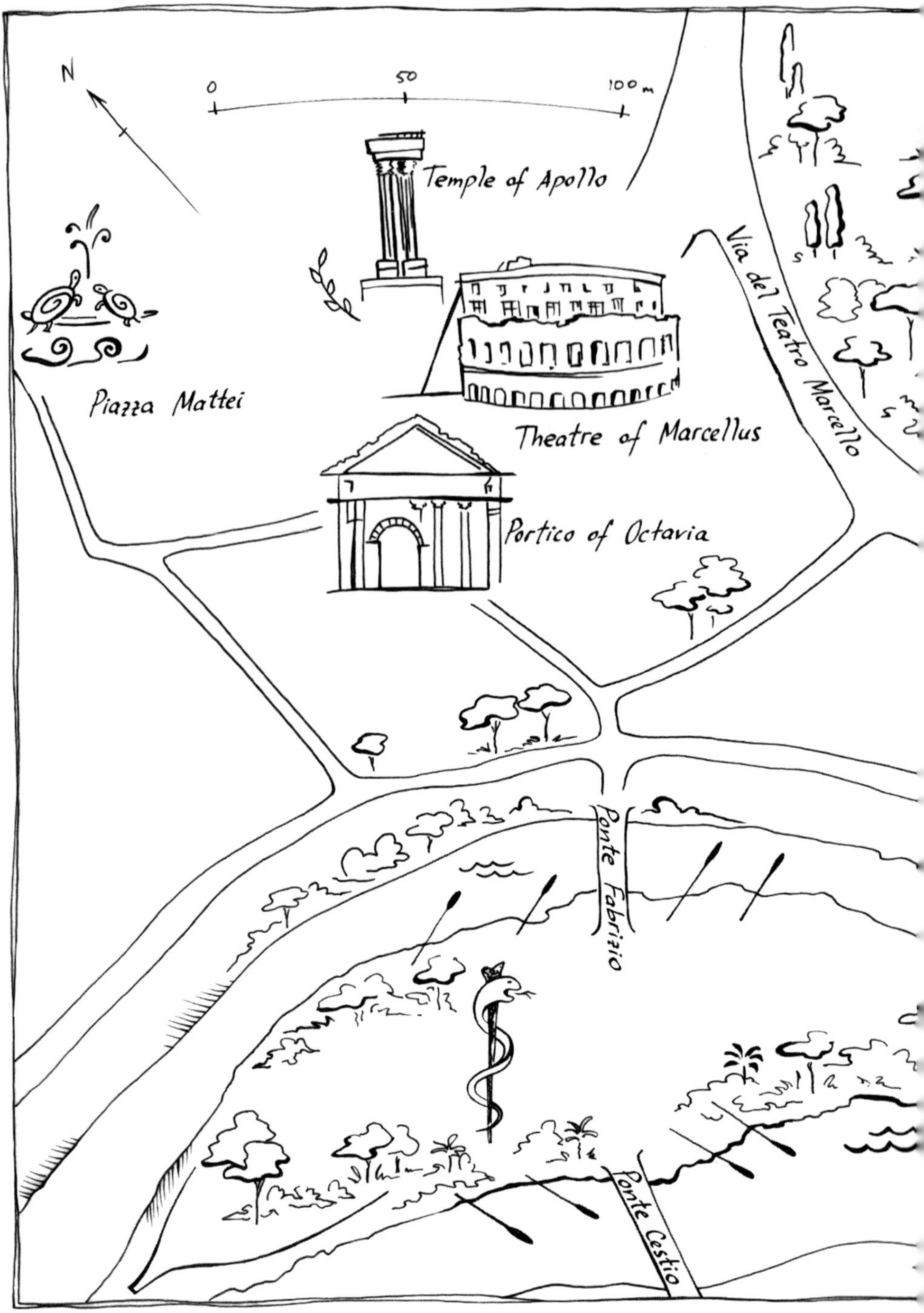

N

0   50   100 m

Temple of Apollo

Piazza Mattei

Theatre of Marcellus

Portico of Octavia

Via del Teatro Marcello

Ponte Fabrizio

Ponte Cestio

IN THE BEND OF THE TIBER

San Nicola in Carcere

San Giorgio in Velabro

Sant'Omobono

Arch of Janus

Temple of Portunus

Ponte Rotto

Temple of Hercules

Santa Maria in Cosmedin

e Palatino

C H A P T E R   V I I

IN THE BEND OF THE TIBER
(THE CRADLE OF ROME)

T he small sector of urban tissue tucked away in the bend of the river and densely studded with ancient monuments is perhaps the most mysterious part of historical Rome. Some of the earliest myths played out there. It was also the commercial hub of the ancient city, and a gloomy place of ethnic segregation in the Middle Ages. Unglamorous and untouristy (in Roman terms), it provides an inquisitive traveller with that rare experience of meeting the city face-to-face in unofficial, intimate settings.

THE GHETTO

We begin our walk on Piazza Mattei – not because it is very ancient (it is not), but simply because it is a charming and unusual spot, a quiet encircled space in the middle of noisy Rome.

The fountain in the centre is called "The Turtle Fountain" (*Fontana delle Tartarughe*), but the original design featured dolphins. They were spouting water, but the water pressure was very weak, and they were removed. Now, without the animals, the postures of the youths (who supported the dolphins with their hands) became somewhat meaningless, and turtles were installed there instead (the reptiles might have been designed by Gian Lorenzo Bernini). In 1979 one of the turtles was stolen, and both the missing one and its remaining brethren were replaced by replicas.

A local legend says that the Duke of Mattei, a spendthrift and gambler, was courting a wealthy girl, but was rebuffed by her father's icy disapproval. To prove his financial solvency and general amiability, the Duke constructed a fountain under his girlfriend's windows in just one night, which broke the family's resistance. In memory of his victory, the Duke for some reason walled up one of the windows of the palace looking on the fountain. The walled-up window is still there; whether setting up a complex artistic and engineering structure overnight is possible, judge for yourselves.

The Mattei were good Roman Catholics, but their palazzi stood in the middle of the Jewish ghetto. When in mid-16th century Pope Paul IV decided to resettle all Jews of Rome in this quarter – close to the river and hence unsafe due to constant threat of flooding – the Mattei family were provided with keys to the ghetto's doors.

The segregation of the Jews of Rome ended later than in any other Western European city, only with the collapse of papal temporal authority over Rome in 1870. The Jews had been living in Rome for a longer time than in any other European city (at least since the 1st century BC), but in Classical times this district, known as "Flaminian Circus," did not have any special ties with the Jewish community.

CIRCUS FLAMINIUS

A Roman circus is a venue of entertainment, usually taking the form of horse races. In English, 'circus' means a different kind of show, and we would call the Roman circus a race-track or hippodrome. But there is every possibility that the Circus Flaminius was not a circus – either in the English or Roman sense.

First, literary sources seem to indicate that the area of Circus Flaminius was huge, but at the same time the neighbouring Circus Maximus was considered a better place for the shows. Second, many buildings in this general area are mentioned as "a temple in the Flaminian Circus" – not 'by,' not 'at,' but exactly 'in.' Third, it contained a market and numerous shops. Fourth, popular assemblies sometimes convened in the Circus Flaminius, and the Romans, as we remember, made a point of standing during their assemblies (excepting the Senate) and despised the pampered Greeks who discussed state business sitting on theatre benches.

These oddities will not seem at all odd if we make an assumption (as some archaeologists did) that the Flaminian Circus, in full compliance with the word's etymology (*circum* means 'around') simply encircled a portion of urban space, as it happens in many city areas (think Piccadilly Circus in London). Sources never mention pens for chariots, a dividing barrier, or any other signs of a race-track. There is a report about Augustus filling the Flaminian Circus with water in the year 2 BC, where hunters butchered 36 crocodiles celebrating the unveiling of the Forum of Augustus. But it would not be too difficult to imagine that a small pond was dug somewhere within the 'circus' in an empty field (the place used to be called "Flaminian field" before it was ever called a circus).

This hypothesis, if true, does not mean that the place called "Circus Flaminius" could not be encircled with walls. Its walls stood until the 16th century, when the Mattei family started to clear ground for their palaces.

OCTAVIA

In Nikolai Gogol's unfinished novella "Rome," the characters "keep asking: 'Where's Rome? Where is grand, ancient Rome?' Only gradually, as it begins to emerge from the cramped alleyways, do they recognize it – ancient Rome, in a dark arch, in a marble cornice embedded in a wall, in a stained porphyry column, in an attic in the middle of a smelly fish market." The attic in the middle of a fish market is the Portico of Octavia, once the geographical centre of the Roman ghetto. There is no market there now, but its past existence is betrayed by the Via del Foro Piscario ('Street of the Fish Market') and the Latin inscription on the right side of the portico: "The heads of fishes that are longer than this tablet are to be given to conservators (i.e. municipal officials) inclusive of the first fins."

The Portico of Octavia is a rather scary sight: the attic is crumbling, marble columns are gaping with holes, brick patches cover up (unsuccessfully) some old damage. This is not even a portico (a covered colonnade), but an entrance to a portico that no longer exists. In its day, it was one of the prettiest architectural structures in Rome. There were two temples inside the portico – of Juno the Queen (*Iuno Regina*) and Jupiter the Stayer (*Iuppiter Stator*). Pliny the Elder tells a curious anecdote: when the movers brought statues to the newly erected temples, they made a mistake and put all male statues in the sanctuary of Juno and all the female ones in the sanctuary of Jupiter. The Romans, with their neurotic attitude to omens, decided to keep it like that, since the gods seemed to have chosen their new abode for themselves. There were also many equestrian bronze statues, brought by the general Caecilius Metellus Macedonius from Greece as war booty. They were said to be by Lysippos, the great Greek sculptor, and to portray the comrades-in-arms of Alexander the Great, those who died in the Battle of the Granicus River. There was also a statue of Cornelia, the mother of the Gracchi brothers – the first statue in Rome portraying a real woman (not a goddess or a mythological figure). The base of that monument was found during excavations, and it is now kept in the Capitoline Museums.

The Portico of Octavia is several times mentioned in Ovid's poetry; in his famous "Art of Love," one of the reasons for his banishment, he admires its opulence, and in "Tristia," written in exile, he complains that Augustus forbade librarians to keep his books in their collections, and the new scroll from the Black Sea shores cannot find a place either in the Palatine book storage or in the new library of Octavia's Portico.

"YOU WILL BE MARCELLUS!..."

The place was previously occupied by a Portico of Metellus; Augustus rebuilt it and dedicated it to his sister Octavia and her son Marcellus who had died tragically at a young age. Octavia Minor was one of the most dignified and influential women in Roman history. Her politically motivated marriage to Mark Antony gave Augustus the much-needed respite from civil strife. When Antony came under Cleopatra's spell and became a mortal foe of Augustus (again!), Octavia, miraculously, managed to remain loyal both to her prodigal husband and to her princely brother. By the end of her life she voluntarily removed herself from society and focused her efforts on raising her children – both her own and Antony's orphaned offspring, including his children by Cleopatra.

A biographer of Virgil tells a story: when the poet was reading his recently written books of "The Aeneid" at the court of Augustus, he chose a fragment from Book Six, where a string of future Roman heroes shown to Aeneas in the underworld culminates in the appearance of the young Marcellus; on the enigmatic phrase "You will be Marcellus" (*tu Marcellus eris*), Octavia fainted; when she came round, she ordered that the poet be amply rewarded.

Augustus did not have sons, and the question of succession was of paramount importance to him. That was perhaps the only major political problem that he could not solve to his satisfaction and in the end fate (and his wife Livia) prevailed. The problem was especially sensitive given that Augustus did not possess any crown, and he could not pass on his authority on formal grounds. All he could was influence the people and Senate with his authority.

Marcellus, a descendant of a famous general in the paternal line (it was the soldiers of that general who murdered Archimedes during the siege of Syracuse), became a pawn in the political game from his childhood. He was only three years old when Augustus betrothed him to the daughter of Sextus Pompey with an eye on forming an alliance with the future in-law. The betrothal failed to reconcile the adversaries, and after Pompey's defeat everyone was eager to forget it. When Marcellus reached the age of seventeen, Augustus married him off to his only daughter, the fourteen-year-old Julia. A handsome boy with excellent pedigree, he soon became popular with the crowds. The ruler's closest associate, his childhood friend Agrippa, felt slighted; he left Rome and secluded himself on the island of Lesbos. Marcellus was increasingly active in public life, even though according to legal standards and accepted practice he was not old enough yet (but after Augustus's own precocious career this was no longer an obstacle).

The dynastic dream of Augustus failed to come true. In the year when Marcellus accepted his first magistracy, he fell ill and soon died in the resort town of Baiae.

THE THEATRE OF MARCELLUS

The Theatre of Marcellus is one of the best-known ancient monuments in Rome. Inexperienced tourists sometimes even take it for the Colosseum. This is not entirely illogical: the Theatre of Marcellus has several tiers, too, and they are not identical, just like on the Colosseum. Unfortunately, we do not know what the third tier looked like, because it does not survive. Like the Colosseum, the Theatre of Marcellus had rows of seats, and some of them were strictly assigned to specific social groups. The shows were different, of course, but Roman entertainment was eclectic, and there was bound to be some overlapping. After all, an amphitheatre is nothing but a 'double theatre' ('theatre on both sides' for etymology fans).

Pliny the Elder says that the first amphitheatre in Rome was set up by one Gaius Scribonius Curio, an associate of Julius Caesar. He was organising funeral games for his father, and for that purpose he built two wooden theatres that stood with their convex sides toward each other and were used for shows with actors and musicians; when time was ready for gladiatorial combat, a complex mechanical contraption turned both structures 180 degrees, creating an amphitheatre.

It was Julius Caesar who first intended to erect a stone theatre on this location – to rival the achievement of Pompey. Pompey had just built Rome's first permanent theatre, also near the Circus Flaminius. Caesar did not live to see this project through, but the space was cleared. Many people thought that the cavalier way he went about it – tearing down temples, burning the wooden effigies of gods – was a bad omen.

The young Marcellus, who invested his money in the construction project, also did not live to see it finished. Augustus dedicated the building to the memory of his untimely departed nephew. During the opening celebrations the Romans had their first chance to see a live tiger.

The Theatre of Marcellus was a venue for games, theatrical and musical performances. The emperor Vespasian restored it, adding a new stage, and provided his favourite performers with huge money bonuses.

In 370 AD, when the nearby Cestian Bridge was in need of repair, the restorers took travertine blocks from the theatre; it is possible that the theatre was no longer functioning in its primary capacity by the time. Mediaeval pilgrims knew the place well, though, and recorded the existence of plinths with dedicatory inscriptions (but, apparently, not the statues that used to stand on those plinths). In the 10th century the building was known as the "Temple of Marcellus."

In Renaissance times, the Theatre of Marcellus formed a part of defensive fortresses that were built upon and around it by a few successive noble families of Rome. The most amazing thing of all is that it is still used as a residential house. In 2012, British newspapers reported that the theatre (under one of its Renaissance names of "Palazzo Orsini") was for sale with a price tag of £26 million. If you walk past the Theatre in the evening and see that the windows in its upper floor are lit, you will know that the deal went through – a unique example of non-museum use of a building that is over 2000 years old.

TEMPLES OF THE VEGETABLE MARKET

Three white columns stand near the Theatre of Marcellus. Notice their fluting: usually the vertical grooves are identical, but here wide and narrow ones alternate. That is all that is left of the Temple of Apollo the Healer (also known as Apollo Sosianus).

The place used to be encumbered by a cluster of mediaeval houses. The "liberation" of the Theatre of Marcellus was the first and one of the most ambitious architectural and archaeological projects of Mussolini's regime. From 1926 to 1930, the whole space had completely changed. While the area was being cleaned, a pediment and some fragments of a temple were found and identified as the Temple of Apollo. In 1940 three restored columns were set up on the pediment.

The cult of Apollo was distinctly non-Roman and very old. Each of these two characteristics was not unusual for Ancient Rome, but their combination was unique. The last Roman king, Tarquin the Proud, troubled by an ominous dream, sent his two sons to the most celebrated Oracle at Delphi. The king's nephew, Lucius Junius Brutus, tagged along. He had been playing dumb for a long time to avoid being detected as a political hopeful, which was mortally dangerous (that earned him his cognomen, Brutus, 'the stupid'). When the young Tarquins, obsessed with the idea of power, asked which of them would rule Rome, the Pythia (the priestess meting out Apollo's oracles) said: the one who will be the first to kiss the mother. Among the three of them, Brutus was the only one to have correctly interpreted the oracle: once out of the sanctuary, he stumbled, as if accidentally, and kissed the earth, the mother of all living things. A few years later, there were no more kings in Rome, and Brutus became one of the first two consuls of the newborn republic.

This is a legend, of course, but it is possible that the cult of Apollo was indeed thriving in Rome as early as the time of kings (characteristically, Apollo is the only major Greek god without a matching Latin name). The cult was probably not imported directly from continental Greece but borrowed from the Etruscans or the Greek settlements of south Italy.

The first temple of Apollo was erected here in the 5th century BC to mark delivery of the city from a plague (it is usually impossible to say which contagious disease ancient authors refer to). For that reason, the temple was dedicated to Apollo in his healing capacity and so it was called *Apollo Medicus*). Its other name, *Apollo Sosianus*, derives from Gaius Sosius, who rebuilt and restored the temple in the 1st century BC, probably after a victory in Judaea. Sosius fought against Augustus in the Battle of Actium (and it was in that battle that Apollo supposedly helped Augustus: it was Apollo's sanctuary overlooking the naval battlefield from a mountain on the coast). Augustus pardoned Sosius, so much so that fourteen years after Actium Sosius was the presiding official of the organising committee in charge of the Secular Games ('secular' here does not mean 'non-religious' or 'lay,' it refers to the Latin *saeculum*, 'century,' the longest possible term of human life – such games were supposed to be celebrated once in a hundred years, give or take, and their renewal in 17 BC was the most ambitious state festival of the Augustan era).

Augustus also dedicated a new temple to the Greek god on the Palatine. Before that, the temple near the Theatre of Marcellus was the only temple of Apollo in Rome.

Preserved fragments of the internal frieze (currently in the Montemartini Museum) show battle scenes involving some northern barbarians. This might mean that it was Augustus himself who oversaw the completion of works, because in 29 BC he celebrated a triple triumph for German victories. On the outside, the temple is adorned with typical attributes of Apollo, leaves of laurel.

The Senate often convened in this temple, and, like many other Roman sanctuaries, it was full of works of art. This collection was subject-oriented: statues and paintings all had some connection to Apollo. The best-known among them was a sculpture group of Niobe's children, though Roman historians were even in that time unsure which of the great Greek sculptors had carved it.

The myth of Niobe stressed the bellicose and vengeful nature of Apollo and his sister Artemis (Diana). Niobe, daughter of Phrygian king Tantalus, had spurned the traditional festival of the goddess Leto (Latona), because Leto had only two children compared to Niobe's fourteen. The children of Leto, Apollo and Artemis, avenged their mother, shooting all of Niobe's children with their arrows. The inconsolable Niobe turned into a rock weeping salty water; this rock is to this day shown in the Turkish province of Manisa (the Greek Magnesia). The ancients called a sudden death the arrow of Apollo, if the deceased was a man, or of Artemis, if it was a woman.

In Palazzo Massimo, part of the National Roman Museum, there is an expressive statue of a Niobid (one of Niobe's daughters). The naked girl is curved in the throes of death, trying unsuccessfully to pull the deadly shaft from her back. The statue was found in the gardens on the Esquiline hill.

Niobe protecting her daughter from Artemis's arrow. Greek statue

In the 1930s, a podium of another temple was excavated near the Theatre of Marcellus – chunks of concrete and tufa, nothing more. It was suggested that it could be the temple of Bellona. Bellona was a typically Roman goddess, without a direct analogue in the Greek pantheon. She symbolised battle frenzy – not simply a goddess of war, but a goddess of carnage. When sacrificing to Bellona, the priests had to cut their arms and legs (in ancient times in earnest, later symbolically). The temple was vowed by the famous Appius Claudius Caecus (we will tell his story in Chapter 9) during a war with Etruscans and Samnites.

The temple had preserved close ties with its founder, and as such was of interest to Augustus who had married into the Claudian clan. Throughout history, the Temple of Bellona never lost its battlefield aura. When the Senate convened there, it was often for a discussion of whether to award a triumph. In front of the temple, a small column stood; that column played a special role in military ceremonies of the Roman state.

In old times, when Rome wanted to go to war with one of its neighbours, a member of the special college of fetial priests, who were mostly responsible for foreign and diplomatic affairs, went to the enemy city and, following a strictly defined procedure, announced Roman claims and conditions. If after thirty-three days the issue was not settled peacefully, the fetials approached the border of the hostile state and threw a spear into enemy territory. This counted as an official declaration of war. But in the 3rd century BC potentially hostile lands grew too distant: one could not throw a spear from Rome and hope that it would land in Sicily or Carthage. So the Romans made a captive Greek soldier buy a small plot of land near the Temple of Bellona. Now it was formally enemy territory, and the fetials could throw their spears into that parcel without breaking the tradition. To make the ceremony more solemn, a War Column (*Columna Bellica*) was erected in front of the temple, and that was where the spear was launched from.

San Nicola in Carcere in the 18th century. Engraving by Giuseppe Vasi

Another typically Roman building stands a little further along the Via del Teatro Marcello. This is the church of San Nicola in Carcere ('St. Nicholas in prison'). The name of the saint who is especially popular in eastern Orthodox tradition was given to it by the Greeks who used to live in the area in large numbers. The place now occupied by the church – between the Theatre of Marcellus, Capitol and Tiber bank – served as a vegetable market (*Forum Holitorium*) in antiquity, and the name of the street that goes along the southern side of the church all the way to the river – Via del Foro Olitorio – is a reminder of that fact.

The church is old – it might have been founded in the 6th century. Most of the surviving walls date back to the 10th and 12th centuries. The façade was built by Giacomo della Porta at the very end of the 16th century, and the bell-tower is a relic of mediaeval fortifications.

The unusual features of this church are immediately visible: ancient columns are built into its walls, and two more protrude forlornly nearby, between the church and the Theatre of Marcellus. Three very old temples had stood there side by side since republican times, but it is very difficult to say which was dedicated to whom. Most specialists think that to the north of today's church building (to the right looking at its façade) was the oldest of the three, the Temple of Janus, built after Rome's first naval victory over Carthage in 260 BC. On the south side (to the left of the church) was the Temple of Hope (*Spes*), also dating to the First Punic War. The fragments of these two temples form parts of the southern and northern walls of the church. And finally, the central position, currently fully covered by San Nicola in Carcere, was occupied by the largest of the three temples, the Temple of Juno Sospita ('the Saviour').

In 90 BC the temple of Juno was reconsecrated after a dream that a noblewoman, Caecilia Metella, had: in the dream, women polluted the temple with "an indecent and dirty trade," and a bitch with a litter of pups made her home at the feet of the cult statue. After zealous prayers and purification rites Juno deigned to return.

The Roman temple of Juno Sospita was secondary to the sanctuary in Lanuvium, about 30 kilometres to the southeast of Rome. In the cave of the Lanuvian grove, sacred to the goddess, lived a sacred snake. A specially selected girl brought a sacrificial bread to the snake on the festival day. If the snake ate the bread, it counted as a good omen.

The bell tower of the church had once been a part of fortifications of the Pierleoni family, rich Jews converted to Christianity who had bought or built the best real estate in the area. Across the road is another of their mansions (11th century, also with a tower), and next to it are ruins of arcades (the poorly preserved left one has two arches of volcanic tufa). It is possible that the arcades once supported a roof over a section of the Triumphal Road which took victorious generals to the Capitol.

There was yet another temple between the three that huddled together near and on the footprint of San Nicola in Carcere and the Theatre of Marcellus. It was the Temple of Piety (*Pietas*). We have already mentioned that the connotations of the Latin word are immeasurably broader and deeper than its English equivalent. The temple housed Rome's first gilded statue, erected by the politician Acilius Glabrio for his father – the father was the person who had vowed the temple but did not live to see it built. This gesture of filial devotion was most appropriate for this temple, because Roman *pietas* stressed respect for parents above all other virtues. Pliny the Elder connected the location of the temple with another story that in his eyes was at the very core of *pietas*. A long time ago, there had been a prison on that spot (its memory might be reflected in the name of San Nicola in Carcere; but a competing version says that ancient ruins beneath the church were once thought to be the Mamertine prison). A woman of low birth was jailed there. Every day this woman's daughter, herself a new mother, came to visit the prisoner; every day the guards searched her because the prisoner was condemned to be starved to death, and bringing food into her cell would have thwarted the punishment. In the end, the daughter was caught in the act of nursing her mother with her breast-milk. The jailers, stunned by this show of filial love, let the convict go and assigned a state pension for the whole family.

*"Roman Charity." Engraving by German artist
Sebald Beham, 16th century*

The original story is recounted by Pliny in striking detail, but there was a more scandalous version already in antiquity, with a convict father instead of mother (in this version, father and daughter have names, Cimon and Pero). In the Renaissance and Baroque era the subject, usually called "Roman charity," gained immense popularity, especially with Dutch and Flemish painters: it provided them with an opportunity to paint a pious subject using very *risqué* visuals. Rubens alone painted several versions.

Either in memory of this virtuous act or simply because a cattle market was nearby, a Dairy Column (*Columna Lactaria*) was erected in the Vegetable Market, with a dairy kitchen nearby, where children from poor families received a free handout of milk. Information about the column is sketchy; most likely, it was demolished during construction work on the Theatre of Marcellus site.

THE ANTIQUITIES OF SANT'OMOBONO

In the 1930s the space southwest of the Capitol alongside the Tiber embankment was actively redeveloped (part of it was the 'liberation' of the Theatre of Marcellus from later accretions). Mussolini laid another avenue parallel to the river – Via del Mare – which was intended, like his other new straight streets, for military parades and ceremonial processions. (It is now divided into two streets, Via Luigi Petroselli and Via del Teatro Marcello.) A noticeable trace of this activity is the former building of the Fascist administration – *Governatorato* – in today's Via Petroselli. It is built in a style typical of Fascism, with marble insets (one of the tablets still has the words 'Mussolini' and 'Duce' on it), a big-headed Capitoline she-wolf and other imperial paraphernalia. It is now a municipal registry office (*Anagrafe*).

Other similar buildings were planned in the quarter, but in the course of preparatory works Roman ruins were discovered near the small church of Sant'Omobono. The ruins ranked among the oldest in the whole city. Mussolini respected Roman antiquity: development was suspended, excavations began.

> Saint Homobonus (meaning 'good man' in Latin) was a wealthy tailor from Cremona, known for his piety: he never missed communion, donated a large portion of his income to the poor, was faultlessly accurate with his customers and died during a mass, prostrating himself on the church floor in the shape of a cross. By urgent demand of his compatriots, he was canonised almost immediately after death (at the end of the 12th century). In recent years, St. Homobonus became a popular mascot of commercial activity, especially in the US; figurines of him are a popular souvenir in some business circles.

It became obvious in the course of excavations that near the church and under it two almost identical temples are concealed. The site is a layer cake of archaeological strata, from the 7th century BC to imperial times, but the most interesting phase in the life of these sanctuaries was in the 6th century BC, the time of the last Roman kings. The buildings were identified as the temples of Mater Matuta and Fortuna, built and consecrated by that most enigmatic of Roman kings, Servius Tullius.

Servius Tullius was a man of humble origins, and veneration of Fortune came naturally to him. One of the legends ascribed his luck to secret intercourse with the goddess who visited his bedchamber through a special window. Scholars who love to rationalise fairy tales interpreted this story as a ritual 'intercourse with a goddess.' Such rite exists in many ancient cultures; sometimes the intercourse is only implied, but sometimes priestesses or special temple prostitutes stand in for a goddess.

An ancient gilded statue stood in the Temple of Fortune. It was clad in two real togas. They covered the figure so successfully that no one could say for certain who was under them. It was thought to be Servius Tullius, but there was no consensus about why he needed to be hiding like that. Pliny the Elder claims that the togas on the statue had stood the test of time (and clothes moths) for over five hundred years.

Various other wonders were found during excavations of the Sant'Omobono area: an Etruscan inscription, the oldest in Rome, as well as fragments of multiple terracotta statues. One of them is especially interesting: it portrays Heracles (Hercules in Roman version), easily recognisable by the lion's hide, and the warrior goddess Athena (Minerva) next to him. The figurine is now in the Montemartini Museum. This must be an illustration of a popular mythological motif: Minerva introduces the freshly dead Hercules who has just ascended to heaven to the Olympians. Interestingly, many Greek tyrants of the time dressed themselves up as embodiments of Heracles and tried to persuade their people that Athena was especially benevolent toward them. If this terracotta figurine was not simply a piece of decoration but a part of Servius Tullius's ideological programme, that might mean that he was attentive to Greek and Near Eastern models of 'god-anointed' rule, and the chasm between the 'mystical' East and 'rational' Rome was smaller than it seemed.

A curious example of appealing to the authority of Athena is found in the first book of Herodotus's "Histories." When the tyrant Peisistratos decided to return to Athens from where he had been exiled, he devised a ruse, which Herodotus recounts with puzzlement: "The Hellenes had long ago set themselves apart from barbarians by enlightenment and being averse to silly superstition, while the Athenians were considered most level-headed even among the Hellenes, and yet the trick aimed at them worked like a dream." The trick was this. In an Attic village, the agents of Peisistratos found a young woman who was uncommonly tall and striking to look at. She was given a full set of armour, put on a cart and driven to the city. Heralds were running ahead, shouting: "The goddess Athena is coming to her city with Peisistratos in tow!" The people, amazed, came running and prayed to the goddess; the woman was silent — she was instructed to be — which made the procession even more solemn. Peisistratos climbed the Acropolis and assumed power in Athens.

The goddess Matuta personified dawn, and did shifts as a protectress of new beginnings and childbirth. "The ancients called the goddess of Dawn 'Mother' for her generosity," wrote a Roman antiquarian. In the 2nd century BC a painted table was set up in the temple of Mother Matuta; it described the conquest of Sardinia by consul Tiberius Gracchus. The tablet, containing a boastful dedicatory inscription ("over eighty thousand enemies killed or taken prisoner") was a map of Sardinia with the principal battles marked and illustrated.

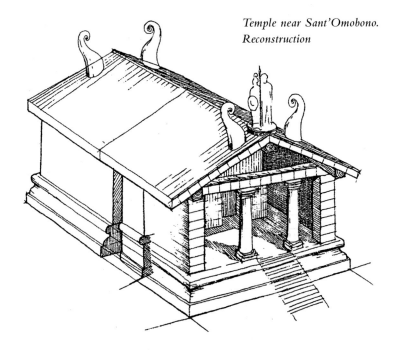

Temple near Sant'Omobono.
Reconstruction

Of those temples, few fragments survive: pieces of foundations, a round stone base which probably used to support numerous statues, taken from pillaged Etruscan cities, a barely discernible altar, shards of columns. Still, the area is a treasure trove for archaeologists. Excavations have been going on and off and with varying intensity, for close to eighty years, but Sant'Omobono remains one of the most promising Roman sites.

Some of the fragments found near Sant'Omobono definitely did not belong to either the Temple of Mother Matuta or the Temple of Fortune. Archaeologists think that landslides and similar natural phenomena might have pulled these fragments down from the Capitol, and they are the remains of the Temple of Fides (like with *pietas*, the Roman notion of *fides* does not translate easily – it is faith, loyalty, honesty, trust all taken together). Any temple on the Capitol was by definition very solemn and official, and the Temple of Fides was no exception. Its walls were covered in international treaties that Rome had made with neighbouring and faraway states (set in stone, not metaphorically). Legionaries submitted bronze tablets which confirmed their honourable discharge to this temple's treasury.

VELABRUM

From Sant'Omobono a short walk takes us to a square with a mediaeval church and a strange-looking squat arch. This square is the heart of Velabrum, and it is the place where, the legends say, Rome began.

Velabrum was the spot where the river spat out the basket with Romulus and Remus and where the she-wolf found them. The name of the area has not been explained satisfactorily. Plutarch explained it by frequent use of boats with sails ('sails' are *vela* in Latin) which was needed due to frequent flooding, but linguists find this version untenable.

The Arch of Janus standing in the middle of the square is Rome's only surviving quadrifrons, or tetrapylon arch (which means that it has four faces). Its present-day name is likely to be a result of confusion: in the Middle Ages the generic *ianua* ('doors' or 'passages') was taken to mean the name of the god. In a late imperial document an "Arch of Divine Constantine" is mentioned; perhaps this is the one. Like the Colosseum, the arch suffered from the depredations of mediaeval metal scavengers: holes gape where heavy iron or bronze clamps used to be. Statues once stood in spacious niches. Keystones above the spans are adorned with the images of gods: Minerva on the north side, Roma (the embodiment of Rome) on the east side. The squat appearance of the arch is deceptive: sketches of the 16th–18th century show that it was topped by another graceful tier.

In 1830 it was dismantled as a mediaeval superstructure (which it probably was not). In the 13th century the arch was used for defence purposes, a fate all too common in Rome, by the Frangipane family.

The Arch of Janus. Engraving by Luigi Rossini, early 19th century

Next to the Arch of Janus is an early mediaeval church, San Giorgio in Velabro, with another piece of Roman antiquity inset in its wall. This structure is usually called "The Money-Changers' Arch" (*Arcus Argentariorum*, or *Arco degli Argentari* in Italian), though erroneously. (In an episode of "The Simpsons," a presenter of an educational film explains to a child the workings of a slaughterhouse: "Let's take a peek at the killing floor. Don't let the name throw you: it's not really a floor." Well, the Money-Changers'

Arch is not really an arch.) It is not known of which larger building it was a part; perhaps it served as a portal for entry to the Cattle Forum.

THE CATTLE FORUM

The Cattle Forum (*Forum Boarium*) was spread out between Velabrum and the Tiber, all the way to the Circus Maximus. The name of the area seems to hint that it was a space for cattle trading, but some scholars are sceptical: they think that the Field of Mars, spacious and less prone to flooding, was a better venue for such activity. To support their version, they quote Ovid, who wrote that the Cattle Forum was named after a bronze statue of a bull, brought from Greece and set up near Velabrum.

This version, however, is contradicted by the long inscription on the Money-Changers' Arch, which says that the structure was dedicated to the emperor Septimius Severus and his household by "money-changers and cattle traders of this place" (*argentari et negotiantes boari huius loci*). There is another clue from the domain of agricultural husbandry. The Money-Changers' Arch is made completely of marble (apparently businessmen could afford expensive materials) except for the lower travertine section, which was much larger in antiquity. Could it be that the lower section was made of a cheaper material and had no decorations because cattle herds were regularly driven through the portal?

The inscription and reliefs on the arch were several times redacted, because during the Severan era various members of the clan were from time to time subjected to a procedure known as *damnatio memoriae*. This practice, well known from Ancient Egypt to the Stalinist habit of airbrushing executed officials from group photos, involved the striking of an undesirable name from all official dedicatory inscriptions and, preferably, destruction of any visual information concerning this person. A number of members of the imperial family were murdered and their names were prohibited – as a result, their names and figures disappeared from the arch. (Notice the character spacing in line five of the inscription; somebody really needed to rewrite whatever was there originally.) The most interesting reliefs are on the inner sides of the 'arch': on the left the emperor Caracalla performs a libation on a portable field altar (next to him is a smooth space that used to have the figures of some disfavoured courtiers); on the other side the sacrifice is performed by the emperor Septimius Severus and his wife Julia Domna (and again, a figure is airbrushed away, and a priestly staff appears as if from nowhere).

A mediaeval legend claimed that money-changers had concealed their treasures inside the arch. There was even a rhyme about it: *Tra la vacca e il toro, troverai un gran tesoro* – "Lies a bag of money full 'twixt the heifer and the bull." (The sacrificial bull is on the left outside part of the arch, the heifer with a skittishly raised tail – on the right inside part.) That is why the arch is so full of holes. No treasure was ever found.

A view on San Giorgio in Velabro and Arch of the Money-Changers through the span of the Arch of Janus. 19th century drawing

The San Giorgio church, whose bell tower is propped up by the Money-Changers' Arch, is full of columns and other traces of antiquity and the early Christian era. The columns are mismatched: notice the gimmicks that the architects had to employ to make them more or less even in height (some have parts sawn off, some are sunk into the floor, some are standing on extra supports). A few of the columns, especially those on the right, bear the traces of ancient graffiti. The painted ceiling visibly narrows down toward the altar – possibly because the church is standing on a foundation of older buildings, and that had to be taken into account when building it.

On the night of July 27, 1993, a car bomb left near the church almost completely destroyed its portico. Simultaneously, another bomb went off near the basilica of St. John Lateran. Both churches were severely damaged. The wreckage of the San Giorgio portico was carefully documented, and now only a small photo exhibition inside the church recalls the terrorist attack.

Fortunately, no one was killed in Rome (while a bomb in Milan killed five people that same night). The attacks followed a bombing that had hit Florence exactly two months earlier, killing five people, injuring more than forty, inflicting severe damage to the Uffizi Gallery and completely destroying the archives and art collection of the unique Accademia dei Georgofili, the world's first learned society of agronomy and scientific agriculture. The police connected the bombings to the nation-wide investigation into the Sicilian mafia (*Cosa Nostra*).

In the Victorian era, many Anglican priests and laypeople began to advocate a return of the Church of England to its Roman Catholic roots. Among the more prominent and vocal proponents of this shift were the members of the so-called 'Oxford movement' (so called because it centered on certain colleges and dons of the University of Oxford), or 'tractarians' (because the philosophy of the movement was exposed in a series of 90 "Tracts for the Times" published between 1833 and 1841). One of the leaders of the movement was John Henry Newman, a tutor at Oriel college and an Anglican priest. His spiritual quest led him to convert to Roman Catholicism in 1845. For decades, he championed the cause of English Catholics, but was not formally acknowledged by the Roman curia until the election of the new pope, Leo XIII, in 1878. Urged by prominent English Catholic laymen, the pope made Newman a cardinal deacon, in spite of the fact that he was neither a bishop nor a resident of Rome (cardinal deacons were typically members of the Roman curia, the Vatican's administrative machine). A cardinal is supposed to have a titular church in the City, and Newman was given San Giorgio in Velabro. There is a plaque inside the church recording this connection and stressing that he was *ante omnia Christianus*, 'before all things a Christian.' His motto was *Cor ad cor loquitur* ('Heart speaks unto heart'). In 2010, on a visit to the UK, Pope Benedict XVI proclaimed Newman's beatification.

BOCCA DELLA VERITÀ

Walking from Velabrum towards the river, we will find ourselves in the Piazza della Bocca della Verità ('The Square of Truth's Mouth'), Japanese tourists' favourite spot. Here, we encounter two ancient temples – one rectangular, one round – and a Christian church with a long history.

The rectangular temple was long called the "Temple of Male Fortune" (*Fortuna Virilis*). Nowadays most specialists agree that it was a temple of Portunus, a god who shared many functions with Janus: both were responsible for doors, borders, passages and crossings, a key was a symbol of both. As time went by, they divided their responsibilities: Janus continued to be in charge of doors, while Portunus took upon himself the new meaning of portus, which now not only meant 'door,' but also 'a sea-port' or 'river-port.' A place by the river was most appropriate for such a temple.

The temple is sitting on a strikingly tall podium. Excavations have shown that the earlier temple in that spot was raised even more, to a six-metre height. This was a necessary anti-flooding measure: floods remained a danger for this neighbourhood for almost the whole time of its existence.

In architectural language, the Temple of Portunus is pseudoperipteral. A peripteral building is, for example, the Parthenon of Athens: it is surrounded by columns on all sides. Here, however, the columns are only in the portico, while half-columns clinging to the side and rear walls only imitate a free-standing colonnade. The same is true of the so-called 'Square House' (*Maison Carrée*), the Roman temple in the centre of Nîmes, France, which might be the best-preserved ancient temple in Europe.

Both the Square House and the Temple of Portunus owe their excellent state of preservation to their timely transfer to the Christian church. The Tiber temple was associated with the Virgin Mary in the 9th century; later it was dedicated to Mary of Egypt, the patron saint of penitents, who was especially popular among Christians of the Eastern Rite. In the 16th century, the church was handed over to the Armenian community and renamed, somewhat confusingly, "The Church of Saint Maria of Egypt of the Armenians" (*Santa Maria Egyziaca degli Armeni*). In the 1930s, Mussolini's campaign of deconsecrating ancient Roman buildings stripped the temple of later outside embellishments, but fragments of 9th-century frescoes inside were preserved.

Saint Mary of Egypt is venerated as patron saint of penitent women, sharing this function with Mary Magdalene. According to some sources, she was a professional prostitute, while others claim she did it out of pleasure. Once, she met a group of pilgrims heading for Jerusalem who made a stop in Alexandria, the city where she lived. She decided to join them and find new business along the way. Once arrived, she was not able to enter the Church of the Holy Sepulchre: an invisible force repelled her from the entrance. Standing before an icon of Virgin Mary, she realised the depth of her depravity. Repentant, she made another attempt to enter the church, this time successfully (there is a small chapel inside commemorating this event). On her return to Egypt, Mary renounced her former life of sin and devoted herself to austerity and prayer.

Opposite the Temple of Portunus is a small temple with tile roof (the roof is not ancient). For a long time, it was called a "Temple of Vesta" only because all circular temples were automatically considered to be dedicated to Vesta. This attribution, doubtlessly erroneous, is still found on some tourist maps and even in popular literature.

It is difficult to say with certainty to what deity this very old temple was dedicated. Many years of research and boisterous arguments of archaeologists have led to a consensus of sorts: this is a temple of Hercules. The problem is, there were two (if not three) temples of Hercules near the Forum Boarium, and indeed the whole commercial port area was under the auspices of this famous demigod. One hypothesis suggests that the temple was dedicated to Hercules of the Olives (*Hercules Olivarius*), patron of olives and oil merchants. Another prefers Hercules Victor, the hero in his guise of warrior and hunter. With reasonable cautiousness, many guidebooks prefer a descriptive label: "round temple near the Tiber."

The only reliable written evidence of the dedication of the temple to Hercules Victor is an inscription on a slab of grey volcanic rock (peperino) found in the 18th century on the Caelian hill. It says that the consul Mummius Achaicus, the conqueror of Greece and the destroyer of Corinth, built and dedicated the Temple of Hercules Victor. This find threw many archaeologists off the trail: if the tablet was found on the Caelian, they reasoned, the temple was also in that area. But there is no evidence of the cult of Hercules ever present on the Caelian (unlike the Forum Boarium), and the journey of the tablet in the course of twenty centuries could have been quite convoluted.

Lucius Mummius Achaicus was one of the "new" plebeian politicians. The military feat of dubious valour which immortalised his name occurred in 146 BC. It is not very clear why his army dealt with one of the wealthiest and most celebrated Greek cities so brutally, even by ancient standards. All Corinthian men were slaughtered, women and children sold into slavery, temples pillaged. Economic reasons may be part of it: Mummius might have followed the instructions of the Senate aimed at removing a powerful trade competitor.

Corinth was one of the most cultivated and beautiful cities of Greece, but Mummius, according to ancient historians, was not a great connoisseur of fine Greek arts. Sending a batch of priceless Corinthian statues to Rome, he gave a stern warning to the sailors that in case of loss of or damage to the cargo they would have to replace any missing statues with identical ones.

The round temple was one of the first buildings in Rome to be built almost entirely of marble. The marble was imported from Greece (it is Pentelic marble, from the Athens region), which supports the hypothesis of Mummius's involvement. The temple was restored for the first time shortly after it was built. The builders were almost certainly Greek: in those times, Roman engineers and developers simply did not have the experience of working with marble.

The original structure had a door that faces due east and two windows on either side. If you walk round the temple, you will see that not all of its columns are identical. Initially there were twenty; today, one is missing, and some others are replaced by later replicas. They are hewn from a different kind of marble – not Greek but Italian (from Carrara); they also look slightly different, and this is especially noticeable in their capitals. If you position yourself right before the entrance, between the two columns, and walk left (clockwise), the fifth column will be different from its flanking neighbours. In the centre of the high tufa podium is an empty space – a so-called *favissa*, which is more or less like a crypt in a Christian church: a place where statues or other sacred relics were kept.

On the other side of the square stands a church with a tall mediaeval bell tower. This church is called Santa Maria in Cosmedin, and it contains two ancient Roman relics.

One of them is an international celebrity. It gave its name to the square, it is reproduced on countless postcards, guidebook covers and posters. It is "The Mouth of Truth" (*Bocca della Verità*). In parentheses, we usually provide Latin names of ancient monuments rather than Italian, but there is no record of "The Mouth of Truth" in antiquity. The relief owes its fame in large part to "Roman Holiday."

Apparently, the scene where Gregory Peck draws his arm out of the ancient mouth with the hand eaten off was improvised: Audrey Hepburn did not anticipate the partner's trick and her horror was genuine. In the *Oxford Archaeological Guide to Rome*, Amanda Claridge writes: "the mouth of Truth who will bite off the hands of those who tell lies." No 'according to legend' or some such; you have been warned.

The relief is certainly Roman, made of beautiful Phrygian marble with coloured streaks (in Italian, this type of marble is called *pavonazetto*, from *pavone*, 'peacock'). It might have been a part of a fountain or a decorative manhole. It is not known for certain whom the face represents. Today's Romans favour the god of the Tiber, though a recent study identified it as Oceanus (it does have dolphin-like shapes in the lower part of the beard).

The other relic is much less known. It is hidden in the least accessible part of the church, the crypt, and, frankly, it is not visually striking. A large platform of tufa blocks, it might have once supported the Great Altar of Hercules (*Ara Maxima*).

In the chapter on the Palatine, we told the story about the conflict between Hercules/Heracles who was returning with the cattle of Geryon from the far-away Spain and the giant Cacus, son of Vulcan, who attempted to steal them. The commercial area around the Tiber and market squares had always been under the protection of Hercules, so this was the logical place for his altar. In a poem by Propertius, Hercules sets the cattle free and sends them to roam the future city: "Rome's noble Forum will be your pasture." Ironically, that was not so much a prediction of the Forum's greatness in its heyday as of its decline and transformation into "Cattle Field" in the Middle Ages.

When Hercules, tired after the struggle, heard the gurgling of a stream and went to the nearby grove to have a drink of water, an old priestess blocked his way, saying that men were forbidden from entering the sanctuary. The enraged Hercules promised that when his Great Altar would be standing in that place, women would be forbidden from coming anywhere near it, because they left him thirsty in a difficult situation. And, indeed, women (and dogs) were not allowed to take part in the rites at the Altar.

The first fruits of any commercial activity were sacrificed on the Great Altar of Hercules. The ritual was unusual: participants sat, not stood, and their heads were not covered (that was the Greek way; Romans, when performing sacrifices and other rites, pulled a corner of the toga over their heads).

The church of Santa Maria in Cosmedin (the meaning of the last word is not quite clear – perhaps it is the mangled Greek 'decorated,' the same root as in 'cosmetics') had incorporated the front section of a Roman building of the 4th century BC. Once inside the church, you will see that not only some of the columns, but even the walls are ancient. The ornamental floor, though, is mediaeval. Stone inlays of that kind are called 'cosmatesque' after the family of Cosmati who were craftsmen and architects. In the 13th century, the Cosmati decorated many Roman churches in that style.

THE ISLAND AND THE BRIDGES

Passing by Santa Maria in Cosmedin and the round Temple of Hercules along Via della Greca, we will find ourselves by the Palatine Bridge (*Ponte Palatino*). This bridge is quite new (in Roman terms), it was built in the late 19th century. A quirk of urban planning makes its traffic left-handed, which earned it a nickname *Ponte Inglese* ('English Bridge').

But on the right, at an angle to the Palatine Bridge, a fragment of the ancient Aemilian Bridge protrudes from the river. Today it is better known, for obvious reasons, as "The Broken Bridge" (*Ponte Rotto*). It is the oldest stone bridge in Rome, present at that place since the 2nd century BC (though, of course, renovated many times). The entrance to it was once adorned with an arch. After violent floods in the 16th century, one third of the bridge collapsed; three centuries later, engineers dismantled almost everything else, leaving only the central span as a relic of antiquity.

There is a 12th-century house near the Temple of Portunus (to the right of it, if you face toward the river). When the Aemilian Bridge was intact, it virtually abutted it. This house deserves the name of "Aesop's magpie" just as much as the Arch of Constantine, so richly and fancifully is its façade decorated with fragments of Roman monuments. For a long time, and for reasons unknown, it was called "The Pilate's House"; in the 19th century, trying to make sense of the flowery Latin inscription above the portal (which says, to cut the long story short, that life is brief and death inevitable), scholars thought that it had belonged to the hapless Roman tribune Cola di Rienzo. Today it is usually called "the House of Crescentius" after an influential mediaeval family, but this is no more than a guess.

As soon as we venture on the right bank, we immediately turn back along the Cestian Bridge (*Ponte Cestio*). This bridge had first connected the Tiber island with Trastevere in the 1st century BC, but it is not known which member of the important Cestius clan gave it his name. In the 4th century the bridge was radically refurbished (it was then that the travertine blocks from the Theatre of Marcellus were used to patch it up) and rededicated by Gratian, the emperor of the moment. In the late 19th century, when new embankments were created, it transpired that Gratian's bridge was too short for the new layout. So a new bridge was built, but the architects tried to preserve the appearance of the central span and even used building blocks from the old bridge.

The island in the middle of the Tiber, strictly speaking, does not have a name. It is often called Tiberina, which simply means "of the Tiber," in feminine gender (because the implied noun, 'island,' is feminine in both Latin, *insula*, and Italian, *isola*). Ancient Romans simply said 'the island' or 'between the two bridges' (*inter duos pontes*), later – 'the island of Aesculapius' (we will shortly explain why). Legend said that the island appeared when the Romans expelled the last king from the city. The grain belonging to the king's house could not be used for food (the chronicler does not explain why), and the Romans threw it into the river. It was summer, and the Tiber, as usual, grew shallow. Silt and sand began to accumulate around the heap of grain, and that was how Tiberina appeared.

The island and two bridges. Drawing by anonymous English
artist of the 19th century

But in fact the island is, of course, older. It is conveniently placed in the spot where the river is not too deep and where the natural waterway intersects with a trade road from the river estuary to the Sabine hills, and it was that intersection that gave birth to Rome.

The island had always been a somewhat separate and un-Roman place. Mysterious and ancient gods found refuge there. One of the first was the healer god Aesculapius (Asclepius in Greek). After a horrible epidemic of 293 BC the Romans consulted the Sibylline Books and sent an embassy to the Greek city of Epidaurus, the principal cult centre of Asclepius. The embassy returned with a strange gift: a snake, the sacred animal of the healer god. The ship docked near the bank on the Field of Mars, in a place called Navalia, site of a naval base on the Tiber. The snake escaped from the ship, swam all the way to the island, and disappeared there. It was considered an omen, and this is where the Temple of Aesculapius was built. When you see a snake on a pharmacy sign, remember the legend that is the origin of this symbol.

No signs of the temple have been discovered so far, but the archaeologists are almost certain that it had stood exactly on the site now occupied by the church of San Bartolomeo all'Isola, and the mediaeval well near the altar is a direct descendant of the sacred fountain of Aesculapius. The portico of the temple was used as a reception ward: confirming inscriptions and gifts were found there. The island's isolation from the rest of the city justified its medical containment use. It continued to receive the sick throughout the Middle Ages; actually, a hospital (called *Fatebenefratelli*, 'brothers do good') stands there today. It has been in continuous operation since 1548.

The long, narrow island with two bridges stretching perpendicularly to the shores like oars resembles a sailing ship. Somebody had this idea in antiquity, too, and a travertine ship prow was constructed on the eastern tip of the island (quite possibly there was also a stern on the western tip). The prow is quite worn down over time, but still visible. Beneath it is Aesculapius with his staff and snake; above it is a police station.

On our way back, we take the Fabricius Bridge (*Pons Fabricius, Ponte Fabrizio*). This is the only ancient Roman bridge within the city that is still functioning in more or less its original form. The dedicatory inscription is repeated four times: under two spans of the bridge on each side. It says that the bridge had been built by Lucius Fabricius, supervisor of roads (*curator viarum*). The arch facing the Field of Mars holds a smaller inscription (but also in duplicate): forty years after the construction of the bridge the consuls checked its condition and found it satisfactory (the inspection was necessitated by a devastating flood).

In the Middle Ages this bridge was often called 'The Jewish Bridge' because it was close to the ghetto; now it is called 'The Bridge of Four Heads' (*Ponte dei Quattro Capi*) for the sculptural heads of two four-faced Januses (eight faces in total) that were installed on the bridge in the 19th century and remain there to this day.

The most celebrated bridge across the Tiber is the first one. It is known as *Pons Sublicius* ('Girder Bridge'). It had been built from wood without a single nail, probably before the time when the Latins could confidently work bronze and iron. A special college of priests was in charge of it, and it was thanks to this fact that the word for 'bridge-maker' (*pontifex*) became synonymous with 'priest' and then 'bishop.' Now it is mostly used as one of the titles of the pope (he is *Pontifex Maximus*, or the Roman Pontiff).

When exactly the Sublician Bridge ceased to exist is not known; in late imperial times it was still standing somewhere close to the Forum Boarium. However, the most important adventure on the bridge occurred in antiquity, in the first years of the republic. After the expulsion of the last kings, who were Etruscan, Rome was in a state of constant skirmishes with the Etruscans. At one point, the enemy had completely occupied the high right-bank hill of Janiculum. The soldier Horatius Cocles urged his comrades to dismantle the Sublician Bridge post haste: if the Etruscans crossed the river, they would capture the Capitol and Palatine as easily as they had captured the Janiculum. The engineers set to work, while Horatius with two other daredevils made a stand on the right bank, prepared to repel the attack of the Etruscan troops, many thousand strong. While the bridge still stood, Horatius was able to withstand the onslaught: enemy darts were harmlessly stuck in his huge shield. But when the bridge finally collapsed leaving him without an escape route, he addressed the river with a prayer:

> "Oh Tiber, father Tiber,
> To whom the Romans pray,
> A Roman's life, a Roman's arms,
> Take thou in charge this day!"
> So he spake and, speaking,
> Sheathed the good sword by his side,
> And, with his harness on his back,
> Plunged headlong in the tide.

Thus wrote Thomas Babington Macaulay, 1st Baron Macaulay, an early Victorian politician who was instrumental in making English an official language of India, and a prolific writer. His "Lays of Ancient Rome" were immensely popular in his day, learned by heart by boys in public schools. The story of Horatius Cocles, a verbose retelling of Livy, remains the most-quoted, especially Horatius's mega-patriotic proclamation:

> Then out spake brave Horatius,
> The Captain of the Gate:
> "To every man upon this earth
> Death cometh soon or late.
> And how can man die better
> Than facing fearful odds,
> For the ashes of his fathers,
> And the temples of his gods?"

In the 2013 Hollywood movie "Oblivion" set in post-apocalyptic space, the character played by Tom Cruise finds a tattered book of "Lays of Ancient Rome" and makes his final stand with the words of Horatius Cocles on his lips.

The stand of Horatius Cocles. 17th-century engraving

As for ancient authors, they told different stories about the fate of Horatius. Polybius said he drowned; Dionysius of Halicarnassus said he survived. Livy, the author of the most detailed account, says that he did swim to survival, was given as much land as one can plough in a day, and had a statue to him erected in the Comitium. That was his reward for "a proof of valour," Livy adds sceptically, "which was destined to obtain more fame than credence with posterity."

CIRCUS MAXIMUS

No buildings, in fact almost no ruins, survive on the site of the Great Circus (*Circus Maximus*), and yet it remains one of the most vital Roman sights: people lie on the grass there, kiss, walk their dogs, jog, sometimes organise concerts, demonstrations and fairs (once, checking on a lonely tree that grows there, I was shocked to see the site full of tents and helicopters in some new satellite photos).

The valley between the Palatine and Aventine hills was ideally suited for sporting events. The first to adapt it for such purposes was Romulus himself, when he invited people from the neighbouring villages, allegedly to enjoy architecture and sports competition, but in actual fact to steal the brides for his cutthroats. "When the time came for the show, and people's thoughts and eyes were busy with it, the premeditated attack began," says Livy. King Tarquin the Elder erected a permanent circus on the site, and later rulers never stopped to expand, embellish, reconstruct it or rebuild after frequent fires. Like the Colosseum, the Circus Maximus was split into sectors, each assigned to people of a certain status (senators, equestrians and so on). Unlike in the Colosseum, Circus Maximus was not gender-segregated: women and men sat together, and Ovid jumps on this opportunity in his "Art of Love" to explain how exactly one should go about wooing a girl in such perfect conditions: offer a pillow to sit on, prevent a ruffian in the next row from poking her back with his knees, remove specks, real or imaginary, from her dress. Busy with all that, our beau completely ignores the arena: Ovid says very little about the actual circus games.

The Circus was majestic in its heyday. Pliny the Elder considered it one of the three most beautiful buildings in Rome. Under Julius Caesar, a protective moat was dug around the arena; under Augustus, a red granite Egyptian obelisk was set up (now in Piazza del Popolo); under Nero, the whole perimeter of the arena was enclosed with wooden banisters with oblong ivory covers that freely rotated around the wood. It was a security device: the claws of lions or tigers who turned their attention to members of the audience would have slipped on it. Among the tribunes stood a special elevated emperor's box – *pulvinar*. However, if the emperor was not in the mood for baking in the sun among his subjects, he could easily enjoy the show from the windows of his own palace: the slopes of the Palatine are a natural extension of the northern tribunes. Finally, a triple arch was erected at the east side of the arena in honour of Vespasian's and Titus's Judaic victories (not to be confused with the surviving Arch of Titus on the Forum).

It is hard to say how many spectators the Circus Maximus could accommodate. Pliny the Elder says 250,000. That means a major show could attract one quarter of the whole urban population.

During the otherwise trouble-free rule of Antoninus Pius, the largest sports-related disaster in recorded history occurred: collapsing stands killed 1112 people. (To compare: the second-worst disaster, the Happy Valley Racecourse fire in Hong Kong in 1918, claimed the life of 590 people; the Hillsborough stadium crush in Sheffield in 1989 of 96.)

The last games in the Circus Maximus were held in 550 under the Gothic king Totila, and it was also in the 6th century that the structures of the Circus began to be slowly pillaged for building blocks. The process was so successful that almost nothing survives, except scanty remains of 'cages' (on which more in a bit) on the east side.

Circus games (*ludi circenses*) were varied: athletic competitions, naumachia (mock naval battles), animal hunts (*venationes*), staged fighting, and "Trojan games," which was something like dressage, only horses were ridden by boys of pre-conscription age (a tradition allegedly going back to Rome's Trojan roots). Sometimes, especially before the Colosseum was built, even gladiatorial combat was staged in the Circus. But the main entertainment and to a great extent the whole *raison d'être* of the circus was chariot racing.

A long time ago, in the heroic era of Homer's tales, chariots were formidable weapons, the tanks of the Bronze Age. But they had long gone out of military use, and for the Romans who wanted bread and circuses (*panem et circenses*, as the satirist Juvenal wrote without much sympathy), chariots were primarily associated with entertainment.

Before the start of the race, all participants paraded before the spectators in a solemn procession called *pompa* (the source of our pomp and circumstance). Then chariots lined up in special enclosures called 'cages' (*carceres*). The cages were positioned so as to give each participant an equal distance to the takeoff line. The number of horses in harness varied from two to ten (we remember that Nero tried to wield ten horses at the Olympic Games), but usually there were four. The presiding official signalled the start by dropping a white cloth called *mappa* from his hand; the cages opened, and the chariots shot forward.

The Roman race-track was neither circular (though called a circus) nor oval; if we try to find a similar shape in today's world, that would be a paper clip, rectangular on one side and round on the other. A high dividing barrier was set, length-wise, in the middle of the arena (it was called *spina*, 'the spine'). On each end of the spina were three conical pillars, each of them a *meta* ('goal'). The charioteer needed to turn his team around these turning posts. The closer to the barrier and *metae* was the trajectory of the turn, the shorter was the distance travelled by a chariot, which improved its chances to reach the finish line faster. However, the risk of crashing into the barrier also grew.

The spina was decorated with sculptures and obelisks, but apart from purely decorative embellishments, it had appliances for recording the progress of the race. These were seven eggs and seven dolphins. When all chariots made a full circle, attendants removed one egg and lowered the nose of one dolphin.

The shape of the appliances had a meaning. The eggs referred to the egg from whence the horse-taming brothers Castor and Pollux had sprung. This unusual form of delivery was caused by their somewhat avian parentage – they were engendered by Zeus/Jupiter in the shape of a swan. But the two eggs born (or should we say laid?) by their mother Leda contained four babies, a girl and a boy in each. One egg was fertilised by Zeus, another by Leda's mortal husband Tyndareus (it is unclear why his children also hatched from an egg). The children of Zeus were Polydeuces/Pollux and Helen (to be known in the future as Helen of Sparta, and later, more famously, as Helen of Troy). The children of Tyndareus were Castor and Clytemnestra; so there were actually quadruplets. But there is more confusion: Greek mythical characters were often called by the name of their earthly father, so all four were technically Tyndarides. Polydeuces renounced his immortality, unwilling to part with his brother, and the gods turned them into a constellation. This is the zodiacal constellation called *Gemini*, 'the twins.'

The dolphins on the spina were a tribute to the sea god Neptune, who was also a patron of horses.

There were usually seven laps in a chariot race, always run anticlockwise. Up to twelve chariots might begin the race, but not every one reached the finish line. The charioteer could lose control of the team, crash into the spina or a meta, crash – accidentally or on purpose – into another chariot; those spectacular accidents were certainly among the most tempting aspects of the races for the audience. The Romans called such a crash *naufragio*, 'a shipwreck.' A charioteer strapped his whole body and wrists with the reins; that enabled him to rein in the horses using his whole body mass, but it also meant that in case of a crash his chances of surviving intact were very slim indeed. Every charioteer had a dagger which he could use to quickly cut off the reins in case of a fall, but there was usually no time to reach for it. The life of a charioteer could be quite short.

Successful sportsmen, though, became the darlings of the public, just as today. Charioteers were usually men of humble origins – slaves, freedmen; but after even a short string of victories they had enough money to buy themselves out of slavery and retire. No one used that option: vanity and adrenaline blocked the path. Many sportsmen had hundreds of victories under their belts. An imagined poetic epitaph of one such hero is preserved by Martial:

> *I am Scorpus, the glory of the noisy Circus,*
> *the much-applauded and short-lived darling of Rome.*
> *Envious Fate, counting my victories instead of my years,*
> *and so believing me old,*
> *carried me off in my twenty-sixth year.*[43]

It was not just skilled charioteers who had fans; experienced horses had their share of glory and adulation as well. The best stud farms were in North Africa, Spain and Lusitania (Portugal). Special marine vessels were used to ship horses to Rome. They only started to race when they were three years old. When a stallion (mares were rarely used for racing) reached a certain length of service, he was honourably released to graze free. That was probably a rare occurrence. An ancient veterinary treatise describes the many troubles that could happen to a circus horse: lashes (inflicted by one's own team driver or by an adversary), tongue injuries resulting from overdrawn bit, injuries from wheels and axles. Special skill was required from the horse on the inside of the team (the leftmost): when a meta was perfectly skirted, he had to be virtually motionless so that his three companions could describe an arc. It was, most likely, that innermost racer who was marked with a name, along with the charioteer, on mosaics and frescoes dedicated to the victors.

Competition between charioteers alone could not heat up the atmosphere of the races to the levels of battle frenzy that are evident from surviving records. The reason for that was in the team nature of the sport. A team was called *factio*, plural *factiones* – the same word that denoted something like political parties or factions in republican times. There were four *factiones*: white, red, blue and green. Late Christian authors who reported many interesting technical details in the course of their passionate rants against sinful pagan entertainment tell us that the colours symbolised the seasons (blue for autumn, for example). Under Domitian, purple and gold were added, but this novelty was short-lived.

Sports fans are the same in all eras. So are people who like to be grumpy about other people's excessive interest in sports. This is Pliny the Younger, writing to a friend in the early 2nd century AD. Notice the 'seen one, seen them all' argument.

Pliny greets his Calvisius.

All these recent days I have spent in the most agreeable tranquillity among my tablets and my books. 'How could you manage that in this city?' you ask. The races were on, and I take not the slightest interest in that type of performance. There is no novelty, no variation, nothing for which a single viewing would not suffice. This makes me wonder all the more that so many thousands should be so childishly keen, time after time, to see horses galloping and drivers hunched over their chariots. If the attraction for them lay in the speed of the horses or the skill of the riders, there would be some justification for it, but as it is they show their support and affection for the colour of the shirt, and if in mid-course, while the race was being run, the colours should be changed, then the enthusiasm and support of the crowd will be transferred, and in a moment they will forsake the drivers and the horses which they identify repeatedly from afar, and whose names they repeatedly bawl. So devout is the popularity and the authority residing in a single shirt of the cheapest kind, not merely among the common crowd (which is cheaper than the shirt), but among certain men of dignity. When I call these men to mind settling down so insatiably to watch the pointless, tedious, continual pursuit, I get some pleasure in not being captive to such low enjoyment, and I feel the utmost delight in devoting my leisure to literature during the days which others are wasting on the idlest of pursuits. Farewell.[44]

The rivalry was bound to lead to clashes, fights, bloodshed now and then. The Roman passion for horse-racing was inherited and fuelled even more powerfully by the Byzantines. In 532 AD, the sporting passions of Constantinople's fans ignited a rebellion that torched half the city and almost deposed the emperor Justinian I.

Interestingly, the loyalty to a certain faction (the most popular were the blue and the green) was a feature of the fans' life, but not of charioteers'. Their epitaphs and other evidence show that many sportsmen were capped with different teams in different periods of their lives, some even for all four. The fans, however, have left for posterity lead tablets with such instructions: "I call upon you, spirit of an untimely deceased, whoever you are, bind up the horses whose names and likenesses I hereby confide in you. From the team of the Reds: Silvanus, Sevator, Lues… From the Blues: Imminens, Dignus, Linon… Deny them victory, tangle their feet, obstruct them, so that tomorrow morning in the Hippodrome they are unable to run or even to walk slowly. May they fall down, along with their drivers, Euprepes, son of Telesphorus, and Gentius and Felix and Dionysisus the scrapper… Pull them out of their chariots and onto the ground, so that they fall and are dragged all around the track, especially through the turns, and are gravely injured, along with their horses. Do it now, quickly."[45]

BEN-HUR

In 1880 a retired US General Lew Wallace published a novel about a nobleman from Judaea, whose life is transformed through contact with Christ and the early Christians. The novel was called "Ben-Hur: A Tale of the Christ." Wallace had spent years in libraries, trying to find out every possible detail about the life in Roman Judaea – the fabrics used, local flora and fauna, architecture and construction practices. Critics have always been condescending to "Ben-Hur," but the novel's commercial success was phenomenal. It quickly replaced "Uncle Tom's Cabin" by Harriet Beecher Stowe in the top position of bestseller chart and remained America's No. 1 bestseller until the publication of "Gone with the Wind." The success of Ben-Hur changed the perception of the godless novel-writing craft among America's devout, which means that Wallace was not an unimportant figure in the history of American literature. But he was perhaps even more important in the history of cinema. The scene of the chariot race from the 1959 film, with the protagonist competing against his childhood friend turned bitter enemy, the Roman Messala, became legendary.

It is not universally known that before the famous "Ben-Hur" starring Charlton Heston, the film that had garnered eleven Oscars, saved MGM Studios from financial ruin and revived the interest for the sword-and-sandal Roman sagas on the big screen, there was a silent 1925 film starring the outstanding Ramón Novarro. The chariot race was also central to that version. It lacked the unbelievable leap of Ben-Hur's white steeds over the wrecked chariot, but camera work and tightness of the shots are perhaps even more intense in the old movie than in the famous remake. In preparation, the film crew had to reinvent the technology of Roman circus racing, since there was nothing of the kind in modern sport. The shooting of both Ben-Hurs are major achievements of the so-called "practical archaeology."

Even that was not the beginning. In 1907, when the genre of cinema was in its infancy, a fifteen-minute-long version of "Ben-Hur" was shot, and it also featured a chariot race. Firemen with their water-carrying nags played the charioteers, and a beach in New Jersey stood in for the circus of Jerusalem.

Though the 'peplum' genre (strictly speaking, a movie with a plot from antiquity, popular in Italian cinema of the early 1960s) fell out of vogue, attempts never cease; the year 2016 saw the release of a new 3D version of "Ben-Hur," directed by the special effects magician Timur Bekmambetov and starring Jack Huston in the title role and Morgan Freeman in an important supporting role. Though the film turned out to be a "box office bomb," not even grossing its budget, the race scene, about ten minutes long (as in both preceding films), was powerful: the director's intention was to make the viewers feel they were riding inside the chariot.

After the decline of the Roman Empire, the Great Circus slowly sank into oblivion under the layers of sand and mediaeval buildings. However, even in drawings of the 16th century, a thousand years after the last chariot had raced around the spina, one can see that many vaults and walls were still standing, albeit overgrown with vegetation. In mid-19th century, an Anglo-Italian company built a gas works in the circus valley, and it continued to chug, poisoning air and the view, for over fifty years. Only in the 1930s all later accretions were removed, and the Circus Maximus transformed into a ghost-like but lofty shadow of itself.

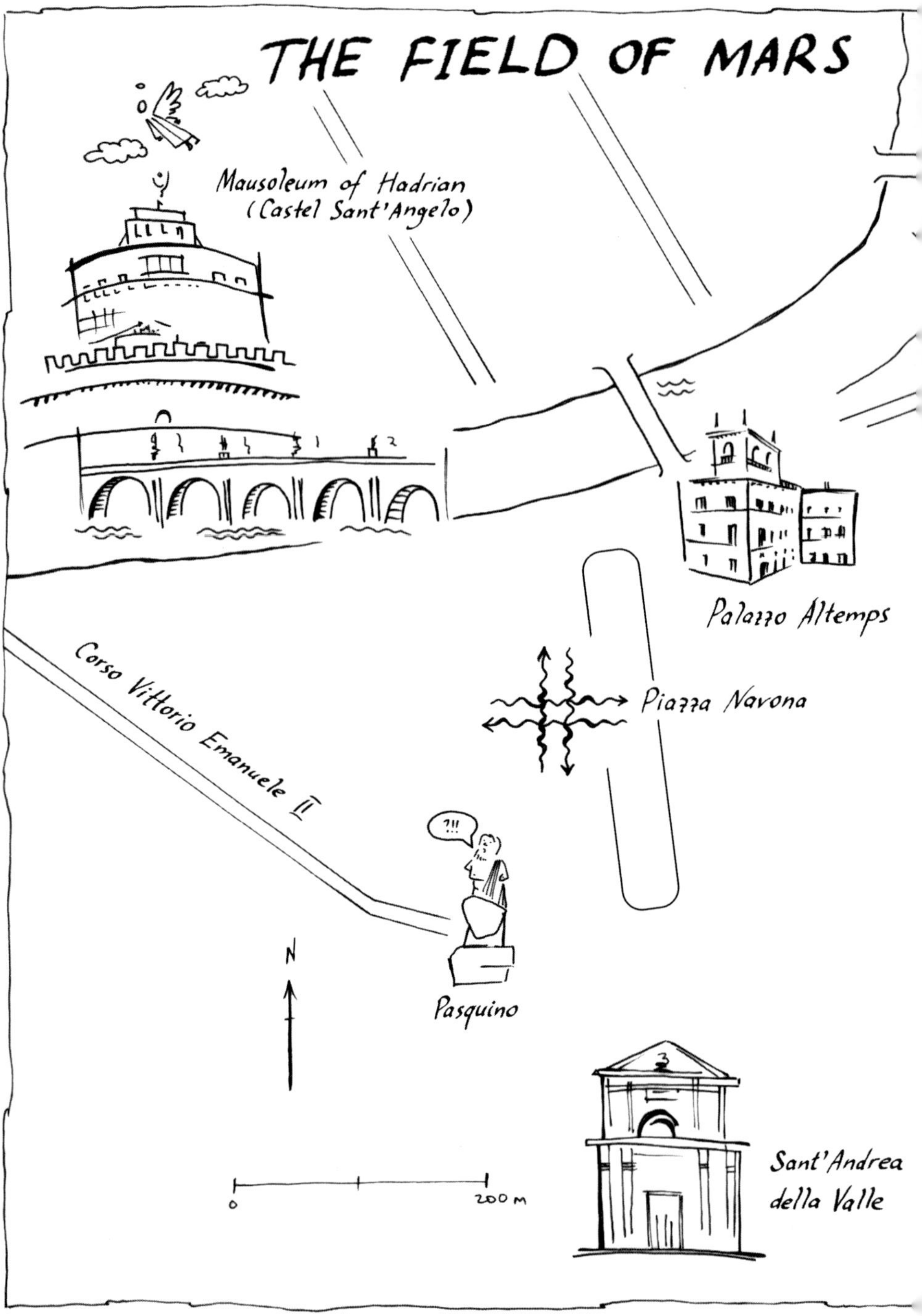

THE FIELD OF MARS

Mausoleum of Hadrian
(Castel Sant'Angelo)

Palazzo Altemps

Corso Vittorio Emanuele II

Piazza Navona

Pasquino

N

0   200 M

Sant'Andrea
della Valle

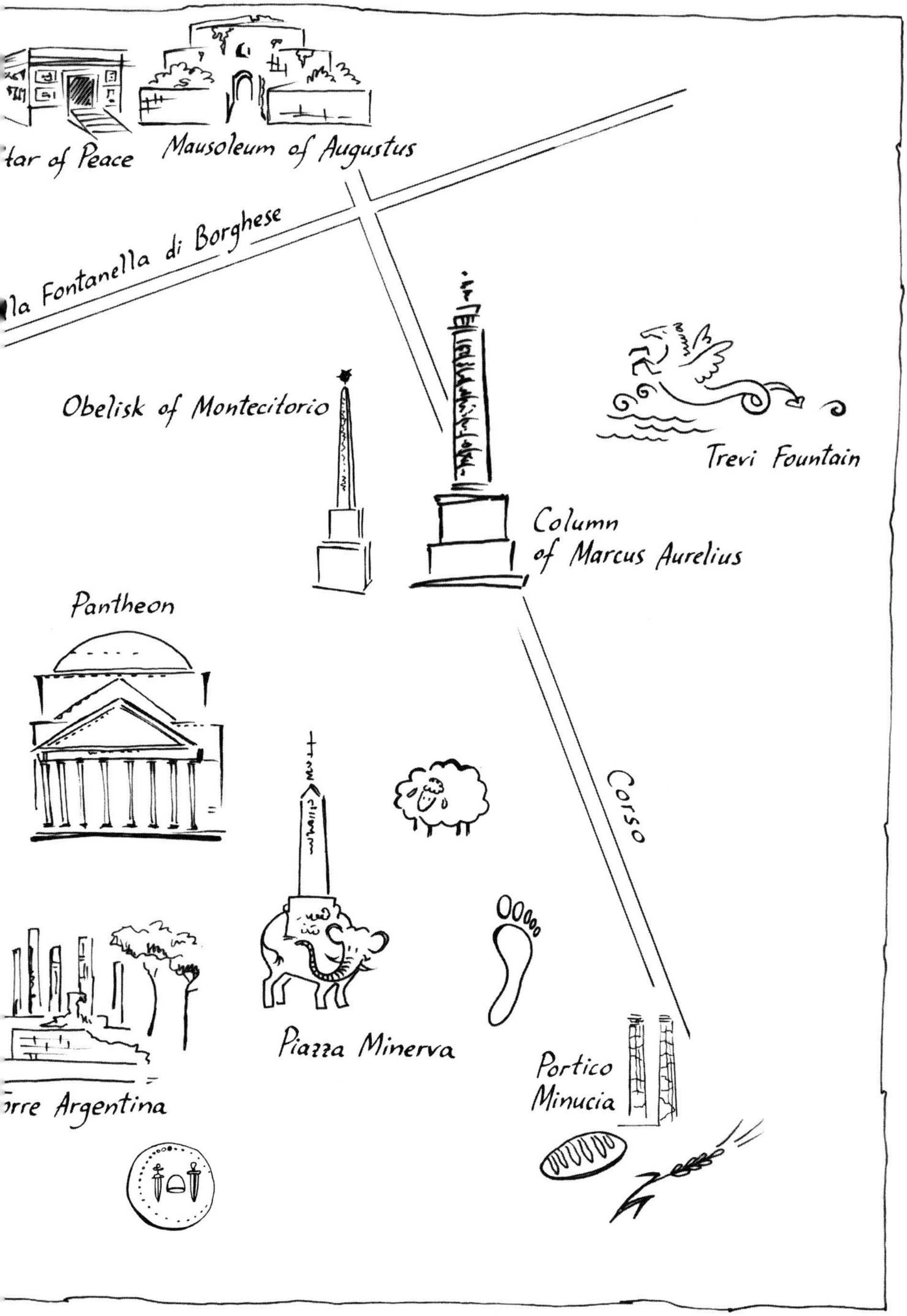

Altar of Peace   Mausoleum of Augustus

la Fontanella di Borghese

Obelisk of Montecitorio

Trevi Fountain

Column
of Marcus Aurelius

Pantheon

Corso

Piazza Minerva

Portico
Minucia

Torre Argentina

C H A P T E R   V I I I

THE FIELD OF MARS
(OBELISKS AND MAUSOLEUMS)

The Forum, Palatine, Capitol, Colosseum – all these places are steeped in legend, crowded with history and, as a consequence, with tourists. When the throngs of multilingual visitors and stentorian tour guides disperse, the places appear rather deflated.

The Field of Mars, on the contrary, is living the real life. Early in the morning, coffee-houses open up in narrow streets; a white-collar stockbroker dismounts from his bike and swallows the scalding drop of espresso at the bar counter (it is cheaper if the customer remains standing) before riding on, past the monument to a marble foot, toward his workplace, the offices that occupy the Temple of Hadrian. On Campo dei Fiori, greengrocers set up stands with wild strawberries and tomatoes. At five in the morning, the only people near the Trevi Fountain are a travelling photographer with a huge camera on a tripod and a young woman with a paper notebook and a box of crayons. Dustcarts speed around the Pantheon square, removing the leaflets after a political rally held here the day before.

It is not a coincidence that most directors of movies set in Rome, while paying respectful lip service to the Forum and Colosseum, prefer to frame the most important events in their characters' stories within the Field of Mars settings.

THE FIELD

Ancient Rome was a huge city, much bigger than mediaeval or Renaissance Rome. When the empire began to dwindle and the population shrank a hundredfold, life had seeped out of monumental neighbourhoods and abandoned palaces, concentrating in a triangular area described by the sharp bend of the river that roughly corresponds to the Field of Mars – roughly, because there are no universally accepted distinct limits of it.

Here is a strange thing. The Greek scholar Strabo who used to spend long stretches of time in Rome under Augustus wrote a monumental opus, "Geography," describing the whole of the known world. First of all, there is no more than a few paragraphs about the capital of the universe. Second, he focused his attention on this plot of land, which was far from the most solemn or celebrated:

> In fact, Pompey, the Deified Caesar, Augustus, his sons and friends, and wife and sister, have outdone all others in their zeal for buildings and in the expense incurred. The Campus Martius contains most of these, and thus, in addition to its natural beauty, it has received still further adornment as the result of foresight. Indeed, the size of the Campus is remarkable, since it affords space at the same time and without interference, not only for the chariot-races and every other equestrian exercise, but also for all that multitude of people who exercise themselves by ball-playing, hoop-trundling, and wrestling; and the works of art situated around the Campus Martius, and the ground, which is covered with grass throughout the year, and the crowns of those hills that are above the river and extend as far as its bed, which

present to the eye the appearance of a stage-painting – all this,
I say, affords a spectacle that one can hardly draw away from.

This passage is followed by a detailed description of Augustus's Mausoleum, then by a few perfunctory words about the Forum, Palatine and Capitol and the final conclusion: "Such is Rome."[46]

According to a legend (the only way to introduce stories about Roman beginnings), the Field of Mars had belonged to the family of Tarquins, the last Roman kings. When the Tarquins were banished from the city, their property passed into public possession, and the grain harvest was for some reason (as recounted in the previous chapter) thrown into the Tiber.

The first (and for a very long time the only) public building in the Field of Mars was called just that – "public building" (*Villa Publica*). No traces of it were ever found, which makes it rather difficult to say what it looked like; some images on coins and on the *Forma Urbis Romae* suggest that it was a wide walled enclosure with a two-storeyed building in the middle. In Republican times, this place was used for the census and call-up.

It was in Villa Publica that several thousand Samnite POWs were slaughtered on Sulla's orders. Sulla himself was at that moment presiding over a Senate meeting in the Temple of Bellona; when cries and groans floated from the Villa, he coolly said to terror-stricken dignitaries: "Let us proceed with business, father Senators, this is nothing more than a bunch of rebels being executed on my order."

We will begin our ramble around the Field of Mars from the south, the side of the Forum Boarium (which is sometimes considered a part of the Field of Mars and not an area in its own right). Our starting point is a sector between Corso Vittorio Emanuele II and the small street with a Gothic name of Via delle Botteghe Oscure ('the street of dark shops'). This sector is bordered on the west by Via di Torre Argentina, and along it, on a noisy street with trams, lies one of Rome's oldest archaeological areas.

The name of the street and square have nothing to do with Argentina the country. It is derived from the name of the tower of a nearby house in Via del Sudario built by Johann Burchard, a Master of Ceremonies who survived four popes and left a record of the most important papal ceremonies, including the infamous 'Banquet of Chestnuts' of 1501, when members of the papal court were rewarded with expensive prizes in accordance with the number of their copulations with prostitutes. The prizes were distributed by His Holiness himself and his children Cesare and Lucrezia.

Burchard was a native of Strasbourg; there had been a Roman outpost in Upper Germany since at least 12 BC under the name of Argentoratum (hence Argentina). In 1988, the citizens of Strasbourg celebrated the bimillennial anniversary – commonly for events that happened before the accepted date of Christ's birth, with a one-year error.

The tower in the corner of the archaeological area is not Torre Argentina, but the so-called Torre del Papito ('little pope') ascribed to antipope Anacletus II of the 12th century, who was a man of small stature.

TEMPLES OF TORRE ARGENTINA

Ancient buildings were found here in the 1920s, during the work aimed at widening the streets and clearing the site for future development. The development never materialised: Mussolini was very happy about the find and, it was reported, promised to execute anyone who would insist on a more practical use for the plot. Unfortunately, the excavation was carried out hastily and sloppily; even with recent advances in archaeological technique, many questions remain. The main problem is failure to securely identify the ancient temples that used to occupy this small space. Even tour guides, often prone to fantasising, use the unimaginative names from scholarly books: temples A, B, C and D.

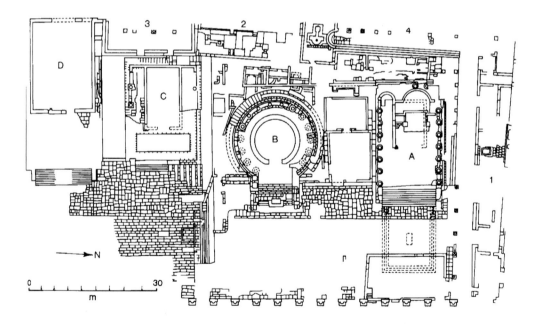

Temple A – leftmost, if you look at the archaeological area from Via di Torre Argentina – is preserved somewhat better than the others, because in the 12th century it had housed the church of San Nicola dei Cesarini (or 'dei Calcarari,' of lime-burners). One possible identification is the Temple of Juturna, the old Latin deity. If that is correct, this would be Rome's first temple of Juturna (a later one, on the Forum, was discussed in Chapter 1), vowed by general Gaius Lutatius Catulus during a victorious battle of the First Punic War.

The round Temple B is the latest of the four. It is also the only one attributed with some degree of reliability. It is the Temple of Today's Fortune (*Fortuna Huiusce Diei*), built by another Lutatius Catulus — one Quintus, a decendant of the aforementioned. Today's Fortune is the goddess that controls the delicate balance of things, able to shift it toward either salvation or destruction. Catulus thanked Fortune for the victory at Vercellae in 101 BC, when the Germanic tribe of Cimbri was routed, and a barbarian march on Rome averted. The victory over an external enemy did not stop internal feuds, but, as it were, fanned them further: another general, Marius, disputed the laurels of Catulus for the Vercellae victory, while Catulus was supported by an enemy of Marius, Sulla, himself a lucky general and ambitious politician. Several years later, Rome was engulfed by the first of the murderous civil wars that were to continue for almost a whole century. Catulus, among others, was soon disfavoured by Fortuna. When Marius defeated (temporarily) his adversaries, Catulus was charged with a variety of crimes, and, knowing full well that the judgement would not be impartial, he committed suicide.

Fragments of a giant cult statue were found near that temple — a head, a hand and a foot, now on display at the Montemartini Museum. The head's ears are pierced — apparently, to accommodate precious earrings of appropriate size. Pliny the Elder informs us that many Greek statues stood under the portico of the Temple of Fortune — seven young men and one old man; and three more statues by the great Phidias were inside.

Temple C — a very ancient one, dating to the 3rd century BC — had once stood on a podium twenty steps high (note again how much the cultural layer has risen). There is still an old altar under the travertine masonry in front of the temple. An inscription on it says that it was restored according to such and such laws by Aulus Postumius Albinus, son of Aulus, grandson of Aulus. There are a few matching Postumii Albini in the historical record (with a dispersion of about half a century), but we do not know which of them left us this inscription.

Temple C is claimed by the goddess Feronia — an Italic deity absorbed into the Roman pantheon after the nation that used to venerate her received the rights of Roman citizenship (they were either Etruscans or Sabines, according to different sources). The goddess was connected to agriculture; she was the patroness of slaves and especially freedmen. Titus Livius describes endless omens of the Hannibalic war, from the truly ominous ("glowing stones had fallen from the sky at Praeneste; at Arpi bucklers had appeared in the sky and the sun had seemed to be fighting with the moon; at Capena two moons had risen in the daytime") to the outright comical ("a hen had changed into a cock and a cock into a hen") and concludes that the priests told all the orders to make sacrifices to their respective 'corporate' gods; in particular, freedwomen were to "contribute money, in proportion to their abilities, for an offering to Feronia."[47]

The rightmost temple D is the largest, but it is almost completely concealed by the pavement of Via Florida. It was rebuilt several times, but even its earliest podium is made of concrete, which means that it can hardly be older than 2nd century BC (concrete was very rarely used in Roman buildings before then). Like many other edifices in the neighbourhood, temple D was restored around 80 AD, after a major fire. In scholarly literature, this temple is claimed by a host of obscure deities: Juno Curita, Jupiter the Lightning Thrower, nymphs and marine lares (of which more later).

If you stand directly opposite the round temple and look down, beyond the enclosure of the archaeological area, you will see the site where one of the most momentous events of Roman history had occurred – the place where Julius Caesar was assassinated.

By a cruel irony of fate, Caesar was murdered in the portico named after his sworn enemy, Pompey. Pompey, who built Rome's first stone theatre and a wide shadowy colonnade (portico) next to it, was long defeated by Caesar in battle and treacherously murdered by the Egyptians, in whose kingdom he hoped to find refuge. By the fateful Ides of March, the portico was a favourite spot for a stroll, especially among the younger people. Roman poets hint that it was one of the best pick-up places in town. Martial says as much using a proof by contradiction:

> He never goes to Pompey's Porch
> As many others do,
> Or Isis' shrine, where whores hang out,
> –He does not wish to screw.[48]

The Portico of Pompey, like many public buildings in Rome, had special rooms for Senate business (called "Pompey's Curia" in this case), which was quite handy at times when the proper Curia was unavailable (see Chapter 1).

So much has been said and written about the assassination of Caesar that retelling the story for the millionth time seems unnecessary. Even if each of the many classical authors who reported the dictator's death invented some details, the general outline of the events is still supernaturally dramatic: the long-ago prediction about the Ides of March; the omens on the night before the assassination; Caesar's wife has a bad dream, he wants to stay home but is persuaded to come by one of the conspirators; before the Senate session he receives a message with a warning but puts it aside to read later; the conspirators cleverly manoeuvre Mark Antony away from Caesar, because aside from being Caesar's friend and staunch supporter, he is so strong physically that it can interfere with their plans, in spite of their numerical superiority; having directed Caesar into one of the rooms of Pompey's portico, they surround him, pretend to pester with various requests and finally assault him, inflicting over twenty stab wounds (seeing that resistance is futile, Caesar pulls his toga over his head in a gesture of resignation); the dictator in his bloodied toga succumbs at the foot of a statue of Pompey. Suetonius quotes the first coroner's report that has come down to us: only one wound, the expert says, was lethal, and death occurred from blood loss; vital organs were not damaged.

Caesar's famous last words – "You too, Brutus?" – were also immortalised by Shakespeare; in the play, Julius Caesar says it in Latin – *Et tu, Brute?* – like Russian mobsters in Hollywood movies, who sometimes switch from accented English into accented Russian. Suetonius reports that Caesar said "And you, child?" in Greek – in tune with the rumour that Brutus was his illegitimate son – but himself considers it a romantic invention.

A coin issued by the conspirators. On the face side, a portrait of Brutus;
on the reverse, daggers, a Phrygian cap (also known as 'liberty cap,'
worn by manumitted slaves) and the inscription "The Ides of March."
17th-century drawing

The "Liberators" (that was how the conspirators chose to style themselves) misjudged the people's mood. The indignation was such that the room where the murder took place was set on fire (though not before the statue of Pompey was safely evacuated). Later, under Augustus, the site was walled up as "cursed" *(locus sceleratus)* and a public loo was installed nearby. Its remains are still visible to the right of the portico (looking from Via di Torre Argentina).

The baroque Villa Arconati near Milan boasts a statue of Pompey in the 'heroic nudity' style. It is thought to be the very statue at whose feet Caesar was murdered. The Romans, however, prefer to think that the statue never left the Eternal City, and is standing today in Palazzo Spada, the seat of the Italian Council of State, while the Milanese simply got hold of a copy.

THE THEATRE OF POMPEY

Pompey's portico was only an annexe to a much more monumental building, a theatre erected by Pompey on the Field of Mars. It was Rome's first permanent theatre, which was never surpassed in terms of size. Christian author Tertullian writes that the Romans of the time were wary about the idea of theatre: it smacked of dissolution, of suspicious Greek entertainment, and of a morally dubious method of glorifying the sponsor. To counter allegations of self-interest, Pompey combined the theatre with a temple of Venus Victrix (or the goddess of Victory plain and simple, according to other sources): the seats of the theatre were supposed to double as the steps of the temple. Such a practice was known in the Greek East, though the temple was usually on a summit of a hill, and the steps/seats were dug into the slope. Perhaps a transfer of this idea into the low-lying Tiber valley wouldn't have worked, or maybe pretend piety was no longer necessary – be that as it may, the other two of Rome's stone theatres (of Marcellus and of Balbus) no longer disguised themselves as temples.

When Pompey was dedicating the new theatre, a curious linguistic problem occurred: he could not decide how to style himself in the dedicatory inscription, *consul tertio* or *consul tertium* (roughly speaking, 'consul for the third time' or 'thrice consul'). Experts, as usual, offered contradictory advice; Pompey turned to Cicero for the final verdict. The cautious Cicero, unwilling to offend previous advisers, wiggled out brilliantly, saying – write *'consul tert.'* Aulus Gellius who retold the story from the words of Tyro, Cicero's secretary, reports that the final inscription was even simpler: consul III.

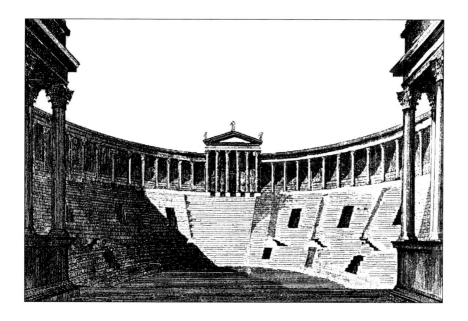

Festivities were organised for the theatre's dedication, including a mass-scale elephant battle. Spectators were duly impressed, but their sympathies were firmly with the noble animals who fought valiantly, and not with their human tormentors.

Today, no traces of the theatre are visible above ground, but there are lots in the basements of nearby houses: whole quarters were built on the foundations of the auditorium and the stage. Concrete vaults and tufa-lined walls can be observed in the restaurants *Costanza* in Piazza del Paradiso and *Da Pancrazio* in Piazza del Biscione. The curve of the seating area is still visible in the contour of streets and squares west of Largo di Torre Argentina (between the church of San Andrea della Valle and the Campo dei Fiori) and in the façade of palazzo Orsini Pio Righetti on Via di Grotta Pinta. The mediaeval tower next to the palazzo is standing on the foundation of the temple of Venus. The baroque building had long stood abandoned, but today it houses the Rome campus of Washington State University.

The theatre's underground remains probably date to Augustan reconstruction, large-scale enough to find its way into the emperor's brief autobiography: "The Theatre of Pompey, involving great expense, I rebuilt without any inscription of my own name."[49] Later builders continued to add to the edifice under Tiberius, under Nero, under Septimius Severus, and later, up to the 5th century AD, when the theatre and its portico were destroyed by an earthquake.

THE THEATRE OF BALBUS

The Field of Mars was really Rome's theatre quarter – all three of the city's permanent theatres were there or very close. We have covered the Theatre of Marcellus in the preceding chapter and the Theatre of Pompey just now; the remaining one is the smallest, the Theatre of Balbus.

Lucius Cornelius Balbus Junior (his uncle is Balbus Senior) hailed from the city of Gades (now Cádiz) in Spain. He was Julius Caesar's subordinate in the civil wars; after that, his trace gets lost, and we hear of him again a few decades later, during the late years of Augustus: he is the proconsul of the province of Africa. In this capacity, he defeated the Saharan tribe of the Garamantes and was awarded a triumph. That event was not special in itself, but it happened to be the first and last of a kind. Balbus became the first triumphator who was not born a Roman citizen, and the last who was not a member of the imperial family. After him, the tradition that had meant so much to generals and people with political ambitions passed into the category of courtly favours.

The theatre was inaugurated in 13 BC. It so happened that at exactly the same time Augustus was returning to Rome after a long state visit to Western provinces. This coincidence made Balbus leap into action: he was happy to imply either that the theatre's inauguration was connected with the emperor's return or that the emperor's return was specifically timed to give him a chance to grace the new theatre with his presence. The Tiber untimely flooded again, and the VIPs had to sail up to the theatre in boats.

The Theatre of Balbus was the smallest and the poshest of the three. Even its décor was more sumptuous. Pliny the Elder mentions four small onyx columns, known across Rome as an architectural wonder.

For a long time, the position of the Theatre of Balbus was only approximately known, but in the end excavations and scrutiny of the Forma Urbis Romae bore fruit. The theatre itself is buried under later buildings (as many ancient remains on the Field of Mars), but a fragment of its quadriportico is opened to the public. A quadriportico is a small building next to the stage, where spectators could relax, have a chat, wait out a boring performance and, perhaps, have a snack. The museum is called "The Crypt of Balbus" (*Crypta Balbi*), and it is one of the rare Roman museums with emphasis on the complex posthumous life of ancient structures. There was an aggregation of many cultural layers above the theatre and the crypt in the course of centuries, and the museum patiently attempts to unravel and explain them.

A large and lavish lavatory was built in the exedra of the portico in the times of Hadrian. In the 2nd century AD, such establishments sprang up all over the empire (in Rome, apart from the Theatre of Balbus, they can be found at the portico of Pompey, on the Forum of Caesar, in the palace on the Palatine): at the time, the Roman elite developed a taste for communal bowel movements, accompanied by discussions of philosophy, healthy life and digestion.

Starting from the 16th century, this neighbourhood was the hub for Rome's large Polish community centred around the church San Stanislao dei Polacchi on the same street.

Via dei Polacchi leads to the picturesque Piazza Margana, surrounded by 16th and 17th-century houses, and Via Margana, where a late Roman Ionic capital is built into the wall of a mediaeval tower (No. 40a); three fragments of a graceful entablature, also ancient Roman, can be seen next to it. In the 12th century, such use of ancient fragments (instead of burning them for lime, which was done right on the location of the crypt) became a sign of prestige, especially among house owners who aspired to education.

Almost directly opposite the museum, on the other side of Via delle Botteghe Oscure, two columns of an unknown temple stand behind the standard 'archaeological' enclosure. The temple was discovered in the late 1930s (as usual, during works on the foundation of a new house, which in the end was never erected), the columns were restored in 1954. The Forma Urbis Romae gives us a general idea of the temple: it was huge, peripteral (with columns on all four sides), with an inner colonnade and a large pediment where, probably, the deity statue was standing or sitting. Perhaps there was a large solemn portico surrounding the temple. Some archaeologists think that it is the portico of Minutius, built by Marcus Minutius Rufus, consul of 110 BC. Later, apparently, another portico was built next to it, because from a certain time, our sources mention two porticoes of Minutius – the 'old' one and the 'cereal' one.

What does 'cereal' (*frumentaria*) mean? It is known that the Romans had clamoured for bread and not just for the circuses. Supplying citizens with grain was considered the task of the state since time immemorial; the Romans were the first to introduce the practice of caring for the poorest which would be later called 'the welfare state.' It was legally required that the government provide its citizens with a certain amount of grain either free of charge or at prices well below the market. These 'grain laws' had quickly destroyed Italy's agriculture: Roman citizens stopped cultivating corn, and grain now had to be imported from the provinces. Some emperors made feeble attempts to correct the situation, but these attempts invariably failed.

It would be wrong to imagine that the grain handout was only intended for Rome's poorest, those who gave history the term 'proletariat' (which means 'people who do not produce anything except children,' from the Latin *proles*, 'offspring'). Basic statistics show that it was not so. Augustus writes that under his rule, over 200,000 people were receiving grain rations, while other sources cite even higher figures. At one point, the right for the dole was given to everyone except senators, and the distribution of grain was handled by a special arm of bureaucracy with ruthless Roman efficiency: every citizen had a 'ration card' (not on paper, of course, but on a pottery shard) which he or she could use to receive a certain amount of grain on a certain day at a strictly defined location. Apparently, the Porticus Minutia was one of such places, but there were many counters (*ostia*) in operation, and every recipient was assigned a counter for life. An astounding testimony of this practice is an epitaph on a burial chest of a little boy in the British Museum (room G70):

"To Gaius Sergius Alcimus, son of Gaius, who had lived three years, three months and three days. He received grain on the 10th of each month at counter 39."

If the temple opposite the Crypta Balbi indeed stood inside the Porticus Minutia, it might have been the temple of the Sea Lares (*Lares Permarini*). It was vowed in 190 BC by the praetor Lucius Aemilius Regillus during the sea battle against Antiochus the Great. Some archaeologists, however, place the Porticus Minutia around today's excavations on Largo di Torre Argentina, which make the temple of Sea Lares one of the square's four (possibly Temple D).

The Lares are the guardians of household hearths, which makes the Sea Lares the keepers of the sailors' homes, the ships. It was natural for an admiral to vow a temple to these deities during a sea battle – especially a sea battle against a foe as formidable as Antioch III the Great, the ruler of the Seleucid kingdom. It was a mighty Eastern state that had appeared when Alexander the Great's empire was divided by his generals. The portico of the Sea Lares temple sported a plaque with celebratory verses that told how the invincible Seleucid fleet was smashed in plain view of "king Antiochus, his army, horses and elephants."

In all fairness, Antiochus had been forewarned. After Hannibal had been definitively defeated by the Romans, he roved from one oriental court to the other, offering consulting services, like Tony Blair many centuries later; Antiochus was among those who welcomed him. One day, Antiochus paraded his troops before the famous consultant: infantry with gleaming shields, horses with golden bridles, elephants in lavishly embroidered saddle-blankets. "What do you think," the king said, "would that be sufficient for the Romans?" – "I guess it would," said Hannibal, "even though they are extremely greedy."

PANTHEON

If you walk due north from Largo di Torre Argentina or from Crypta Balbi, you will almost inevitably reach the Pantheon.

The Pantheon is one of the best known architectural monuments of the Classical world. The Parthenon and Colosseum are perhaps the only other contenders for top position on that chart. Michelangelo called it "a creation of angels and not of human hands"; Pope Urban VIII who played an important part in Pantheon's destiny called it "the most celebrated building of the whole world" (*edificium toto terrarum orbe celeberrimum*). Add to that the fact that the Pantheon has survived in a state of preservation that neither the Colosseum nor the Parthenon can dream of. Several generations of popes have rebuilt the roof of the portico, restored the east corner of the pronaos (pronaos is the open section of the portico between outer columns and the entrance into the temple proper); bronze tiles were stripped off the roof and lead tiles put there instead – and that is about it. Even the interior decoration has not changed that much since ancient times (excluding, of course, paintings and tombs that appeared much later). There is no classical edifice in the world that is more authentic than the Pantheon.

History loves paradoxes, and piled them abundantly in the case of the Pantheon. We can see the building, we can touch its ancient stones and study them using the most advanced modern technology, and yet we know next to nothing about its initial purpose and functions. Classical authors give us only tiny scraps of information. It is not even known what its name means. Of course, the etymology is quite clear, 'Pantheon' is a combination of two Greek words that mean 'all' and 'god,' but whether it means 'the temple of all gods' or 'the holiest temple' – this, we simply do not know. Cassius Dio, one of the few ancient authors who mention the Pantheon at all, thought that the name is derived from the dome that looks like the heavens.

Most likely, Dio was wrong, and not just about that. He ascribes the Pantheon to Marcus Vipsanius Agrippa, a friend and associate of Augustus. Indeed, there is an inscription in huge letters on the attic of the portico: M. AGRIPPA L. F. COS. TERTIUM FECIT ("Marcus Agrippa, son of Lucius, three times consul, made [this]"). Bronze letters were restored in late 19th century at the suggestion of Minister of Education Guido Bacelli, but the placement of holes made the inscription easily legible even before.

However, seeing is not necessarily believing. In 1892 Georges Chedanne, an archaeologist working at the French Academy (with its seat, then as now, in Villa Medici, up the Spanish Steps), found that the Pantheon was largely made of bricks dating to 120–125 AD. Agrippa had died a hundred years earlier.

Roman bricks were produced using an industrial process, and in industrial quantities. Before heat processing, the bricks were stamped with manufacturer stamps and often a date. (The Roman dating system was based on consuls of a given year. There were more general systems, like counting years from the foundation of the city, but, just like the Greek system of dating by Olympic games, it was a scholarly gimmick that was never used in everyday life or bureaucratic record-keeping.) Brick stamps helped to date many Roman buildings. In the case of the Pantheon, most bricks studied by Chedanne were produced during the consulship of Quintus Articuleus Petinus and Lucius Venuleus Apronianus, which is 123 AD by our reckoning.

This meant that the Pantheon was built under the rule of the emperor Hadrian. It was a well known feature of his rule that he never signed his reconstruction projects (except the Temple of Deified Trajan), preserving the original dedication. Agrippa's Pantheon seemed to have perished in a fire of 80 AD, was restored under Domitian, burned down again after a lightning strike, and appeared in its present form only after that. Not even a foundation was preserved from its first two incarnations.

The Pantheon is a very unorthodox edifice. To what extent it has acquired the features of its predecessors is hard to say. Ancient sources say that Agrippa had wanted to adorn the temple with a statue of Augustus, but Augustus, driven by modesty (or hypocrisy), refused that honour; in the event, Agrippa installed a statue of Julius Caesar, while a statue of Augustus (and of himself to boot) was placed under the portico. Pliny the Elder reports that a statue of Venus, decorated with one of Cleopatra's earrings cut in two, also stood under the portico, while between the columns (or "on the columns," the language is ambiguous) stood caryatids of Greek craftsmanship, the prettiest in the world.

What happened to Cleopatra's other earring? It became the stuff of legend as an ingredient of history's most expensive dish. When Cleopatra was entertaining Mark Antony and his retinue for the first time, she made a bet with one of the guests, claiming that she would be able to easily concoct an astronomically expensive drink. To prove her point, she took out her huge pearl earring, of the kind that cost a fortune, dropped it into a cup of vinegar, and drank it up to the astonishment of her dinner companions.

The story is not very plausible: it is not that easy to dissolve pearl, even in concentrated acid, and drinking concentrated acid is, well, unsafe; do not try this at home. On the other hand, pearls are easily crushed; having crushed an earring with something heavy, one can easily wash it down with something more palatable than vinegar. This is exactly what Sir Thomas Gresham, an English merchant and banker, did at a feast given by Elizabeth I. But Cleopatra's legend was preserved and perpetuated in paintings and poetry.

Hadrian's Pantheon consists of two clearly distinguishable parts: the portico and the round domed cylinder ('rotunda'). They share a common low foundation (it is less than one metre high), but their interrelationship is complicated, if not strained. The traditional genre of temple architecture – a portico – is connected to a round concrete wall and vault, an architectural feature previously used in baths and palaces.

The tension between the portico and rotunda is obvious in design as well. Viewed laterally, they are seen to be joined by a transition unit of sorts, which has two cornices; the upper continues a similar cornice on the rotunda, and the latter coincides with the cornice of the portico, while on the rotunda there is nothing whatsoever to correspond to it. This awkward combination might have been caused by a logistics problem. For example, if the initial plan was to erect taller columns, but they were never delivered (lost, damaged en route) and the builders had to replace them with what was available. Quartz diorite, the material of most columns of the portico, was quarried in Roman times from a single mine in East Egypt; delivering huge stone slabs to the Field of Mars in Rome was a task both very demanding technically and very cost-intensive.

In ancient times, the Pantheon stood in an environment that was very different from today's. Its entrance, oriented due north, opened onto a huge rectangular square that covered a whole block, almost all the way to where the church of Santa Maria Maddalena stands today. On the sides and from the rear, the rotunda was, on the contrary, constrained by neighbouring buildings – the voting precinct and the Basilica of Neptune. The colour deviation of the front left columns is not a part of the original design. In the Middle Ages, after a number of earthquakes, the left portion of the portico was severely damaged, and in the 17th century the problematic columns were replaced with others, carved from pink Aswan granite (the one in the corner was pillaged from Hadrian's villa in Castelgandolfo, the other two from the neighbouring baths). The roof space, empty and full of holes today, used to be decorated with something, and the position of the holes suggests that it was an eagle with a wreath, symbols of Jupiter. The concrete of the rotunda was covered with stucco to imitate marble.

Most likely, the vault was also decorated on the inside. Its rectangular depressions are not purely decorative, they make the heavy dome lighter. Many cunning techniques were employed to reinforce and lighten the dome. The thickness of concrete decreases from the foundation up: in the lower part, it is six metres, in the upper just above a metre. The opening – called *oculus*, the eye – also makes the structure lighter. Finally, from the bottom up, the concrete itself becomes lighter: in the upper part of the dome, aggregate with the lowest possible density is used – pumice, the porous volcanic rock.

The result was a true architectonic wonder. The dome of the Pantheon to this day remains the world's largest unreinforced concrete dome. The proportions of the building accommodate a perfect sphere: it is 43.3 metres from the oculus to the floor, and the diameter of the rotunda is exactly the same. The plumbing system under the floor easily deals with the rainfall through the oculus. On those rare days when it snows in Rome, few things are as pretty as the whirling of snowflakes in the beam of light from the oculus.

On the lower level, trapeze-shaped and semi-circular niches alternate in the massive wall. There are seven of them (a magic number); the door takes the place of the eighth (and the deepest niche is directly opposite the door). The Pantheon's bronze doors date from Classical times, though they are not likely to be the original doors of Hadrian's edifice. Note that the upper part of the portal is covered by a decorative grill – the original doors must have been taller. In any case, this is one of the three pairs of functioning ancient doors in Rome (the other two are in the "Temple of Romulus" on the Forum and in the cathedral of St. John Lateran). The threshold is marked by a large slab of African marble, and the tiles of the floor are made of granite, porphyry and other types of coloured stone.

We know little of the uses of the Pantheon in ancient times. The ancient college of the Arval Brethren, priests in charge of food supply, used to convene there. Hadrian himself held court there. In 399 AD, the emperor Honorius (or his advisors – Honorius himself was fifteen years old at the time) prohibited the performance of pagan rites in the Pantheon. The building would have stood desolate and abandoned, slowly chipped away for building materials, if not for a happy chance. During his brief visit to Rome, the Byzantine usurper Phocas, the very one in whose honour a column was erected on the Forum, offered the Pantheon as a gift to Pope Boniface IV. In 609, the pope consecrated the Pantheon with the name Santa Maria dei Martiri, and the relics from early Christian tombs (catacombs) were transferred (the technical term is 'translated') there. The correct name of the church is rarely used, and the people of Rome have usually called the church Santa Maria Rotonda. Unlike some other classical buildings that were preserved thanks to being converted into Christian shrines, the Pantheon was not deconsecrated into a museum.

Soon after its transformation into a church, the Pantheon lost its gilt bronze tiles from the roof. An attempt was made to evacuate them to Constantinople, but the Saracens intercepted the cargo in Sicily and sent to Alexandria to be melted down. In the 8th century, Pope Gregory III covered the roof with lead; that cover was many times renewed, but has, by and large, survived until today. In the 13th century, a small bell tower was annexed to the church, only to be demolished later.

In the Renaissance era, an interest in ancient monuments sprang up with renewed force. The Pantheon was surrounded by excavations – which were very far from modern archaeological standards, of course. Pope Eugene IV cleared the portico from rubble and shops that had accumulated; a bronze quadriga was found but later lost. Other finds included a large red porphyry vase, now housing the ashes of Pope Clement XII at St. John Lateran, and lions (also of porphyry, only grey), dispatched by Pope Sixtus V to guard the Aqua Felice fountain on the Piazza San Bernardo. In the late 16th century, Pope Gregory XIII redesigned the square to make it more or less what we see today, down to the fountain in the middle, with the exception of the Egyptian obelisk which was inserted into the fountain in the early 18th century.

Perhaps the most massive intervention in the Pantheon's appearance was initiated by Pope Urban VIII, previously known as Maffeo Barberini. He occupied the Holy See from 1623 to 1644. First, he stripped the building of its inner bronze decorations that had survived since antiquity (even that was a remarkable feat of longevity) and sent them to be melted down for cannons that were needed for the protection of Vatican's Castel Sant'Angelo. This unexpected spoliation enraged the Romans and inspired the most famous pasquinade (see below) of all times: "What the barbarians did not do, the Barberini did" (in Latin, the pun is even more direct: *Quod non fecerunt barbari, fecerunt Barberini*). To save face, Urban VIII pretended that the bronze was needed for a pious enterprise – the Bernini-designed canopy over the altar of St. Peter's (Bernini never saw the Pantheon bronze, which was used up for the cannons). The lie, however, is perpetuated in Latin inscriptions on marble tablets on either side of the Pantheon door. Urban VIII remarks on his other exploits in remodelling the Pantheon, "once impiously dedicated by Agrippa, Augustus's son-in-law, to Jupiter and other false gods." One of them is the construction of twin towers (*binae turres*) at the sides of the portico. The design was again by Bernini, but the towers turned out to be awkward and out of place and soon earned the nickname of 'ass's ears' (*orecchie d'asino*). They were torn down in the late 19th century.

TALKING STATUES

A pasquinade is a short satirical utterance, often in verse, as if on behalf of a statue. The tradition dates back to the 16th century, when a cardinal set up a time-worn chunk of ancient sculpture in the vicinity of Piazza Navona. How the practice got going and why such name, is difficult to say. One of the versions says that a tailor, master Pasquino, lived in this neighbourhood, and people used to come together at his workshop and freely discuss whatever and whomever they wished to discuss; when Pasquino died and people were stripped of a venue for self-expression, they began writing caustic verses on a statue, which they called Pasquino in memory of the deceased freethinker. Other people said that Pasquino was not a tailor, but a barber (or perhaps a teacher), and was not known as a supporter of free speech – he simply looked like the statue (which is hard to believe, given the state of the statue's preservation). Be as it may, the custom became popular; other 'talking statues' sprang up and some of them began to engage in friendly arguments with Pasquino. Among the most talkative, six statues stand out.

- Pasquino himself. A piece of a Hellenistic sculpture, possibly depicting a scene from the Trojan war, Menelaus with the body of Patrocles. It stands on Piazza Pasquino, a bit to the west of Piazza Navona. "Talks" to this day – mostly in long and boring rants on social and political issues.

- Marforio. A huge statue of a river god. It used to stand (or, rather, recline) near the Mamertine Prison by the Forum, and later on Piazza del Campidoglio. Today it is one of the centrepieces of the inner courtyard of the Capitoline Museums; as a result, it does not talk anymore.

- Abbot Luigi. A late Roman statue of an unknown toga-clad man; received its name because it looked like a local priest. It stands on Piazza Vidoni, by the wall of the church of Sant'Andrea della Valle. Its head has been lost countless times; the current version is made of concrete.

- Madam Lucrezia. A huge late Roman bust, which might be the goddess Isis, a priestess of Isis or the empress Faustina. It stands on Piazza San Marco (the one in Rome, not in Venice – but it is quite close to Piazza Venezia by the foot of the Capitol hill).

- Babuino ('the baboon'). A poorly preserved Roman statue of Silenus (a goat-legged forest god); the name reflects its ugliness. It is located in the luxury shopping district, in a street that used to be Via Paolina but is now called Via del Babuino. It used to talk until recently, but then the authorities decided that graffiti amid boutiques were incongruous, and they were removed.

- Facchino ('the porter'). The only member of the family not dating back to antiquity: a 16th-century relief (sometimes attributed to Michelangelo) of a water carrier; such people used to draw water from the Tiber into barrels and sell it in the city. This small decorative fountain stands on the corner of the Corso and Via Lata.

During the Renaissance, the Pantheon was put to use as a mausoleum (apart from the bones of the martyrs that were already there). The most famous burial in the Pantheon is that of Raphael (second chapel on the left side). His Latin epitaph was recycled by Alexander Pope for the memorial of Sir Godfrey Kneller, a German-born painter who made his home in London and painted some of the most famous personalities of the late 17th century, including John Locke and Isaac Newton:

> *Living, great Nature fear'd he might outvie*
> *Her works; and dying, fears herself may die.*

Dr. Johnson was not particularly impressed: "not only borrowed from the epitaph on Raphael, but of a very harsh construction."

Apart from painters and sculptors, the Pantheon is the final resting place of the short-lived Italian royal dynasty – Victor Emmanuel II, the first king of unified Italy, and his son Umberto I with his wife Margherita of Savoy.

Starting with the 15th century, the Pantheon was decorated with paintings; the most notable among them is a charming *Annunciation* attributed to Melozzo da Forlì.

The Pantheon of Rome has influenced Western culture in two important ways. First, the meaning of the word 'Pantheon' in European languages has shifted: from the hypothetical 'temple of all gods' to 'the resting-place of great people.' The shift was promoted by the French experience: in the early years of the Republic, the newly built church of St. Genevieve in Paris was turned into a mausoleum for the great sons (and, later, daughters) of France. This is where Voltaire, Rousseau, Victor Hugo, Alexandre Dumas père, Pierre and Marie Curie and many others are buried (some tombs only contain urns with the hearts of the deceased, and at least one – that of Jan Willem de Winter, a Dutch Napoleonic admiral – the body without the heart, which is buried elsewhere). An even later enterprise, the National Pantheon of Portugal, was only inaugurated as such in 1966, and its central crossing is beset with cenotaphs – pretend tombs of the country's great personalities (Prince Henry the Navigator, poet Luís de Camões, explorer Vasco da Gama). After the death of Joseph Stalin in 1953, plans were made to erect a Soviet Pantheon and transfer both Lenin's and Stalin's bodies there, but they have never materialised.

A design project of the Soviet Pantheon, by A. Vlasov, 1954

The second direction of influence was architectural, and at least as important. Many architects from the Renaissance on have been trying to rethink the unusual structure of the Pantheon and to reinvent and recreate the great edifice. According to biographer Giorgio Vasari, Michelangelo tackled St. Peter's Basilica with the idea of putting the dome of the Pantheon onto the vaults of the Basilica of Maxentius. Andrea Palladio built a small church (*Tempietto Barbaro*) based on the Pantheon's design on the grounds of Villa Barbaro in the Veneto region. Other famous variations and hommages to the Pantheon include the former Reading Room of the British Museum (in the middle of the Great Court, currently used as exhibition space), Killian Court of Massachusetts Institute of Technology in Boston, the Thomas Jefferson Memorial in Washington, D.C., and lots of other buildings around the globe.

AROUND THE PANTHEON

The back of the rotunda is abutted by a wall of another Hadrianic building, which, in its turn, replaced another Agrippan structure that had burned down. Well-preserved decorations of the marble frieze – dolphins, sea shells, tridents – suggest that it is the Basilica of Neptune, mentioned by Cassius Dio. The building of Agrippa was erected in celebration of naval victories (pointedly so: it was a naval victory at cape Actium, under Agrippa's command, that turned Augustus into an indisputable master of the universe). Inside the basilica, to complete the marine theme, were paintings about the argonauts' travels.

The Basilica of Neptune bordered on the Pantheon from the south, and on the west it was crowded by another building – Saepta Iulia. There is a Parkinson's law of institutions: a corporation only builds a perfect building for itself when it is in the throes of petrification and death; this is true of governments as well. There is no clear date and hour for the end of the Roman Republic (or, for that matter, Roman Empire), but few would argue that the political career of Julius Caesar roughly covers that transitional ground. Sure enough, it was Caesar who invested lots of money and efforts into building and renovating landmark Republican institutions – the Curia (Senate building) and the Saepta, the voting enclosure.

Caesar's attitude toward democratic procedure was cynical. "He shared the elections with the people on this basis," Suetonius writes, "that except in the case of the consulship, half of the magistrates should be appointed by the people's choice, while the rest should be those whom he had personally nominated. And these he announced in brief notes like the following, circulated in each tribe: 'Caesar the Dictator to this or that tribe. I commend to you so and so, to hold their positions *by your votes*'"[50] (emphasis mine). However, both he and his successors had been attending to the Republican façade, at least for a while. Caesar did not live to see the Saepta unveiled, but unveiled they were, under Augustus, and with much pomp. It was only Tiberius, the successor of Augustus, who finally did away with the practice of direct popular vote and transferred all elections under the supervision of the Senate, which was by that time puppet enough not to present any threat.

The Saepta were used for outdoor parties, gladiatorial combat, theatrical shows, possibly even naumachia (mock sea battles). The Emperor Claudius, on an anniversary of his rule, presented there a modest gladiatorial show called "A Snack" (*Sportula*). This was the name of a food basket, traditionally given by patrons as a gift to their clients. Claudius explained that the offered show was like a hastily prepared meal.

To the southeast of the Pantheon's rotunda and the wall of Neptune's basilica lies Piazza della Minerva. It is called after a small but important church, Santa Maria sopra Minerva. The name of the church, however, is erroneous: it was supposed to have been erected on the ruins of the ancient temple of Minerva. Indeed, there had been a temple of Minerva somewhere on the Field of Mars, but this specific spot was most likely occupied by a temple complex dedicated to Isis and Serapis.

Santa Maria sopra Minerva is considered to be Rome's only Gothic church. It is famous for a few sepulchres (five popes, the painter Fra Beato Angelico, the body of St. Catherine of Siena – in Roman Catholic tradition, body parts are often buried separately: the head of the saint is kept in Siena) and for works of art: Christ Carrying the Cross by Michelangelo, Madonna and Child Giving Blessings by Bennozzo Gozzoli. The façade of the church is beset with plaques commemorating water levels during the floods of various centuries. Many of them seem to have been moved in the course of restoration works, and should not be taken at face value.

Isis was an Egyptian goddess, but the Romans, as we have seen many times, easily accepted foreign gods into their pantheon. Under Augustus, the cult of Isis and Egyptomania in general became very popular in Rome (foreshadowing the future eruption of international Egyptomania in the 1920s, following the discovery of Tutankhamun's tomb by Howard Carter). A couple of Egyptian obelisks were found in the area; they might have adorned the entrance to the temple. One of them is currently set into the fountain in front of the Pantheon, the other stands on the back of the elephant on Piazza della Minerva.

The elephant (endearingly called "Minerva's chicken" – *pulcino della Minerva* – by the Romans) was made after a sketch by Bernini in the 17th century. The idea might have come from a printed book of 1499, a romance called *Hypnerotomachia Poliphili* ("The Dream of Poliphilus"), in which the protagonist pursues his love through a series of dreamlike land- and cityscapes; lavishly illustrated, it features among other wonders a figure of an elephant pierced by an obelisk.

Elephants were well known to the ancient Romans, both as war animals (used first by Pyrrhus, later by Hannibal) and as circus entertainment. According to historians (admittedly writing a couple of centuries after the events they were describing), both Julius Caesar and the emperor Claudius used elephants (or at least one elephant each) in their invasions of Britain (Caesar's was abortive and ultimately failed, Claudius's was successful and resulted in 350 years of Roman occupation). After the fall of the Western Roman Empire, trade routes between Europe and Africa (or India) were severed, and in the Middle Ages, a live elephant was an almost unheard-of marvel. The few animals who managed to make it to royal or papal palaces died very soon of unsuitable climate and incompetent handling. In the 9th century, an elephant called Abul-Abbas, a gift of the legendary caliph Harun al-Rashid, lived at the court of Charlemagne. Six centuries later, a white elephant called Hanno was given to the Medici pope Leo X by the Portuguese king Manuel I. Hanno quickly became the pope's favourite pet, and when the animal fell ill and died (probably as a result of botched treatment), Leo X remained with the animal until his last breath, buried him in Vatican's Belvedere court, and wrote a lengthy epitaph extolling the noble Hanno. Raphael painted a fresco for the elephant's tomb; it has not survived, but a rough copy has. It shows beyond a reasonable doubt that Hanno was an Indian elephant.

Identifying the species of Bernini's elephant is a harder task. Bernini might have seen a live animal: in his lifetime, a few elephants were brought to different European countries, including Italy. However, the Minerva elephant's anatomy is far from flawless: the trunk is too long, while hind legs have horse-like hocks (elephants have knees that bend forward on both pairs of legs).

As for the obelisk, it was found shortly before the monument was erected, somewhere in the vicinity, by Dominican monks. Its original placement is not known. The obelisk is small by Roman standards (just above five metres) and of a relatively late date: it features an inscription of pharaoh Apries (6th century BC; the Bible calls this Egyptian ruler Hophra). Pope Alexander VII, the insignia of whose family (Chigi), six mountains and a star, cover the elephant's saddle-cloth, ordered his favourite expert in all matters Egyptian, the learned German Jesuit Athanasius Kircher, to interpret the signs on the obelisk and to compose a fitting inscription for the new monument. Kircher set to work with enthusiasm and wrote a whole treatise on the Minervan obelisk, interpreting its hieroglyphs with abandon and brio. Unfortunately, his ideas, like all 'symbolic' interpretations of Egyptian writing, had no relation to reality whatsoever. A breakthrough only came in the 1820s when Jean-François Champollion (with some help from his English rival Thomas Young) unlocked the riddle of the ancient script.

The inscription composed by Kircher, however, was sensible enough. It reads:

> THE LEARNING OF EGYPT
> CARVED IN FIGURES ON THIS OBELISK
> AND CARRIED BY AN ELEPHANT
> THE MIGHTIEST OF BEASTS
> MAY AFFORD TO THOSE WHO LOOK ON IT
> AN EXAMPLE
> OF HOW STRENGTH OF MIND
> SHOULD SUPPORT WEIGHT OF WISDOM.[51]

(The hieroglyphs on the obelisk, in this parable, represent 'the weight of wisdom,' and the elephant 'strength of mind.')

From Piazza della Minerva extends one of those Roman streets whose name is like a poem, Via del Piè di Marmo ("the street of the marble foot"). If you follow its course east, toward the Corso, on the corner of the third street to your right (Via San Stefano del Cacco) you will, indeed, see a lonesome marble foot. The type of sandal indicates it is a man's foot – perhaps its owner was Serapis, the husband of Isis.

PIAZZA NAVONA

To the west of the Pantheon and Piazza della Minerva lies Rome's prettiest square, Piazza Navona. Its shape is unusual: it is oblong and narrow, almost like Circus Maximus. It is because its contour follows almost exactly the outline of a running track that used to be in that place – the so-called Stadium of Domitian.

We have already encountered three types of Roman entertainment, each with its own type of premises: musical and dramatic performances in a theatre; gladiatorial combat and animal hunts in an amphitheatre; chariot races in a circus. The Stadium of Domitian was meant for a fourth type, roughly corresponding to today's athletics. Competitions of that kind (race track, wrestling, discus-throwing) formed the backbone of Greek sports – for example, at the Olympic Games. However, mutual insemination of Greek and Roman tradition was lackadaisical in the realm of sports and entertainment. Gladiatorial fights never really took off in the Greek East, and athletic competitions of naked youths inspired little interest in the Romanised West.

The borders between types of entertainment were porous, and entertainment venues were often used for purposes other than initially intended. The Stadium of Domitian, designed to hold thirty thousand spectators, was no exception. In 217 AD during a violent thunderstorm lightning struck the Colosseum; it was simultaneously engulfed by fire and flooded by rainwater. The upper tier and most underground structures were severely damaged – so severely that for decades, while the amphitheatre was being restored, gladiatorial fights were staged at the Stadium of Domitian.

Places where passions run high attract businesses that make use of overflowing hormones. Lots of brothels were located around Rome's main sporting arenas, the Circus Maximus and the Colosseum. Emperor Helagabalus, known for his eccentricity, once "gathered together... all the harlots from the Circus, the theatre, the Stadium and all other places of amusement, and from the public baths, and then delivered a speech to them, as one might to soldiers, calling them 'comrades' and discoursing upon various kinds of postures and debaucheries."[52] In the early 4th century AD, the Stadium neighbourhood witnessed a dramatic clash between good old Roman debauchery and the nascent – and therefore especially fanatical – Christian chastity. Sempronius, the prefect of the city, decided to marry off his son to a girl called Agnes. Agnes had grown up in a Christian family and by the time she was twelve or thirteen (the right age to be planning marriage) was firmly resolved to devote her life to Christ, and declined the match. Sempronius, using his bureaucratic leverage, sent Agnes to one of the brothels near the Stadium (putting a virgin to death was frowned upon), but no one was interested in a virgin; when some horny man attempted to flirt with her, he miraculously lost his eyesight. The angry Sempronius, scorning the ancient custom, sent an executioner to kill the girl. The description of Agnes's ecstasy at the sight of the executioner as described by the Christian mystic Prudentius is a typical example of a peculiar "martyr erotica," often found in religious texts of the time:

> *When Agnes saw the furious headsman stand*
> *With weapon drawn, in transports of joy she cried:*
> *Far happier am I that a swordsman comes,*
> *A wild uncouth barbarian, fierce and grim,*
> *Than that a languid suitor pays court to me,*
> *A lovesick creature, scented with rare perfumes,*
> *Who would destroy my soul with my chastity.*
> *This butcher is the lover who pleases me:*
> *His bold advances I shall go forth to meet*
> *And will not try to hinder his ardent suit.*
> *I gladly bare my breast to his cruel steel*
> *And deep into my heart I will draw his blade.*
> *Thus as the bride of Christ I shall mount above*
> *The darkness of the world to the realms of light.*[53]

The spot where Agnes of Rome was martyred was marked by a 16th-century church, commissioned by the papal family of Pamphili. The church is called Sant'Agnese in Agone, and its façade was designed by one of the greatest masters of Roman baroque, Francesco Borromini. The ruins of a large Roman house are preserved under the church, and one of the chapels contains the skull of Saint Agnes (the rest of her relics are in a different church dedicated to her name, Sant'Agnese fuori le mura).

In antiquity, the Stadium of Domitian was often simply called "the stadium" (*stadium*), from the Greek word for the classical sprint distance. That word, *stadion*, used to be anglicised as 'stade'; the length of the stadion varied in different traditions, but the typical Olympic stadion was 176 metres. The length of Piazza Navona is somewhat greater, but not by much.

The word Agone in the name of St. Agnes church comes from another Greek word, *agon*, which meant the crowd of spectators at a sporting event and the event itself. (The Stadium of Domitian was also called *Circus Agonalis*.) The word 'agony' comes from the same route (in Greek, its initial meaning was the fight for victory in a sports competition). This word might have distorted into 'Navona.' In its original form, it is preserved in the name of the church and of Via Agonale on the northern side of the square.

If you walk along the Via Agonale and take a left turn, there will be an arch under a wall of a modern building, and in the arch rather imposing ruins of underground structures that used to support the long-gone stadium. They were uncovered in the course of works at the northern boundary of the square. In the late 1930s one of Mussolini's unrealised plans envisaged the demolition of a whole neighbourhood near the square, to open up a vista on the Tiber from Piazza Navona. Thankfully, the plan never came to fruition; otherwise we might have lost Palazzo Altemps. Today it houses a museum with a rare collection of classical sculpture. The rarity derives from the fact that today's museum fashion calls for utmost authenticity, while the Ludovisi collection, on display at Palazzo Altemps, reflects an older fashion for restoring or inventing everything that was lost, damaged or broken off.

In the middle of Piazza Navona stands the famous Fountain of the Four Rivers (*Fontana dei Quattro Fiumi*), a work by Bernini. Among Roman fountains, only the Trevi trumps it in popularity. According to the legend, ill-wishers had squeezed Bernini out of a competition for the fountain's design, but his well-wishers countered that by strategically placing a mock-up by Bernini in a place where it was spotted by the commissioner, Pope Innocent X. When the pope saw it, he called off the competition and gave the commission to Bernini.

The sculptures symbolise four great rivers of the four continents: the Nile, the Ganges, the Danube and Rio de la Plata (North America was pretty much outside the sphere of papal influence, while Australia and Antarctica were not even discovered). A popular Roman story says that the river god of La Plata is cowering in fear, shielding himself from the imminent collapse of the Sant'Agnese façade. It is supposed to be Bernini's quip at his long-time rival Francesco Borromini. The story has a ring of truth to it, though Borromini began working on the façade a few years after the fountain had been installed.

The centre of the fountain is fitted with an obelisk that bears no connection to the square or the stadium, but is linked to Domitian. It used to adorn the Circus of Maxentius near the Appian Way, but before that it had stood somewhere else, perhaps in the temple of the Flavii built by Domitian on the Quirinal hill. It was carved (possibly in Aswan) by masons whose command of Ancient Egyptian was flawed, most likely for the accession of Domitian (his name, in hieroglyphs, is on the obelisk, as well as the names of his deified predecessors, Vespasian and Titus). The obelisk is topped by a bronze dove, the symbol of Innocent X's Pamphili family.

AUGUSTUS

The northern part of the Field of Mars is inextricably linked to the name of Augustus, often called the first emperor of Rome.

Who was Augustus? Why is he considered the first emperor of Rome? These are simple questions, but they are very difficult to answer.

When the conspirators (or 'liberators,' as they preferred to style themselves) were planning the assassination of Julius Caesar, they did not want to go down in history as the instigators of a new bout of civil war. They wanted to be seen as noble tyrannicides in the spirit of ancient Greek tradition. As a result, they did very little to eliminate or neutralise Caesar's closest associates, including Mark Antony. As for Caesar's distant kinsman, the young Gaius Octavius, they probably did not even think of him at all.

Soon, however, Caesar's will, kept with the Vestal virgins, was publicly read. Among a variety of populist provisions (giving some money to each citizen of Rome, bequeathing private gardens to the city), Caesar also announced from beyond the grave that his grand-nephew Octavius was to be his principal heir. For all intents and purposes, this was a posthumous adoption (though technically you could not be adopted by a dead man). Perhaps more important that Caesar's immense fortune (which had to be fought for with creditors and other claimants) was the name that the young man acquired – also being a Gaius, he was now his adopted father's full namesake, Gaius Julius Caesar. With the name came an even more important asset: the loyalty of Caesar's legions.

Octavius was nineteen, and he was immersed in Greek scholarship in Appolonia, an Illyrian city on the Adriatic shore (near Pojani in today's Albania). On hearing the news, against the advice of his mother and stepfather (his father had long been dead), he immediately rushed to Italy, ready to claim the name and everything that came with it.

The name of this man changed throughout his long life, and historians have always been confused about the naming conventions that relate to him. His father came from a respected but obscure plebeian *gens* of the Octavii which had not hitherto produced any great men. Thanks to his successful career in business, army and politics he rose to senatorial rank and died soon afterwards, having not attained the consular rank. When the boy was born, he was named Gaius Octavius Thurinus (the cognomen was probably awarded to Octavius père to commemorate his victory over a band of runaway slaves near the town of Thurii in Magna Graecia). On becoming Caesar's adopted son, his name changed to Gaius Julius Caesar. In such cases (which were numerous: adoption was a popular dynasty-building device in Roman life), an adoptee often preserved his own family name – nomen – as a cognomen, or at least a second cognomen; thus, the son of general Aemilius Paulus, adopted into the Scipio family, became Publius Cornelius Scipio Aemilianus.

Following this logic, our young man could become Gaius Julius Caesar Octavianus. Quite possibly, this is exactly what he did; however, he never used that last name and, also possibly, made an effort to prevent others from doing so. 'Octavianus' reminded the world that the family of the master of the world was not distinguished, that his link with Caesar was not tied to direct descent. In 27 BC, when the 35-year-old ruler told the Senate he was planning to retire from politics but then agreed to be persuaded otherwise, he was given an honorific name 'Augustus.' 'Augustus' comes from the Latin verb *augere* meaning 'grow, expand'; the name has the overtones of 'majestic, solemn, famous, glorious' – its primary connotations were religious rather than political. By that time Augustus had squashed all internal enemies and probably wanted to stress the advent of the new era of prosperity and peace. The change of the name focused attention on this transition.

The so-called Augustus of Prima Porta, a two-metre marble statue discovered in 1863 during excavations at the suburban villa of Livia, the wife of Augustus. Was probably lavishly painted. Currently on display in the New Wing of the Vatican Museums

Apart from a new name, Augustus was also offered a new title. The word princeps meant a formal leader of the Senate (*princeps Senatus*), the most senior senator who traditionally opened the sessions. In less terminological use, it was also a title offered to statesmen and generals for special achievement. Now it was permanently bestowed on one man, stressing the unofficial nature of Augustus's power: "I exceeded all in influence [*dignitas*], but I had no greater power than the others who were colleagues with me in each magistracy."[54] In other words, Augustus wanted to dress up his power as an almost informal contract between himself and the Roman people.

It was certainly the decisive step toward changing the structure of Roman government. A Soviet historian wryly notes that it was "an example of regime founded on political hypocrisy, the first in history" (and Soviet historians should know). It was officially called "republic restored" (*res publica restituta*), even though it was neither restored – the republic was never overthrown – nor very republican. Augustus claimed that he held no magistracy incompatible with ancient customs, and technically it was almost true (though not quite: for example, his first consulship which he wrought more or less at swordpoint at the age of 19 was a slap in the face of all customs and traditions). And yet, after the times of the kings, no Roman ruler had ever performed so many governmental functions simultaneously and irremovably. The secret of his authority was not his consular power (which he had largely relinquished at a certain point), nor a dictator's *imperium* (which he never assumed), nor his permanent tribune's power, nor even his proconsular authority which gave him command over immense military resources. Strictly speaking, there was no name for his grip on power – that is why he uses such vague words as 'dignity' and 'influence' in his autobiography. The record of subsequent rulers who were left with this precarious construction to handle was uneven. Tiberius, the immediate successor of Augustus, handled it pretty well; some of the later principes, such as Caligula or Nero, were less lucky.

A strange thing had happened: a very young man without serious political connections, without any military or government experience, purely by the force of his new name and his ambition, became a rightful player among the top public officials. He formed an alliance with the associates of his adoptive father, Mark Antony and the general Marcus Lepidus, forming the so-called 'second triumvirate' (the first unofficial triumvirate had united Julius Caesar, Pompey, and Crassus in the previous generation). Just like the first one, the second triumvirate was short-lived: Lepidus was soon edged out from the political stage and only kept the ornamental office of the supreme pontiff, while the future Augustus and Antony engaged in a series of armed stand-offs interspersed with periods of uneasy truces. The finale occurred in 31 BC: Augustus, commanding the forces of the West, including Italy, and Antony, the ruler of the rich Hellenised East, fought a pitched naval battle near Cape Actium off the coast of Greece, and the West won. From the military standpoint it was not a crushing defeat for Antony, but it dealt a death blow to the morale of his troops; his allies scattered, and shortly after both Antony and Cleopatra were forced to commit their famous suicides.

THE ALTAR OF PEACE

On the 4th of July in the year 13 BC, Augustus returned to Rome from his three-year-long expedition in Western provinces, where he had successfully restored Roman administration and general stability (Balbus, as we have seen, was trying to time the opening of his theatre to coincide with the emperor's return). The mere fact that the ruler could be absent from the capital for such a long time went to show how stable his new system of governance was. On hearing the news, courtiers scurried to display their loyalty and proposed to build an altar in the princeps's honour in the heart of the state, on the Roman Forum.

Augustus thwarted the sycophants by slipping into the city unnoticed, at night, and rejected the proposed location for the altar. Instead, the new edifice was erected on the northern confines of the Field of Mars, where Augustus was creating a cluster of monuments celebrating his rule (those included his future mausoleum and an obelisk commemorating his Egyptian victory, both discussed later in this chapter). The altar was meant to become the central hub of the whole complex.

Its symbolism was clear: the altar was called *Ara Pacis Augustae*, 'the altar of Augustan peace'; peace and Augustus were thus imprinted as synonyms on the Roman psyche.

The Latin word *pax* (cognate to the English 'page') originally meant 'agreement, contract, treaty,' but since most international agreements of Roman times were aimed at maintaining peace, often on Roman terms, it gradually came to mean 'peace.' In the post-Augustan era, the concept expanded further, covering the whole Roman dominion; we know this meaning from the set phrase *Pax Romana* and its direct descendants (*Pax Britannica*, *Pax Americana*).

In Russian, the word for 'peace' and 'world' is exactly the same (*mir*), but before the orthographic reform enforced by the Communists in 1918, they were spelled differently. This led to a curious misconception: in a 1980s TV quiz show, immensely popular among entertainment-starved Russian TV viewers, it was claimed that Leo Tolstoy's famous novel "War and Peace" actually meant "War and the World," and the pre-Communist spelling allegedly made it clear. This is not true: there is only one example of such spelling in Tolstoy's lifetime, and it's likely a typo. Still, the idea stuck, and traces of it are still to be found in Russian Internet battles. Though the Tolstoy story is a myth, this polysemy is very similar to the Roman complex concept of *Pax*.

Augustus's new neighbourhood was a bold exercise in urban development, but it stood right in the middle of the Tiber's flood plain. After the fall of the Western Roman Empire, the Altar of Peace was submerged under layers of silt and debris. By the Middle Ages, all memory of it was gone.

The Field of Mars was a far-off militarised suburb of the ancient metropolis, but in the Middle Ages, when the former centre was abandoned and transformed into *disabitato* ('the uninhabited'), it became the focus of city. A church dedicated to Rome's patron saint, St. Lawrence, appeared next to the location of the Ara Pacis as early as the 4th century AD – it is now believed that some of reliefs from the Ara Pacis might have been removed or damaged during its construction. In the 13th century, a British cardinal built a palace over the altar. Through the ensuing centuries, the palace passed from one noble Roman family to another, changing names each time – it was known as 'Palazzo Peretti' (after the family of Pope Sixtus V), 'Palazzo Almagià,' and, most commonly, 'Palazzo Fiano.'

From the 16th century on, stone stabs with reliefs began to be found in the underground structures of the palace. Some were kept in the courtyard of the palace, others were later sold to the Medicis in Florence and found their way to the Uffizi gallery. A few ended up on the walls of yet another Medici haunt, their Roman villa (now the seat of the French Academy). One slab turned up in the Vatican museums, and another one was found in the Louvre. A relief panel with ornamental décor, turned face down, had served as the tombstone of a priest's grave in a nearby Jesuit church for a few centuries.

In the 1880s, a young German classicist, Friedrich von Duhn, published a series of papers arguing that the various reliefs depicting a solemn Roman procession, an allegory of abundance, and other motifs all belonged to an important monument of the Augustan age, likely the Altar of Peace.

First attempts to excavate the altar began in the early 20th century. It soon became apparent that the excavation endangered both the workers and the palace, and, just a few months into the project, the dig was abandoned. However, a few pieces of the altar were unearthed and some others were documented for the first time.

With Mussolini's rise to power, the operation was given a new lease of life. The Duce envisioned himself as the second embodiment of Augustus, creator of the new Italian Empire, and promoted everything that sounded imperial. The bimillennial anniversary of the birth of Augustus, falling in September 1938, was the perfect occasion to showcase this continuity with a grandiose archaeological experiment.

Preparations began years in advance. In 1933 the *New York Times* waxed lyrical on the subject: "Never before have Italians been so conscious of being descendants of the ancient Romans as they are today. Not the least of the effects of the spiritual revolution achieved by fascism ... is the reawakening of the Italians' pride of race."

Meanwhile, the problems were still present and pure political will, even backed by serious money, could not solve them. In Campo Marzio, many buildings stood on posts lodged into waterlogged soil. Some of the posts under Palazzo Fiano were resting on the altar, and removing its pieces could topple the building.

Giuseppe Moretti, the archaeologist in charge of the excavation, circumvented this problem by supporting the most vulnerable corner of the palazzo with an improvised trestle. But in order to extract the altar, the area had to be drained. Pumping out the water from the soil proved useless, since no pump could match the power of the groundwater. A dyke to stop the influx of water was needed, but creating a cement structure under the pavement of a busy residential quarter in the midst of the cultural layers of two millennia was impossible.

Moretti's engineers came up with an ingenious solution – freezing the waterlogged soil around the altar by pumping compressed carbon dioxide through 55 steel pipes laid into a trench dug for this purpose. The frozen trench acted as a dam, allowing the altar pieces to be safely removed. Mussolini's government brought back the missing pieces from the Uffizi and made plaster copies of the fragments they could not obtain (such as the ones in the Louvre).

Ara Pacis. Reconstruction by Guglielmo Gatti from 'Ara Pacis'
by Giuseppe Moretti, 1948

The altar was then reassembled at a new location, on the bank of the Tiber, near Augustus's mausoleum, also refurbished and 'liberated' from mediaeval accretions for the occasion. The architect Vittorio Morpurgo designed the new Piazza Augusto Imperatore in a style typical of fascist architecture of the time. The new square sported a pavilion for the altar.

By the late 20th century the pavilion was in disrepair. At the 1995 Davos Economic Forum, the mayor of Rome approached the American architect Richard Meier with an offer to design a new structure for the Ara Pacis. Meier's model showed his favourite geometric minimalism at work – a glaring white rectangular structure, all glass and open spaces. The Italians were furious: the first major project in the historic centre since Mussolini's time was secretly given to a foreigner, and look at the horror he created! The subsequent Italian governments alternately greenlighted and scrapped the project, but after all the scandals the new museum finally opened in 2006.

In the time of Augustus, Ara Pacis was a functioning sacrificial altar – the Roman poet Ovid vividly wrote about "the white victim falling, its brow well-soaked in blood." The famous reliefs adorning the long sides of the reconstituted altar most probably depict dignitaries attending a sacrifice. The procession is of course idealized – the Roman officials are stately and tall, the matrons comely and statuesque. Leading the priests (recognizable by the togas that cover their heads), first among equals, is Augustus himself. His figure on the relief is damaged because, ironically, Palazzo Fiano's weight was concentrated at this very point, but that is unmistakably him, easily recognizable by hairstyle and the distinctive fold in the corner of the mouth.

The reliefs depict many historical figures – Augustus's right-hand man Agrippa, his 'minister of culture' Maecenas, his wife Livia and his daughter Julia. His sister Octavia is pressing a finger to her lips, shushing the children. The images of children are everywhere on the reliefs – a unique detail for Roman portraiture of the time. These attributions, of course, are tenuous and many are hotly disputed. One thing is certain – the sculptors depicted the crème de la crème of Augustan society in a manner guaranteed to please Augustus.

Relief from the side panel of Ara Pacis. A drawing from the collection of the Italian scholar and patron of art Cassiano del Pozzo

The reality of life, typical of Roman art of the era, is nevertheless evident on the reliefs. It is not a coincidence that Octavia is pressing a finger to her lips: the children (perhaps the grown-ups as well) noisily misbehave, disrupting the solemnity of the occasion. On the other side of the monument, spontaneity is even better visible: a child aged about five asks his father to lift him up. (One hypothesis says it might be not a Roman child but a young hostage from the conquered lands.)

The adjoining sides of the enclosure are covered with mythological reliefs and rich ornamentation. The best preserved of these (it was substantially restored by Renaissance craftsmen) depicts an allegorical figure of a full-bosomed woman with plump babies in her arms and two other allegories (of air and water) by her sides. It is not quite clear which deity she represents – she may be Earth (*Tellus*), Rome (*Roma*), or Peace (*Pax*). On the other side, a serious bearded man sacrifices a sow. This could be Aeneas, the proto-founder of Rome and Augustus's mythological ancestor, or the king Numa Pompilius, who instituted almost all of Rome's religious cults.

Two other reliefs on the shorter sides are poorly preserved, and the reconstructions that accompany them are conjectural. To the left of the entrance is the god Mars and, probably, Romulus and Remus with the she-wolf. On the back, a goddess (the embodiment of Rome?) sitting atop a pile of captured weapons.

The ornament around the enclosure is full of unexpected details. Children will love looking for the frogs, lizards, worms, butterflies and scorpions hiding amongst the acanthus leaves and heraldic swans (swan being the sacred bird of Apollo, the patron god of Augustus).

In contrast to the lavish outer enclosure, the altar itself is austere. It was, as we have said, a working altar, where sacrifices were performed; as such, it was fitted with water and blood-draining grooves. A small decorative relief on the lateral side of the altar shows robust young men leading bulls and rams to the slaughter – some by the horns, some grabbing a tail and pushing from behind.

THE OBELISK

Augustus had erected another unique monument next to Ara Pacis. It was of the kind that stressed the subtlety of the Roman way of thinking and "ancient wisdom." Under Augustus, Egypt became a part of *Pax Romana*, the Roman world (an event commemorated by minting a special coin featuring a crocodile and an inscription 'Egypt Conquered,' *Aegyptus Capta*). The conquest was accompanied by the first appearance of Egyptian obelisks in Rome – a marvel of Egyptian engineering and Roman logistics that stressed the power and wisdom of the ruler. One of the first such obelisks was set up on the Field of Mars. It was employed in the unusual function of a gnomon (indicating device) of a huge sundial and calendar. On the day of the autumnal equinox (coincidentally Augustus's birthday), the shadow of the obelisk with a bronze sphere on its top for better visibility pointed at Ara Pacis, as if confirming that the emperor was "born for the peace."

Pliny the Elder says that after a mere fifty years the readings of the gnomon were seriously off. To explain this annoying fact, Pliny advances two hypotheses: either the movement of the earth and stars got disrupted, or the obelisk sank into the ground under its own weight and diverged from the dial.

The obelisk remained standing for many centuries, but finally collapsed and broke into several pieces. It was rediscovered, but not excavated, in the 16th century. In the mid-18th century Pope Benedict XIV displayed interest in it again, but it was only finally re-erected by Pius VI in 1792. The material for restoring it was borrowed from the already half-destroyed column of Antoninus Pius.

The obelisk was erected in a new place, on Piazza Montecitorio, in front of a baroque palace that now houses the Italian parliament. An identical dedicatory inscription adorns the base on the north and south sides. It says that the emperor Caesar Augustus, the Supreme Pontiff (this title is given a line of its own, probably to stress its special importance for the occasion) dedicated the obelisk to the Sun in honour of Egypt's return under the power of the Roman people. Another identical inscription is on a twin obelisk that used to stand in Circus Maximus. Today it stands in the middle of Piazza del Popolo. Under Augustus, both obelisks were taken from the Egyptian city of Heliopolis, famous for its obelisks and towers. The restoration of the Montecitorio obelisk is recorded in the inscriptions of the popes who sponsored it: the one by Benedict XIV is on the outer wall of the parliament, the one by Pius VI on the obelisk base.

In the 1970s the German archaeologist Edmund Buchner had an idea. Knowing the original placement of the Augustan obelisk and the laws of planetary motion (which are less frivolous than Pliny the Elder thought), it would be possible, he reasoned, to figure out the position of the dial that marked the months and zodiacal signs. Knowing the positions, it would be possible to try to dig for them. The problem with any excavations in the Field of Mars is the density of urban tissue. However, Buchner managed to receive permission to explore a basement of a house in Via del Campo Marzio – and, to his immense joy, at a depth of six metres, where the gnomon-like obelisk was supposed, according to his calculations, to point at the zodiacal sign of Virgo, he found a travertine floor and a bronze letter A.

But where's an A in Virgo? The riddle was a simple one: anything related to wisdom, philosophy, and especially celestial bodies and astronomy, was discussed and written in Greek; Virgo in Greek is *Parthenos* (compare the Parthenon, temple of the virginal Athena), and what Buchner found was the letter alpha of that word. Buchner's discovery was a major achievement of "analytical" archaeology, when an object is first predicted and then its existence is confirmed – not unlike the discovery of Neptune and Pluto, whose existence was predicted by calculations.

Since 1982, when Buchner's results were first published, his hypothesis was often criticised. One of the objections was practical: the readings of this giant sundial would have been undetectable at ground level.

However, we have seen many Roman monuments whose decorations and reliefs seemed not to be intended for human eyes (like Trajan's column). Also, the dial might have been visible from the surrounding hills.

MAUSOLEUM OF AUGUSTUS

In 1918, shortly after the Communist revolution, Vladimir Lenin signed a decree setting in motion a plan of "monumental propaganda," ordaining the removal of monuments to "tzars and their servants" and the development of ideologically correct Socialist monuments. In this, the Communists had solid predecessors in the ancient Romans. And, like the famous Lenin's mausoleum in Moscow's Red Square, the mausoleum of Augustus became the pinnacle of Augustan monumental propaganda. It was not a fluke that the geographer Strabo dedicated almost as much space to it as to all other Roman sights put together.

Augustus began building the sepulchre soon after his final victory over Antony, at the same time as adopting the name Augustus. The name of the sepulchre, 'mausoleum,' was fraught with meaning: it hinted at the absolute power of oriental rulers and at the splendour of Alexander the Great – a hero whom Augustus revered just as Julius Caesar did.

The word 'Mausoleum' derives from the name of one Mausolus, a 4th-century BC Persian satrap of Asia Minor, who built a monumental tomb for himself and his sister-wife at Halicarnassus. One of the seven wonders of the world in ancient times, the original mausoleum has been reduced to nondescript rubble near the Turkish resort of Bodrum. Some of the sculptures that adorned the mausoleum were brought to England in the 19th century and are now kept in the British Museum.

Another famous mausoleum was in the Nile Delta. After the death of Alexander the Great, one of the king's generals, Ptolemy, stole the coffin with the body and spirited it away to Egypt, where a majestic tomb was built to house it. Embalmed after the Egyptian fashion but put on display, the corpse of Alexander attracted dignitaries of the world, including Julius Caesar and Augustus. Augustus made a point of snubbing an invitation to see the tombs of the Ptolemy rulers: "I came to see the king, not some dead men." When he touched the hero's body, he accidentally broke off a piece of his nose.

After the establishment of Christianity, around the 5th century, the tomb of Alexander was no longer mentioned, and the destiny of its mummies, books and treasures is unknown.

Augustus placed his mausoleum in an elevated location near the river. Its shape echoed the luxury of oriental tombs, and at the same time the severe simplicity of ancient burial hills, such as the ones still standing in the valley around Troy. It seems that Etruscan tombs served as the immediate source of inspiration. The concrete core of the structure was a warren of interconnected chambers and passages, and the central part, apparently, was designed to hold the ashes of Augustus himself. The concrete was faced with some bright stone, travertine or marble. The upper levels of the mausoleum have not survived, and their exact shape is difficult to guess. There are two main versions: either they rose in steps, like in some eastern mausoleums, or formed a tumulus with a colonnade at the top, a reference to old burial mounds. The mausoleum was surrounded by a dense forest of evergreen trees and topped by a colossal statue of Augustus. To the north of it, Augustus laid out a vast park open to the general public.

Augustus had survived many of his associates and relatives, and his mausoleum began to serve as a burial place long before his own death. The first to be interred there was his nephew Marcellus, whom we have met in the previous chapter. He was followed by Augustus's close friend and companion Agrippa, the sister Octavia, the stepson Drusus, the grandsons Gaius and Lucius.

Finally, in 14 AD, the princeps's turn came.

Augustus died in the home of his biological father in the Campanian city of Nola, not far from Naples. He died a month short of his 76th birthday – a venerable age, though not uniquely advanced even in classical terms. The peculiarity of Augustus's political career was not its late end; it was its extraordinary early beginning. According to strict Republican rules, a man could only stand for consulship after turning 45, while the young Octavian ruled the empire at the age of 19 on a scale that put any consul to shame. In various forms and guises, the power of that man over Rome had continued for 56 years, and by the end of his rule there were very few people who had any clear recollection of pre-Augustan times.

Historians tell us that he died peacefully: asked for a looking-glass, adjusted his slack jaw, asked if he had played the comedy of life well; quoted an appropriate Greek verselet: "Since well I've played my part, all clap your hands / And from the stage dismiss me with applause." He drew his last breath addressing his wife Livia with tender words.

The emperor's last journey from Nola to Rome took several days. To avoid scorching sun, the body was carried at night, and during the daytime it was placed in a temple or basilica of the nearest town. Normally, temples were completely off-limits to dead bodies, and the exception made for Augustus is significant. Senators vied to offer the most lavish and outlandish ceremonies for the state funeral. Some suggested that the body be brought into the city through Triumphal Gate, an honour only given to triumphant generals. Others wanted to take the statue of Victory from the Senate House and put it at the head of the funeral procession. Girls and boys from the best families were supposed to sing dirges. A proposal was aired to forbid all gold decorations on the day of the funeral and replace them with iron ones. It was also proposed to rename the month of August, which had acquired the emperor's name a long time ago, back into Sextilis, and to change September into Augustus instead, because Augustus was born in September (but died in August).

Moderation, the eternal Classical virtue, had won in the end, and the funeral was luxurious but not extravagant. The relatives of the deceased said their eulogies, and the body was burned on a pyre not far from the mausoleum.

In his will, Augustus explicitly forbade the burial of his daughter and granddaughter, both called Julia, in the mausoleum; both had damaged the reputation of the imperial household, and both were banished by Augustus to remote islands. After Augustus, the mausoleum received the ashes of his grandnephew Germanicus, another Julio-Claudian who never became an emperor, and of his widow Livia, Tiberius and a few more people. The emperor Nerva was the last to be buried in the Mausoleum of Augustus.

THE DEEDS OF THE DIVINE AUGUSTUS

The entrance to the Mausoleum was flanked by two unusual Egyptian obelisks: both were huge and uninscribed, without any hieroglyphs. Both have survived: one stands on the square in front of Santa Maria Maggiore, the other on the Quirinal hill, near the residence of the President of the Italian Republic.

Even more interesting were two bronze columns also installed by the entrance. They contained a brief autobiography of Augustus, in which the princeps looked back on his life journey, recounted his achievements, reported the good deeds he had performed for the benefit of the Roman people, and boasted of the honours he had received for them.

Of course, the bronze columns have not survived (few metal objects of serious size have). However, Augustus was deified immediately after his death, and temples to the imperial cult sprang up all across the empire. The ruler's autobiography was an appropriate decorative device in such buildings. One such temple was erected in Galatia, a province in Asia Minor, in the city of Ankyra. A full and exact copy of Augustus's autobiography was inscribed on its walls – not just in Latin, but in Greek translation as well for the benefit of the locals.

When Asia Minor fell to the Turks, the Europeans lost sight of Greek and Roman treasures so abundant in those lands. It was only in the 16th century that a Flemish diplomat Ogier Chiselin de Busbecq, a member of an embassy of the Holy Roman Empire to Sultan Suleiman the

Magnificent, found the temple, saw the inscription for what it was (the Augustan autobiography was mentioned by ancient writers) and made the first copy. In this endeavour, he and his followers were faced with major obstacles, quite literally: a Turkish village had long overgrown the ruins of the temple, and the inscriptions were partially obscured by the houses.

Full replicas of the Ankyra inscriptions were only made in the late 19th century (a few more temples similarly decorated were discovered, all of them in Asia Minor, but the Ankyran inscription was the best preserved). In 1883 the great German historian Theodor Mommsen, one of the few authors who received a Nobel Prize in literature for a work of nonfiction, published a detailed critical edition of this document, which he called "the queen of Latin inscriptions."

Since Mommsen's time, this short autobiography has been called either "The Deeds of the Divine Augustus" (*Res Gestae Divi Augusti*), or simply "The Monument of Ankyra" (*Monumentum Ancyranum*). This is not, strictly speaking, a historical source; it is a propaganda document, where Augustus studiously avoids any mention of his participation in civil wars, never even mentioning his rivals – Sextus Pompey, Mark Antony, the murderers of Julius Caesar – by their names. He exhibits prodigious dexterity in word-juggling in an attempt to paint his political system not as a monarchy with a republican façade, but rather as a republic blessed with an authority of a supreme ruler.

The temple with its inscriptions, with the huts now removed, can be seen in the same place, near the former Ankyra, now Ankara, the capital of Turkey. In Rome, "The Deeds" were inscribed in Latin on a travertine wall of the new pavilion of the Ara Pacis designed by Vittorio Morpurgo; over 15,000 bronze letters were cast for the project. When Morpurgo's pavilion gave way to the new Richard Meier building, the wall was the only part of the fascist-era structure to be incorporated in the new museum design.

According to a mediaeval legend, Augustus ordered every visitor coming to Rome from faraway lands to bring a handful of his native soil and throw it on top of the mausoleum, so as to perpetuate his memory across the empire. Indeed, the Mausoleum of Augustus had lived on together with the city, and, importantly but very uncommon in Rome, the link connecting the monument with the name of Augustus was never completely severed.

In the 12th century, the influential Colonna family converted the mausoleum into a section of its ramparts – a fate that befell many ancient Roman monuments. In 1354, the body of Cola di Rienzo was burned atop the building. In the 16th century, the monument was purchased by

Cardinal Francesco Soderini. He turned it into an open-air museum and laid a garden inside, where he installed many statues from his collection. In the 18th century, the mausoleum served as a bullring, and in 1909 it was refurbished to serve as a concert hall called "Augusteo."

On October 22, 1934, Mussolini, standing on the roof of a house on Via Soderini with a pickaxe in his hands, personally signalled the launch of the clearing-up campaign that did away with the late Renaissance quarter around the Mausoleum. By the bimillennial anniversary of Augustus in 1938 the work was finished, and the façade of a new building on Piazza Augusto Imperatore with its typical fascist architecture and reliefs displayed the following inscription:

"After the emperor's mausoleum had been saved from the shadows of the centuries, and disjointed fragments of the Altar of Peace set together, the *duce* Mussolini ordered the clearance of this place, still graced by the presence of the *manes* of Augustus, of narrow old streets, and adorn it with beautiful avenues, houses and buildings as befits human mores in the year 1940, the 18th year of the Fascist era."

The word 'fascism' comes from the Italian *fascismo*, and in Italian, in its turn, it is derived from the Latin *fasces*. The fasces were a bundle of wooden rods, the symbolic weapon of lictors who served as bodyguards to top magistrates of the Roman state. The higher the rank of a magistrate, the more lictors followed (and/or preceded) him. Outside the sacred boundary of Rome, an axe was inserted into the bundle, making the weapon less symbolic.

> The beginning of the "fascist era" in Mussolinian Latin was described as *a fascibus restitutis*, 'since the restoration of the fasces'. Such inscriptions are to be found on monuments to the emperors that line the Via dei Fori Imperiali.

"Liberated" from the concert hall and other late accretions, the Mausoleum of Augustus has not, unfortunately, become an interesting tourist site. However, recently an Italian telecommunications company has contributed money for its renovation, and there is hope that some day it will become accessible to the public.

THE MAUSOLEUM OF HADRIAN

This book does not have a separate chapter on Trastevere or the Vatican, because classical sites and monuments on the Tiber's right bank are few and far between, not enough to fill a whole chapter without becoming too technical. However, some of them are unmissable, and the most important among them, the Mausoleum of Hadrian, better known as Castel Sant'Angelo, is near the top of any chart of Roman sights.

When the Mausoleum of Augustus ran out of burial space, the emperor Hadrian started building a new resting place, less than a kilometre away from the old one. With reverence typical of "good emperors," Hadrian took special care not to make his new mausoleum wider than the one of Augustus.

Hadrian's monumental tomb was similar in shape to traditional Roman burials that lined the Appian Way; we will visit them in the next chapter. But in size and décor, the mausoleum was much grander. The lower tier was faced with white Italian marble, the upper featured a frieze with bucrania (ox heads) and wreaths; its fragments are preserved in the Castel Sant'Angelo museum. The side facing the Tiber had marble panels affixed to it, on the sides of the entrance, with the names of those who were buried inside.

Members of the imperial household were buried in this tomb for about eighty years. The last one to be awarded this honour was the emperor Caracalla, who died in the early years of the turbulent 3rd century, in 217 AD.

Strategically placed, the Mausoleum of Hadrian was very soon converted into a defence installation. First it was incorporated into a new section of Rome's military perimeter (Aurelian walls), then it was used as the main fortified location during the Gothic siege of 537: huge bronze

and marble statues (even equestrian) were hurled on the barbarians from the upper tiers of the building. Later, in its role of papal citadel, it remained in the service of Vatican defence for many centuries (as evidenced by the bronze of the Pantheon used for its cannons). In the 13th century the castle was connected to the Vatican by a covered passage, the *Passetto di Borgo* (a fact that was used and abused by Dan Brown in "Angels and Demons"); it was used for escape by popes whose life was in danger. The castle was finally decommissioned as a military facility only in the early 20th century.

The Mausoleum of Hadrian got its present-day name in 590. In the midst of a plague epidemic that had engulfed Rome, Pope Gregory I saw the archangel Michael sheathing his sword on top of the building, and realised that the worst was behind the people of Rome.

The mausoleum and its neighbourhood have changed dramatically since ancient times, and nothing here reminds us of classical antiquity today. The upper part of the round superstructure, the palace, the bronze St. Michael on top, the moat, the curtain between the ramparts, the ramparts themselves – all of that was erected between 13th and 16th centuries. Even the elements of interior decoration were not spared by papal architects and restorers. However, the concrete plinth and the ring of inner walls date back to Hadrian's time, though they have grown lots of new layers since then.

Something similar happened to the bridge across the Tiber that leads to the mausoleum. It was built at the same time, with the name of the Aelian bridge (Hadrian's full name was Publius Aelius Hadrianus), but was subjected to countless reconstructions and embellishments in the intervening centuries. Three events in its turbulent life stand out. In the Jubilee year of 1450, the crowd of pilgrims was so huge that the overburdened bridge partially collapsed, killing lots of people; during its subsequent restoration, the ancient railing and triumphal arch on the bridge were removed. In the 1660s the bridge, by then synonymous with the castle (the Sant'Angelo bridge) was adorned with ten statues of angels made to a design by Bernini. The statues have whimsical names: "Angel with the Superscription," "Angel with the Sponge," "Angel with the Nails." Finally, the large-scale upgrade of Tiber embankments in the late 19th century required a complete rebuilding of the bridge, and only three of the original spans remained in place in its central portion.

THE TEMPLE OF HADRIAN

Some of the streets and squares on the Field of Mars bear traces of Hadrian's name and activities. The most obvious among them is, of course, the Temple of the Deified Hadrian, or Hadrianeum on Piazza di Pietra, just around the corner from Piazza Montecitorio with the Augustan obelisk. What remains of it are eleven huge one-piece columns made from Proconnesian marble with distinctive greyish horizontal veins. There were more, perhaps thirteen or fifteen, and the temple's façade was turned toward today's Corso. The lower part of the architrave has survived, while the upper was restored much later, a fact that is apparent at once. Behind the grating near the building wall one can see the depth – of five metres – of the tufa podium that used to be faced with white marble. This depth is another reminder of the cultural layer that has risen on the Field of Mars since ancient times.

The temple is not fitted with any inscriptions; for a long time it was believed to be the Basilica of Neptune, but it is listed among other buildings of Hadrianic times in roughly that area. It was not built by Hadrian himself, but by his adopted son Antoninus Pius. Numerous holes in the travertine wall are not the traces of a battle (even though they look very much as if they are), but openings used for affixing decorative marble slabs.

The Temple of Hadrian is one of the few ancient buildings that remain fully functional, though the function has obviously changed. In the 17th century, the famous architect Domenico Fontana built a papal customs house inside the remains of the temple. In the late 19th century, that baroque palazzo was much simplified – by that time it was housing the Roman stock exchange. It was in the interiors of the stock exchange that one of the most iconic scenes in all of cinema history was shot, the minute of silence from Michelangelo Antonioni's *L'Eclisse* (1962). After a recent reorganisation of stock exchange activity in Italy, the Temple of Hadrian came to house the mission of the Rome Chamber of Commerce. A part of the temple's cella with a vaulted dome has survived, and can be viewed inside the palazzo.

The Italian archaeologist Filippo Coarelli writes that Hadrian might have been the only man in history who made his mother-in-law a goddess. Indeed, there is information about Hadrian dedicating a temple to Matidia, the mother of his wife Vibia Sabina. A piece of a plumbing pipe with the inscription "For Matidia's temple" (*templo Matidiae*) was found near the church of Sant'Ignazio, which places the temple itself somewhere in the vicinity of Piazza Capranica. It is quite likely that the two columns built into house No. 76 on that square, and another shaft on Via della Spada d'Orlando, are spoils from that temple that has not survived. If so, then, judging by the circumference of the columns, Hadrian must have erected a very monumental temple to his mother-in-law.

Via della Spada d'Orlando, 'the street of Roland's sword,' is named after this column trunk or, rather, a crack in it. For some reason, the Romans connected this flaw with the legend of Roland, the paladin of Charlemagne. During the Battle of Roncevaux, Roland tries to destroy his famous sword called Durendal to prevent its falling into enemy hands, but cannot even blunt it. The crack in the piece of greenish marble is supposed to be a trace of that sword.

THE COLUMN OF MARCUS AURELIUS

The area of Rome comprising Piazza Capranica, the square with the Augustan obelisk and Palazzo Fiano, under which the Altar of Peace was found, is called "Colonna." The name derives from the column that stands on Piazza Colonna. It is a triumphal monument erected at the end of the 2nd century AD to celebrate the victories of emperor Marcus Aurelius over northern barbarians.

It was Trajan's Column, of course, that served as the model for the column of Marcus Aurelius. Art historians never tire of stressing the dissimilarity of these two monuments. Superficially, they are very much alike: both are made from huge drums of Carrara marble set upon one another; each is carved with a relief band depicting battles of the Roman army in two separate campaigns. Inside both there is a spiral staircase lit by narrow windows; both had a corresponding emperor's statue on top, and in the late 16th century Pope Sixtus V installed a statue of an apostle on each: St. Peter on Trajan's column, St. Paul on Marcus Aurelius's. On the

Aurelian column, just like on its model, the first and second campaigns are divided by the figure of Victory with a shield (at the tenth whorl, on the side of the Corso). Both are time-worn, but the newer column more so: it was struck by lightning, shaken by earthquakes and, since metal clamps had long disappeared, the 'drums' rotated against each other, resulting in some jagged images in places.

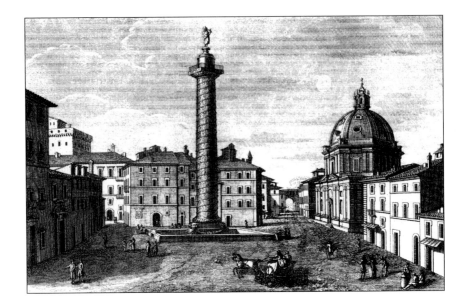

This is where similarities end and differences begin. They are technological: the relief on Marcus Aurelius's column is much higher than on Trajan's. Artistic: the images are more sketchy, with heads enlarged relative to the bodies. Finally, and most importantly, subject-related: the column of Marcus Aurelius depicts war as an activity that is much bloodier and more frightening. In Trajan's relief, one of the most frequent motifs is construction: of a bridge across the Danube, defensive ramparts, military camps. On the Aurelian column there are just two instances of construction and many more battle scenes. Trajan's Dacians are depicted as weak but dignified adversaries, while the Germans and Sarmatians never offer any sensible resistance: they flee, panicked, cower in terror, have their heads chopped off (including at least one case when it is obviously done on the explicit orders of the emperor). Violence against civilians – almost absent on Trajan's column – also features prominently: Roman legionaries haul barbarian women by their hair, snatch children from their hands, scorch villages. Finally, while the long sequence of images on Trajan's column ends with an image of a peacefully grazing deer, the

Aurelian relief also ends in a quadruped, but it is so awkward and bizarre that even its species is unidentifiable.

Romantically inclined art historians of the past wanted to explain such aesthetic dissimilarities by the dissimilar nature of the two emperors, but immediately ran into problems. After all, wasn't Marcus Aurelius the only ruler of Rome who wrote a large philosophical treatise in Greek? Usually titled "Meditations," these rather abstruse notes paint a picture of a stoical emperor, whose only desire is to follow the moral law.

By the late 2nd century the Roman Empire was not in such good shape as a century earlier. For the first time since Hannibal, barbarians were threatening an invasion of Italy. The borders, expanded by Trajan and fixed by Hadrian, gradually began to weaken. Epidemics ravaged the empire, their cumulative effect comparable to the "Black Death" of the mid-14th century, when a huge portion of European population perished. The empire's excellent connectivity – its system of roads, waterways, staging grounds, military camps, a source of deserved pride for the Romans, worked for, rather than against the disease. All in all, it was certainly not the best of times, and Marcus Aurelius, however philosophically-minded and benign, spent a major portion of his rule on military campaigns. A biographer, noting the emperor's magnanimity, writes that no senator was ever executed on his direct orders – a back-handed compliment if there ever was one.

In the face of overwhelming evidence, romantic researchers still wanted to airbrush the imaginary contradiction between the bloodthirsty reliefs and the good-natured emperor. Perhaps, they said, the column was erected after the death of Marcus Aurelius by his son Commodus, a quintessential bad apple. That was probably so: there is an inscription dated 193 AD (when not only Marcus Aurelius, but Commodus were dead), where a freedman of the imperial household proudly reports that he was appointed the guardian of the column and as such given the right to build a hut on public land nearby. Be as it may, explaining artistic features through someone's personal qualities, though romantically attractive, is not always the soundest of ideas.

The Aurelian column's reliefs were a step in marking the transition from classical style to late antiquity, edging increasingly closer to mediaeval canons. Soon, realism and knowledge of anatomy would give way to symbolism and piety.

We know virtually nothing of the original architectural environment of the column. Perhaps behind it was the temple of the deified Marcus Aurelius and his wife Faustina, who followed her husband on the military trail and was nicknamed "The Mother of Camps," *Mater Castrorum*, by the soldiers. She died on campaign, in Cappadocia. The remains of marble ceiling, possibly from that temple, were found under Palazzo Wedekind on Piazza Colonna.

By the Renaissance, the base of the column had partially sunk into the ground. When it was excavated, the original relief was chiselled off and replaced by an inscription that commemorated the restoration under Sixtus V. Part of the base is still concealed underground, and even lower there are probably stone steps leading up to it, but no one has seen them since ancient times.

Close by was another column, dedicated to the apotheosis of the emperor Antoninus Pius. Unlike the columns of Trajan and Marcus Aurelius, it did not have a relief band: it was a simple granite shaft on a carved base, topped with the emperor's statue. By the 18th century the base had submerged deep underground; only a tip of the column protruded above surface. The base was excavated, and there were plans to restore the column, but they never materialised, because the column's newly excavated fragments were destroyed by fire. What was salvaged was used to mend the Augustan obelisk in Piazza Montecitorio.

Cortile della Pigna, a part of the Belvedere courtyard of the Vatican palace, holds a number of famous ancient artefacts. Most important among them is the giant bronze pinecone. It used to stand in a fountain on the Field of Mars, near the Temple of Isis. In its honour, the small square area of Rome that holds, among other things, the Pantheon, is called 'Pigna' to this day. Before taking up permanent residence in the Belvedere courtyard, it had stood for a while near the old St. Peter's basilica, where it was spotted by Dante ("As large and long his face seemed, to my sense, / As Peter's Pine at Rome").[55]

The peacocks are copies of the birds that stood in front of Hadrian's Mausoleum (the originals are inside the Vatican museums). The lions, on the other hand, are genuine Egyptian sculptures, while their copies adorn the Aqua Felice fountain not far from the Baths of Diocletian.

The base survived, and it made a strong impression on the public. It had an inscription on one side and a very lively scene on two other sides – Roman knights solemnly riding around a funeral pyre, a procedure known as *decursio*. The fourth side featured an apotheosis – the ascension of the emperor's spirit heavenward. An allegorical figure symbolising the Field of Mars was watching it from below, hugging the Augustan obelisk.

It was near the obelisk, on Piazza Montecitorio, that the base had stood for a while before being transferred to the Vatican museums. It had long occupied pride of place in the famous "Courtyard of the Pinecone" (*Cortile della Pigna*), but was later moved near the entrance to the Vatican Pinacoteca.

AQUA VIRGO

Most fountains on the Field of Mars are fed by an aqueduct called Aqua Virgo. It was one of the few Roman aqueducts that continued to function throughout the Middle Ages. By renaissance times its output dwindled to a trickle, but when in the 15th century pope Nicholas V decided to restore its functionality, he could do so without too much trouble.

The original aqueduct was built by Agrippa about 19 BC to supply water for a new bath compound near the Pantheon. Legend has it that the source of water was pointed out to his soldiers by a young girl, and it was she who gave the name to the structure. At 20 kilometers' length, the gradient between the starting point and the terminal was only four metres, a testimony to the amazing skill and precision of Roman engineers. For most of its course, the aqueduct was concealed underground. One of its supporting arches can be seen – much lower than today's ground level – behind a grating in the courtyard of house No. 14 on Via del Nazareno. The arch is made of deliberately rough travertine in an archaic manner typical of the time of the emperor Claudius.

The power of Aqua Virgo is visible in the turbulent waters of Rome's most iconic fountain, the Trevi. On the right side of its 18th-century façade is a relief where the girl (*virgo*) shows the water source to Agrippa's men.

Santi Giovanni e Paolo

Santi Quattro Coronati

Arch of Dolabella

Clivo di Scauro

Santa Maria alla Navicella

Santo Stefano Rotondo

Santi Nereo e Achilleo

Caracalla Baths

Tomb of the Scipios

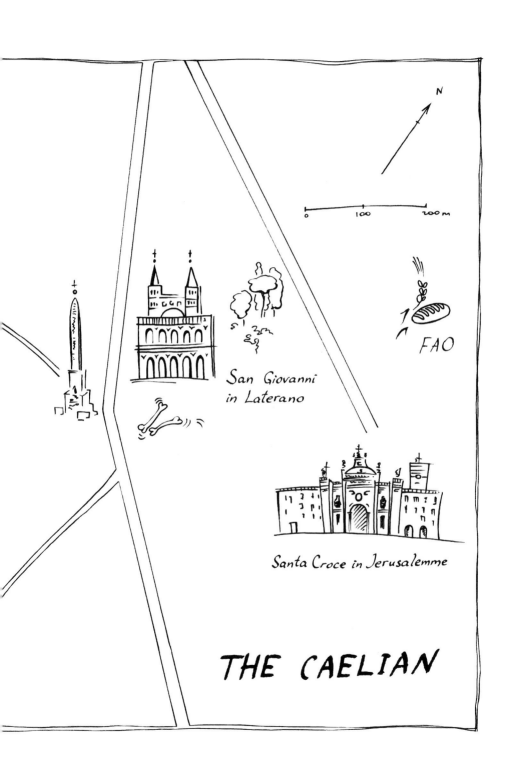

San Giovanni
in Laterano

FAO

Santa Croce in Jerusalemme

THE CAELIAN

CHAPTER IX

THE CAELIAN AND APPIAN WAY
(BATHS AND TOMBSTONES)

I n 48 AD, emperor Claudius addressed the Senate. In his speech, he put forward a motion to open access to the Roman Senate to noblemen from the further Gaul (*Gallia Ulterior*, the area behind the Alps, also called 'the hairy Gaul,' *Gallia Comata*). The ensuing discussion was replete with the same xenophobic feelings that are typical of discussions today on immigration. Senators were saying "why should they be stealing our jobs," "they do not respect our customs," "give them an inch and they'll take a mile" and so on.

Claudius replied along these lines: Sparta and Athens had gone to seed as a result of self-imposed isolation, while Romulus, our founding father, was keen on accepting conquered peoples into a close-knit family; some time ago, Italians, too could not hold top magistracies, and before them Latins, and before them plebeians, and, to tell you the truth, Conscript Fathers, everything we revere as hoary antiquity was a shocking novelty in its day.

Claudius might have been interested in new legislation for sentimental reasons: he was himself a native of the Gallic Lugdunum (now Lyon), the first emperor to have been born outside Italy. He succeeded in persuading senators, and the law was adopted. The story is itself fascinating, but even more fascinating was a historical detour Claudius made in his speech.

Claudius found himself the ruler of the empire almost by chance: he was never power-hungry, and during the rule of the cruel Tiberius and the half-mad Gaius Caligula made a point of playing an idiot: it was the easiest way to avoid being killed in some palatial intrigue. When Caligula was assassinated, a praetorian soldier found the disoriented, trembling Claudius behind a curtain (one of the favourite subjects of the Pre-Raphaelite painter Sir Lawrence Alma-Tadema) and took him to their military camp, where the Praetorian Guard proclaimed him the new princeps. The senators were indignant for a while, but then decided that a limp and geeky ruler would be better for them than the previous two.

One of the things that helped Claudius earn the reputation of an idiot was his scholarly pursuits. As a young man, prompted by historian Titus Livius, he delved into ancient manuscripts and archives and composed many historical works in Latin and Greek, including a voluminous history of Carthage and a history of Etruscans. He was one of the last Romans who knew the Etruscan language (there are no Etruscan documents or inscriptions postdating Augustus). It was his Etruscan research that furnished him with a colourful example for his speech in the Senate, an Etruscan king called Mastarna.

Among the seven Roman kings was the mysterious Servius Tullius, who came from nowhere and left an important trace in the history of Rome's oldest institutions. Citing Etruscan sources, Claudius claimed that Servius Tullius was actually an Etruscan called Mastarna, a companion of the Etruscan *lucumo* (king) Caelius Vibenna. When they were forced to leave their native places and settle in Rome, they chose the hill that was now called Caelian in his memory (but used to be called Querquetulanus, 'the oak hill'). Mastarna adopted a Roman name and "took over the kingdom for the greater good of our fatherland."

THE MYSTERIOUS MASTARNA

One of our sources for Claudius's speech in the Senate is the so-called Lyon Tablet found in 1528 in a vineyard on Croix Rousse Hill, the old silk industry neighbourhood of Lyon. The tablet records the proceedings, including the senators' impatient remarks "Get to the point!" The tablet was installed in the Sanctuary of the Three Gauls, because the result of the hearing was, of course, very advantageous for the Gallic aristocracy.

The tale told by Claudius was unexpectedly confirmed in mid-19th century, when a rich Etruscan necropolis was found near the ancient town of Vulci. One of the tombs, called "the François Tomb" after its discoverer, the Italian polymath and archaeologist Alessandro François, contained two large murals, one depicting a mythological scene, the other a historical one. The mythological scene was from the *Iliad*, and something that would have been termed a war crime today: the ritual burning of Trojan prisoners on the funeral pyre of Patroclus. The historical scene is also rather unsavoury: in it, a group of armed men, some of them naked, slaughter unarmed opponents caught off-guard. The artist inscribed the names above the participants of the scuffle; the victorious group contains Caile Vipinas (Caelius Vibenna) and Masterna (possibly Servius Tullius); one of the defeated is Cneve Tarchunies Rumach, possibly Gnaeus Tarquinius the Roman. Unfortunately, the frescoes from the tomb were detached shortly after their discovery on the orders of Prince Torlonia, and are kept in Villa Albani, one of the Torlonia's properties. The Italian state has for decades fought to make the innumerable Torlonia treasures accessible to the public, with limited success; apparently, you may try to call Villa Albani and request a visit.

Traditional Roman historiography considered Servius Tullius a man of Latin origin: his mother, Ocrisia, was taken prisoner at the Roman siege of Corniculum, a town not far from Rome, and accepted into the household of king Tarquinius Priscus and his wife Tanaquil (his fatherhood was problematic even for Roman historians). The Claudian hypothesis corrects this view: Tarquinius Priscus, he says, who was an Etruscan, had an Etruscan military advisor and condottiere called Mastarna, who later united with other Etruscans, overthrew his patron and established himself as the Roman king under the name of Servius Tullius.

The Caelian Hill occupies the south-eastern portion of Rome – or, rather, that part of Rome that sits inside the oldest Servian walls (the Field of Mars, and of course the Vatican and other right-bank districts are outside this boundary). Its western part stretches from the Colosseum to the Baths of Caracalla, and the eastern part tapers off near the Porta Maggiore city walls; these two parts are divided by the street that bears the name of the inquisitive emperor, Via Claudia.

AQUA CLAUDIA AND THE ROMAN AQUEDUCTS

Urban planning projects undertaken by Claudius ("great and essential rather than numerous," says Suetonius) were all of an aquatic nature one way or another. He built an aqueduct, an outlet draining Lake Fucinus through an underground channel, and a new harbour at Ostia.

Even in summer, when it is very hot, it is not necessary to carry a bottle of supermarket water around Rome, which is the city's marked advantage over other European capitals. There are lots of drinking fountains around Rome, and each produces a constant stream of ice-cold, fresh, potable water. They are called *nasoni* because their tap resembles a long nose and, of course, these days there is an app that helps tourists to locate them. Using them, however, requires a certain skill – but it is not difficult to acquire.

In ancient times, more than ten aqueducts supplied the city with water, and the one bearing Claudius's name was the largest among them. "If anyone will carefully calculate the quantity of the public supply of water [carried by Aqua Claudia]," wrote Pliny the Elder, "for baths, reservoirs, houses, trenches, gardens, and suburban villas; and, along the distance which it traverses, the arches built, the mountains perforated, the valleys levelled; he will confess that there never was anything more wonderful in the whole world."[56]

Roman aqueducts are a true engineering wonder. Their only technological principle is incline: the beginning of the aqueduct (its source) must be higher up than its end without any bumps along the way; the huge masses of water are moved by the force of gravity alone. The results are amazing feats of precision: for example, the Roman aqueduct that fed the Gallic city of Nemasus (Nîmes) is about 50 kilometres long, and only loses 17 metres in height from beginning to end, which means that its incline is as small as 0.02 of a degree.

The small part of the Nîmes aqueduct that is supported by stone arches is now called Pont du Gard. It is one of the most famous landmarks in all of France, a UNESCO World Heritage Site. Its construction used to be credited to Agrippa, but recent excavations moved the date closer to the middle of the 1st century AD, which was, again, the time of Claudius.

At the word 'aqueduct,' most people picture majestic arches of stone or brick, silhouetted high against the luminous skies. This image is only partially correct. Conduits of Roman aqueducts were overwhelmingly concealed underground. Arches were only used when relief (sometimes coupled with ideas of monumental propaganda) demanded it.

However, the Claudian aqueduct (*Aqua Claudia*) has a few stretches that are raised on striking arches. This aqueduct had its source about sixty kilometres east of Rome. Ten kilometres from the city, near one of the most important Roman roads (Via Latina), was its reservoir. Many aqueducts were fitted with reservoirs, where, passing through a complex system of several multi-storeyed chambers, water was filtered, leaving sand and other sediments on its bottom. After the reservoir, the Claudian conduit met another aqueduct, Anio Novus, and from that point on they flowed, one under the other, in channels set in overground arches. Closer to the city, the ground level was gradually falling, and the arches were becoming increasingly higher.

The location where the Claudian aqueduct looks especially magnificent in the meridional landscape is a separate zone inside the archaeological area of the old Appian Way. This zone is called "The Aqueduct Park" (*Parco degli Aquedotti*). The famous Italian film studio Cinecittà is next door, which is why the aqueducts of Claudius often get in the shot of historical and other movies. Perhaps one of the best examples is the first shots of Federico Fellini's *La Dolce Vita*: a helicopter is transporting a huge statue of Christ, followed by another helicopter carrying a crew of journalists – all that against a majestic background of Claudian ruins and pine trees.

PORTA MAGGIORE

The next place to look at Claudian aqueducts is Piazza di Porta Maggiore, where the north-eastern spur of the Caelian tapers off. Today a few important thoroughfares of Rome criss-cross on this spot, but in antiquity it was an even more complicated crossroads. Two major roads forked off here, Via Labicana, leading south-east from Rome, and Via Praenestina, going east (stretches of both roads have preserved their ancient names); plus, the lines of six aqueducts crossed right there. The structure we are seeing today is part of the same construction that carried the waters of Aqua

Claudia and Anio Novus all the way from the Park of the Aqueducts and beyond. The holes for water conduits are easily visible if you look at the arch at an angle. When in the second half of the 3rd century AD Aurelian walls were constructed, the arch turned into a gate, and it is in this capacity, first as the "Praeneste Gate" (*Porta Praenestina*), and then, in Italian, simply as "the big gate" (*Porta Maggiore*) that it is known today.

Travertine blocs that make up the gate seem rough-hewn, unfinished. This is done deliberately. We know already that the emperor Claudius was a fan of all things ancient, and the architecture of his time is stylised to look old. We will soon encounter another example of this fashion for archaic things.

This proclivity of Claudius was not limited to architecture, and there is something on the Porta Maggiore façade to testify to that. This is how Claudius is styled in the first line of the dedicatory inscription: TI. CLAVDIVS DRVSI F. CAISAR AVGVSTVS GERMANICVS – "Tiberius Claudius, son of Drusus, Caesar Augustus Germanicus…" Note how the word 'Caesar' is spelled: not Caesar, as in Classical Latin: Claudius restored a much earlier spelling. By the way, this is one of the clues that helps to reconstruct actual Latin pronunciation: inscriptions like this make it evident that the name which later became an imperial title was pronounced 'kay-sahr' rather than 'see-sahr,' 'tseh-sar,' or even 'chezahrreh,' like in modern Italian.

THE THREE LETTERS OF CLAUDIUS

That was not the end of Claudius's orthographical experiments. He introduced three new letters to the Latin alphabet. These letters were meant to deal with ambiguity in certain words. Thus, for example, the capital Latin V in inscriptions is sometimes a consonant (v), sometimes a vowel (u). As a result, words like *voluit* ('he wanted') and *volvit* ('he rolled') are written exactly the same, *VOLVIT*, in traditional Latin orthography. Claudius wanted to solve the problem by introducing Ⅎ, a letter that was supposed to replace the "consonant" v.

An example of this usage can be seen on a unique tablet which marks the extension of pomerium, the sacred boundary of Rome, under Claudius. This tablet is tucked away in a corner of the Field of Mars that is usually tourist-free, where four streets meet (they are Via del Pellegrino, Via dei Banchi Vecchi, Vicolo della Moretta and Via di Monserrato). The inscription on the tablet ends with the words FINIBVS POMERIVM AMPLIAℲIT TERMINAℲITQVE, with the unique Claudian letter where a modern edition would have written 'v'.

Two other letters invented by Claudius were also meant to eliminate ambiguity: he suggested to use one symbol (Ↄ) for endings in words like *celebs* and *anceps*, which were pronounced the same anyway, and introduce a new symbol (Ⱶ) where different grammarians recommended using either *u* or *i* (*monumentum* and *monimentum*).

After the death of Claudius, his innovations were immediately dropped (it is well known that any orthographic reform meets with violent opposition – the nightmarish spelling of modern English is a living proof of that fact). Mankind only matured into consistent differentiation of *V* and *U* by the 17th century, but some scholarly editions (like the Oxford Latin Dictionary, for example) have not adopted it to this day and continue to write all lowercase *u*'s and *v*'s as 'U' and all uppercase as 'V.'

Interestingly, two other inscriptions on Porta Maggiore indicate that something was wrong with the Claudian aqueducts: they had to be repaired for the first time barely twenty years later, under Vespasian, and then ten after that, under Titus. In that latest (and lowermost) inscription Titus claims that he had restored the aqueduct "ruined to its foundations from old age" (*a solo vetustate dilapsae essent*).

Before we follow the further route of Aqua Claudia across the Caelian, let us linger for a while more on Piazza di Porta Maggiore. Behind the Claudian arch, almost abutting it, stands one of the strangest and loveliest ancient monuments of Rome – the tomb of Eurysaces the baker.

In 1838, pope Gregory XVI decided to remove mediaeval accretions that had grown over the Aurelian wall, and a large monument, previously almost invisible, was uncovered under one of the towers. Its concrete core is faced with travertine, and there is an identical inscription on all of the surviving sides:

EST HOC MONIMENTVM MARCEI VERGILEI EVRYSACIS PISTORIS REDEMPTORIS APPARET

The inscription is mostly clear: "This is the monument of Marcus Vergilius Eurysaces, baker and supplier," but the last word is mysterious, and probably refers to some obscure inside joke. The baker was certainly an eccentric man: a relief depicting a man and a woman was found nearby, with a funerary urn shaped like a bread-basket and another inscription: "Atistia was my wife and an excellent woman, whatever is left of her body is in this bread-basket." The relief and inscription are in the Capitoline museums, but the "bread-basket" is sadly lost.

The baker had a Greek cognomen (Eurysaces), and his tomb does not mention his father or grandfather, which was almost obligatory on the epitaphs of free-born Romans; this means that he was most likely a freedman. This fact has for a long time influenced the treatment of his tomb in scholarly literature: it was considered an example of nouveau riche taste, denial of traditional Roman austerity, and even compared with the tomb that the vulgar parvenu Trimalchio imagines for himself in the famous "Satyricon," the novel by Petronius: "I want fruit trees of every kind planted around my ashes … and me, in my robes of office, sitting on my tribunal, five golden rings on my fingers … and my favourite boy, and large jars … as for the inscription, see if you think this is appropriate: HERE RESTS GAIUS POMPEIUS TRIMALCHIO FREEDMAN OF MAECENAS; HE COULD HAVE BEEN A MEMBER OF EVERY DECURIA OF ROME BUT WOULD NOT; HE GREW RICH FROM LITTLE AND NEVER HEARD A PHILOSOPHER."[57]

In recent years, the tomb of Eurysaces has been looked at with more sympathetic eyes – as a testimony of typically Roman social mobility; as a story of life (and death) of a man who had earned money, social acceptance and respect using his own labour, and who was unashamedly proud of his trade. The reliefs that gird the upper part of the tomb show various stages of bread preparation: workers carry grain, pour it into large measures, weigh it, sell to wholesale dealers; then it is ground (the mill is powered by gloomy-looking donkeys) and riddled; finally, the dough is kneaded, rolled, and baked in an oven. The very structure of the monument is reminiscent of the baking industry: vertical pipes in the lower level are possibly meant to represent grain silos, while horizontal openings, never explained to anyone's satisfaction, may be imitating kneading-machines.

If you walk due south from Porta Maggiore along the Aurelian wall, the road will very soon bring you to the church of Santa Croce in Gerusalemme ('Holy Cross in Jerusalem'), which stands side by side with impressive ancient ruins that usually remain overlooked by tourists (as a rule, they can be only looked at from behind the fence). This is the so-called "Camp Amphitheatre" (*Amphitheatrum castrense*) and the Sessorium, a building used by Saint Helena, mother of emperor Constantine, as her personal palace.

The amphitheatre had been built of concrete and brick, without any marble embellishments, and today, only its lower tier remains. Even in it, the arches had been walled in when the construction was integrated into Aurelian walls. The amphitheatre officially belongs to the neighbouring church, and, while it is difficult to get inside, satellite photos show that a formal garden is laid out inside the ancient walls.

The church of Santa Croce in Gerusalemme, as the legend has it, was built in the early 4th century AD around one of the rooms of Helena's palace – an important room, where the so-called Relics of the Passion were kept, brought by Helena from her journey in the Holy Land: a fragment of the trilingual inscription on the cross ("Jesus the Nazarene, King of the Jews"), two thorns from the crown of thorns used to torture Christ, a piece of a nail, three small wooden chips of the True Cross, the one used to crucify Christ; and a large piece of the cross of the "wise thief," the one who had acknowledged the divine nature of his crucifixion neighbour; also, a bone from the index finger of St. Thomas ("the doubting": he inserted that finger into the wound of his resurrected Master); pieces of a column near which Christ was flagellated, and so on. By the way, the name of the church is parsed not as "The church of the Jerusalem cross," but as "The church, holding pieces of the True Cross, is actually standing in Jerusalem": Helena brought Jerusalem soil to Rome, and the footprint of the church was covered with it to make it actually stand "in Jerusalem."

On the first pages of Mikhail Bulgakov's "The Master and Margarita" (a book that defies the notions of a typical Russian novel: it is relatively short, fast-paced and delightfully funny), the incarnate devil on a visit to the 1920s Moscow says that he was invited there as the only specialist in the world who could consult on a manuscript of the famous necromancer Gerbert of Aurillac. That was the birth name of Pope Sylvester II, the first Frenchman in St. Peter's see. According to a legend, the church of Santa Croce in Gerusalemme turned out to be fatal for him. He had once received a prophecy that he would die after celebrating a mass in Jerusalem. He got the message and never ventured into the Holy Land. Once, after a service at the Roman church of St. Cross he felt out of sorts; when the full name of the church was revealed to him, it was too late.

THE LATERAN

Walking west from Santa Croce along the Viale Castrense, you will reach a place where the bones of Sylvester II had been laid to rest – though, it seems, with mixed results.

Pope Sylvester II was buried in the cathedral of St. John Lateran, and his rather clumsy Latin epitaph begins thus: *Iste locus mundi Silvestri membra sepulti venturo Domino conferet ad sonitum*, which means "at the trumpet's sound, this neighbourhood of the world shall convey the limbs of the buried Sylvester to the Lord at His coming." The folk explanation vividly reimagined the coming Lord as a new pope, and the sound as the rattle of bones. This gave birth to a legend: before the death of a pope, something quietly rumbles in the tomb of Sylvester II.

The location of today's Lateran compound (the basilica, baptisterium and palace) used to be covered by the estates of the Lateran family. Little is known about them, though there is evidence that one Lucius Sextius Lateranus possibly had had the honour of being Rome's first plebeian consul. In the late 2nd century AD, emperor Septimius Severus founded here a camp of cavalry guards (*Castra Nova equitum singularium*). About a hundred years later, this élite mounted regiment that had protected members of the imperial household outside Rome and in the provinces, had bet on the wrong side of an internal squabble, namely on co-emperor Maxentius. Immediately after the battle of the Milvian bridge the victorious Constantine disbanded the cavalrymen, and handed their barracks and the neighbouring palace to the Christian church.

It was an important event in Christian history. The followers of the new Middle Eastern religion, recently persecuted and despised, were not only supported by the state machinery, but could now establish themselves on a prestigious (albeit suburban) spot of the Eternal City. To this day, the cathedral of St. John Lateran enjoys a special status among the world's Christian (or at least Roman Catholic) churches. It is that church, and not St. Peter's Basilica which is the cathedral of the city of Rome, which means that it is the location of the throne (cathedra) of the Roman bishop, commonly known as the pope (the previous ornate chair was replaced by Francis I by a much simpler white affair). This special status is described in a Latin inscription at the entrance: "The sacrosanct Lateran Church, Mother and Head of all churches of the City and the World" (*Sacros<ancta> Lateran<ensis> eccles<ia> omnium urbis et orbis ecclesiarum mater et caput*).

> The President of the French Republic is *ex officio* the "first and only honorary canon" of the Lateran cathedral. This title is held by the head of the Fifth Republic by virtue of his (or her? that's an interesting hypothetical) succession from the French kings, who had been the cathedral's benefactors since the times of Henry IV (late 16th century).

Simple Roman Christians, however, never took to the Lateran cathedral. Throughout the Middle Ages there were tensions between the Lateran hub of papal power and improvised Christian communities that usually sprang up outside city walls – in the catacombs, and in places where popular saints had been martyred and churches were erected to commemorate it. (The Vatican was one such centre.) In the early 14th century, the papal court was forced to leave Rome and settle in the French city of Avignon for about seventy years, which lead to further decline of the Lateran palace and surrounding buildings. The nexus of Catholic hierarchy never returned to the Lateran: after Avignon, the Roman curia was in Trastevere (at Santa Maria in Trastevere), on the Esquiline (at Santa Maria Maggiore), until it finally put down roots on the Vatican hill.

The eyes of the world's Roman Catholics were on the Lateran once again in 1929, when the "accords" were signed in the Lateran palace between the Kingdom of Italy (represented by Prime Minister Mussolini) and the Holy See. The accords definitively settled the so-called "Roman Question" of the popes' temporal power and formalised the relationship between the papal court (now officially presiding over its own sovereign state) and the Italian state. The Lateran Accords remain in force to this day, with slight modifications. The cathedral of St. John Lateran, though standing on Italian soil outside the Vatican, is nevertheless extraterritorial and belongs to the Holy See.

The compound of the Lateran's Christian sanctuaries is filled with relics and trophies (*spolia*) of ancient times. The bronze doors of the main east portal are taken from the Senate building on the Forum (they are one of the three pairs of functioning ancient doors in Rome). The organ is propped up by two columns of yellow marble, one of them taken from the Arch of Constantine. Finally, in the portico stands a huge marble statue of the emperor in full battle attire, once thought to be of Constantine though it is actually Constantine's son, Constantius II. It seems that all imperial statues in the Lateran neighbourhood were traditionally recognised as Constantines: before settling on the Capitol, it was here that the famous equestrian statue of Marcus Aurelius, also under the name of Constantine, had stood.

The baptistery called San Giovanni in Fonte, or simply the Lateran Baptistery, for a long time the only structure of its kind in Rome, was founded in the 5th century. It is sometimes incongruously called the place where Constantine was baptised, though Constantine, if he was baptised at all, did so only on his deathbed in Nicomedia, a town near Constantinople.

The baptistery has obviously survived many restorations and rebuildings since the 5th century, but its general structure and porphyry columns date from that time. Inside, the building is lavishly decorated with columns, reliefs, pieces of frieze, mosaics of ancient times. Under it is a foundation of a 1st century AD residential house that was replaced by a small bath complex some time later; the long squat structures with brick-faced arches near the baptistery, next to the entrance to the Pontifical Lateran University, are the remains of those baths.

On the other side of the square, inside the old Lateran Palace, is hidden the so-called Scala Sancta (Holy Stairs). According to the legend, these are the marble steps of the Roman palace in Jerusalem, the residence of the governor, where Christ had stood during his conversation with Pontius Pilate. The stairs were brought to Rome with other Christian relics by the same tireless St. Helena. Enclosed in a protective wooden framework, the steps should be ascended on one's knees as an act of penance followed by absolution (indulgence). Charles Dickens witnessed the scene on a Good Friday, and was not happy: the sight seemed to him "unpleasant in its senseless and unmeaning degradation." The tradition survives to this day.

Finally, the largest Egyptian obelisk – not just in Rome, but in the whole world – stands on Piazza di San Giovanni in Laterano. It is one of the city's oldest obelisks (work on it started under the pharaoh Thutmose III of the 18th Dynasty, in the 15th century BC). Constantine had endeavoured to take it out of Egypt (probably to Constantinople rather than to Rome), but could only arrange the delivery of the obelisk to Alexandria from its original position near the temple of Amun in Karnak. After Constantine's death, his son Constantius II showed interest in the project. The ship taking the obelisk to Rome was record-breaking in size and tonnage. The wonder of the world was delivered to Circus Maximus, where it was erected with superhuman effort. In the Middle Ages the obelisk fell down and broke into three parts and disappeared from record for a long time, until Pope Sixtus V had it excavated and restored in the present position, in the 16th century.

Returning to the Claudian aqueduct, its urban portion, about two kilometres long, was finished in the time of Nero and is often called "Arches of Nero" (*Arcus Neroniani*). Entering the city at Porta Maggiore, the aqueduct continues along Via Statilia on the grounds of Villa Wolkonsky. Then it disappears for a while in a thicket of modern development, and the arches reemerge only on Via di Santo Stefano Rotondo – first a long stretch on the left (on the north side), then a shorter one on the right, on the south side of the street.

VILLA WOLKONSKY

In Italian, as in Classical Latin, the word 'villa' does not mean simply a large house, but the grounds of the estate. In the 1830s, the Russian princess Zenaïde Wolkonsky bought such an estate – a distinguished one featuring ancient arches. The princess also had an urban residence – Palazzo Poli; its façade features one of the most famous landmarks of the city, the Trevi fountain.

Wolkonsky was used to being in the centre of public attention; her Moscow salon on Tverskaya street had been one of the most glamorous, and celebrities vied to be invited; Alexander Pushkin wrote her a somewhat formal but wildly complimentary poem.

*Princess Zenaïde Wolkonsky. After a portrait by
Jean Désiré Muneret (1814)*

By the late 1820s, Princess Wolkonsky began feeling somewhat ill at ease in Russia. She had recently converted to Roman Catholicism, and her intimacy with key figures of the failed 1825 Decembrist revolt against the tsar and their wives (one of the ringleaders, Sergei Wolkonsky, was her brother-in-law) caused royal displeasure. She left for Italy, never to return. Her Roman estate became a centre of émigré life: in the shadow of Nero's arches, Nikolai Gogol thought out his "Dead Souls," the painter Karl Bryullov, a European celebrity after "The Last Days of Pompeii" that had inspired the (in)famous novel by Edward Bulwer-Lytton, painted portraits of the hostess, and the villa's grounds saw a host of other European and American illuminati, the likes of Walter Scott, Fenimore Cooper, and Gaetano Donizetti.

For about a hundred years, the villa remained the property of Wolkonsky's heirs, until in 1922 it was sold to the government of Germany. After World War II, it passed into the joint control of Allied Command and the Italian Government. When in 1946 the Zionist terrorist organization Irgun blew up the British Embassy on Villa Torlonia, the Italian government offered the Villa Wolkonsky to the British. It has remained a UK property ever since, though it no longer serves as an embassy: it is the residence of the Ambassador and other high-ranking diplomats.

From antiquity to today, historians have been vicious toward Nero, so much so that it takes an effort to picture this emperor in any constructive role. Take the story about his bathing in the source of the Marcian aqueduct, a gross offense not just against public hygiene, but against piety: Tacitus thinks that it was that incident that brought the wrath of the gods upon Nero's head. However, even Nero's ill-wishers concede that after the famous fire Nero worked hard to restore order and dignity to the city. Among other things, he commissioned the development of stricter building regulations and forbade unlawful siphoning of water from aqueducts (wherever there is a poorly guarded pipe, there will be those wishing to exploit the opportunity).

Nero's building projects did not only serve the greater good – they also fed his own megalomania. An example can be spotted on Via Claudia: on its western side, on a hill, one can see the ruins of a huge fountain known as Nero's Nymphaeum (we have discussed the difference between a nymphaeum and a regular fountain in the chapter about the environs of the Colosseum). Function-wise, this was a decorative fountain like the one in Nero's Palatine palace, only twelve times as large. It is hard to say exactly what it had looked like, but it is easy to imagine lavish decorations: coloured marble, exquisite Greek statuary. The gigantic cascades were fed by the restored aqueduct.

After Nero's "personality cult" was debunked under the Flavian emperors, the fountain, together with the whole Golden House compound, fell into disrepair and was soon built over. The nymphaeum was completely forgotten, all until the late 19th century, when the cutting of a new street uncovered the mounds of concrete.

One end of Nero's Nymphaeum faced a small valley between the Caelian and the Esquiline, while the other abutted a spot with the urban reservoir of the Claudian aqueduct. After Claudius's death, the spot was earmarked for the temple of the freshly deified emperor. The moving force of the project was the emperor's widow Agrippina, rumoured to have poisoned her husband with the goal of enthroning her son by a previous marriage, Nero. Having risen to power, Nero did away both with his mother and with the memory of his predecessor, razing the new temple to the ground. In the course of his de-Neronification campaign, Vespasian rebuilt the temple and the whole neighbourhood.

The Temple of Claudius, standing on the highest point of the Caelian Hill, became for a while the architectural centrepiece of that part of Rome. Unfortunately, it survives only in fragments of a huge platform, largely concealed in the gardens of the Passionist priests (members of a religious institution with a special emphasis on the Passion of Christ), who own the monastery next to the church of Santi Giovanni e Paolo. The corner of the platform forms a part of the bell tower of that church on the north side of the small square. It seems that the platform (and probably the whole temple) was stylised in the spirit of the rough-hewn antiquity so dear to the learned emperor.

PIAZZA CELIMONTANA AND CLIVO DI SCAURO

The principal streets of the Caelian converge on Piazza Celimontana, and a branch of the Claudio-Neronian aqueduct also passes here. In antiquity it was a lively place as well, a crossroads in front of the entrance to the "old town." A gate, known as the Arch of Dolabella and Silanus, leads inside the Republican walls. It is not simply a gateway into the city, but also another aqueduct support (there are some ruins of water-carrying structures on the other side of the square, too). From here, branching water conduits brought water from the Claudian source to a number of Rome's districts: the Esquiline, the Palatine (where the main consumer was Nero's Golden House, and after its destruction – its successor, the Flavian imperial palace), to the Aventine and even to what is today Trastevere on the other bank of the river. The branches that had fed the Palatine still adorn central Rome; others have disappeared completely. The water of the Claudian aqueduct was considered of superior quality, second only to the water from the very old Aqua Marcia. The emperor Alexander Severus never touched his food before drinking half a litre of ice-cold Claudian water.

A small street leading from Piazza Celimontana to Circus Maximus is one of the quaintest corners of the old Caelian. The concentration of ancient and mediaeval history (and their entwining) is very dense here. The street has a double name: closer to Piazza Celimontana it is called Via di San Paolo della Croce, closer to Circus Maximus it is Clivo di Scauro. It is an Italianised version of the Latin name, *Clivus Scauri*, "the Scaurus lane."

St. Paul of the Cross (San Paolo della Croce in Italian) was an Italian mystic of the 18th century. In his youth, his experience of prayer made him devote his life to Christ. The central point of his teaching was the concept of the Passion of Christ as the principal symbolic expression of God's love for people. The numbers of the new order grew slowly, because ascetic simplicity and austerity of the "Passionists" was at odds with the spirit of the "Gallant Age." Paul did not mind. By the end of his life, there were twelve Passionist monasteries and one nunnery. He was canonised in 1867.

The rare Latin word *scaurus* means someone suffering a disease of the feet (either 'lame' or 'gouty' or 'swollen'). This word became a cognomen in the noble patrician Aemilia *gens*. One of the members of the family, Marcus Aemilius Scaurus, was a very prominent politician of the Republic (his son, though, also made a name for himself by suppressing a Jewish revolt and collecting carved stones). It is possible that a street leading up the Caelian was named in honour of one of them back in ancient times (though the name is only attested since the Middle Ages). In the 20th century, based on this scant antiquarian information, a portion of Via di San Paolo della Croce was renamed Clivo di Scauro. Unless a mistake occurred, this is one of the rare streets – rare even in Rome – that still bear the original name after two thousand years' time.

Our short walk begins at the church Santo Stefano Rotondo. St. Stephen has a special place among all the Christian saints: he is a protomartyr. This is a title given to the first saint martyred for his or her religious beliefs in a certain country (thus, the British protomartyr is St. Alban, believed to have been beheaded in the 3rd or 4th century in the Romano-British city of Verulamium, now St Albans). St. Stephen, though, is the very first Christian martyr in the world: he was executed by the Jewish religious tribunal for blasphemy shortly after the crucifixion of Christ, and the execution itself, by stoning, is described in the Acts of the Apostles. Interestingly, among those who actively participated in the persecution of Stephen and his fellow believers was Saul of Tarsus – the future Apostle Paul, the main promoter of international Christianity. The relics of St. Stephen are in Rome, but for some reason not in this church but at San Lorenzo fuori le mura.

In the 15th century, Pope Nicholas V handed Santo Stefano, by that time rather decrepit, over to the order of Pauline monks – the only Roman Catholic order to have been founded by Hungarians. Since then, the church has become an unofficial centre of the Hungarian community in Rome and acquired another heavenly patron – Stephen I of Hungary (known as *Szent István király* in his original language), the king who baptised Hungary at the very end of the 10th or beginning of the 11th century. The Hungarian István and the Greek-derived Stephen are one and the same name and, incidentally, it means 'a wreath' in Greek.

Santo Stefano Rotondo is one of Rome's oldest churches. It was rebuilt multiple times both inside and outside during the last millennium and a half, but the general layout has survived from the 5th century. The layout is very unusual: it combines a circle and a "Greek" cross with arms of equal length. Round outer walls concealed two rings of internal supports. The arms of the cross spread out from the space beneath the dome; they were quite visible until the reconstructions that altered the church in the 12th and 15th centuries. The original architects obviously drew their inspiration from certain Eastern churches, such as the rotunda in the Church of the Holy Sepulchre in Jerusalem.

An etching by Giuseppe Vasi (18th century) shows the ruins of the Claudian aqueduct, Santo Stefano Rotondo (on the right), San Tommaso in Formis and Santa Maria in Domnica

In Renaissance times it was thought that Santo Stefano was standing on the foundation of an ancient building – probably the Temple of Faunus; some went so far as to say that it had actually been originally the Temple of Faunus (which was pure fiction: there is no mention of such a temple anywhere in classical sources). Another candidate was Nero's food market (*macellum*), which was, indeed, somewhere in the vicinity. Excavations of the 1970s have shown that the church was built from scratch, and the only thing found beneath it were the ruins of a mithraeum, which had been functioning on that spot for about two hundred years, and then was hastily walled up, probably giving way to the increasing sway of Christianity. Objects preserved in the vault – altars, figurines, reliefs, some still with traces of paint and gilding – were transferred to the collections of the National Roman Museum.

MITHRAISM

The word 'mithraeum' is used for the cult-related premises used by the followers of a mysterious sect which had flourished all across the Roman Empire from the 1st to the 4th century AD (that is, simultaneously with the spread of Christianity). Unlike Christians, the Mithraists have not left any sacred texts or explanations for posterity. Archaeologists and philologists have to reconstruct the details from second-hand reports, including Christian condemnations. Mithrea were abundantly decorated with cult images – of those, we have quite a lot. These images (mostly reliefs, sometimes frescoes) feature the killing of a bull (the so-called tauroctony) as their main motif; the bull-slayer is a heroic-looking man in a Phrygian hat, most likely the very Mithras who was revered by the members of the sect. Other reliefs and sculptures depicted a feast on the hide of the slain bull, the birth of Mithras from stone, his two servants, and a mysterious character with the head of a lion.

The cult of Mithras (like the cult of Christ) almost certainly arrived from the East; it is not quite clear whether this Mithras and the Indo-Iranian deity called Mithra are identical or even related.

The followers of Mithraism met in underground sanctuaries. The nature of their rites is uncertain, but they certainly ate a lot during the sessions – both meat and fruit. The cult was especially popular among the legionaries: many mithraea have been preserved on the outskirts of the empire, in military camps. Women were excluded from the mysteries (that could be one of the reasons for their ceding ground so fast to the Christians, in whose early church women played a pivotal role). The structure of the sect was semi-military, with a rigid hierarchy and seven levels of initiation: Raven, Bridesman, Soldier, Lion, Persian, Sun-runner and Father.

After Christianity had been established as the official state religion, Mithraism went even further underground and gradually withered away. It had always been more of a provincial fad, but there are a number of mithraea in Rome, including the one under Santo Stefano Rotondo. The best known and most easily accessible among them is under the church of San Clemente. Others are in Palazzo Barberini, under the Santa Prisca church on the Aventine, in the Baths of Caracalla and near the Circus Maximus. Outside Italy, there are many mithraea in Germany, a few in France.

The Mithraeum of London is perhaps the best-known Roman find in 20th-century London; it was discovered during construction work for a financial services company building. With no Mussolini to stop the works, the developers proceeded with their plans, while the mithraeum was relocated and reassembled, in the Ara Pacis style, at Temple Court. In the last decade, there have been intermittent plans to restore the mithraeum to its original place, which have recently received a new lease of life. The artefacts found during the dig, including a fine head of the Roman-Egyptian composite god Serapis (readily recognizable by a strange device on his head – *modium*, a measure of grain, which symbolises eternal life) are on display at the Museum of London.

In the 16th century, Pope Gregory XIII commissioned artists to paint Santo Stefano with frescoes that would depict the life and (primarily) the death of Christian martyrs. In the 19th century they were heavily restored in a realistic style, and it was in that guise that they made an unforgettable impression on Charles Dickens:

> St. Stefano Rotondo, a damp, mildewed vault of an old church in the outskirts of Rome, will always struggle uppermost in my mind, by reason of the hideous paintings with which its walls are covered. These represent the martyrdoms of saints and early Christians; and such a panorama of horror and butchery no man could imagine in his sleep, though he were to eat a whole pig raw, for supper. Grey-bearded men being boiled, fried, grilled, crimped, singed, eaten by wild beasts, worried by dogs, buried alive, torn asunder by horses, chopped up small

with hatchets: women having their breasts torn with iron pinchers, their tongues cut out, their ears screwed off, their jaws broken, their bodies stretched upon the rack, or skinned upon the stake, or crackled up and melted in the fire: these are among the mildest subjects.

Santo Stefano's western wall faces a small square whose opposite side is occupied by another old church, Santa Maria in Domnica. It was built not later than the 7th or 8th century on a place previously used by the firefighters of Ancient Rome. When Augustus divided the city into 14 regions, seven fire brigades were established, each to serve two regions; one of them was quartered on the Caelian.

The name of the church sounds as if it were related to Latin words *dominus* ('master') or *domenica* ('Sunday'), but it is not, and it is unclear what it means. The church has an unofficial name, too – Santa Maria alla Navicella. Navicella ('a boat' in Italian) is a rather large (4.5 metres) fountain shaped as a marble boat. Today, a 16th-century copy stands on the square, but the original dated back to classical times and could have been a votive offering of sailors who survived a shipwreck.

Votive objects – from the Latin *votum*, 'a vow' – are ritual gifts to a deity. In Ancient Greece and Rome such objects (figurines, amulets, pictures) were left in temples and shrines when the bearer asked for something or thanked for promises kept. Especially interesting are votive offerings to Asclepius/Aesculapius and other medicine-related gods: they are often shaped like the organs that are supposed to be healed. Such models show what the ancients knew about human anatomy, and many of them are surprisingly accurate.

If you make a sharp left after the Arch of Dolabella, you will find one of those Roman churches whose façade is set back so far that it is hard to see. It is the church of San Tommaso in Formis, also dating back to ancient times but rebuilt in the 13th century by Trinitarians (the order that venerates the Holy Trinity). The church is hiding behind the ruins of the Claudio-Neronian aqueduct, which is reflected even in its name (*forma* means aqueduct in late Latin). The façade facing the open space in front of the Arch of Dolabella is not that of the church, but of a hospital attached to it. A mediaeval mosaic is set above the door: Christ liberates two slaves, one white and one black (their slavery is apparent in the chains they are discarding). That New Testament Christianity should not, at least in theory, tell a Jew from Gentile, has been always known, but the racially blind message of this mosaic is well ahead of its time: the first serious protests of enlightened Europeans and Americans against slave trade occurred more than five hundred years later.

The Trinitarians' political correctness was limited to slaves of Christian faith. The crusades, like any war, produced lots of prisoners who were used as slaves. The new order aimed at liberating (by way of buying out) prisoners from Christian lands from the hands of the unfaithful.

A large chunk of land between Circus Maximus, the Baths of Caracalla and the Colosseum is taken up by Villa Mattei. The name indicates that it owes its existence to the very Mattei family whose activities on the Tiber banks were covered in one of the previous chapters. In the 1920s this plot was purchased by the Italian government and made accessible to the general public (the main entrance is near Santa Maria in Domnica), and it is now usually simply called Villa Celimontana ("the Caelian villa"). An interesting detail of the grounds is a small Egyptian obelisk (so small that it had to be installed on a granite pillar to increase its visibility). Dating to the time of Ramesses II, it was meant for the Temple of Isis on the Field of Mars. In the 14th century it was set up on the stairs leading up to the Capitol, and an urban legend claimed that the bronze sphere on its top contained the ashes of Augustus, just as the ball on the Vatican obelisk, now in St. Peter's Square, allegedly preserved the ashes of Julius Caesar (the architect Domenico Fontana made a point of opening up the sphere and studying its contents, which was nothing more than some dust accumulated throughout the centuries).

A more plausible legend says that when the obelisk was being erected in the Mattei gardens, some of the scaffolding collapsed, pinning down the arm of a labourer. The limb had to be amputated in the field, and has remained buried under the base of the obelisk ever since.

At the point where Via di San Paolo della Croce transforms into Clivo di Scauro, the street is spanned by seven striking brick arches. They are mediaeval (except the last one, probably dating back to antiquity), and their purpose is to prop up the south wall of the church of Santi Giovanni e Paolo. The wall is made up from façades of houses that used to face the street in the 3rd century AD. The church with its long history boasts an intimate and somewhat mysterious connection with ancient Roman times.

SANTI GIOVANNI E PAOLO

The church of Santi Giovanni e Paolo does not commemorate the apostles John and Paul, but martyrs of the same names who allegedly perished on this spot during persecutions instigated by the emperor Julian. This is not a very plausible tale: the short-lived pagan renaissance of Julian (later called 'the Apostate') of the 4th century AD was not particularly bloody and focused mostly on eastern provinces. A Christian sanctuary appeared on this spot in the late 4th century, in the house of Christian senator Pammachius. As we've seen, such a home church was called a *titulus*. Pillaged more than once during barbarian raids on Rome, the church had acquired its more or less present-day shape, with the monastery and bell tower, in the 12th century, through the efforts of the popes Paschal II and Adrian IV (the latter pope, born Nicholas Breakspear, to this day remains the only Englishman to have ever occupied the Holy See). The church still maintains a connection to the Anglo-Saxon world: it is considered a titular church of the archbishops of New York.

One of the tablets near the church entrance commemorates the service of Francis Spellman, the Archbishop of New York, as the Cardinal-Priest of Santi Giovanni e Paolo. The Latin inscription offers a rare chance to work out the name of the largest US city in Latin. It is Novum Eboracum (adjective *novoeboracensis*) – because the 'old' York, one of England's most ancient cities, had grown around a large Roman military camp called Eboracum.

The bell tower of the church, rising directly above the bearing wall of the Temple of Claudius, is adorned with ceramic plates (a while ago, the originals were removed to the museum and replaced with replicas). The provenance of those plates is unexpected: almost all of them were made in Muslim-ruled Spain and often decorated with verses of the Qur'an. This mediaeval multiculturalism was not intentional, of course: few people in Rome could read Arabic script at the time, let alone recognise sacred texts of a different religion.

In 2002, the excavated space under the church was opened to the public. The resulting museum is called simply "Roman Houses on the Caelian" (*Case romane del Celio*). The museum is surprisingly large: it is dedicated to the Christian "titulus" and the mediaeval church, and the story of its development and restoration. However, its most interesting exhibits are the mysterious frescoes, painted in abundance on the walls of ancient Roman houses under the church.

In the so-called "room of the genii," the walls are decorated with cheerful winged figures with wreaths in their hands and plump Cupids gathering grapes in the company of numerous birds. In the "prayer room," amid the grotesques resembling similar art of Pompeii and the Golden House, there is a human figure with arms spread wide. Art historians love to draw far-fetched conclusions, and this figure is sometimes interpreted as evidence of early (not postdating 3rd century AD) penetration of

Christianity among Roman home-owners. The small 'confession room' is very likely to have been painted by Christian artists indeed: here, we see a beardless Christ and two people lying prostrate at his feet; on the other wall, three martyrs are being executed. They are two men and a woman, and there is some confusion regarding their identity: they are usually listed as Saints Crispin, Crispinian and Benedicta, but Benedicta seemed to have been martyred jointly with two other saints with similar names, Priscus and Priscillianus – and under Diocletian rather than Julian. Be as it may, the three people in the fresco had certainly met a gruesome death: they are blindfolded, with arms tied behind their backs. This is probably the earliest depiction of Christian martyrdom in history.

The most interesting (and least understandable) painting is in the so-called "nymphaeum" (there used to be a fountain in the room). Its centrepiece is a woman who is either feasting or simply sailing in a boat accompanied by two more characters, while Cupids cavort around her in smaller boats. Ancient painting is known to us mostly from verbal descriptions (except for Pompeian frescoes, which are less numerous than one would have wanted); this marine scene is, therefore, an important and rare example of ancient Roman painting. It is interpreted in various ways, among which two are more accepted than most. According to the first, the central heroine, who somewhat resembles the central figure of Édouard Manet's *Le Déjeuner sur l'herbe* (a naked woman with two clothed men), is Proserpine who returns from the underworld with the spring. The other version casts her in the role of Venus as the protectress of seafarers.

Opposite the church, on the other side of Clivo di Scauro, are the remains of a semicircular apse. It used to be the large ceremonial hall of a late Roman house, but in the 6th century AD pope Agapetus I used his brief pontificate to transform it into the first major Christian library, along the lines of multiple libraries of the pagan Greco-Roman civilisation. The Einsiedeln Itinerary, which we have mentioned in Chapter I, has preserved the dedicatory inscription over the entrance:

> A venerable company of saints sits in a long line
> teaching the mystical precepts of the divine law.
> The priest Agapetus is appropriately seated among them.
> He has built with art this beautiful place for books.[58]

Somewhat later, a church and monastery were founded on this site by Pope Gregory I, also known as St. Gregory the Great. It was largely through his efforts that Rome became the main pivot of Western Christianity and remained the centre of an independent papal state all until the 19th century.

The large space behind the "Agapetus's library" is taken by a church that bears St. Gregory's name and its adjoining chapels. The present building was erected in the 12th century, but fully refurbished from inside and outside in the 17th and 18th centuries. These grounds also contain a small museum (*Antiquarium Comunale,* or *Antiquarium del Celio*) with archaeological finds of the Caelian and Esquiline.

Leaving behind the picturesque Clivo di Scauro and emerging into Via di San Gregorio, we find ourselves in a spot where the collision of historical names, eras and allusions is so dense as to be possible only in Rome. On the right is the Colosseum; straight ahead, the Palatine; a little to the left, Circus Maximus; further left, the Aventine; and, finally, behind your back is Porta Capena, with the Baths of Caracalla lying behind it.

THE AVENTINE

In a guidebook that offers its readers the fiction of time travel ("How to survive in Ancient Rome on five sestertii per day"), the Aventine Hill would have merited a chapter of its own. Unfortunately, today this low-lying hill with two summits has virtually no traces of antiquity left. (Roman hills are also a fiction of sorts – they can be defined and classified in lots of different ways; however, most historians and archaeologists agree that the neighbourhood to the west of Via Marmorata is not a part of the Aventine but a separate place called Testaccio, which we will cover later.)

Since the most ancient time, the Aventine was clothed in an aura of unorthodoxy, opposition to state order, even rebellion. This had begun in the very first days of the nascent city, when Romulus and Remus were quarrelling about its name, and Remus, who was watching the flight of birds on the Aventine, lost to Romulus (who made camp on the Palatine for the same purpose). The king Servius Tullius continued the tradition by building a temple of Diana on the hill. Diana was considered the patron of slaves and plebeians, who accepted the goddess wholeheartedly. In early republican times, the plebeians, back then quite disenfranchised, several times organised "an Italian strike" taken to its logical conclusion: not only did they stop working, they collected all their things and, taking their whole families with them, moved out of Rome to one of the neighbouring hills, threatening to secede in earnest and establish their own state. Apart from political implications, this action was a very palpable economic disaster: since the plebeians constituted the absolute majority of the labour force, their absence led to the immediate collapse of everyday life: no one sold anything in the market, or swept streets, or delivered goods, or forged, or sewed, or baked (imagine all migrant workers disappearing overnight from any large city).

*A view of the Aventine Hill, 19th-century drawing. On the summit of the
hill is the church Santa Maria del Priorato, the only major architectural
monument built by Giovanni Battista Piranesi. He is buried in that church*

Not all of these rebellions used the Aventine as their stronghold,
but it was the Aventine secession (withdrawal) of 449 BC that became
the turning point in the plebeian struggle for rights: for the first time
ever, Roman authorities passed written laws (the so-called "Laws of the
Twelve Tables"), known to everyone and applicable to every citizen.
In the previous system, trials were conducted in secret, almost like a
religious rite, with outcomes usually unfavourable for those less well-
born and poorer.

The secession aura of the Aventine was further supported by the events
of the 2nd century BC, when the followers of the Plebeian Tribune Gaius

Gracchus, anticipating an imminent defeat, made a desperate attempt to find refuge in the Temple of Diana.

In 1923, the Socialist Party withdrew from the Italian parliament, protesting at the assassination of one of its leaders by Fascist thugs. This action was called "the new Aventine secession," even though there was no topographical link to the hill. Unfortunately, the socialists' actions were futile: after the secession, there was no parliamentary opposition at all, and Mussolini consolidated even more authority in his hands. In the Italian political vocabulary, a boycott by a minority is called *Aventino* to this day. As for the Aventine Hill, it has undergone a radical change, turning into a quiet and affluent neighbourhood with luxurious villas and expensive hotels.

BATHS OF CARACALLA

Our route takes us past the southeastern edge of Circus Maximus (where its only visible remains have survived) down the Via di San Gregorio to the square called Piazza di Porta Capena. The Capena gate was perhaps the most important city gate in the old Servian walls: it was where the Appian Way started, and the count of miles from the city began. In the 1860s, fragments of masonry were found in the square, but they are no longer visible. The most conspicuous building in the square is the huge compound of the United Nations Food and Agriculture Organization, FAO; its logo is a stylised head of wheat and the Latin motto, *Fiat panis*, which means "Let there be bread." This dubious masterpiece of Fascist architecture was initially intended for the Department of Italian East Africa during the short stretch of time when Mussolini's government, burning with imperial ambition, made attempts to colonise Ethiopia and Somalia.

In 1937, a monumental obelisk, taken from the Ethiopian city of Axum as a trophy, was erected in front of the building. (Strictly speaking, it is a stele, not an obelisk, as it is not topped by a pyramid.) The obelisk remained there for almost sixty years before the government of Italy gave it back to Ethiopia. The restitution procedure dragged on for years: a huge granite obelisk, even divided in three parts, is just as difficult to transport these days as it was in the times of the emperors. To facilitate the return, the runway of the Axum airport had to be refurbished to accommodate the huge transport An-124, the only aircraft able to carry even a third of the stele. After a few years spent in storage limbo in both countries, in 2008 the Axum obelisk was finally reassembled on the original spot.

In ancient times, the Capena gate was not the final limit of the city, but the Appian Way was quite narrow here (about four metres wide) and certainly very crowded. The alley of today, Viale delle Terme di Caracalla, was only cut in the 1930s. Those walking toward the city saw the huge wall of Septizodium on the Palatine slope, and could feel the appropriate empire-inspired awe. Those walking in the other direction could also experience their own sensation of grandeur, at least from the early 3rd century AD: immediately after the Servian wall, the emperor Caracalla had built a huge bath complex, the most monumental of all monuments near the Appian Way.

No other sight, not even the Colosseum, gives a better idea of Roman imperial gigantomania. Under the empire, Roman baths were generally planned with abandon, but of the baths of Agrippa, virtually nothing survives; the ruins of Trajan's baths are scattered across a large park, while the baths of Diocletian house numerous successors of the Ancient Roman civilisation, from a museum to the church of Santa Maria degli Angeli. The Baths of Caracalla, on the other hand, have survived better than most, and they form a designated museum space without any other development that could hinder the imbibing of Roman grandeur. Grandeur, in this case, is directly linked to sheer size.

The level of personal hygiene enjoyed by Romans has been only recently re-attained by modern civilisation, and even that is not ubiquitous. In very old times, the Romans did not bathe in luxury either: an agricultural treatise advises the landowner that his farm labourers should not wash more than once a week. The Romans used to perform their ablutions privately, but in the late years of the Republic, public baths were already widespread. The novelty was aimed at the poor who could not bathe at home, but it spread to other strata of society very quickly. Suetonius says that Atia, the mother of Augustus, and a very proper lady, was rumoured to have consorted with the god Apollo and received a snake-shaped mark as a consequence, which forced her to abstain from public baths.

In the imperial era, the baths were no longer limited to providing their obvious hygienic functionality: they became clubs of sorts, where idle people could spend days on end in physical exercise, pleasant conversation, reading (libraries were often attached to baths) and even eating.

A bath visit followed a well established ritual. First of all, a visitor paid for the visit (the fee was symbolic and affordable even for the poorest) and took off his clothes, which could be then given to an attendant (a surviving epitaph of a married couple says that the husband used to be a cloakroom attendant at the Baths of Caracalla). After that, the visitor started a routine that is called 'cardio workout' in today's gyms, since the Romans had by trial and error reached the same conclusions as the sports medicine of today. Their workout mostly consisted of ball games; before hydrotherapeutic procedures, it was necessary to properly sweat. Then the visitor slowly progressed through a series of rooms with different temperature: first a warm one, then the hottest one, then another warm one, then a cold one (the exact sequence might have differed in different baths). Each of those rooms could have a pool with water of appropriate temperature. At one of the stages (it is not known when exactly) the actual washing occurred; at some other stage the visitor meticulously scraped off sweat and dirt with a special brush or *strigil*. Then one could dry off, anoint himself with oils and fragrances, talk to friends and, donning a set of clean clothes brought from home, leave.

Many of the procedures described above unfolded differently for people in different income brackets. Rich men visited baths attended by a slave, or sometimes a whole retinue. Once, when the emperor Hadrian was bathing, he saw a retired legionary scratching himself against a column, because he could not afford a slave who would scratch his back with a brush. The empathetic emperor dispatched his own slave to help the veteran. Next time, Hadrian found his ablutions invaded by a whole company of the destitute, meaningfully scratching against columns. "Well, there are lots of you now," said the emperor, "why don't you scratch each other's backs?"

There were two names for baths in Latin – *balneum*, plural *balnea* (hence balneology, the study of therapeutic bathing and healing springs) and *thermae*, from the Greek word 'warm' that has produced lots of English derivates. Perhaps *balnea* used to denote a small bath in a private house and *thermae* referred to specialised public premises, but later they were used interchangeably. In old times, which the Romans liked to romanticise like the rest of us, it was considered improper for a man to visit baths with his grown-up son, or son-in-law; even less thinkable was co-bathing of men and women. Later such prudishness was tossed away, though a number of emperors made vigorous but apparently unsuccessful attempts to ban promiscuous bathing.

The all-important role of baths in Roman consciousness is obvious in a couplet which an imperial freedman of the Julio-Claudian dynasty considered important enough for his tomb:

> *Baths, wine and Venus corrupt our bodies,*
> *But they make life – baths, wine and Venus.*[59]

Not everyone accorded baths such deference. In his "Moral Epistles," the philosopher Seneca wrote:

"Beshrew me if I think anything more requisite than silence for a man who secludes himself in order to study! Imagine what a variety of noises reverberates about my ears! I have lodgings right over a bathing establishment. So picture to yourself the assortment of sounds, which are strong enough to make me hate my very powers of hearing! When your strenuous gentleman, for example, is exercising himself by flourishing leaden weights; when he is working hard, or else pretends to be working hard, I can hear him grunt; and whenever he releases his imprisoned breath, I can hear him panting in wheezy and high-pitched tones. Or perhaps I notice some lazy fellow, content with a cheap rubdown, and hear the crack of the pummelling hand on his shoulder, varying in sound according as the hand is laid on flat or hollow. Then, perhaps, a professional comes along, shouting out the score; that is the finishing touch. Add to this the arresting of an occasional roisterer or pickpocket, the racket of the man who always likes to hear his own voice in the bathroom, or the enthusiast who plunges into the swimming-tank with unconscionable noise and splashing. Besides all those whose voices, if nothing else, are good, imagine the hair-plucker with his penetrating, shrill voice, – for purposes of advertisement, – continually giving it vent and never holding his tongue except when he is plucking the armpits and making his victim yell instead. Then the cakeseller with his varied cries, the sausageman, the confectioner, and all the vendors of food hawking their wares, each with his own distinctive intonation."[60]

Baths planned with imperial abandon were an engineering wonder. Water supply alone was staggering (the cisterns of the Baths of Caracalla held over eight million litres). The giant buildings and awe-inspiring vaults required pinpoint accuracy in dealing with construction materials, including the all-important concrete. Finally, bath premises had to be heated. To make it possible, an ingenious system was invented: pipes were laid in cavities beneath the floor, and air, heated by fire, was pumped through them. The invention of the method (called *hypocaust*) was credited to one Sergius Orata, an entrepreneur who was also famous as the first oyster breeder in the Bay of Naples.

When building baths, the Romans had first used environmental power planning: the buildings were aligned so as to maximise the exposure of warm and hot sections to the sun. An estimate of workforce claims that nine thousand labourers toiled in the construction of the baths every day for five straight years. The central unit was completed during the rule of emperor Caracalla from the Antonine dynasty, which gave the monument its two names – the older Latin one (*thermae antoninianae*) and the more familiar "Baths of Caracalla."

Seeing the Baths of Caracalla as they are today, it is easy to imagine their original scale, but not their original luxury. All that remains in place are brick-faced concrete structures, some stumps of columns and some mosaics, unimpressive and fragmentary. The aqueduct that used to feed the baths (a separate branch of the Claudian waterway) was cut off, like most Roman aqueducts, during the Gothic siege of Rome in the 6th century. By the 7th century, a necropolis had appeared in the eastern part of the complex – a blasphemy by pagan standards, but apparently acceptable in the new Christian age; it was probably a cemetery related to the local church (of Saints Nereus and Achilleus – this very ancient Christian basilica stands opposite the present-day main entrance to the baths). In the Middle Ages, the structures were gradually pillaged for stone, but an especially heavy blow was dealt under Pope Paul III (born Alessandro Farnese) in the 16th century: he removed almost all remaining columns and giant statues from the baths. These treasures were used for embellishment of the Palazzo Farnese in the Field of Mars, which Alessandro Farnese had begun to build while still a cardinal but substantially extended after ascending to the papacy. The extension work was headed by chief papal architect Antonio da Sangallo the Younger and after his death resumed by Michelangelo.

PYRAMID OF CESTIUS AND TESTACCIO

One of Ancient Rome's most bizarre remaining monuments stands near the San Paolo Gate. It is the pyramid of Gaius Cestius. This is one of those tombs that have forever preserved the name of the deceased without any other information about him. All we know of Gaius Cestius we know from his extravagant grave. There is an inscription there which says that he was a pretor, a people's tribune and an epulon (which means a member of a priestly college in charge of solemn feasts honouring certain gods), and that the pyramid was built according to his will in only 330 days. Later the monument became part of the Aurelian walls as an extra fortification; in the middle ages, it overgrew with ivy, and Cestius's name was forgotten – up to the 17th century the tomb was called "The Tomb of Remus," paralleling an even larger "Tomb of Romulus" on the Vatican Hill which was destroyed in the beginning of the 17th century. In 1663 the Pyramid of Cestius was cleared and restored on the orders of Pope Alexander VII (which is recorded by the lower, large-letter inscription on the pyramid's façade). When the tomb was excavated, two marble pediments with the remains of bronze statues were found; the pediments told the gripping story of how the statues were erected. It turns out that Cestius ordered in his will that he should be buried with luxurious cloths from Pergamon (attalici), but new anti-luxury laws made this impossible. The descendants were forced to sell the cloths and erect statues with the money they received.

To the modern eye, used to the proportions of Egyptian pyramids in Giza, the pyramid of Cestius looks somewhat narrow and elongated. Not long ago, this would not have been the case: Cestius's pyramid was the only ancient pyramid known to the Europeans. As a result, even those artists who had been to Egypt started to doubt their own recollections and drew the pyramids near Cairo as more prolonged vertically. A form like that is typical for the ancient kingdom of Meroë, only rediscovered by the Europeans in the 19th century. This similarity gave birth to a hypothesis about the participation of Cestius in some punitive action or trade mission in Africa further to the south than Egypt.

Recently, the Pyramid was cleaned and restored at the expense of a Japanese clothes tycoon, and its interior is available for visit if agreed in advance.

The Pyramid of Cestius overlooks over a big cemetery which is usually called "Protestant," even though it is actually "non-Catholic" (Cimitiero acattolico). Apart from well-known Protestants (like the poets John Keats and Percy Bysshe Shelley) and atheists (like the Marxist thinker Antonio Gramsci), many Orthodox or Greek Catholics who decided to live in Italy found there their last repose – these include the Russian painters Karl Bryullov and Alexander Ivanov, the poet Vyacheslav Ivanov.

The non-Catholic cemetery is bordered by a military one with the graves of soldiers who died during World War II. The relics of that cemetery include an Ancient Roman one – a small portion of Hadrian's Wall honouring the servicemen of Cumbria, a gift from the citizens of Carlisle.

To the north, the cemetery is bordered by a fifty-metre hill called Testaccio, which gave its name to the whole quarter. It is not a part of the ground's layout – it is an artificial mountain made of the shards of old amphorae. An old legend said that the whole world paid taxes to Rome in kind, and the amphorae were broken to make the mountain, another sign of Roman greatness. When Testaccio (the name that comes from the Latin *testa*, a shard) began to be studied by archaeologists, they found that things were more complex. First of all, almost all amphorae came from the Spanish province of Baetica (which more or less corresponds to today's Andalusia) and used to carry one thing only: olive oil. Second, clay shards were not discarded haphazardly, but in constructed terraces: the shards were covered by lime to conquer the stench of rank oil.

It is not very clear why this was done; apparently, ancient sources claimed that vessels used to store oil cannot be reused. When Testaccio was studied by Heinrich Dressel, a disciple of Theodor Mommsen, he found that the amphorae provided excellent epigraphic material, with inscriptions and seals surviving on many of them. After his Roman work, Dressel worked out the classification of amphorae and other vessels which, with some additions, survives to this day. In the 1990s, Testaccio was inspected by an international Italian–Spanish team of archaeologists, who traced many of the shards to ceramic workshops of Roman Spain.

The Farnese Treasures

Palazzo Farnese stands on Piazza Farnese, a few steps from Campo dei Fiori. In its upper tier, the brickwork forms strange diamond-shaped patterns that are never repeated. In Giacomo Puccini's *Tosca*, the most Roman among classical Italian operas, the heroine stabs the villainous policeman Scarpia in this palazzo (while the final scene with the execution of the *jeune premier* Cavaradossi and the subsequent suicide of the heroine, mockingly described in Gerald Durrell's *My Family and Other Animals*, takes place at Castel Sant'Angelo). Palazzo Farnese currently houses the French Embassy: the building was leased under Mussolini to the French until 2035 for the equivalent of one euro per month.

Spoils plundered by Pope Paul III and other art lovers from the Baths of Caracalla have been dispersed all over Italy. On Piazza Farnese itself stand two huge granite bathtubs, transformed into fountains by the architect Girolamo Rainaldi. The nave of the opulent mediaeval church Santa Maria in Trastevere is decorated with eight Ionic columns with Isis, Serapis and Harpocrates, the gods of Graeco-Roman Egypt (Harpocrates, derived by Greeks from the Egyptian Horus, is the god of silence, and its distinctive gesture is a shushing finger pressed to his lips). These columns had probably stood in the library of the baths. The cathedral of Pisa received columns from the palaestrae (gyms) with eagles and lightnings, the symbols of Jupiter. The Vatican Museums were given a mosaic (actually, parts of two different images) from the palaestrae with extremely vicious-looking athletes and, in compensation, a docile clothed bearded man, perhaps a referee or coach.

The Farnese Hercules

A famous sculptural group stood in the centre of the palaestra: two young men tying a woman to the horns of a huge bull. That was the punishment meted out by the twins Amphion and Zethus to queen Dirce (it had begun with Dirce ordering the men to tie her maid Antiope to the horns of the largest bull in the royal herd, but a shepherd who had once found Zethus and Amphion as babies told them that Antiope was their mother, which resulted in Dirce getting her just deserts). The statue, according to a report by Pliny the Elder, was hewn from a single marble block by two brothers from Rhodes, and then made its way to the collection of Asinius Pollio, a friend of Virgil and Horace. The Farnese Bull is the largest surviving classical sculpture. It was heavily restored during the Renaissance, and its many depictions – engravings, sketches and photos – have since spread to many books. A string of dynastic marriages brought the bulk of the Farnese collection into the possession of the Neapolitan Bourbons (who greenlit full-scale excavations of Pompeii and Herculanum). The Farnese Bull and the equally famous Farnese Hercules (also found in the Baths of Caracalla) are currently residing in the Naples National Archaeological Museum that houses what is probably the best collection of classical art in the world.

When you visit the Baths of Caracalla, keep in mind that the museum area does not only cover the central bath unit, but the adjacent area as well, mostly to the south (furthest from the entrance). This humongous lobby is flanked by the ruins of two semicircular apses, and two other symmetrical buildings stood in the corners – possibly they were libraries (you may remember that libraries in Rome were usually designed in pairs, for Greek and Latin books). Finally, an elongated stadium-like oval lying parallel to the Viale di Guido Bocelli used to conceal huge water reservoirs from prying eyes. Midway along the eastern wall, where the semicircle of the apse begins, a mithraeum, Rome's largest, was found.

The walls of the central unit have survived reasonably well, and the archaeologists have convincingly reconstructed the layout of bath premises.

The ruins of one more large semicircular hall looking in the southerly direction is the caldarium, the hottest room in the baths. At its sides were probably other hot rooms, forming a Turkish bath of sorts. Behind the caldarium was the tepidarium, and further still the central hall, which certainly must have dazzled visitors with its opulence. Laterally from the central hall were two palaestrae, also symmetrically positioned, and, finally, there were cloak-rooms near the entrance, with a large pool (*natatio*) between them. Visitors used the baths at their own peril: ancient authors often warn against the dangers of the heat, and a surviving tomb inscription of an eight-year-old boy informs us that he had drowned in the pool of the Baths of Caracalla.

Since the 1930s, the Teatro dell'Opera di Roma holds its summer season in the Baths of Caracalla. Accompanied by music of Verdi or Puccini, the ruins cease simply to be pieces of buildings and brick walls, being transformed into a majestic stage set. In July 1990 the baths hosted the first (and, connoisseurs claim, the best) concert of the "three tenors" (Placido Domingo, José Carreras and Luciano Pavarotti). It was watched live by 800 million people, and the recording made the Guinness Book of Records as the bestselling classical disc of all time.

Baths of Diocletian

The Baths of Caracalla served the southern neighbourhoods of the city, the Baths of Trajan served the centre, but the densely populated north of Rome had long remained without its own bath complex. The problem was solved in the early 4th century AD, when after a long period of turmoil stability was reasserted across the empire. The new baths were given the name of the restorer of order, the emperor Diocletian – shown by the wording of a dedicatory tablet, assembled from fragments of four identical copies.

The surviving remains of the baths of Trajan and Caracalla parade their ancient bareness in archaeological areas. Things turned out differently for the Baths of Diocletian: their fragments became a part of the urban environment that grew around them. They were huge, like the Baths of Caracalla, and surviving parts are sometimes separated by large distances. Architects of new eras were conditioned to respect antiquity, and the contour of the square (Piazza della Repubblica), shaped by 19th-century façades, follows the line of the bath exedra. The main hub of bathing units, designed according to a typical plan along one axis and oriented to maximise sun exposure, was transformed more radically. These units, the frigidarium and pool, were turned by Michelangelo into the church Santa Maria degli Angeli. The church still stands, though in the 18th century it was turned 90 degrees and decorated in late Baroque style. Christianisation did not conceal the grandeur and sheer size, and the inner space of this church, along with the Pantheon, is one of the few places where Roman architecture can be observed almost in its original splendour.

Other remnants of the baths are scattered in the neighbourhood. Two well preserved rotondas flank the Piazza della Repubblica; one of them houses the church San Bernardo alle Terme, another a restaurant. Between Via Cernaia and Via Parigi stands an octagonal hall with a concrete dome. It used to be a planetarium, now a branch of the National Roman Museum, and also a part of the baths. The main building of the National Roman Museum (Palazzo Massimo) stands nearby, on Piazza dei Cinquecento. On the other side of the square is the part of the same museum that focuses on the Baths of Diocletian and exhibits a unique collection of ancient inscriptions. Next to the Termini railway station (whose name might be linked to Termae) is a section of an ancient Roman wall. The wall is not related to the baths, it is much older, dating to Republican times. Looking at it from the outer side (from Via Marsala or one of the restaurants in the railway station), one can see marks on the wall in the shape of Greek letters, chiselled into tufa blocks at the quarry. These marks show that the wall was erected by Greek migrant workers from South Italy or Sicily.

TOMB OF THE SCIPIOS

Between the Baths of Caracalla and Porta San Sebastiano there is another curious archaeological site; for twenty years it was closed for long-term restoration, but currently it is open for prebooked group visits. It is the Tomb of the Scipios. The family of the Scipios, an offshoot of the very ancient patrician clan of the Cornelii, gave Rome many statesmen, consuls, senators, generals and conquerors. However, the most famous representatives of the family, Scipio Africanus, who triumphed over Hannibal, and his brother Scipio Asiaticus, who beat King Antioch III, were not buried in this tomb: their sepulchre was in the grounds of the family villa in Campania, in the town of Liternum, which went into decline before the fall of the Roman Empire. As for the tomb near Rome, for centuries many Scipios were buried there. Eight sarcophagi survived to this day (the ones in the tomb are replicas – the originals were removed to the Vatican Museums) but, judging by the configuration of niches and passages, there were about thirty burials in the tomb, and not just of family members – Ennius, the favourite poet of the Scipios, was buried there as well. The earliest sarcophagus is that of Lucius Cornelius Scipio Barbatus, consul of 298 BC (*barbatus* means 'bearded'); it is lavishly decorated in the style of Greek colonies of South Italy, and the epitaph in verses, extolling the stature, career and conquests of the deceased, though added by descendants two hundred years after the death of Barbatus, still remains one of the most archaic Latin texts that had come down to us.

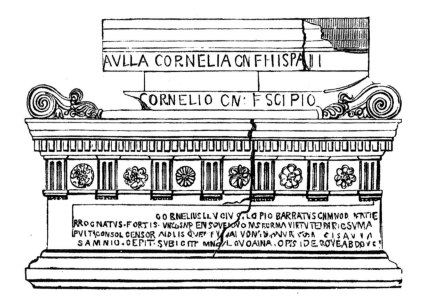

The Romans, as a rule, cremated their dead, but they practiced burial too; the ancient "Laws of the Twelve Tables" mention both customs: "do not inter or burn the dead within the city." Full-body inhumation was considered an older ritual, practiced by the poor who had no money to arrange a funeral pyre, and some aristocratic families who used it to stress the antiquity of their pedigree. All branches of the Cornelii gens, including the Scipios, did not burn their dead. The first to break the family tradition was the dictator Lucius Cornelius Sulla: he was afraid that his numerous political enemies would despoil his remains, and opted for the 'cleaner' procedure of cremation.

The tomb of the Scipios was famous. In his treatise "Tusculan Disputations," Cicero writes about disdain for death (and the author's unbearable fear of nothingness seeps through the calm dialogues). He turns to the tombs of great men for an example: "When you go out at the Capene gate and see the tombs of the Calatini, the Scipios, Servilii, and Metelli, do you look on them as miserable?"[61]

By the 1st century AD, the Scipios' family line died out, and another branch of the *gens*, the Cornelii Lentuli, took upon themselves the care of the monument, but by the 3rd century the monument was irrevocably forgotten and overbuilt with a three-storey house. The owners of the plot discovered the grave in the early 16th century, but soon forgot about it for another two hundred years. It finally became a site of archaeological importance in the 1920s.

PORTA SAN SEBASTIANO AND THE AURELIAN WALLS

After the Baths of Caracalla, the Appian Way continues as Via di Porta San Sebastiano. In this part of the city, the distance from the old Servian walls to the new Aurelian walls is short. We have mentioned both circuits many times, and near the St. Sebastian Gate (the former Appian Gate) one can get to know them better: there is a museum in the fortress towers covering the history of Roman defensive walls.

After the Servian walls had been erected in the late 4th century BC, the city continued to grow quite briskly. The Romans felt increasingly at ease on their land: neighbouring tribes, then Italy, and then almost the whole world (whatever was known about it) had fallen under their command. Even when Hannibal with his troops was erratically prowling around Italy and once came within a very short distance of Rome but then turned back, the Romans did not entertain the idea of building new ramparts. This status quo had held for a very long time, more than five hundred years. Then the crisis of the 3rd century came, and it turned out that legions' stations on the borders could no longer hold off the barbarian push, and sometimes they even joined in the slaughter and pillage. For the first time in centuries, enemies had penetrated the borders of Italy. The emperor Aurelian mustered all available resources and within a very short time – a few years – the new boundaries of the city were secured with new walls (the work was completed after Aurelian himself had died as a result of a petty court plot).

The work went quickly and efficiently because the builders used existing structures and incorporated them in the ramparts. This happened to a section of the Claudian aqueduct near Porta Maggiore, with the Camp Amphitheatre, with the Pyramid of Cestius (and later with the Mausoleum of Hadrian). The walls underwent continual modification – under Maxentius, the height of some of the sections was doubled, and under Honorius, in the early 5th century, walls and gates were radically refurbished.

The defensive value of Aurelian walls was questionable, and this was further brought into question by subsequent barbarian raids of late Antiquity and Middle Ages. A Greek inscription on the keystone of the Appian gate archway praises the Saints Conon and George, as well as God's grace, for the victory over Goths in 403. The joy was short-lived: the Goths thoroughly sacked Rome seven years later, in 476 the German chieftain Odoacer deposed the last Western Roman emperor, and in the 6th century the whole of Italy and Sicily, as well as a large portion of the

Balkans, fell under the dominion of the Gothic kingdom, with its capital in Ravenna. At this point, the Eastern Roman Empire (the "Byzantium" of later historians) went after Italy, too. After a series of hard-fought battles and a protracted siege of Rome (whose most bloody episode occurred by the Aurelian walls, near Castel Sant'Angelo), the Goths were defeated, but the war depleted the resources of Byzantium and laid waste to North Italy, now thrown centuries behind its Roman-era prosperity.

The Goths and all Things Gothic

The Goths were an East Germanic tribe with a Scandinavian homeland, according to not very reliable mediaeval sources. Rome had first come into contact with them in the turbulent 3rd century AD, during large-scale migration of barbarian tribes. The scale of that migration is attested by the fact that one of its waves rolled as far as the northern shores of the Black Sea; in the 16th century, there still were settlements in the Crimea where a Gothic language was spoken. (Incidentally, this amazing fact is known from a report of the same Flemish diplomat Busbecq who also found the will of Augustus in Turkey.) In the 5th and 6th centuries, Goths divided into two branches, Ostrogoths and Visigoths. Both managed to grab juicy chunks of the collapsing empire for themselves, if not for long. Ostrogoths founded a kingdom on the territory of present-day France but were soon displaced by another Germanic tribe, the Franks. Visigoths retreated into Spain and ruled it until the appearance of the Arabs.

The architectural term "Gothic style" was born out of a misunderstanding. In the Middle Ages it was known as "French" (*opus francigenum*); the term "Gothic" was introduced by Italian Renaissance men as a taunt (meaning, roughly, 'barbaric'). As often happens, the mocking word stuck and lost its original derogatory aura.

In the English language, the word 'Gothic' was actively used in the 18th and 19th century as a synonym for 'horrible, uncivilised, unbridled.' A genre of English literature pioneered by Horace Walpole, the author of *The Castle of Otranto*, was called 'Gothic' in that sense. Today, the pleasant titillation derived from reading scary stories is usually categorised as 'horror,' while the old, 18th-century sense of the word 'Gothic' was appropriated by a subculture that had originated in the music world of the 1970s and survives to this day, though its main stamping ground has moved from the UK to Germany. Taken together, the modern usage of words like "Gothic" and "Goths" has nothing whatsoever to do with the historical Goths.

The Appian Gate, also known as Porta San Sebastiano, is largely a result of restoration of Honorius's time. Twenty metres from it on the road stands an arch that is traditionally called "The Arch of Drusus," even though it bears no relation to Drusus, the father of the emperor Claudius. Right here, the Appian Way was crossed by a branch of the Claudian aqueduct that used to feed the Baths of Caracalla. The Walls Museum (*Museo delle mura*) displays a broad range of decorative motifs on late Roman bricks, including Christian symbols (crosses and Chi-Rho, the monogram of the first two letters of Greek *Khristos*, 'Christ'). In 1942–43, the interior of the gate was used as an office by the aviator and Party Secretary of the National Fascist Party Ettore Muti; black-and-white floor mosaics and a spiral staircase date back to that time. A ticket to the museum gives you a right to walk on top of the wall in the western direction (this is called *passegiata*, 'a walk') and survey the surrounding gardens and fields, little changed since the Middle Ages. The total length of the *passegiata* is 400 metres, though sections of it are often unavailable due to reconstruction work.

THE CATACOMBS

The Appian Gate was renamed Porta San Sebastiano to commemorate an important Christian shrine – the church of San Sebastiano fuori le mura; the designation *fuori le mura*, 'beyond the walls,' is used for those Roman churches that stand outside the perimetre of Aurelian ramparts. This church, built in the 4th century (today's version is largely an 18th-century remake), two and a half kilometres from the Appian Gate, is also called San Sebastiano ad Catacumbas. The word 'catacombs' is of obscure origin, possibly a mixture of the Greek preposition *kata* and Latin *tumba*, 'tomb.' Later, the name spread to cover all secret subterranean Christian burial places, and later still, other underground warrens, but this is where the original catacombs were.

St. Sebastian was an officer of the Praetorian Guard (an elite force of imperial bodyguards) under Diocletian. Diocletian, one of the handful of Roman emperors who actually persecuted Christians, was not aware of the religious proclivities of his subordinate, and when he learned about it, he got very angry and ordered that Sebastian be executed. The legend says that Sebastian was executed by a shooting squad (shooting arrows), and the scene of his martyrdom became a favourite subject of Italian Renaissance painters from Mantegna to Titian.

The church was only dedicated to St. Sebastian in the 9th century; it was previously called "Basilica of the Apostles" (*Basilica apostolorum*), because the local catacombs were said to have kept for a while the relics of Saints Peter and Paul.

A detailed story of the catacombs and other early Christian sites of Rome deserves a book of its own (and there are, indeed, many such books). The density of those sites is especially high along the Appian Way. Almost immediately after the Aurelian walls stands the church of Santa Maria delle Piante, better known as Domine Quo Vadis. The apocryphal Acts of Peter tell a story of how St. Peter, fleeing Nero's persecution, met Christ on that very spot and asked him: "Lord, where are you going?" (*Domine, quo vadis?*), to which Christ answered: "To Rome, to be crucified again" (*Eo Romam iterum crucifigi*). This put Peter to shame, and he returned to Rome to meet his martyr's death on a cross. The original text of the Acts of Peter was written in Greek, and Jesus must have spoken Aramaic to his disciples, but only the Latin translation has survived in full. In spite of being uncanonical, Acts of Peter remained very popular in the Christian world, and the famous phrase provided the title for an 1895 novel *Quo Vadis: A Narrative of the Time of Nero* by the now largely forgotten Polish author Henryk Sienkiewicz, who went on to win the Nobel prize in 1905. The novel was adapted for the screen a few times, including a lavish, three-hours-long Hollywood version of 1951.

A fresco from the catacombs of St. Callixtus

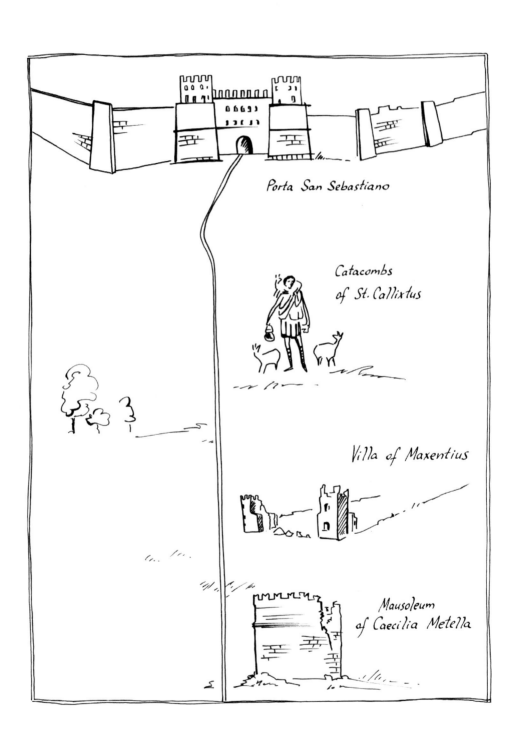

Porta San Sebastiano

Catacombs
of St. Callixtus

Villa of Maxentius

Mausoleum
of Caecilia Metella

The Horatii
and
the Curiatii

Villa of the Quintilii

Casal Rotondo

VIA APPIA

Next to St. Sebastian are the catacombs of St. Callixtus, where very interesting Christian sacrophagi are adorned with allegoric ornaments. It used to serve as "the crypt of the Popes," a tomb for Roman bishops of the 2nd through 4th centuries. Gradually, as the ancient Roman taboo against inner city burials began to slacken, the remains of the popes were removed to various churches in Rome.

Not far away are the catacombs of St. Domitilla (the only catacombs where tourists can see existing graves) and the so-called "Jewish catacombs," the burial place of Roman Jews.

THE APPIAN WAY

The Appian Way led from Rome to the seaside town of Brundisium (now Brindisi) in the southeast region of Apulia. It was the first major road built by the Romans. The poet Statius wrote: "The Appian Way is the queen of long roads" *(Appia longarum teritur regina viarum)*.

In antiquity (and, to some extent, today), roads served a dual purpose: trade and military. In the late 4th century BC, the latter was more important to the Romans: Italian tribes had not quite yet succumbed to Rome's supremacy and fought incessant wars against Rome all over the Apennine peninsula. Which nation could gain an immense advantage over the others? The one that could deploy troops fast, set up temporary and permanent supply bases, and keep soldiers at the ready wherever necessary. That nation, of course, was Rome, and her success was brought about to a large extent thanks to the art of military engineers who had covered the whole of Italy, and later the whole of the empire, with a road network.

APPIUS CLAUDIUS

The first and most important section of the Appian Way, from Rome to Capua, was built by a senator named Appius Claudius Caecus. He is often called 'the first personality of Roman history.' Of course, there were many heroes, kings and generals before him, but they were all partly, and sometimes completely, legendary. The historicity of Appius Claudius is beyond doubt.

Appius was a charismatic and resolute politician. Tradition has preserved both gushing praise and scathing criticism aimed at him. He became a censor without serving as a consul previously, in contradiction of an old custom; in this capacity, he introduced lots of lower-class citizens into the Senate, including freedmen's sons, and earned himself a crowd of ardent supporters and no less ardent haters. When his censorship colleague made a show of resigning to protest Appius's politics, everyone expected Appius to do the decent thing and follow suit, but he thwarted all expectations. In the end, he served as a censor for five years instead of the customary one and a half, building Rome's first aqueduct and first major road in the process. He gave his name to both projects: Aqua Appia and Via Appia. He lived a long and turbulent live, completing the whole Roman 'course of offices': consul, dictator, interrex and so on.

The cognomen 'Caecus' means "blind," and calling Appius the builder of roads and aqueducts by that name is anachronistic, because he only lost his sight when he was very old. But posterity remembered his old age best of all. At that time, Rome for the first time encountered a military foe from mainland Greece. Pyrrhus, the king of Epirus (a state on the western shore of the Balkan peninsula), drawing his strength from the support of Greek colonies in South Italy, the so-called Magna Graecia, was threatening Roman interests in the region. An envoy of the king, one Cineas, arrived in Rome to negotiate peace. The senators – not without reason – feared Pyrrhus with his Macedonian training and battle elephants, and were inclined to make peace on Pyrrhus's terms. At that point, the frail, blind Appius was brought into the Senate house on a litter. "It's a good thing I'm blind, Father Senators," said the old man, "and cannot see this disgrace. You're going to negotiate with an enemy whose army has not left the Italian soil? You must be crazy." The shamed senators rejected the peace, Cineas returned to the king empty-handed and reported to Pyrrhus that he had found the Senate an assembly of kings and the Roman people a Learnean Hydra that grows two new heads in the place of a chopped-off one. Pyrrhus went on to win a few battles against Roman troops, but it is easy to guess that those victories were Pyrrhic, and the Romans had preserved their strategic advantage and later defeated him completely.

A speech given by Appius Claudius in the Senate is the first prose text in Latin that was ever recorded. It did not survive, but it was taught in schools for centuries, and the famous expression "every man is the artisan of his own fortune" (*quisque faber suae fortunae*) is taken from it.

The merits of Appius moved the hitherto undistinguished Claudian gens to the front of the political scene, where it remained for centuries down to the Julio-Claudian emperors – Tiberius, Caligula, Claudius and Nero.

With very rare exceptions, the Romans did not bury people within city walls, which made the sides of the roads, especially near big cities, a natural place for burials: on the one hand, they were easy to reach, on the other, they afforded travellers ample food for thought. Addressing a potential reader of a tomb inscription ("Good friend for Jesus sake forbeare / To dig the dust enclosed here") is a genre with a reputable Classical pedigree. Roman epitaphs often engaged posterity in a lively chat, signing off with the formula "There, I said it; now go."

There are few places in Rome where stepping into a past era is as simple as on the Appian Way. There are four reservations to be made about that statement, though. First of all, latter-day engineers have built a new road parallel to the Via Appia, which is called exactly that, "The New Appian Way" (Via Appia Nuova). This is a regular highway with nothing to look at. We are interested in the old Appian Way (Via Appia Antica). Second, the first couple of kilometres of the Appian Way are virtually impassable – that section is open to traffic and lacks pavement at the sides. To enjoy the walk, start it from the Catacombs of St. Sebastian or the mausoleum of Caecilia Metella. Third, numerous noisy tourists may spoil your time-travelling experience; choose the season and time of day wisely. Finally, the Appian Way is an archaeological park, with permanent ongoing work of some kind, and you may find major sections closed off.

On the third kilometre of the Appian Way, approximately opposite the church of St. Sebastian, lies the huge Villa of Maxentius. It was only in the early 19th century that the archaeologist Antonio Nibby determined the original owner – it was previously thought that the villa had belonged to Caracalla.

We touched upon the hapless career of the emperor Maxentius in the chapter on the Forum (where a huge basilica which he had commissioned stands) and in the one on the Colosseum (this is he who was styled 'a tyrant' on the Arch of Constantine, his luckier rival). A scion of the imperial family, Maxentius was initially passed over by older relatives when successors were appointed, and retired to live here, in the estate on the Appian Way. He built for himself a palace (now almost completely covered in vegetation) and, for some reason, a circus.

The Circus of Maxentius is second in size only to Circus Maximus, but it is much better preserved. Its state today owes much to the restorers' skill, but there were more materials to work with. Among the surviving details are twelve "cages" that released the competing chariots, two flanking towers, concrete brick-faced walls, chunks of columns, a referee box and an emperor's box. The dividing barrier (*spina*) is also quite visible; its length is 296 metres, exactly one thousand Roman feet. It was from here that the Obelisk of Domitian was snatched and moved to Piazza Navona (it is not known how it got to the Villa of Maxentius in the first place).

It is hard to say whose idea it was to build a huge sports venue in such a remote place. There is virtually no evidence that the Circus of Maxentius was ever used for actual races. Moreover, recent excavations by American archaeologists suggest that the villa might have been left unfinished and never housed anyone. Perhaps Maxentius had intended to return the original funerary flavour to the circus games: his son Romulus died aged four, and Maxentius spared no effort to immortalise his memory; a circus might have been one of such monuments. Next to the circus, on its east side (near the 'cages') stands the Mausoleum of Romulus – a huge round tomb that was probably originally covered with a dome, Pantheon-style. Judging by the number of niches, the mausoleum was intended to accept the whole imperial family in addition to the little Romulus.

Not far from it are the ruins of another tomb that is even older – a cylindrical drum on a square base. Starting from the 16th century, it was very arbitrarily called "Tomb of the Servilii" (probably on the basis of the passage from Cicero's "Tusculan Disputations" which we have quoted earlier). In the Middle Ages it housed a lime-kiln. Inside was a cross-shaped burial chamber with a circular passage around it. Such a structure was typical of Julio-Claudian mausolea (like the one of Augustus). Visitors to the tomb made two revolutions in the passage: one way when they went in, the other when they went out. That was a ritual for commemorating important people, like generals and former consuls.

Some inscriptions and fragments of sculpture found near the villa confirm the idea that the estate of the billionaire Herod Atticus, the so-called Triopion, was in the vicinity.

HEROD ATTICUS

Herod Atticus cuts a very colourful figure. He belonged to the old Athenian aristocracy and traced his lineage from almost every historical and mythological Hellenic hero, all the way from Theseus, the founder of Athens, and the god Zeus. In his time (2nd century AD) that was more or less all that Greeks could be proud of – all the levers of political power were in the Romans' hands. The Atticus family seemed to have adapted to the new situation; one of his ancestors must have been adopted by a Roman from the Claudian gens (Herod's full name was Lucius Vibullius Hypparchus Tiberius Claudius Atticus Herod), and his father was a Roman senator of consular rank. Herod himself, an heir to a huge fortune, studied history and oratory and became one of the principal exponents of the so-called "Second Sophistic" (unfortunately, his speeches have not survived). He shared his time between Athens and Rome; Athenians had mixed feelings about him, but appreciated his grand-scale development projects for the good of his native city. Some of them are still standing, like the famous Odeon – the stone theatre on the slope of the Acropolis hill.

Herod married a Roman noblewoman, one Aspasia Ania Regilla, a relative of a few emperors and empresses. They were a perfect couple: both rich, independent, well-educated, both eager to spend money on charities. When they got married, Regilla was fourteen, Herod over forty. Their marriage lasted for about twenty years and produced a number of children. Herod had a stint as a mentor of children of the imperial household (the future emperors Marcus Aurelius and Lucius Verus) and as a Roman consul (thus appointed by the emperor Antoninus Pius for his educational service). In 160 AD Regilla suddenly died. Evil tongues put the blame on Herod's temper; Regilla's brother even took Herod to court, but after the emperor's intervention he was acquitted.

To put his slanderers to shame, Herod laid out a huge estate, Triopion, at the third mile of the Appian Way, where Regilla ('neither a mortal nor a goddess,' according to one of the found inscriptions) was posthumously worshipped.

In his old age, Herod fell in love with a youth called Polydeuces, and when he, too, died an untimely death, Herod arranged sports games in his memory, decorated Athens with statues of him, and then, disconsolate, passed away.

MAUSOLEUM OF CAECILIA METELLA

The most famous of all the tombs on the Appian Way stands near the third milestone. This structure, like the Mausoleum of Romulus, is a huge cylindrical drum on a square base. The brick wall with dovetail castellation on the top was added in the Middle Ages by the Caetani family who, as was the custom of the time, turned the Roman monument into a fortress at the border of their estate. In antiquity the tomb was most likely covered by a plain conical roof.

Travertine slabs that used to cover the whole mausoleum did not survive on the base, but partly survived on the cylinder. Inside the walls that are up to ten metres thick is a relatively narrow vertical shaft that tapers off toward the top. The burial chamber was not at its bottom, but at the end of a separate lateral passage. In the 16th century, a large sarcophagus was found in the neighbourhood; the tireless Farnese pope Paul III moved it to his Roman palace, where it stands to this day. The archaeologist Antonio Nibby was inclined to think that it was the sarcophagus of Regilla, the wife of Herod Atticus.

The mausoleum is decorated with a relief featuring wreaths and bull's heads. It is thought that this decoration gave rise to the popular name of the mausoleum and the whole area around it – *Capo di Bove* (Bull's Head). However, there is an equally compelling alternative version: the coat of arms of the Caetani family, visible on neighbouring structures, also features a bull's head.

Inside the mausoleum is a small museum with reliefs and sculptures from different tombs on the Appian Way. Its main attraction is the chance to go up to the roof of the monument and survey the environs (if the staff let you).

We often know precious little about the most famous and best-preserved monuments of antiquity. All the available information about the mausoleum of Caecilia Metella is on the wall of the building itself: on the side facing the road, the circular frieze is interrupted by a relief with wartime spoils, and under the relief is an inscription: CAECILIAE Q. CRETICI F. METELLAE CRASSI, meaning "To Caecilia Metella, daughter of Quintus Metellus of Crete, wife of Crassus." The problem is, in the family of the Caecilii Metelli all women without exception were called Caecilia Metella, and that noble and rich plebeian gens produced lots of officials, generals and politicians in republican times. The word 'Creticus' offers a clue: such nicknames were usually given to generals who had managed to subdue a province to Rome's authority. The conflict of Rome with the island of Crete occurred in mid-1st century BC, when the Cretans were helping Rome's bitterest enemy in the East, King Mithridates, and offered shelter to Mediterranean pirates who managed for a while to completely disrupt Roman military and trade maritime routes. Metellus successfully smashed Cretan troops and converted the island into a Roman province. In this case, the husband of our Caecilia is probably not the famous Marcus Licinius Crassus, the suppressor of the Spartacus revolt and Rome's richest man, but his son or grandson. The authors of guidebooks cherished the thought that he was the "main" Crassus all until the 20th century: they thought it was more romantic that way.

The travellers of old were fully aware of the beauty and charm of Caecilia Metella's mausoleum and its picturesque surroundings. The countryside around Rome – Roman Campagna, *Campagna Romana*, not to be confused with Campania, the region around Naples – was a star destination of the Grand Tour and the most-painted European landscape in the 18th and 19th centuries. Unfortunately, Rome's recent urban sprawl has all but destroyed it, and a swathe of greenery along the Appian Way is almost all that remains of the old Campagna. The tomb of Caecilia Metella was one of its most powerful symbols; Lord Byron waxes lyrical about it in *Childe Harold's Pilgrimage*, and Johann Tischbein paints the young Goethe in his famous portrait against a background of Italian greenery and ruins, including the faraway, sfumatto-shrouded silhouette of Metella's tower.

> There is a stern round tower of other days,
> Firm as a fortress, with its fence of stone,
> Such as an army's baffled strength delays,
> Standing with half its battlements alone,
> And with two thousand years of ivy grown,
> The garland of eternity, where wave
> The green leaves over all by time o'erthrown;–
> What was this tower of strength? within its cave
> What treasure lay so locked, so hid? – A woman's grave.
>
> But who was she, the lady of the dead,
> Tombed in a palace? Was she chaste and fair?
> Worthy a king's, – or more, – a Roman's bed?
> What race of chiefs and heroes did she bear?
> What daughter of her beauties was the heir?
> How lived, how loved, how died she? Was she not
> So honoured, and conspicuously there,
> Where meaner relics must not dare to rot,
> Placed to commemorate a more than mortal lot?

Near the fifth milestone, the road veers slightly to the left. Here, close to each other, stand four large burial mounds (all of them on the right side of the road, facing away from Rome). Legend has the ancient "Cluilian trenches" here, defence works dug on the orders of Cluilius, the king of Alba Longa; the famous battle between the Horatii and the Curiatii also occurred here.

Tradition assigned this event to very hoary antiquity, early 7th century BC. Alba Longa was (hereinafter add "according to legend" to every statement) Rome's mother city, the birthplace of Romulus and Remus. Rome had quickly outgrown its metropolis, and the issue of supremacy over Latium became a burning one. It should be noted that at the time the territory at stake was tiny: the distance between Rome and Alba was in the range of 20 miles or so.

While the opposing armies (the Albans under king Cluilius, the Romans under king Tullus Hostilius) were preparing for the battle, an Alban emissary came to the Roman camp. "Look," said the envoy, "whoever wins, the strength of our both states will be depleted. Do not forget that we are surrounded by enemies: cunning Etruscans would be delighted to grab our lands. What if we try to settle the matter in some other way, in accordance with our ancestors' customs?" The Romans put their thinking caps on: after all, the Albans were their relatives (often quite literally), they spoke the same language and worshipped the same gods; the Etruscans, on the other hand, were a dangerous and alien force. It was decided that the conflict would be resolved by combat of the bravest warriors that each side could provide; the defeated city would peacefully submit to the victorious one. Each army brought forward a set of triplets – Alba the Curiatii, Rome the Horatii (some ancient historians claimed it was the other way around). The battle began near the Cluilian trenches; very soon, two of the Horatii were dead, all three of the Curiatii were more or less gravely wounded, while the only surviving Horatius remained intact. He resorted to a tactical ruse: he started running away from the enemies, but half-heartedly, hoping that the Curiatii would not reach him simultaneously, but one by one, in accordance with the gravity of their wounds, and he would take care of them one by one. That was exactly what happened. The Romans who had all but despaired welcomed the national hero with abandon; only a sister of the Horatii did not join in the festivities, mourning one of the fallen Albans, her fiancé. Outraged by such an unpatriotic display, the victorious Horatius stabbed his sister as well.

The mounds on the site are traditionally called the tombs of the Horatii and Curiatii. Titus Livius reports that the Romans were buried together, closer to Alba Longa, while the Albans were buried separately, each on the spot where the warrior met his death. He also writes that in his time (under Augustus), the tombs of the five brothers could be still seen on the same spot. The mounds we see today were constructed using materials unavailable in the 7th century BC, but it is possible that they are a deliberate 'antiquarian' restoration of the Augustan age, and that was what Livius was describing.

THE VILLA OF THE QUINTILII

Beyond the Horatii mound, on the other side of the road, are the remains of another huge estate. This is the Villa of the Quintilii.

The Quintilii brothers (one was called Sextus Quintilius Maximus, the other Sextus Quintilius Condianus – note that two male siblings were given the same personal name, *praenomen*) lived in the 2nd century AD and were famous for their handsomeness, intellectual prowess, education, wealth and other fine qualities. Brothers often form creative tandems; the Quintilii were like that. They even served a consulship together. Under "good emperors," they led a peaceful life. But it was during their lifetime that the string of good emperors came to an end with the death of Marcus Aurelius, and the throne was ascended by the troubled Commodus.

The outcome of this dynastic change for the Quintilii is recounted by the historian Cassius Dio. Commodus decided to lay his hands on the brothers' huge fortune and ordered that they be executed and their property confiscated. The brothers, who never separated in life, died together. But tyrants are seldom satisfied and like to destroy their subjects in droves. Sextus Maximus had a son, also called Sextus. He was in Syria when he learned that he had been declared an outlaw. He drank some hare's blood, and then deliberately fell from a horse and was sick all over the place; everyone thought it was his own blood and he was dying. The young man was taken to his house, from where he escaped, aided by faithful slaves; a ram was burned on his funeral pyre instead of him. The trick played by the younger Quintilius became known, and a manhunt ensued. Every day a new severed head was brought to Commodus as the head of Quintilius; all the friends of the family were suspected of harbouring a fugitive and were persecuted as a result. It is not known whether the real Quintilius Jr. was ever apprehended or not; what is known, though, is that shortly after the dishonourable death of Commodus an impostor came to Rome claiming that he was Sextus Quintilius Jr. and a lawful owner of the clan's huge fortune. When asked about some matters of Greek politics, an area of expertise for Quintilius, the impostor failed to even understand the question and was thus unmasked.

The Quintilii brothers could have anticipated their demise, especially since it had been prophesied to them. In the province of Cilicia lived a soothsayer who made predictions in an unorthodox manner: he had prophetic dreams and then made sketches of them. The Quintilii received a drawing of a boy strangling snakes. It was a reference to the well-known myth about Heracles who strangled the snakes set upon him by the jealous Hera. Since Commodus considered himself an embodiment of Heracles (there is a famous sculptural bust in the Capitoline museums, where he is depicted with all the paraphernalia of the hero – a lion's hide, a club, and the apples of the Hesperides in his palm), and since the brothers were strangled, the meaning of this prophecy becomes obvious.

The brothers' estate passed into the ownership of the imperial house and after a couple of centuries fell into disrepair. Under the Quintilii, though, it had amazed contemporaries with luxury and convenience. A large fountain, partly visible to this day, stood on the Appian Way, where a weary traveller could have a drink of water and praise the owners of the estate. A separate aqueduct branch fed the baths of the villa, and there was even a private race-course.

In 1485, a sacrophagus was accidentally discovered on the premises of the villa. When it was opened, it revealed, to everyone's amazement, the perfectly preserved body of a young woman in splendid garments, with hair pulled up into a topknot ("like the Hungarians wear," a contemporary observes) and gold decorations. The jewellery was immediately stolen, while the sarcophagus and the mummy were later put on display in the Palazzo dei Conservatori on the Capitol. It was attributed – without any foundation whatsoever – as Tulliola, the daughter of Cicero, whose untimely death was bitterly lamented by the famous orator in his letters.

The estate was so huge that for centuries, people from nearby villages used to call it "old Rome," *Roma vecchia*: it seemed that kind of space was fit only for a whole city. In the 20th century, the villa had for a long time stood deserted and crumpling; it was bought by the Italian government and turned into a museum only in 1985. Excavations are under way at the villa, and many ruins are off-limits, but it is a large and mostly deserted chunk of land, where one can sit under an ancient brick wall while watching the planes take off and land at the nearby Ciampino airport.

After the Villa of the Quintilii, fewer large tombs line the Via Appia, giving way to humble graves of Republican times. But it is near the sixth milestone that the Appia's largest round mausoleum stands. It is called Casal Rotondo, which means 'round farm,' which is a misunderstanding: indeed, a farm had overgrown the tomb a long time ago, but it was not round; the tomb was. This is probably a monument of the Augustan era, but it is not known who is buried in it. In the 19th century, the archaeologist and architect Luigi Canina made an assumption, based on a fragment of an inscription, that it was the tomb of Messala Corvinus, general, author and mythological ancestor of Hungarian kings, but it was little more than a fantasy.

Another fantasy of Canina's decorates a large brick wall next to Casal Rotondo: it is a collage of marble sculptures and architectural details. It is worth remembering that it was largely through Canina's efforts that the Appian Way was transformed into an archaeological area in mid-19th century.

Few tourists venture further down the Via Appia than Casal Rotondo: there are fewer tombs, and the landscape is ill-kempt. This is where we, too, conclude our journey.

IN LIEU OF AN AFTERWORD

[Avunculus meus] dicere etiam solebat nullum esse librum tam malum ut non aliqua parte prodesset.

Pliny the Younger about Pliny the Elder, I century AD

[My uncle] used to say that no book was so bad that some good might not be got out of it.

Prima urbes inter, divum domus, aurea Roma.

Ausonius, IV century AD

First among cities, the home of the gods, is golden Rome.

Dumque offers victis proprii consortia iuris,

Urbem fecisti quod prius orbis erat.

Rutilius Namatianus, V century AD

By offering to the vanquished a share in thine own justice,

Thou hast made a city of what was erstwhile a world.

Translated by J. Wight Duff and Arnold M. Duff

Si fueris Romae, Romano vivito more,

Si fueris alibi, vivito sicut ibi.

Mediaeval proverb

If you are in Rome, live in the Roman style;

If you are elsewhere, live as they live there.

Par tibi, Roma, nihil, cum sis prope tota ruina;

Quam magni fueris integra fracta doces.

Hildebert of Lavardin, XI century

Nothing can equal Rome, Rome even in ruins:

Your ruins themselves speak loud your former greatness.

Translated by George B. Parks

Sive favore tuli, sive hanc ego carmine famam,

Iure tibi grates, candide lector, ago.

Ovid, I century AD

Whether I earned my good name or not
— thank you, reader.

RECOMMENDED READING

The list of literature about Ancient Rome and about Rome the city is boundless and inexhaustible. The following short list cannot be even called the tip of the iceberg: it is very concise and subjective, which is why the reader is warned to treat it cautiously.

Lesley and Roy Adkins. *Handbook to Life in Ancient Rome.* Oxford University Press, 1994.

Peter J. Aicher. *Rome Alive: A Source-Guide to the Ancient City.* Bolchazy-Carducci Publishers, 2001.

J. P. V. D. Baldson. *Life and Leisure in Ancient Rome.* McGraw-Hill, 1969 (reissued by Phoenix Press, 2002).

Mary Beard. *The Roman Triumph.* Harvard University Press, 2009.

Mary Beard, John Henderson. *Classics: A Very Short Introduction.* Oxford University Press, 2000.

Mary T. Boatwright, Daniel J. Gargola, Richard J. A. Talbert. *The Romans: From Village to Empire.* Oxford University Press, 2004.

Amanda Claridge. *Rome. An Oxford Archaeological Guide.* Oxford University Press, 2010.

Filippo Coarelli. *Rome and Environs. An Archaeological Guide.* University of California Press, 2007.

T. J. Cornell. *The Beginnings of Rome.* Routledge, 1995.

Tim Cornell, John Matthews. *The Cultural Atlas of the World: The Roman World.* Time Life, 1991.

Adrian Goldsworthy. *How Rome Fell: Death of a Superpower.* Yale University Press, 2010.

Martin Goodman. *The Roman World. 44 BC –AD 180.* Routledge, 1997.

Michael Grant. *The Roman Forum.* McMillan, 1970.

Keith Hopkins, Mary Beard. *The Colosseum.* Harvard University Press, 2011.

Rodolfo Lanciani. *Ancient Rome in the Light of Recent Discoveries.* Houghton, Mifflin and Co., 1898.

Rodolfo Lanciani. *Pagan and Christian Rome.* Houghton, Mifflin and Co., 1892.

Tyler Lansford. *The Latin Inscriptions of Rome: A Walking Guide.* Johns Hopkins University Press, 2009.

Alta Macadam, Annabel Barber. *Blue Guide Rome.* Blue Guides, 2016 (11th edition).

Paul MacKendric. *The Mute Stones Speak. The Story of Archaeology in Italy.* Norton & Co., 1983.

The Oxford Classical Dictionary. Oxford University Press, 2012 (4th edition).

Samuel B. Platner, Thomas Ashby. *A Topographical Dictionary of Ancient Rome.* Oxford University Press, 1929.

Lawrence Richardson, Jr. *A New Topographical Dictionary of Ancient Rome.* Johns Hopkins University Press, 1992.

Margaret Steinby (ed.). *Lexicon Topographicum Urbis Romae.* Vol. 1–7. Oxford University Press USA, 1995–2014.

Ronald Syme. *The Roman Revolution.* Oxford University Press, 1939 (was reissued).

David Watkin. *The Roman Forum.* Profile Books, 2009.

Greg Woolf (ed.). *Cambridge Illustrated History of the Roman World.* Cambridge University Press, 2003.

ENDNOTES

1   Humanists in the Roman Forum. Frances Muecke, *Papers of the British School at Rome*, Vol. 71 (2003), pp. 207-233.

2   Translated by A.J. Woodman. Tacitus, The Annals, Hackett Publishing Company, Inc., Indianapolis/Cambridge, 2004.

3   Translated by B.O. Foster. Livy, Books I and II With An English Translation. Cambridge, Mass., Harvard University Press; London, William Heinemann, Ltd. 1919.

4   Ovid's Fasti, or the Romans Sacred Calendar, Translated into English Verse With Explanatory Notes By William Massey, Master of a Boarding-School at Wandsworth. London, 1757.

5   Plutarch. Plutarch's Morals. Translated from the Greek by several hands. Corrected and revised by William W. Goodwin, PhD. Boston. Little, Brown, and Company, Cambridge, Press of John Wilson and son, 1874.

6   Saint Augustine. The City of God, books I-VII. Translated by Demetrius B. Zema and Gerald G. Walsh. Washington D.C., 1950.

7   Translated by W. D. Hooper and H. B. Ash, Loeb Classical Library, 1934.

8   Translated by Bernadotte Perrin, Loeb Classical Library 1919.

9   Translated by Frederick W. Shipley, Loeb Classical Library, 1924.

10 Translated by P. G. Walsh, Oxford University Press, 2006.

11 Translated by J. C. Rolfe, Loeb Classical Library, 1913.

12 Translated by J. C. Rolfe, Loeb Classical Library, 1913.

13 Aulus Gellius, "Attic Nights" 1,12. Translated by J. C. Rolfe, Loeb Classical Library edition, 1927 (rev. 1946).

14 Translated by Constance Garnett.

15 The Letters of Gustave Flaubert, 1857-1880. Selected, edited and translated by Francis Steegmuller, Belknap, 1982.

16 Theodor Adorno, "Cultural Criticism and Society" 1949. Translated by Samuel and Shierry Weber. The quote is often misunderstood and misrepresented, and I only cite it as an example of a feeling typical of the post-war generation.

17 Translated by William Thayer.

18 Livy Books I and II with English translation. Translated by Benjamin Oliver Foster, Harvard University Press, 1919.

19 Translated by Earnest Cary. Loeb Classical Library, Harvard University Press, 1937.

20 Translated by J.C. Rolfe. The Lives of the Twelve Caesars by C. Suetonius Tranquillus, Loeb Classical Library, 1913.

21 L. Annaeus Seneca, Minor Dialogues Together with the Dialogue "On Clemency" translated by Aubrey Stewart.

22 Translated by J. C. Rolfe. Suetonius, The Lives of the Twelve Caesars, Loeb Classical Library, 1914.

23 Translated by J.C. Rolfe. The Life of the Twelve Caesars, Loeb Classical Library, 1914.

24 Translated by Peter J. Aicher. Rome Alive: A Source-Guide to the Ancient City, Volume I, Bolchazy-Carducci Publishers, 2004.

25 Translated by Francis Fawkes (1721–1777) from an epigram ascribed to Anacreon.

26 Translated by David Magie. Augustan History, Loeb Classical Library, vol. II, 1924.

27 Translated by Walter Hamilton. Ammianus Marcellinus, The Later Roman Empire (A.D. 354–378). Penguin, 1986, reprinted 2004.

28 Translated by Mark Reasoner.

29 Translated by David Magie. Augustan History, Loeb Classical Library, 1921.

30 Translated by Tyler Lansford. The Latin Inscriptions of Rome: A Walking Guide. The Johns Hopkins University Press, 2009.

31 Translated by J.C. Rolfe. Sallust, The War with Catiline, Loeb Classical Library, 1928.

32 Translated by Peter J. Aicher. Rome Alive: A Source-Guide to the Ancient City, Bolchazy-Carducci Publishers Inc., 2004.

33 Ovid's Fasti, or the Romans Sacred Calendar, Translated into English Verse With Explanatory Notes By William Massey, Master of a Boarding-School at Wandsworth. London, 1757.

34 The Heroides, or Epistles of the Heroines, the Amours, Art of Love, Remedy of Love, and Minor Works of Ovid, Literally translated into English prose by Henry T. Riley. London, 1869.

35 Translated by Tyler Lansford. The Latin Inscriptions of Rome: A Walking Guide. The Johns Hopkins University Press, 2009.

36 Horace: Odes, epodes, and Carmen Saeculare. Translated into English verse by G. J. Whyte Melville, Esqu., London, 1850.

37 Translated by J. C. Rolfe. Suetonius, The Lives of the Twelve Caesars, Loeb Classical Library, 1914.

38 Translated by J. Jackson. Tacitus, Annals. Loeb Classical Library, Harvard University Press, 1925-37.

39 Translated by James Elphinston (1721–1809).

40 Translated in: Robert Goldwater, Marco Treves. Artists on art: from the XVI to the XX Century. New York, 1945.

41 Translated by Tyler Lansford. The Latin Inscriptions of Rome: A Walking Guide. The Johns Hopkins University Press, 2009.

42 Translated by John Addington Symonds.

43 http://www.vroma.org/~bmcmanus/scorpus2.html

44 Translated by P. G. Walsh. Pliny the Younger. Complete Letters. Oxford World's Classics, 2006.

45 Fik Meijer, trans. Liz Waters. Chariot Racing in the Roman Empire, Johns Hopkins University Press, 2010.

46 Translated by H. L. Jones. Loeb Classical Library, Harvard University Press, 1917 – 1932, Volume 5.

47 Livy. Books XXI-XXII With An English Translation. Cambridge, Mass., Harvard University Press; London, William Heinemann, Ltd., 1929.

48 Translated by Dorothea Wender. Epigrams of Martial Englished by Divers Hands. Selected and edited with an introduction by J. P. Sullivan and Peter Whigham. University of California Press, 1987.

49 Translated by Frederick W. Shipley. Velleius Paterculus and Res Gestae Divi Augusti, Loeb Classical Library, 1924.

50 Translated by J. C. Rolfe. Suetonius, The Lives of the Twelve Caesars. Loeb Classical Library, 1914.

51 Translated in: Maurice Pope, The Story of Decipherment. L., 1999.

52 Translated by David Magie. Historia Augusta, Loeb Classical Library, 1924

53 Translated by Sister M. Clement Eagan. The Fathers of the Church, a new translation, vol. 43. The poems of Prudentius. The Catholic University of America Press, Washington, D.C., 1962.

54 Translated by Thomas Bushnell, BSG.

55 Translated by Dorothy L. Sayers.

56 Translated in: William Smith, A Dictionary of Greek and Roman Antiquities, L., 1875.

57 Translated by W. C. Firebaugh. NY, 1922.

58 Translated by Dorothy Hoogland Verkerk. Imaging the Early Mediaeval Bible, ed. John Williams. The Pennsylvania State University Press, 1999.

59 Valery M. Hope, Death in Ancient Rome. A sourcebook. Routledge, 2007.

60 Translated by Richard Mott Gummere. Loeb Classical Library, 1917.

61 Translated by C. D. Yonge. Harper's New Classical Library, New York, 1877.

INDEX

D